William Henry Thomes

The Whaleman's Adventures in the Sandwich Islands and California

William Henry Thomes

The Whaleman's Adventures in the Sandwich Islands and California

ISBN/EAN: 9783744712491

Printed in Europe, USA, Canada, Australia, Japan

Cover: Foto ©Thomas Meinert / pixelio.de

More available books at **www.hansebooks.com**

The Kanaka Girl. Page 125.

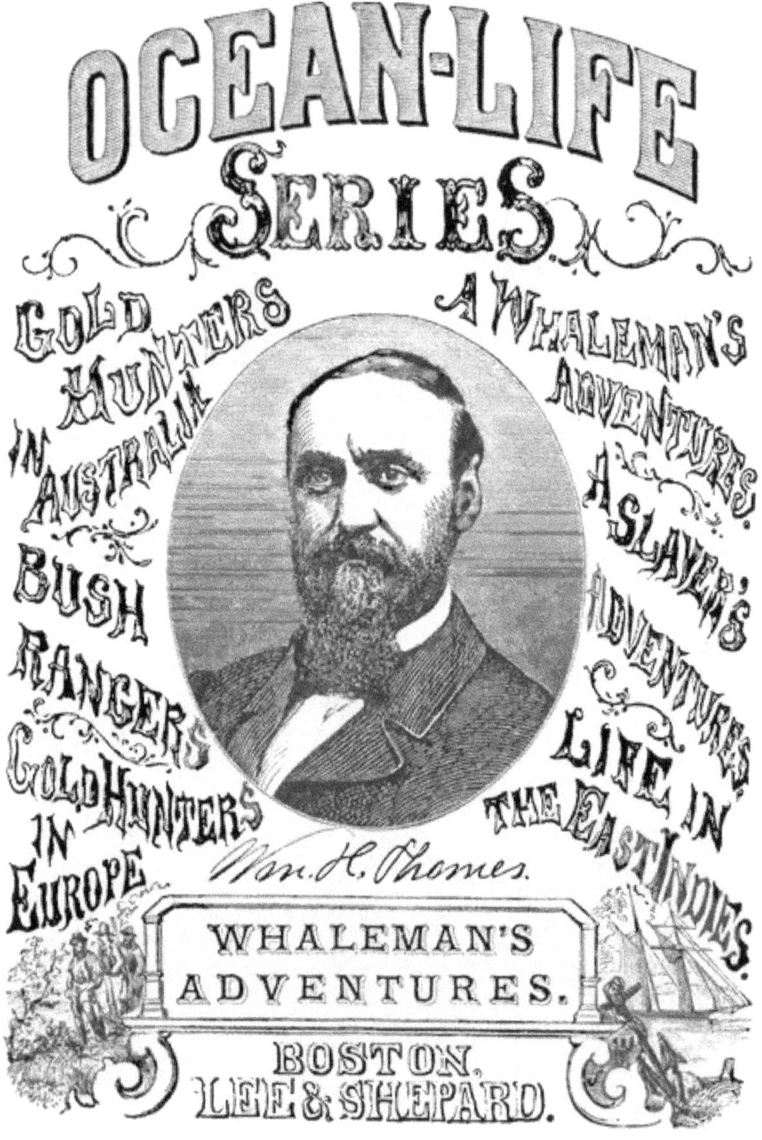
OCEAN-LIFE SERIES.
GOLD HUNTERS IN AUSTRALIA
BUSH RANGERS
GOLD HUNTERS IN EUROPE
A WHALEMAN'S ADVENTURES.
A SLAVER'S ADVENTURES.
LIFE IN THE EAST INDIES.
Wm. H. Thomes.
WHALEMAN'S ADVENTURES.
BOSTON.
LEE & SHEPARD.

THE OCEAN LIFE SERIES.

THE

WHALEMAN'S ADVENTURES

IN

THE SANDWICH ISLANDS

AND

CALIFORNIA.

By WM. H. THOMES,

AUTHOR OF "THE GOLD-HUNTERS' ADVENTURES," "THE BUSHRANGERS," "THE GOLD HUNTERS IN EUROPE," "ADVENTURES OF A SLAVER," "LIFE IN THE EAST INDIES," ETC., ETC.

ILLUSTRATED.

BOSTON:
LEE AND SHEPARD, PUBLISHERS.
NEW YORK:
LEE, SHEPARD AND DILLINGHAM.
1873.

Stereotyped at the Boston Stereotype Foundry,
No. 19 Spring Lane.

BOOKS BY THE SAME AUTHOR.

THE GOLD HUNTERS' ADVENTURES IN AUSTRALIA.

THE BUSHRANGERS; or, LIFE IN AUSTRALIA.

THE GOLD HUNTERS IN EUROPE.

ADVENTURES OF A SLAVER.

LIFE IN THE EAST INDIES.

All Handsomely Illustrated.

CONTENTS.

CHAPTER XI.

CHAPTER XII.

CHAPTER XIII.

CHAPTER XIV.

CHAPTER XV.

CHAPTER XVI.

CHAPTER XVII.

CHAPTER XVIII.

CHAPTER XIX.

CHAPTER XX.

CHAPTER XXI.

CHAPTER XXII.

CHAPTER XXIII.

CHAPTER XXIV.

CHAPTER XXV.

CHAPTER XXVI.

CHAPTER XXVII.

A WHALEMAN'S ADVENTURES;

OR,

LIFE IN THE SANDWICH ISLANDS.

CHAPTER I.

A FAIR STATEMENT OF THE CAUSE OF LEAVING HOME.

If a man intends to relate the adventures which have befallen him through a life that has had some of the ups and downs necessary to make existence endurable, it is incumbent upon him to give some account of his early history.

I will state, therefore, that in the year 184–, I was an only son of parents residing in Boston, and that my father carried on the wholesale grocery business in Broad Street, was director of a bank, was reputed to be worth about two hundred thousand dollars, and had twice served the city as an alderman, and was only defeated when he ran for the third time, because the miserable opposition placarded the city, saying that he sanded the sugar which he sold, and watered his rum, and mixed herbs with his black tea.

I was young then, but I well recollect my father's honest indignation when he related the circumstance to my mother; and I also have a vivid remembrance of his red face turning nearly black as he strove to eat his dinner, and wished at the same time that he had the author of the handbills by the neck, so that he could crush him.

Two days after my father's defeat, I fell in love with the prettiest little school-girl that I had ever seen. Her name was Jenny Fairchild, the only daughter of old Fairchild, in the leather business, on Shoe and Leather Street, and estimated worth five hundred thousand dollars. He was, therefore, more aristocratic and more pious than my father, and, never having been elected to any office, pretended to look down upon our family in a patronizing manner, which made my father mad and my mother virtuously indignant.

I remember even at this time where I was introduced to Jenny. It was at the corner of Tremont and Park Streets. I was finished at a glance, and wished that I had had my best coat on. She was on her way to a private school, and, although only fourteen, had the airs of a countess. I can hardly recollect what I said as I walked along with her, but I have a vivid recollection of asking her if she loved bunch raisins and figs, and she said that she did, and I said that I should be most happy to supply her with those articles any morning if she would meet me on the above-named corner, and I remember that she agreed to the proposal without much opposition. I think that she feared it would give me too much trouble, but I rejected the idea with scorn.

I walked with the young lady to school. How sorry I was that my parent had not done as well with sugar and tea as her father had with sole and upper leather!

But to return to the figs and raisins which I had promised Jenny. I knew that it would ruin me to fail in my offer; so I meditated upon the subject, and my meditations were rewarded by finding that in my mother's store-room were a box of raisins and a drum of figs, always under lock and key, on account of the filibustering disposition of the "help." To obtain the key of that store-room was no easy matter; but I accomplished it by relating a fanciful sketch of having seen a mouse at work there when I had visited the room some weeks before. I was intrusted with the key for the purpose of destroying the vermin. The next morning I had the happiness of presenting to Jenny about two pounds of the productions of southern climes, and in return was rewarded with a smile and information that "she and the girls would have nice times during school hours," and that "she should be exceedingly pleased to see me the next morning in the same place."

I was bewildered with joy. Poor goose that I was! She cared more for the figs and raisins than for me; and as long as her appetite was supplied, she was willing to furnish me with such weak and cheap food as smiles.

But such a state of things could not last forever. The figs and raisins came to an end, and there was a terrible howl in the house, and the "help" were blown up. In the midst of the storm in walked my father. It was only a month after his defeat at the polls, and he had not recovered his temper.

"What's the row?" he asked.

"Here's a whole box of raisins and a drum of figs gone, no one knows where," answered my mother.

"Who's had the key of the store-room excepting yourself?" he demanded.

"No one," my mother answered.

"O, yes, mum. Master Charley Allspice has had the kay to kill mouses, and sure he carried off dead ones in a paper. I seed him," answered one of the help.

"Has he had the key?" the ex-alderman asked.

"I have let *him* have it several times," mother answered.

"Then he has taken the fruit. Serve up dinner. I'll settle with him when he comes in."

My mother trembled as she gave the order. She knew that it would be useless to remonstrate.

I entered the house five minutes after dinner was on the table, and before my parent had satisfied the first pangs of his hunger.

"So, sir," said my father, shoving his soup-plate away, "you have been behaving in a pretty manner — haven't you?"

I replied that I had, and that my teacher thought I was one of the smartest boys in school.

"Smart at stealing, you mean," thundered the ex-alderman, and then I knew that I was discovered, and that the figs and raisins were to be brought in judgment against me; but although my heart sank, yet I determined to quail not.

"Don't, pa," entreated my mother.

"I will!" exclaimed the ex-alderman. "I won't have a boy of mine growing up and learning to steal. What will become of him when he arrives at my age?"

"I should be competent to act as an alderman," I said in a low tone; but the old gentleman heard it, and for a moment he gasped for breath.

"Do you hear him, madam?" he cried. "Did you hear what he said? Did you hear that boy cast reflections upon his own father?"

Father scowled at me for a moment, and then cut off a slice of beef and scowled at that; but his heart was too full to eat just then, he pushed his plate away.

"To think that a child I have been so particular in bringing up, should take to stealing, is not a consoling reflection, madam, and I must nip this passion in the bud."

I thought that he meant Jenny, and I determined to die before I gave her up.

"She is as good as our family," I said, with a sniffle, "and her father is richer than you."

The ex-alderman glanced at me in a state of bewilderment, and shook his head as though he found ideas in that operation.

"Do you know, madam, what he means?" my father asked.

"La, I suppose that he has got a girl, and I'm sure that if she is of good family, and her father is rich, I don't think that it will hurt Charles in the least."

"Well, if this don't beat even the mayor's veto," my respected parent said, looking first at my face and then at my mother's. "Here's a school-boy, hardly through his multiplication table, has got a girl, and talks of it as though it was something creditable. There is where the figs and raisins have gone. He's been stealing 'em for the girl, as true as I'm an honest man."

"Well, there's no harm done," remonstrated my mother.

"But there is harm, madam. It's not a few raisins that I care for, but it's the principle of the thing, as I told the mayor, when we caught one of the clerks stealing.

"Well, well, eat your dinner now, and talk of the matter hereafter," suggested my mother.

"But I will talk of it now, or at any time when it suits my convenience," roared my father. "Now, I want to know who the boy has been fooling with. By the Lord Harry, things have come to a pretty pass, if I have got to supply all the school-girls in town with fruit. I'll send a bill in to the fathers of the young 'uns, and they shall pay it."

This frightened me. I would rather have died than Jenny should have heard of such a thing.

"Now," said my father, squaring off at a joint of meat which was before him, and scowling at it as though it had defeated his election, "I want to know the name of the girl who has induced you to steal."

I resolved that I would not tell, and I considered how novel heroes would act under like circumstances.

"Are you going to answer me?" yelled my father. "Will you tell me this minute?"

"I will not," I answered, quite firmly.

My father pushed away his plate, and looked at me fiercely, and I returned his look with one of firmness.

"Will you tell me?" he shouted, dashing his fist upon the table, and making the glasses ring.

"No, sir, I will not," I answered.

"Then go to your room, and mind, you shall have nothing to eat until you do answer me. I'll nip your obstinacy in the bud."

I left the table without a word. My mother was shedding tears. I went to my room, and considered what I should do. I was resolved not to involve Jenny in my disgrace, and I knew enough of my father's disposition to be aware that he would keep me under lock and key for weeks, unless I yielded, and conformed to his wishes.

At length I heard my father leave the house for his store, and then my mother came to me.

"Charles," she said, "your father is very angry, and has cause for it. You must tell him, when he returns, all that he desires, and ask his pardon. If you do not do this, he will keep you on bread and water for a week."

I refused to make any concessions, and my mother left me with tears in her eyes.

Night approached, and I began to sigh for freedom. I thought how pleasant it would be to roam over the world, and see all that was interesting, and return home after a lapse of many years, rich, and with a mind stored with knowledge. For the first time the idea flashed across my brain that I would run away and see the world. I knew that whale ships were in the habit of receiving green hands, and why should not I join one? Before I had time to consider the subject, I had packed up a few of my clothes in a bundle, taken all the money which my money-box contained, amounting to eight dollars, stole softly down the front stairs, and left the house.

For a moment I paused on the sidewalk opposite my father's house, and thought of the course which I was about to pursue. Tears came into my eyes as I looked up at the room which I had occupied for so many years. A kind word then would have sent me back, but there was no one to utter it.

My dreams were brought to a close by a man staggering against me; and, looking up, I found that during my reverie I had been wandering to the street in which Jenny lived, and that I was standing opposite her father's residence.

I wanted to see Jenny before I left the city, and yet I hardly dared to call at the house; I feared her father would order me out of doors. But at last I mustered courage, and went up the steps and rang the bell.

A young woman opened the door with a flourish, but when she saw only a boy, she appeared to have regretted her smartness, and stood staring at me.

"Is Miss Fairchild at home?" I asked, rather timidly.

"Yes; have you a bundle for her?" the help demanded.

"I have no bundle for her, but I wish to speak with her," I replied with some spirit, for I did not like the idea of being taken for a bundle boy.

She looked at me by the light of the gas in the hall, saw that my clothes were a little better than an errand boy's, and she grew gracious in consequence.

"Will ye walk in till I tells her?" the help said, after a brief scrutiny of my person; and I entered the hall, and then the parlor, which was lighted with but one burner, for old Fairchild was rather particular about expenses. "I'll call her," the help said, and off she started.

While I was waiting my heart beat wildly, and I felt like bolting from the house. Each moment seemed an age; but at length I heard the light step of Jenny, and then she stood before me looking so beautiful and calm, that I felt more timid than ever.

"Why, is it you?" she said.

"Yes, I — I — have called," I gasped.

"To bring me more figs?" she asked. "Why did you not keep them, to give them to me to-morrow?"

"I have no figs," I faltered.

"Ah, raisins, then. I don't like them as well as figs, but I will take them."

She reached out her pretty little hands, and I started forward and seized them, and would have kissed them, but she skipped away in a moment, and stood at some distance from me, looking somewhat astonished.

"No figs, and no raisins?" she asked, after a moment's pause. "Pray what have you brought me?"

"Nothing," I answered.

"Then what do you want?" she inquired, coldly.

Alas, how like lead her words fell upon my heart!

"Jenny," I faltered; but she interrupted me with a proud gesture.

"Miss Fairchild, sir, is my name."

"Excuse me," I replied, with deep humility. "I will not offend again."

"You had better not," she answered, with a toss of her pretty head. "Mr. Sutton would not have dared take such liberties, and I'm sure I think that he is splendid."

Bill Sutton was my rival. He "splendid"! He was always called the clown of the school. That remark was torture to me; but still I managed to bear all without exhibiting the least sign of temper.

"I have already asked pardon," I said, "and now I will say good by, for I have a long journey before me, and many months will pass before we shall meet again."

The little beauty looked incredulous.

"I shall always think of you," I continued, "and whether I make my fortune or remain poor, you will always have the first place in my estimation."

"O, dear, I thank you," she cried; "but I don't want to have anything to do with a poor person."

"I hope that you will learn, as you grow older, that there are many poor people in the world whom you would be proud to know. But I did not come here to argue with you."

"O, didn't you?" and her pretty nose was tossed in the air.

"No; I came here to say farewell, for I am about to leave my home, and I don't know when I shall return."

"When are you going?" Jenny asked.

"I leave this evening."

"And where do you intend to go?"

"I am undecided. I am going to search for my fortune, and I hope that I shall find it. I have not been treated like a gentleman at home."

I expected to see her shed a few tears, but not one made its appearance.

"Well," she said, at length, "if you are going, good by. I

hope you won't tell folks that you was my beau, because you know that you was not."

I bowed and moved towards the door.

"You will at least shake hands with me," I said.

She extended her little hand, and suffered me to touch her fingers. I thought of the many pounds of fruit which she had taken from my hands with enthusiasm, and my heart rose up in my mouth, and I could hardly restrain my tears; but I suppressed them with a mighty effort, took one long look, and left the house. I walked rapidly for a few minutes, for the purpose of giving vent to some of the angry feelings that oppressed me; but after I grew tired I began to think that if the girl was coquettish I could not help myself, and that I had better make the best of it, and with this consoling reflection I was more anxious than ever to leave the city. Where I was to pass the night I had not the slightest idea. I knew that cars left the Boston and Providence station for New Bedford; and as I had heard that that city was the great whaling mart of the state, I determined to get there as soon as possible. As I approached the depot, I saw that it was lighted up, and that people were entering it in haste, as though fearful of being late.

"When does the next train leave for New Bedford?" I asked of the clerk in the ticket office.

"An extra train starts in one minute," he answered. "Never mind the ticket. You have no time to get one. Jump aboard and pay the conductor;" and he jerked a bell, and the conductor shouted, "All aboard!"

After the train was fairly under way, I began to realize the position I had taken, and grew homesick accordingly. A few words from a friend would even then have turned me from my purpose, and sent me home a repentant boy.

There were some fifteen or twenty sailors on the cars, men who had shipped in Boston, and were bound to New Bedford, to join ships which were to cruise in pursuit of whales. I took a seat as near these men as I could get. They were not an attractive lot of sailors; and some of them appeared as though they had fared hard on shore, their faces being bloated, and two of them had black eyes, and a third had a cut upon his face that looked serious.

I supposed that I should hear some interesting stories of the sea; but although I paid strict attention, I can't say that their talk was of the deep and its wonders. Their minds were upon other topics.

"New Bedford!" shouted the conductor, and the train rolled into the depot.

Before the cars had ceased their motion, on entering the depot, half a dozen brawny fellows, smelling strongly of oil and tobacco, jumped upon the platform, and entered the car in which I was seated in company with the sailors.

"Don't you go for to move till I tell you to," cried a runner, addressing the sailors.

"You don't s'pose we is goin' to run for it — do you?" asked Jack.

"Never you mind what I s'pose," answered the runner, dogmatically. "You jist keep still, and then there'll be no trouble atwixt us. That's all."

"Hullo, Ben! is this you?" asked one of the fellows who entered the car, and from whose face oil seemed to exude as naturally as from the oil springs of Pennsylvania.

"Yes, this is me, or what is left of me," the runner grunted.

"Have you got 'em all here?" asked the oily man, casting his eyes over the sleepy sailors.

"Well, I 'spect they is. Did you ever know me to lose a man in my life?"

"Can't say that I ever did, Ben. But pass 'em out, and we'll take care of 'em. Rouse and shine, lads, for there's ile afore ye, and in two years ye'll all be so rich that you won't know what to do with your money."

"That will do for the marines," grumbled one of the men.

"Hullo, old grumbler; you want a little waking up — don't you?" asked the city man. "When you is on the blue water, you won't talk that way. But come along, for the boats is waiting for yer."

"Ain't we to stop on shore to-night?" cried half a dozen in chorus. "We want one more good drink afore we goes to sea."

"We can't trust you, my beauties," answered the oily one. "You goes on board to-night, and the skipper can do as he pleases to-morrow. Come, heave ahead. Let's get on board, and have some supper and a glass of grog. The Sally is awaiting us."

"Then let her wait and be ——," was the indignant cry of the men, who had made up their minds for one more carouse.

"Ah, that's the talk — is it?" cried the oily man; "then we'll put on the irons, and see how you like it."

A perfect howl of rage escaped the sailors at this threat.

"Don't let any one leave the car," shouted the oily one. "Ben, you must lend us a hand here."

"Ay, ay; I'm ready," answered the runner, peeling off his coat and rolling up his sleeves.

I found that my position was not a comfortable one by any means; yet there was no chance to retreat unless I escaped by one of the windows. I threw one of them up, and put out my head, and that act attracted the attention of the oily man.

"That feller is trying to get off," he shouted, and made a jump for me, and caught me by one foot, and jerked me back with some violence; but luckily I struck on the cushion of the seat, and did not get much injured. At any rate, I feared that I was hurt, and shouted most lustily.

"Avast, there, you blubber-hunter," shouted Jack, a sailor, who had sat next to me. "He ain't one of us."

"You lie," shouted the oily man, giving my foot another wrench, which made me yell in earnest.

"Lie, do I?" asked Jack, stretching his stout, compact form, and then letting fly one of his hard fists, and a blow lodged between the eyes of the man of grease, and over he went with a crash and a curse that started his friends to the rescue.

"A free fight," yelled Jack.

"A fight all round," echoed the sailors, and both parties sprang forward to encounter each other.

Over the seats they went as fierce as wolves. They flew at each other's throats, and struck, and bit, and gouged each other, and rolled over and under the seats, and swore; and while the fight was raging most fiercely, out went the lights, and then the men could not tell friend from foe, and all was confusion.

While the battle was raging hottest, I recollected that I had something to look after, and that was my own preservation. I put my legs out of the window and let myself out of the car; but the instant I struck the depot I slipped and fell, and just as I did so, a man, who was rushing towards me, stumbled over my body, and down he went with a crash.

Before he could regain his feet I had regained mine, seized the bundle which I owned and had thrown from the window, and ran.

"Stop him!" shouted the man who had fallen; but the people in the depot were too intent upon the fight in the car to pay much attention to me, and as I dodged out of the building, I skirted an acre or two of oil casks, which were lying near, and broke for the darkest place that I could find.

After walking for some five minutes, I heard the sound of a fiddle, and saw an illuminated sign which informed me that "lodging and meals could be had here;" and as one place seemed as good as another, I entered the building, and found myself in a bar-room, graced with innumerable black bottles, clay pipes, tobacco, and cheap cigars. At one end of the room was a negro, with a violin in his embrace, and he was producing some very nautical airs, while on the bar, with red flannel shirt sleeves rolled up, displaying arms by no means clean, leaned a dirty-looking fellow, from the pores of whose skin whale oil appeared to flow in the form of perspiration. At a table some distance from the bar were seated some three or four men, in half-sailor, half-landsman costume, and they were engaged in drinking ale and smoking very black pipes.

As soon as I entered the room the negro stopped fiddling and looked at me. The bar-keeper slightly changed his position, and also looked at me, and the four men with the ale and pipes also directed their gaze at me. I evidently was a *rara avis* in such quarters.

After looking around for a moment, I stepped to the bar, and as if from habit the bar-keeper placed a tumbler on the bar, so as to be ready to fill it with such liquor as I might want.

"Is there a better hotel than this in the place?" I inquired.

"Why, what is the matter with this?" was asked by the bar-keeper.

"Nothing that I know of," I replied; "only I thought I should like to find a place where I can obtain a good night's rest."

"If you want to stop here to-night, just shell out twenty-five cents, and you can do it; otherwise no."

I took from my pocket a twenty-five cent piece, and laid it upon the bar, and the greasy genius pounced upon it as though it had been a barrel of oil.

"Want anything to drink?" asked the bar-keeper.

"Nothing but a glass of water."

He whirled a tumbler at me as though I had insulted him by

asking for water. I rinsed it with water from the pitcher, and then drank what I wanted, and intimated that I was ready to retire.

"Don't want any grub — do you?" the bar-keeper asked.

"No."

"Well, then, Jake, show him to No. 1, and see that the windows is down, for it may rain during the night. Blow out the light when you are done, and set it out at the door."

I promised compliance, and followed a negro to the room. The bed did not look inviting. The floor of the chamber was not particularly clean, and some portions of it resembled the deck of a whaler while cutting in and trying out. For a moment I stood looking at the bed, the room, and the negro, and the latter looked at me with a broad grin upon his face, and the white of his eyes glistening like ivory.

"Is this the best bed in the house?" I asked.

"Well, sar, it am as good as any," was the reply. "I spect dat you will do berry well dare if you once get asleep."

The negro was about to retire when I stopped him.

"You love a drop of liquor — don't you?" I asked.

He grinned all over, and showed more ivory than a sperm whale in its most angry mood.

"Well, sar, I does like a drop once in a while, dat am a fact."

"Then drink my health with this quarter;" and I put one in his hand.

"I'll do it, by de Lord Harry; you see ef I don't."

He left me in haste to put his promise into execution, and after I had taken off my coat and put the light outside of the door, I lay down upon the bed; but it was a long time before I could sleep, late as it was.

But sleep at length came upon me, and I dreamed that I was a sperm whale, and that I was surrounded by innumerable men armed with lances and irons, and that each one was trying to fasten to me, and at length just as one of the negroes let fly his iron, I awoke with a start. Some one had his hand in my pocket, but not the one which contained my slender store of money. I gave a sudden spring, and struck with my left fist in the direction of the person who was robbing me; and luckily the blow took effect, and lighted upon his nose, for the hand was hastily withdrawn from my pocket, and an oath was muttered, and then I heard the robber move softly across the room and leave it, closing the door.

I sprang from the bed and struck a match, but saw no one. I next tried the door, and found that it had been unlocked, although the key was still in the lock. I did not know how successfully nippers could be used in the hands of the experienced. The house was quiet, and I thought it would be foolish on my part to give an alarm; so I locked the door again, removed the key, and this time determined not to sleep; but before I was aware of it, I was off, and did not awaken until the sun was high in the heavens; and the first thing that I did hear, when I opened my eyes, was the fiddle in the bar-room, playing the same old tunes, with an occasional break-down, as though the performer was attempting to play and dance at the same time.

I arose and looked around for a wash-stand and water; but such things were not to be found, and I was forced to walk down stairs into the bar-room, where I met Jake, violin in hand, and the bar-keeper, with a green jacket on, leaning upon the bar in the same indolent manner as upon the night before. I thought he blushed, but it may have been the oil that was in his system. I imagined that his nose was swollen a trifle larger than the night before, and I wondered if I was the occasion of it. The instant Jake saw me, he laid his fiddle down on a chair, and came towards me, showing every ivory in his head.

"I hopes dat you sleeps well," he said. "Let me hab dat coat ef you please. I brush 'em for you, and den gib your shoes a lick."

He took the coat, in spite of a feeble resistance on my part, and the next moment was improving its appearance.

"Have a drink?" the bar-keeper asked.

"No; I want a place to wash, and some breakfast."

His fish-like eyes brightened as he saw the prospect of getting a few more cents from me. He led the way to a back room, and pointed to a dirty sink, and a huge piece of yellow soap, which was enough to make me wish myself back in my father's house once more.

"I s'pose you slept well," the fellow said, while I was pumping some water.

"So, so," I answered.

He made no reply, but walked off and took his old place behind the bar.

After a wash, I had breakfast, consisting of tough beef steak, and oily coffee, and butter that was strong enough to man a whaler. For this I was modestly charged fifty cents; and after I had paid the bill, I set forth to find a ship, on board of which I could commence my sight-seeing, and experience the pleasure of looking at the world.

CHAPTER II.

HOW I SHIPPED IN A WHALER AS A GREEN HAND.

I HAD got but a few steps from the house where I had passed the night, when I heard some one panting after me; and looking around, I found that Jake was close upon my heels.

"Is you goin' to look for a ship now?" he asked.

"Yes."

"Well, den, I will go wid you ef you has no 'jections. I show you whar de shippin' office am, sure."

I did not like the idea of walking through the streets by the side of a negro, for I had always looked upon colored men as many degrees lower in the scale of humanity than whites, but this was years ago, and before slavery was abolished; but as Jake seemed so respectful, I thought I would humor him.

We walked through the main street, until we came to a store, upon which were signs informing the public that it was "Podgers' Original Shipping Office," and also that "Landsmen are wanted for first-class Whaling Voyages. Good lays. Clothes Furnished on Credit." Opposite this attractive place Jake paused, and then looked at me and grinned.

"Dis de place whar you ship ef you want to," Jake said. "Old Podgers in dar, and tell you all about it ef you ax 'em. Ef you don't like Podgers, den go to Sharky. He keep shippin' office too, and tell you lots of lies, and no mistake."

"I will go in and see Podgers," I said, and in I went.

The store was filled with boots and shoes, tin pots and pans, sheath knives and sheaths and belts, Guernsey frocks, red flannel shirts, thick trousers, pine chests, boxes of cheap cigars and tobacco, fancy shirts, portable looking-glasses, formidable appearing fine-tooth combs, and a hundred other things which go to make up a sailor's chest and stock for a long voyage.

Mr. Podgers was a man about sixty years of age, very bald and very vulgar-looking. He shipped green hands, and supplied them with outfits on credit, but at such exorbitant charges that he calculated that if he got pay for one outfit in three, he made a hundred per cent. profit. He was a member of a fashionable church, and believed that every sailor who did not pay him in full was damned to all eternity; and, in truth, he rather liked the idea, and would have felt sorry if any one had attempted to prove that such would not be the case.

Such was the man whom I saw seated upon a stool, a short, black pipe stuck in his mouth, a greasy cap upon the back of his greasy head, and a pen behind his ear. As I entered the store, he turned his fish-like eyes upon me.

"Well, sir, what can I serve you with this morning?" Podgers asked, coming forward, and scrutinizing me from head to foot.

"I see that you have ships that are about sailing, and I called to consult about the chances of shipping in one," I replied.

"Ever bin to sea afore?" he asked.

"No."

"Green hand, eh? Wal, now, I don't know about it. Seems to me that all the young fellers in the States wants to go to sea jist at this 'ticlar time. Ef you had ever bin at sea, why, I could take you in a minute, and give you a good lay and a good ship. But as it is, why, I don't know."

"Perhaps I can find a ship somewhere else," I said, and moved towards the door.

"Stop!" he shouted. "I didn't say that I couldn't find you a berth — did I? What kind of a vige do you want?"

"What kind do you think best?" I asked.

"I s'pose that you would have no 'jections to sailin' with a pious cap'n?" Podgers asked, after a moment's thought.

"Certainly not," I replied.

"Nor pious mates, I s'pose."

"No."

"Wal, that is one pint towards our bargain, if we make one

The cap'n of the Sally is a professor of religion, and don't have swearin' aboard of his ship."

"The Sally," I repeated; "why, I came in the cars last night with a lot of men intended for that ship."

"O, did you?" Podgers asked; "well, the men had a fight at the depot, I'm told. I fear they are an ungodly set."

"Captain Bunker," Podgers continued, "is a mighty particlar man, and won't have any profundity on board of his ship."

"Profanity, I suppose you mean," I said.

"Wal, sir, I don't s'pose there's much difference; and if there is, I don't parceve it."

I saw that the good man was offended, and I hastened to appease him; but it was a long time before he could get over it and become reconciled to me.

"Wal, how about your clothes?" he inquired. "Have you got any money to buy 'em? Or have you got an outfit?"

"I have seven dollars," I said.

"That is somethin', but not enough. I can trust you for some clothes, and take what money you have got towards paying for 'em."

I laid down my seven dollars, and he pounced upon them like a hungry shark upon a piece of fat pork.

"It is all the money I have," I remarked, "and I don't know what will support me until I go on board of some ship, if you keep it."

"O, I can send you on board of the Sally this afternoon. She sails to-morrow."

He was determined not to give me the money at all hazards.

"You haven't got a father that would be willin' to pay for your traps — have you?" Podgers asked, after a moment's consideration.

I shook my head.

"Ah, well, never mind. I must trust you, I suppose. Ah, if I only had what I have been cheated out of by sailors, I could leave business and devote the remainder of my days to charity."

He beckoned me behind the counter to an awful oily desk, where some papers were spread, and pointed with his fat finger to a line, and put a pen in my hands.

"I hope," he groaned, "that Cap'n Bunker won't be down on me for shippin' you. He is a mighty particlar man, and don't like to take green hands. He is a great man for whalin', and likes short viges. Ah, he is what we call a good man, and no mistake."

I afterwards found out what constitutes a good man in the estimation of the New Bedford whaling portion of the community.

"I s'pose," Podgers continued, "that I shall have to allow you about the one hundred and ninetieth lay, and hope that when you come home with pockets full of money, you won't forget that Podgers gave you a start in life, and consequently make him a handsome present."

I assured the honest man that I should remember him, and I have from that day to this.

I signed my name, and became enrolled as one of the crew of the ship Sally, and for wages was to receive one barrel of oil out of every one hundred and ninety taken on board, which is called, in whaling parlance, the lay.

Then I signed another paper, which secured to Podgers his pay for outfits, in case whale were taken, and I was disposed to leave at some foreign port; and after that the shipping-master began to select my clothes, together with a belt and sheath-knife, a pot and pan, a spoon, and a fork. I insisted upon a fork, although Podgers scoffed at the idea.

"What does a sailor-man want of a fork?" he asked, with an expression of scorn.

"To eat with," I replied.

"Bah! they allers eats with their fingers. But put it in."

"There," said Podgers, throwing in a monkey-jacket of rather coarse material, "there are clothes enough for four years, if you is only keerful of 'em. Otherwise no."

"And what are they worth?" I ventured to inquire.

"Let me see. Shirts, best quality. Gone up within three days. Trousers, such as no man need feel ashamed to wear, even to church. I'm short of 'em, and they can't be had at fair prices. They has gone up like sixty. But I'll be reasonable."

"Perhaps the price of jackets has also gone up," I remarked, as I saw that he was regarding one attentively.

He looked at me a moment to see whether I was joking or not.

"Well, we'll say about eighty dollars for what there is there," he remarked, after a mental calculation. "I don't do right by my family in selling 'em so cheap."

The old rascal! The articles could all have been purchased at a store in Boston for fifteen dollars, and dear at that.

"Now you go on board as soon as you please," the shipping-master said, "and let me advise you to jump and obey orders arter you is on board, or you'll find out that there is some difference 'twixt the land and sea."

The greasy scamp stuck his black pipe in his mouth, and began to smoke, and, while I was looking at him, Jake entered the store.

"Here, you nigger," said the shipping-master, "I want this feller and his traps put on board the Sally; do you get him on board and I'll give you a half pint of whiskey — some of the squealing sort."

"I'll do it, sar," answered Jake. "I's glad dat he's going in de same ship dat I go in. I larn him to be a whaler, sure, and like as not he be boat steerer afore we come back."

"The more hope that I shall get my pay," grunted Podgers.

I took hold of one end of the chest, and Jake the other, and we staggered off towards the wharf, which was about ten rods distant from the store.

On reaching the wharf, I ran up to the lodging-house where I had passed the night, and got my bundle which I had left there; but before I could take my leave of the place, the tallow-faced bar-keeper asked me to drink, and I declined.

"Going whaling?" he asked, with his elbow still upon the bar.

"Yes," I answered.

"Wal," he replied, "you is like a young bar."

"Why?" I asked.

"Wal, 'cos you has got all your troubles afore you;" and with that he laughed most heartily, and while he was laughing I left him and ran down to the dock, where I found Jake sitting on my chest, and singing negro melodies, to the intense delight of a large collection of greasy-looking boys.

"The boat from the Sally no come yet," Jake said, when he saw me. "I is no hurry to get dare — is you? I spect dat we shall see nuff of de old Sally widout being anxious to jine 'em."

About twelve o'clock, a whale boat put off from the ship. As it drew near, Jake exclaimed, —

"By golly, here come de skipper; and now you hab a chance to see 'em."

Upon the strength of that information, I looked quite hard at the man in the stern-sheets, who was working a steering oar with much vigor. He was stout and short, with red hair and heavy beard. As he landed upon the wharf, I saw that his eyes were red, that his hands were dirty, and that his mouth was filled with tobacco; and according to my ideas, he did not look at all like a Christian, or a Sabbath school teacher.

"Well, nigger, what are you doing here?" he asked of Jake.

"I's going to help dis boy get his tings on board, sar," answered Jake.

"What, is this one of my boys?" he asked, with a look at me.

"Yes, sar; Mr. Podgers ship 'em dis mornin' as green hand."

"And green enough he is, I s'pose."

"What is your name, you sir?" Captain Bunker, the pride of whalemen, and the pet of New Bedford, thundered.

"Charles Allspice," I responded.

"That's a —— spicy name; but if you show any pepper on board, I shall apply the salt, and we will see which gets the best of it. You are not going on board the Sally to eat the bread of idleness, by a —— sight; so I give you warning."

"Good gracious," I thought, "if this is a specimen of the Christians of New Bedford, what must the sinners be?"

But it was too late for me to investigate such matters, for I was forced into the boat with my chest, and the next moment was pulling for the Sally.

The Sally, which was to be my future home, looked as though she had been built by contract with a number of other ships, and sawed off at bow and stern, for she was blunt one way as the other, and could sail stern foremost as rapidly as she could go ahead. Sailors who knew her best said that she could make more leeway during a twenty-four hours' gale, than she could make good in twenty-four hours with a fair wind; but I have my reasons for saying that I think such an assertion was greatly exaggerated. Extending from stem to stern was a bright streak of varnish, about a foot wide, and looking as greasy as the majority of whalers generally look. The masts and yards of the Sally were not stepped and slung with mathematical precision. That I could tell at a glance, although I was no sailor, and did not know the name of a single spar at that time.

When the boat was alongside of the pride of New Bedford, and I was requested to "parbuckle" myself to the deck — an invitation that I did not know the meaning of, until Jake put a couple of ropes in my hand, and told me to stick my toes upon some cleats nailed on the side of the ship, and then go up, and I did so after seeing some one try the experiment.

Upon reaching the deck of the Sally, I found what appeared to me supreme confusion. Men with very dirty trousers, and very black jumpers, were rushing about the deck, pulling at first one rope and then another, and then shouting to other men aloft, and the men aloft were shouting to those on deck the most incomprehensible orders, and emphasizing the same with terrible oaths, to which those on deck responded with interest. No one took any notice of me, and I leaned against the rail, looking on amazed, until I was aroused by a fierce voice asking, —

"Whose traps are these?"

I looked up and saw a tall, lank man, with ferocious black whiskers, a flat nose, — a nose that seemed to have been beaten even with his face by some terrible blow, — standing near me and chewing tobacco at a terrible rate.

"Whose traps are these?" the fierce man repeated.

"Mine," I answered.

"Then what in —— is it doing here? Away with it to the forecastle."

"Where is that?" I asked.

"What a —— fool!" the fierce man said. "Take the chest for'ard. It seems as though the race of greenhorns would never die out. Come, look lively, for I want the deck cleared."

I don't know how I should have got out of the trouble if it had not been for Jake, who joined me at that moment, and who grinned at the fierce man in such a kind, good-natured way, that I think his heart, if he had one, was slightly touched.

"Well, darky, have you come on board for good?"

"Yes, sar. I cum off wid dis young man who shipped dis mornin'. Hope you berry well, Mr. Spadem."

"Well, help the feller carry his traps to the forecastle, and look arter him a bit."

"Dat," whispered Jake, as we dragged the chest forward, over sails and barrels, harpoons and lances, grindstones and blocks, just received on board, "is Mr. Spadem, de mate, who kills more whales dan any udder man, and make lots money for de owners."

"Is he a Christian, also?" I asked.

"Ha, ha!" chuckled Jake; "dey is all Christians on shore, and berry devils at sea. But you find 'em out by and by. Now, den, here am de forecastle, and a precious time dey is habin' down dare, sure."

I stepped to the scuttle and looked down. A strong steam of mingled onions, tobacco, smoke, rum, and bilge-water was ascending the narrow passage.

"Wal, dey is having a time, and no mistake," muttered Jake, listening at the scuttle for a moment.

"Is that the place for sailors?" I asked, with a tremulous voice.

"Dat de place, and a berry good place you find 'em; arter you has ben on deck in de wet and cold for four hours, you tink 'em a riglar hotel den, and no mistake."

I had some doubts on the subject; but I afterwards found that his words were true.

"Wal," said Jake, after a moment's pause, "I s'pose we must lower de chest down somehow; so you hold 'em one end and go afore. Now, den, here we goes."

Jake seized one end of the chest, and commenced backing down the narrow, greasy steps, and in an instant there were heard a dozen men shouting, —

"Out of the light, and be —— to you;" "Hit his heels;" "Stern, all;" "There goes flukes;" and many other expressions which were strange to me and incomprehensible.

At length we landed in safety, and then I looked around to see what kind of a place I was in. Although it was midday, there was a light burning between two upright pieces of timber, at the foot of the steps, and I afterwards learned they were called "bitts." Around the den, which was dark and dirty, was a row of chests, and on these were seated sixteen or twenty men, some of them playing cards for piles of tobacco, while others were drinking from tin pots, and refilling them from suspicious-looking black bottles.

A more diabolical looking set of fiends I never saw in all my life. I was a little astonished, and remained speechless while I looked on the scene.

I forgot to mention that around the forecastle, in the form of a triangle, were berths for the men to sleep in, and some of the sailors appeared to be improving their time, and napping away undisturbed by the noise and confusion.

"Who in the devil's name are you?" asked one fellow, shying a pot at my head, which I was fortunate enough to dodge.

I made no answer.

"Can't you speak, you son of a fresh-water dog?" the man thundered, and he raised a black bottle to throw at me, but just then Jake interposed.

"You jist let 'em alone," the negro cried, with some little sign of temper. "You no see dat he jist jine de ship, and no understand much about sailor's life."

"What is that to you, snow-ball?" the sailor asked, and removing a quid of tobacco from his mouth, he threw it at Jake, and the filth lodged upon the face of the negro.

I saw an expression like that of a fiend pass over the negro's face; and then I saw him tear his old Scotch cap from his head, and dash it upon the deck, and then bend his bullet-shaped head, until it was on a level with the sailor's breast; and then, like a thunder-bolt, the darky dashed forward, and with his head struck the sailor upon his breast, and over he went upon the deck, as though he had been shot.

But Jake did not stop with his butting punishment. Before his adversary could rise, the negro had planted his heavy feet upon the white man's breast, and kicked him until some of the men, who, having nothing to do, were a little interested in the fight, interfered, and parted the belligerents.

"Let's have a fair chest fight," roared one man, who could hardly stand, having been drinking all day.

"Tell 'em to fight across a hand'chief," a second cried; "that's the way to settle a quarrel."

In the mean time the sailor, who had been butted to the deck, arose, with face covered with blood, for Jake had planted one of his feet upon that portion of his body, and it had done execution.

"You see what he has done — don't you, boys?" asked the sailor, not appearing to have much desire to renew the battle.

"If we is to be run over by niggers, we had better understand it at once."

"Fight him," one cried. "On the chests in sailor fashion."

But this did not seem to suit the fancy of Charley, as he was called.

"Is you going to fight, or not?" two or three asked; and I mention it as a matter of remark, that the men who were playing cards did not even cease their game, or hardly look up, fights being so common just before the sailing of the whaler.

"I'll fight 'em," cried Jake, his eyes flashing like fire, and his face expressing all the bad nature of his heart. "I'll fight 'em any how, or at any time. Wid de lead, wid fists, wid knives, or wid harpoons. Let 'em cum on, and I'll larn 'em manners. He insult me, and I do nuffin to him. What he insult me for! Des answer me dat. Ef he tink dat he going to pick on dat boy, 'cos he green, he mistaken."

"And who is to prevent me?" asked the white man.

"I do now or by and by. All times I look arter 'im."

"And I will lend a hand, there," cried a voice, which I recognized; and Jack, the sailor I had met in the car, pushed his way through the crowd, and extended his huge fist to the negro. "I tell you, darky, that I'll take a hand with you in any fight when they want to crowd the boy. I ain't forgot the time when I was a boy, and was kicked about the deck like a dog."

The white man and the negro shook hands upon the contract, and it was one that they kept during the time that I was on board, and if it had not been for them I should have fared hard.

By this time the men had resumed their regular occupations, such as drinking and smoking, and playing cards, and left us three to talk as we pleased.

"Let me see," said Jack, looking around the forecastle. "You want a bunk. Have you got any bedding dunnage?"

I looked at one and the other without speaking.

"He don't know what you mean," Jake said, with a grin.

"Wal, I s'pose not. Has you got any bedding? That's what we call dunnage."

No, I had no bedding. Old Podgers had wilfully neglected me in that respect.

"Let me see," Jack muttered; "there's that boy Will, he's got a bunk all to himself. It's large enough for two, if you both is in the same watch. He's got dunnage, and will share it, I think. I'll see;" and up the steps he went, and shouted, "Boy Will," until I heard some one answer, and then Jack returned to the forecastle.

In a few minutes down the steps bounded a lad about my own age, but with regular sailor rig on, and a face that appeared to have seen service in facing the smoke of the try-pots and strong gales of wind.

"Well, who wants me?" Will said.

"I want yer, Will. Here's a shipmate for yer," Jack answered, nodding at me.

We looked at each other rather slyly, as boys always do on first meeting, and each declined to say anything.

"Will," said Jack, "you must give Allspice half of your bunk and dunnage. He'll get some blankets from the slop chest afore long, and make it all right with yer. What do yer say?"

"I agrees to that," the lad answered with much frankness. "I was fearful I'd have to turn in and out with some lubber of a man, or a Portuguese. I's got plenty of bed-clothes, and he shall share with me."

We sat down upon the chest, and had a confidential talk, and I learned that Will had a mother and a sister at New Bedford; that his father followed the whaling business until he was killed by the flukes of a whale, which came down upon the boat and crew unexpectedly; and that, consequently, the widow had to support herself and daughter by doing slop-work for Podgers and others. Will had assisted his mother as much as possible, and his first voyage had realized some fifty dollars, which he had given his parent. This trip, he hoped to do better, as he got a much better lay. He was desirous of rising in his profession, and hoped to command a ship before many years.

"Now," said Will, in conclusion, "let's stick together and be friends, and if the Portuguese picks on one of us, we'll resent it together. They'll want to make us wait on 'em, and do the dirty work; but I rather fancy that a Yankee boy is too good for that — don't you?"

I thought so.

"Now," continued Will, "can you fight?"

I recollected my bloody nose when I had a battle with a school-boy, and said that I could, some, but I was not confident.

"Never mind; you'll have to pretend that you can do some, and that goes a great ways with the Portuguese. You'll soon learn how to fight, for we shall have a few pitched battles 'afore many days, and then every man will have to look after his own head."

I shall never forget my first meal on board of the Sally. It was six o'clock, and the decks were all cleared up, and the Sally was pronounced ready to sail. The mate came forward, and told the cook to "give the people their supper," and then we went to the galley, where the cook, or "doctor," as they called him, presided in greasy dignity, and received one quart of hot mixture; and then two tubs, which they called "kids," were thrust out, and I saw that they contained pieces of beef which had been boiled, and were cold. These were carried to the forecastle by a Portuguese, who was half drunk.

The men were not hungry, and some of them did not even leave off playing cards, for the purpose of tasting the tea or the salt beef.

I must confess that I felt hungry; and while I stood looking at the beef and bread which the Portuguese were hacking at like wolves, Will joined me, and I hinted to him that I felt as though I could eat a little something on deck.

"Pitch in, then," cried my juvenile friend. "Out with your sheath-knife, and hack away at the best that you can get, and then we will go on deck and eat in peace, and afterwards have a comfortable smoke."

Under this advice I timidly approached one of the kids, and stuck my new fork into a piece of beef, when the kid was kicked beyond my reach, and a Portuguese, who did it, scowled at me as he said, —

"You s'pose you eat all fore sailors do. You waite, sar, till men help demselves; den you cut, ef you want to."

I said nothing, but Will whispered to me to "pitch into him;" but the fellow was twice as large as myself, and I feared that would not do.

At length I got what I wanted, and my chum and myself went on deck, where we could eat without molestation, and without the perfume which pervaded the forecastle. I tried to drink my first pot of tea, and nibbled at bread which had made one voyage around the Horn. But the beef was not so bad, and I managed to consume enough to satisfy my appetite, and then turned to Will, who was eating like a sailor.

"I tell you what it is," said Will, pouring some hot tea into his pan, and washing the utensil with that compound; "you should have hit that Portuguese thief when he kicked the kid away from you. You must recollect that we is Americans, and that these Portuguese rascals ain't even Christians; therefore we mustn't let 'em hustle us around like anything."

We sat on deck and talked until a late hour, and Will told me his whole history, and wanted to know mine; but I was shy of confiding it to him, and after he had questioned me and obtained no results, he gave it up in despair, and spun me a few whaling yarns, to show that he was familiar with the art of taking the monsters.

By ten o'clock we began to grow sleepy, and I proposed that we should retire to our berth; but the noise and confusion in the forecastle were so great, that we found it would be useless to attempt to sleep there. Jake had received his violin from the shore, and was tuning it and playing lively break-downs. Liquor was still passed around. Men who could hardly speak half a dozen words intelligibly, on account of a certain thickness of tongue, were roaring out songs. The Portuguese, of whom there were some six on board, were collected in one corner, and gambling for tobacco most industriously, and sometimes even putting up a shirt or two, to make the game more interesting.

Sleep, in such a den, was out of the question; so we took the blankets from the berth, and went on deck, and fouud quarters on the try-works, where some sails were stowed.

I don't know what time it was when I awoke, but I started up on hearing a most frightful noise, and loud oaths and exclamations, which came from the forecastle. I touched Will, and we listened for a moment, and heard cries of murder, and cries of defiance, and cries of triumph, and blows, and kicks, and the overturning of chests and pans. I ran aft to awaken the mate, whom I found lying on the transom of the cabin, and sleeping as quietly as though upon shore.

"Mr. Spadem," I said, touching him on his arm, "the crew are having a terrible fight in the forecastle."

He started up and stared at me for a moment without speaking, and I repeated my information.

"Well, let 'em fight and be hanged," he said. "After they have killed each other, let me know;" and down went his head again, and he was asleep in an instant.

I ran forward and joined Will, who was standing by the scuttle of the forecástle, listening to the row.

"The mate won't come forward," I said.

"Then they must fight it out, and a pretty time they will have."

We did not dare descend into the forecastle, so stood there and listened until we heard some one coming up the steps as though in a great hurry, and then we stepped back and concealed ourselves behind the foremast, and saw one of the Portuguese plunge upon the deck, and then gather himself, run to the rail, and jump overboard: and as he did so three or four of the crew also reached the deck, and looked around for the man who was in the water.

"Where is he?" they asked, getting sight of us.

"Overboard," answered Will.

Their clothes were almost torn from their backs and bodies, their faces were cut, and blood was streaming down upon their breasts, and from their hands, and dripping upon the deck. All this we were enabled to see by the light of the moon.

"Is he overboard?" they asked; and with one accord they rushed to the rail, and saw the Portuguese in the water, swimming for the shore.

"Kill him!" they shouted; and seizing firewood and handspikes, they hurled them at the man in the water; but they fell short.

"Lower a boat and after him," was the next cry, and the three men rushed aft to one of the boats, which had been hoisted up at sundown, and had commenced lowering it, when the mate came on deck with a heaver in his hand, which he began beating the men with.

The battle was an exciting one; but the mate had the advantage. The second and third mates were awakened by the row, and rushed upon the deck *sans* trousers, *sans* everything but flannel shirts.

This re-enforcement was too much for the sailors, and they were compelled to retreat forward with broken heads.

"If you please, sir," said Will, running up to the mate, who was expressing himself in most awful terms, "the Portuguese will get clear."

An explanation was demanded and given.

"Why, blast 'em," cried Mr. Spadem, "I thought they wanted to run for it, and that's the reason I knocked 'em so. Here, you Will and the other boy, — what's his name? Pepper, — go down the falls and unhook the tackles, and haul the boat to the gangway. Be lively, or the cuss will reach the shore."

Will ran to obey, and I followed him, and did as he did. We landed in the boat, and had her alongside in no time, although I must confess that Will did all the work.

The mate tumbled into the boat, and we shoved off. They got out their oars, while I looked on.

"Where's your oar, you Pepper?" roared the mate, who had hold of the steering oar.

"I don't know," I replied.

"Out with one, and pull, you son of a gun," roared Mr. Spadem.

"I don't know how," I replied.

"Then larn, and be hanged to you. Out with one, or I'll hash you into mince meat in no time."

To prevent my meeting such a dreadful fate, I managed to get out an oar and slip it in the rowlock; but the very first stroke I took I missed the water, and up went my feet and down went my head, while my oar struck the back of the second mate, who was aft of me.

"You Pepper, you," roared the mate.

"Yes, sir," I answered, rubbing my head.

"I'll be the death of you before you have been on blue water ten hours. You see if I don't."

"If you don't kill me, the water will," I answered.

"Silence, you rascal! How dare you answer me back? But I'll larn you — you see if I don't."

I dipped my oar into the water this time; but unfortunately, I went too deep, and cramped it, and caused the boat to keel over about two or three streaks, and nearly tumbled the mates and Will from their thwarts. The last disaster was more than the mate could stand, and he blasphemed so loud, and called me such hard names, that I really began to think the Christian-like officer whom Podgers described to me had turned into a devil.

"I couldn't help it," I said, as soon as I could find my breath, and put in a word edgeways.

"Yes, you could help it, too," roared the mate. "But wait until I get on board, and see if I don't sarve you out."

"Perhaps he had better ship his oar," suggested the second mate, a Mr. Lance, and a very fine fellow, as I afterwards found.

"In with it then. Be lively. Give way, the rest of you. And you, Pepper, take the boat-hook and stand by to catch that Portuguese as we get on to him."

The second mate pushed the boat-hook along with one hand, so that I had no doubt that what he had hold of was a boat-hook; and armed with this weapon I stood up in the bows of the boat.

"There he is, just ahead of us," cried the mate. "Give way, boys, and he is ours. One stroke more and we shall be up to him. Now, then, start her with a will. Don't you miss him, you, Pepper."

As he spoke we were close upon the sailor, who ducked his head down, intending to dive; but I caught the seat of his trousers with the boat-hook, and perhaps a little flesh with it, and then recollecting what I had read about whaling, I shouted with the whole strength of my lungs,—

"Stern, all — stern, all! for I've got him."

From long habit the rowers instantly "backed water," and stopped the boat from progressing.

By this time the mate had dropped his steering oar, and come forward and taken the boat-hook.

"O, I no do so more," the sailor cried.

"No, I don't intend that you shall. You are not going to ride over me, and I shall let you know it;" and down went the poor fellow, and after being held under water a few seconds, he was drawn up and told that he might get into the boat.

The Portuguese had not strength enough to do that alone; so assistance was extended, and he was parbuckled over the side and landed in the bottom of the boat, and then we pulled for the ship, where I expected to "catch it;" but I suppose that the mate had found a valve for the escape of his bile, and was satisfied.

When Will and myself went forward, the fight was over. Each man was relating his grievance, and shedding tears,—a state of drunkenness that is quite common with some sailors,—and the three men who chased the Portuguese on deck were having their injuries dressed or washed by those who were sober enough to do such work.

It was quite evident to Will and I that the forecastle was no place for us; so we returned to our blankets on the try-pots, and just as we had covered ourselves up, the mate came forward and looked down the forecastle.

"If I hear any more noise down there," he said, "I'll come down with a lever. Do you understand that?"

"If you come down here you will never go up alive," I heard some one say.

"What is that, you mutinous rascal?" yelled the mate.

He looked down the forecastle with a wishful glance, as though he would have admired to know who was talking to him; but as he could not find out, and an inquiry was answered with slang, he turned away, muttering most terrible threats of "using up their old iron for 'em;" but the meaning of that term I did not know at the time.

I did not awaken till all hands were called in the morning. The men were rather slow to "turn out." But when they did muster on deck, such a looking set of battered faces I never saw.

There did not seem as though in the whole crew there was life enough to move; yet the men, after a drink all round, which was supplied to them by one of their number, who had saved a bottle on purpose to ease off with, improved wonderfully, and even began to joke each other on the bad appearance which they presented.

"Give the people their breakfast," said the mate, coming forward and speaking to the cook. "As soon as they have finished it we get under way."

No sooner was breakfast over than a boat came alongside from the shore, and on deck sprang the redoubtable Captain Bunker, who looked as though he desired to take vengeance on some one for rousing him up so early in the morning.

"Loose the sails, and man the windlass," Bunker growled to the mate, as he passed over the gangway and disappeared in the cabin.

CHAPTER III.

MY FIRST DAY AT SEA.

It is not a very pleasant thing to go to sea at any time, unless homeward bound; but to up anchor and stand out to sea with a crew half drunk and the other half suffering under mild attacks of delirium tremens, is not enviable, but the officers of the Sally seemed to mind it but little. The anchor came up rather slowly, for the strength of the men was not applied to their task. The mate stood upon the top-gallant forecastle, chewed tobacco, and shook his fist at us, and tried to infuse some life into us; but the men were dead to all attempts to force them to work harder, even if they had been able.

"Why don't that chain come in faster?" roared the skipper from the quarter-deck, where he was walking in all the majesty of command; and then, without waiting for an answer, his promenade was resumed.

"Do you hear?" the mate cried. "The cap'n is arter you, and if he cums for'ard there won't be nothing left of you. He won't be trifled with, I can tell you. Now heave with a will, and up she comes."

But this speech did not seem to inspire the men with that energy which was desirable, for they sullenly confined themselves to their work, and exhibited no enthusiasm. My labor on that important occasion was hauling the chain out of the way, and arranging it in layers along the deck; and as it was the first hard work that I had ever done, it told upon me.

"We are short, sir," shouted the mate to the red-headed skipper.

"Short of what?" I wondered.

"Sheet home the topsails, then," the skipper said.

That I found was much easier work, although it made me very short of breath, and hurt my hands awfully pulling at the ropes.

At length our sails were hoisted, and we once more manned the windlass, and up came the anchor from its muddy bottom, but in such a reluctant manner that the Sally did not know that she was free from the ground for some time, and then she commenced moving, stern foremost, towards the shore. The captain raved about the quarter-deck fearfully when he found that the Sally would do nothing but drift towards the shore, and he had just ordered the lowering of a boat for the purpose of towing her head round, when she gradually wore round and pointed her blunt nose out of the harbor; but even the Sally was doubtful about moving ahead, and for a short time remained stationary.

"Is that anchor on the bottom?" yelled the captain to the mate.

"No, sir, it is in sight," was the answer; but the question afforded amusement for the crew for many days, when we were in company with other ships, and they would leave us far astern.

A gentle breeze from the shore filled our sails, and at length the Sally drew ahead, to the great relief of the officers and the chagrin of the men. As the Sally began to show her heels, more sail was made, and by ten o'clock we were out at sea, and had lost sight of the city of oil and oily men. Then I began to experience all the horrors of seasickness; my legs failed me, and I was compelled to sit down upon a spar.

"Hullo! what are you doing there?" roared the mate.

"I'm sick," I answered; and I gave signs that my words were true, but I did not get any sympathy from Mr. Spadem.

"Up with you," he said; "you didn't come aboard the Sally to eat idle bread, I can tell you. Up with you, and rush about. That's what will do you good."

I staggered to my feet, and managed to crawl about the deck; but it was the worst punishment that I ever received in my life. Every few moments I was compelled to seek the side of the ship, and give vent to my feelings and relief to my stomach. But amidst all my troubles Will and Jack were good friends, and as often as they could neglect their duty they would come near me and exchange a few friendly words, and tell me that I should soon feel better and get my "sea legs" on.

"Cheer up, old boy," said Jack; "you will soon be over this, and then you will eat more than any man aboard the ship. Stick to the deck as long as you can, for if you go below you'll be sicker."

Such words of kindness gave me some life, and I made a brave effort to move about, but I could hardly walk. Still I stuck to the deck, and just before supper time I staggered aft with the rest of the men to be chosen into watches for the voyage. Much to my disgust, I found that I was picked for the larboard or mate's watch, while Will was in the second mate's or starboard watch. Then they commenced choosing boat's crews, and I found that I was drafted into the captain's boat, and allotted to the after oar.

After the business for which we were called aft was transacted, we were told to go forward; and we went, the men whispering their comments as they moved along. Jack and Jake laid me down upon some rigging upon the try-works, and told me to keep still; and there was need of it, for I was very weak, and trembled violently from the effect of my vomiting. At sundown Will came and sat by my side.

"Look up, Charley," he said, "and take a farewell view of the land, for it's the last we shall see of our country for many days."

I raised my head, and saw a long, blue line upon the horizon, and that, he told me, was the last I should see of the United States until we returned home filled with oil, and with more money at our command than a cow could eat. I stuck to the try-works until daylight, when I was aroused by Jack.

When eight bells struck, and the starboard watch came on deck, I felt as though I could eat a little breakfast; and my anticipations were realized, for I commenced on salt junk, and found that it was not so bad on an empty stomach; and from that morning I seldom missed a meal while I was on board the Sally.

A week passed on; we were steering an east course, and making slow progress. Men were stationed aloft to look after whales, for sperm whales were sometimes met with between the United States and the Western Islands.

At daylight every morning a boat-steerer went aloft and perched himself on the main-top-gallant cross-trees, where he could command a full view of the horizon, and at the same time a man from the forecastle went aloft and perched himself on the fore-top-gallant cross-trees, and each man was compelled to remain on duty aloft two hours, before he was relieved.

I remember one afternoon, while I was aloft on the lookout, I saw, just ahead of the ship, an immense commotion in the water, and something that looked dark and skinny, which whalemen call "black skin."

"There are whales ahead," I shouted to those on deck.

"What does it look like?" yelled the mate.

"I don't know," I replied. "They keep jumping out of the water."

"It's a school of black-fish," cried the boat-steerer, who had now got his eyes open.

For fear that some should suppose that I mean a very delicious fish caught in the waters of Rhode Island and Connecticut, and weighing from one to ten pounds, I will state that the black-fish which I allude to is from six to twenty feet long, and weighs from seven hundred pounds to a ton, and that the carcass is covered with a thin coating of blubber, about an inch and a half thick, and that a moderate-sized fish will yield a barrel of oil if the blubber is not too dry. The oil is not equal to sperm, but is superior to right whale oil, and brings a higher price.

As soon as the announcement was made that the school ahead was black-fish, the deck became alive with preparations. The tubs containing the lines were lifted into the boats, the harpoons were got ready, and every boat-steerer was alive and on the alert for real business. The ship lazily rolled towards the school, which was some two miles distant; but as we did not move fast enough, we were ordered from aloft to take our stations in the boats.

"Lower away the boats," shouted the captain; and down they went into the water with a rush, and we tumbled into them.

"Give way, men," cried Captain Bunker; "don't let the other boats get the start of us."

We dropped our oars into the water, and shot away from the ship like a bird; for we had practised rowing several times.

"Don't lift your oar so high, and keep it in the water longer," said Captain Bunker to me. "There, just touch the water, then bend your back so that the whole strain won't come on your arms. That's better; now give way, and be hanged to you; for if the mate's boat passes mine, I'll keep you all on bread and water for a week."

We did our best, and I tugged at my oar until my arms seemed as though they would drop from their sockets; yet, owing to the strong manner in which those in the boat with me bent to their work, the skipper's boat kept ahead, and we were enabled to please him, although, for all that, he cursed us for a lazy pack of dogs as ever lived, and swore that we did not earn our salt, and that we were a set of old women dressed in men's clothes; and while he was swearing the hardest, we came up to the school of black-fish, which were sporting entirely unconscious of danger, and I could hear them blow as the captain told the boat-steerer to "stand up."

"Don't you miss," said this Christian Captain. "Pick out the biggest one; and don't you be too long in picking one out. Ef you do I'll come for'ard, I will, and my name is Bunker. Now then, one more pull. That'll do."

There was a moment of breathless suspense on my part, and then the captain shouted, —

"Give it to 'em. Stern, all — stern, all! The rascal will be in the boat if you don't bear a hand."

I ventured to look over my shoulder, and as I did so a shower of water was poured upon us, and close under our bow was the black-fish rolling over and over.

"Stern, all, and be hanged to you!" roared the skipper. "You want him to stave my boat — don't you?"

We backed off the ferocious little fellow. By this time all the boats were fast, and were running in various directions, and just as the captain got out his lance, the fish that we were fast to started for the school, and towed us along at a merry rate. Suddenly he stopped, and came towards us; and as he did so the skipper threw his lance; it struck the fish just back of a fin, and went almost through him. Our prize rolled over once or twice, and then blew up a pale substance mixed with water, which they said was spouting blood, and then the fish rolled over on his back, belly up, and was dead.

"Haul up so that I can cut close to the iron," the skipper said. "I'm bound to have another one."

We hauled up, and the line was cut close to the harpoon in the carcass, bent on to another iron, a flag was stuck in the body of the dead fish, so that we could find it at some other time, and then we went in pursuit of the school which had begun to grow alarmed and was making off. We bent to our oars, and passed the mate, who was just giving his fish a finishing stroke, and were, by hard rowing, enabled to overtake the school, and fasten to a second one, which yielded to its fate without a struggle — a circumstance which so pleased the captain, because he struck it, that he even smiled, and condescended to joke a little.

He even had a tilt at me; but I was not to be led on to my own destruction, for Jack gave me a warning look.

"Well, Pepper," the skipper said, "you now know how to kill black-fish. Do you think that you could eat one?"

"Not a whole one, sir," I answered, with a slight grin, for all in the boat were bound to laugh at what the skipper said.

"Well, ain't this better work than larning at school and saying lessons?"

"It is more exciting, sir," I replied.

"I'll show you excitement if I get arter a seventy barrel whale. Here, pass the line aft, and let's tow the fish alongside, for I see that the *shurks* is gathering for a bite."

I looked over the side of the boat, and to my extreme surprise saw half a dozen six foot sharks had already mustered around the fish. Of us they seemed to have the most supreme contempt, and would frequently roll on their sides, and look at us with their dull, staring eyes.

At length one more bold or hungry than the rest attempted a mouthful, but succeeded in only tearing the black skin; but the signal seemed to have been given for all the others to commence, and they did pile upon the fish and snap at its fins and tail and other portions of its body with refreshing eagerness.

While this continued I saw that the monsters suddenly withdrew from the fish, and swam off a distance of some two fathoms, and there waited for whatever was to occur; and suddenly, as though issuing from the bowels of the sea, came in sight a monster shark, at least two fathoms long, and with a set of teeth that would have delighted a dentist desirous of commencing business.

"Ah," said the skipper, rubbing his coarse hands with delight, as though he had met with a congenial companion, "here comes the president of sharks, and he'll lick the little cusses all to thunder if they don't mind their eyes."

The monster shark was very composed in the presence of his followers, for he moved with a deliberation that was very striking, and the only token he gave that he appreciated the situation in which he found himself placed, was by a slight wag of his tail, and an opening and shutting of a ponderous pair of jaws, as though ascertaining if they were in good working order. At length the monster sailed up to the fish, and laid its head upon one of the fins, and seemed to smell it, and then he slowly opened his mouth, and set his teeth upon the fin, and gave it a jerk; but it did not yield readily, although the shark backed some half a dozen fathoms, and towed the dead black-fish as it did so. But the fin contained too many bones to be severed readily, and the shark dropped that part and attempted the head; and while he was doing all that he could with that portion of the carcass, he was directly under us, and I could have touched his back with my hands.

I had been so much absorbed in watching the movements of the king of sharks that I had forgotten all about the ship and the other boats, and now I took time to glance around the horizon and see what had become of them. The old Sally was about half a mile from us, becalmed, and the other boats, each with a black-fish in tow, were close to her, and would soon have their prizes on board.

Once more I leaned over the side of the boat and examined matters below me. The shark had abandoned the head, and had swam to the tail, as though that part of the carcass offered an advantageous opening.

"What a rambacious old cuss it is!" said the captain, speaking for the first time for a quarter of an hour. "I'm a good mind to send a lance through him, and see how he'll relish it."

"Better do it, sir," said Jack. "There's no knowing how many sailors he has eaten in his time."

The skipper got his lance ready, and then altered his mind.

"I won't spile the edge of the lance with sich a critter," he said. "He's all bone and gristle. I'll cut off his flukes with the spade and see how he'll look cruising round without a starn-piece."

While the skipper was taking off the sheath which covered the sharp spade, the third mate's boat was seen coming towards us.

"Don't come here, 'coz I don't want yer," shouted Captain Bunker.

"We thought you were stove, sir," cried the third mate.

"Wal, I ain't stove, and when I is, I'll ask you to come for me. Jest tow that other black-fish aboard, and I'll look arter this one."

The third mate did not stop to hear more. He turned the head of his boat and went off after the fish which we had first killed, and which could easily be found on account of the small red flag we had stuck in the carcass.

"Now, Bushy, give a slew that way," said the skipper to the

boat-steerer, who was called Bushy for no other reason that I could discover than because he seldom combed his hair.

Bushy, with two or three careful sweeps of the steering oar, did as he was directed, and that brought the bow of the boat directly over the tail of the shark.

Captain Bunker took good aim and let fly with the spade, and I expected to see the shark leave us in a hurry; but it did no such thing. It gently wagged its tail, as though something had stung it, and continued to attempt to take a mouthful of the carcass, although a large gash, a white one, was visible where the spade had cut the sinews.

"Blast 'em, I'll give 'em another one," said Captain Bunker; and he did, but with the same result.

"He's like a rich man; he's got no feelings," Jack muttered.

"Then I'll make him have some," the indignant skipper cried; and he continued spading the shark until by continuous lucky hits, the tail was suddenly lopped off, and then the monster began to realize the want of such an appendage, and leaving the carcass the shark turned round and round, and seemed unable to comprehend its misfortune. If it attempted to go in one direction, owing to the want of a rudder, it would vary some three or four points in a few fathoms distance; and an effort to reach the carcass of the fish was a lamentable failure, for instead of getting there, the shark brought up among its jealous companions, which had been regarding its eccentric movements with some interest, and now made a show of approaching; and one more bold than the rest even had the audacity to put it's square nose close to the wounded member.

Others, also, appeared, and one after another of the petty rascals made attempts to bite their big brother, and then the whole school of sharks turned upon the big one and chased him from our sight.

"That's like the world," muttered Jack; "as soon as you have lost all that is valuable, hundreds of knaves kick you out of favor."

We dipped our oars in the water, and taking the black-fish in tow, made for the ship, and without any other incident arrived on board, hoisted in the fish, and found that we had secured five, which made about six barrels of oil.

During the night watches, Jack used to give me lessons in sparring, and I found they were of much advantage to me even before we reached Fayal; for the morning before sighting that port it was my watch below, and after we had eaten breakfast I took the kids and carried them to the galley for the cook to clean. When I returned to the forecastle, one of the Portuguese, named Antonie, — the same fellow who kicked the kid from me the first night I was on board the Sally, — shouted out, —

"Here, you boy — you no turn in till you clean de forecastle. Scrape 'em all out."

"I'll do my part," I said. "I am not going to spend the whole of my forenoon watch below in doing such work alone."

"S'pose you no do it, I make you," he said.

"I'd like to see you try it," I remarked.

"You would, hey?"

"I should," was my answer.

The fellow muttered something in Portuguese, and made a jump for me, and as he came I put out one foot, and he plunged headlong into a berth, striking his head and cutting it slightly against a board.

"There goes flukes," shouted the men, roaring with laughter.

"Stern, all!" cried Jack. "He's in his flurry. Look out for him, Pepper."

The warning was not lost on me, but I suffered the man to scramble from the berth, and as soon as he had done so I saw that he meant fight by the look of his face. He made a dive at me, like a bull; but I dodged one side, and let him have a blow upon his face that started the claret, and then clinched and threw him upon a chest. The other Portuguese in the forecastle started up to interfere, but Jack kept them at bay with his long and powerful arms.

"Let 'em alone," he said. "They must fight it out. No one shall interfere."

"You let me up," cried the Portuguese, kicking with all his might; but I managed to avoid his feet.

"Let him up," said Jack, "and we'll see if he has got a bellyful yet."

I released my hand from the fellow's throat, and he got up and seemed inclined to try his fortune again, but thought better of it, and joined his companions on the other side of the forecastle.

CHAPTER IV.

WE FASTEN TO A SPERM WHALE, AND THE WHALE FASTENS TO US.

BETWEEN the Western Islands and the equator is favorite cruising ground, even to the present day, for schooners frequently pick up half a dozen sperm whales there in the course of a few months; and as we were compelled to cross this tract on our way around Cape Horn, the lookouts at the mast-heads were cautioned to keep their eyes open, and see how soon they could raise a school of whale. For a week after we left Fayal, we strained our eyes in all directions, and one morning just as our watch had come on deck, the boat-steerer at the main-top-gallant mast head shouted, in clear ringing tones, —

"There she blows."

"Where away?" yelled the skipper, who was walking the quarter-deck with his hands in his pockets.

"Two pints off the lee bow, sir. There she blows."

"What does it look like?" Captain Bunker asked.

"Sparm whale, I guess, sir," was the answer. "A rigular old sojer. There she blows — there she breaches."

Captain Bunker took his hands out of his pockets and looked aloft, and after looking for a moment, he thought that he would leave the quarter-deck to attend to itself, and have a glance at the whale, so that he could pass judgment on it.

He took a position near the slings of the fore-yard, and cast his red eyes upon the waters, far ahead of the ship; and as he did so he manifested some signs of astonishment.

"Keep off two pints," he said to the man at the wheel, "and Mr. Spadem, get a pull at the weather braces."

The boat-steerer, who was perched in the main-top-gallant cross trees, continued to yell every time the whale made a breach, until at last Captain Bunker lost all patience.

"Stop yer blasted noise," he yelled; "I can see for myself — can't I?"

The whale appeared to be terribly excited, and when not lash ing the ocean into foam with its flukes, was breaching most wildly, and throwing its body half out of water. As we neared the whale, and saw its antics, I noticed that the men who had spent most of their lives on board of whale ships, began to look serious and apprehensive. A few words which I overheard Busby and Hunter (the two best boat-steerers in the ship) exchange convinced me that something was wrong, and the whale was acting in a most extraordinary manner.

Captain Bunker was still on the fore-yard, and seemed somewhat undecided and uncertain. He even called the mate in consultation, and they spoke in low tones, but with eyes directed toward the whale, as though they were studying its eccentric movements, and could not comprehend them.

"I tell you what it is," cried one of the men; "that 'ere whale has been fastened to, and he's trying to get the iron out of his body. That's what makes him breach so like blazes."

"I know better," cried another. "That whale is ugly. I don't want to be in the boat that fastens to him, I don't."

"I never seed the whale that I was afeard of yet," replied the other, boastingly.

"Well, I has, and a good many of 'em, and I ain't ashamed to say so. By thunder, look at that feller. He was all out of water that jump. He'd cut in ninety barrels, I'll bet a plug of tobacco."

"Brace up the head-yards," shouted the captain from his place aloft, "and put the helm down."

The mainsail had been hauled up when we edged away for the whale, and now the foresail was also hauled up as the ship came to the wind with main-top-sail thrown to the mast.

"Clear away the boats," the captain next said; and he left the slings of the yard and descended to the deck.

The tubs were placed in the boats and the latter lowered, and in we tumbled and shoved off; but somehow there did not seem to be much excitement among the men as to which should fasten first. In fact, a gloom seemed to settle upon us as we pulled in the direction of the animal.

When we were within half a mile of the whale, Mr. Lance, the second mate, seeing that his superiors were not disposed to press matters, spoke to his crew, and as they had every confidence in him, and liked him better than any officer on board, they bent to their oars, and the second mate's boat shot past us.

"Pull, you lazy rascals," our skipper said, with an oath. "Are you all going to sleep, or what is the matter with you? Do you know that there's a sparm whale ahead of us?"

We obeyed, and the boat went over the long Atlantic swell like a Cape Horn pigeon, just touching a wave and then bounding to another: and in a few minutes we were up even with the second mate's boat, and struggling for the lead.

I can't say that I felt very pleasant or comfortable at that time, for, as we approached the whale, I could hear with awful distinctness the terrible manner in which it struck the water during one of its breachings. At length I could no longer control my will, and round went my head, and the captain saw my motion.

"I'll murder you, Pepper," he roared, "if you look over your shoulder agin, you scamp. You wouldn't pull a sojer off your —."

The balance of his remarks was lost, for just at that moment the whale breached, and was so near the boat that spray flew all over us, and the waves knocked us about as though we were in a cross current with a stiff breeze blowing.

"Lay on your oars," the skipper said, while we were shaking our heads free of the salt water.

I was only too glad to obey.

I saw the skipper's face assume a doubtful look. He squinted at the second mate, who had pulled close to us in obedience to a signal, and the second mate returned the glance with interest.

"What do you think of that 'ere whale?" asked the skipper.

"I don't know whether he is ugly or sick," was the answer.

"Sick be hanged," the skipper rejoined. "Who ever seed a whale sick in that way."

"Shall I fasten, sir?" asked the second mate.

"Wal, perhaps you'd best, and I'll stand by to pick you up if you get stove."

The second mate did not wait for another word. He spoke to his men, and they pulled towards the whale.

I peaked my oar, and all of us turned to witness the contest, which puny men were to wage against the leviathan of the deep. The second mate approached the whale in a slow and cautious manner, and I could see that nearly every one of his boat's crew had their heads over their shoulders to see what they were pulling upon; and for once I think that this departure from strict rules was unrebuked, for Mr. Lance was too much concerned at the danger he was in to think of wasting words at that time.

Slowly the boat moved over the water upon its destination, and it seemed as though no trouble was to be experienced in fastening to the whale, for the animal remained motionless until just as the boat-steerer in Mr. Lance's boat stood up and poised his iron, ready for a dart; and then the whale raised its huge, square head high out of water — a head that was armed with a lower jaw which bristled with long, white teeth — a head so old that upon its sides were clustered white barnacles, large as oysters.

"Starn, all!" shouted Captain Bunker, tearing off his hat, and dashing it into the stern of his boat, so great was his excitement.

"Starn, all!" he repeated, "for your lives, starn, all! That whale's crazy, and be hanged to him."

The second mate had seen the peril before the captain shouted his warning, and just in time, for after toppling for a moment, over the huge body went, and struck the water with a sound like a thunder-bolt; and for a minute Mr. Lancé and his boat were lost sight of, as the water bubbled and boiled in the vicinity of the whale; but as the waves subsided, the mate and boat were seen safe, and I breathed easier in consequence, and I think that the captain did, selfish as he was and seemed.

The mate's boat, with the round-shouldered Mr. Spadem in the stern-sheets, came bobbing towards us, the face of the officer not looking particularly amiable.

"What do think?" asked the captain.

"I don't know," was the answer; and the mate scratched his head and took a huge piece of tobacco, and chewed on it most savagely.

"Do you want to fasten to that 'ere whale?" the captain asked.

"Wal, I should if he would keep quiet," was the non-committal reply.

The captain didn't like the answer; but he scratched his head, and looked at the mate, and then both looked at Mr. Lance; and just as they did so the second mate's boat stole quietly towards the whale, which was for a moment resting in peace upon the water, and before we could take a long breath, we saw the second officer in the bow of his own boat, and hurling two irons through the air with the quickness of lightning. The next instant the boat was hid from our view by foam and spray.

"By thunder, he's fast!" cried Captain Bunker; "and if he ain't stove it's a miracle. Pull a few strokes, and let's see what we can do for him."

We dipped our oars into the water, and the boat was pulled towards the whale, which had not yet ceased its struggles; but as we neared the scene of action, the boat of the second mate was found to be safe and uninjured, and Mr. Lance coolly surveying the contortions of the animal, lance in hand, ready for a dart when an opportunity presented.

In the mean time the whale was sometimes standing on its head, but oftener on its tail, looking around with its small eyes as though to get the range of its tormentors. To approach the whale while fighting in such a manner, was not to be thought of.

We pulled up until we were enabled to speak with the second mate, for the latter had backed off to a respectable distance, and was as much astonished at the actions of the whale as any one; yet he kept his thoughts to himself for fear of imparting alarm to his boat's crew.

"Both irons home?" asked Captain Bunker.

"Yes, sir, and just behind the hump. They won't draw."

"What do you think of him?" the captain asked.

"I think that he is ugly, and will do mischief, unless we are sharp enough to prevent it," was the calm reply.

"Then I won't fasten to him, but will lay by and assist," the captain remarked.

While this conversation was going on, the first and third mates were lying on their oars, waiting for a favorable turn; and it soon came, but was not so favorable as could have been wished, for the whale, after one or two glances around the horizon, suddenly settled, and we could see the men in the second mate's boat contesting every inch of line for fear he should take it in his head to sound deeper than was desirable. It seemed as though the expedient was to be successful, for the strain on the line appeared to cease, and Mr. Lance's boat was whirled around half a dozen times, towed rapidly for a few fathoms towards the other boats, and then, while we were thinking that the whale was at least fifty fathoms beneath us, there was a sudden ripple near, and, to our consternation, the old fox was alongside, and looking at us with his little cunning eyes, as though glad of the interview.

"Starn, all!" yelled the skipper. "Starn, all, I tell ye!"

Up out of the water came the head, with the huge mouth open, and the lower jaw dropped as though dislocated. Up, up went the head until it towered above us like a huge rock, which needed but a touch to fall and crush us to atoms. We forgot our oars, and we forgot everything but the danger that threatened us. I looked at the captain, to see what advice he would give under such circumstances; but that gentleman did not seem inclined to talk much, and I noticed that he paid particular attention to the mouth of the whale. I began to move in my seat, and think how I should retreat from such dangerous company, when one of the men, an old fellow named Davy, suddenly commenced, —

"Now I lay me down to sleep"

but did not stop to finish the appeal, for over the side he went, and struck out for the mate's boat.

"The devil may stay in such company, for I won't," roared Jack; and over he went.

I wanted to go also, but I dreaded to leave without orders; but Captain Bunker did not seem inclined to give any, excepting once or twice he mechanically repeated, —

"Starn, all — hard."

Over towards us came the head, slowly, as though to prolong our agony, and at last even Captain Bunker found that he was for once in a tight place.

"Starn, all — hard!" he yelled; and overboard he went, although even in his retreat repeated the words which were most used while fastened to a whale.

"Here goes flukes," cried the boat-steerer, who was in the stern-sheets, and over he went.

"Now, Pepper," said the last man, the one who pulled the tub oar, and over he went; and then I arose in all the majesty of my strength, and with a bold leap I left the boat about ten feet behind me, and when I landed in the water it was directly across the neck of the tub oarsman.

He opened his mouth to utter a curse, but the water flowed in and stopped it. Down I went, and my companion with me, and when I gained the surface of the water, I struck out for the third mate's boat, which had pulled towards us to render some assistance; but before I reached a place of safety, I heard a crash, and turned and saw that the whale had closed his jaws upon the boat, and that it was a wreck, divided in the middle as easy as though cut with a knife; and then the savage monster threw two thirds of his body out of the water, and came down upon the pieces with a crash that destroyed the last remnants of the boat. I called out for the third mate, but to my surprise, his men commenced pulling from me.

"Look out, Pepper!" yelled Jack, who was in the mate's boat.

I glanced around and saw that the whale had sounded, so I recommenced swimming after the runaways.

"Swim the other way!" cried the mate. While I was wondering what he meant, I felt my feet touch something; and the next instant I was on the back of the whale.

I had only time to notice the wondering looks of the men in the boats which were near, and then I rolled off into the water, and the whale passed on; but the eddy which such a huge bulk caused surged me against his flukes, and I felt them touch my shoulder, but as gently as a lady would tap her lover with a fan, while in sportive mood. To be sure, the under-current drew me beneath the surface of the water, and I swallowed more of it than was agreeable; but I struggled until I once more saw daylight, and then I struck out manfully for the nearest boat, which came towards me none too quick, as I thought.

All were watching the movements of the whale, which was chasing the third mate's boat with considerable perseverance. I don't mean to say that the third mate was frightened at the enemy in his rear, but I noticed that his men bent to their oars as though they were in earnest.

"Don't you run!" yelled Captain Bunker. "Turn and lance him." But the advice was not taken by the cautious officer.

"How are we goin' to kill that whale?" asked the master of Mr. Spadem.

The mate bit off a rather huge chew of tobacco.

"Can you kill that whale?" yelled the master, after waiting for a few minutes impatiently.

"I don't know," was the response. "He's an ugly feller, and I don't want to get stove if I can help it."

"Are you afraid of that whale, Mr. Spadem?" the captain asked, rather sharply.

"Wal, I ain't afeard, sir," was the response; "but I don't want to go near him."

"What kind of a whaleman do you call yourself?" the skipper asked.

"I can kill a whale, Cap'n Bunker," the mate said.

"Wal, then, let's see you do it."

All this was a treat to us, for we hated the captain and the mate, and there was not much to choose between them. The mate was about to make a response; but just at that moment the whale, which had sounded for a moment, showed signs of coming to the surface, and near the boat the captain was in.

"Look out, sir," cried the mate.

"You take keer of yerself," was the ungracious response.

Just at that moment the whale made a break out of the water, and within ten fathoms of the boat in which the skipper was scolding. The captain lost his boasted presence of mind and shouted his ever-rallying cry, —

"Starn, all — hard!"

But as the boat moved the whale advanced, until he put his nose close to the bows of the craft; and then the captain, in an agony of rage and fear, seized a lance, and drove it into the head of the whale clear to the staff.

A roar of rage was the answer to such a salute, and out of the water rose that lower jaw, as though impatient to snap up boat and contents; and then with a powerful effort, the whale headed from the water, in the direction of the boat which contained the captain. The mark which the rascal aimed at was missed, but by not more than a fathom; and the next instant the boat was rolling in a heavy swell which the whale occasioned, and the crew were clinging to the gunwales, as though fearful it would turn over. That last breach was too much for Captain Bunker.

"Starn, all — hard!" he shouted; and after the boat was out of danger he headed for the ship.

"We can't kill that whale," he cried. "He's crazy and ugly. Go on board and let him alone, or we'll have more boats stoven."

"Well, I s'pose we must go," cried the mate; and I thought that he was pleased at the idea; and, though he was inclined to hesitate, the movements of the whale were enough to hurry him, for the rascal headed direct for the mate's boat, and raised that square head of his as though taking aim.

"Pull; blast him, he's arter us," said the mate; and the men did not wait to be told twice. As they passed the third mate's boat, Mr. Spadem shouted to Mr. Lance to go on board; but Mr. Lance had got his blood up, and wanted revenge for the boat which had been destroyed.

On we went, the whale in our wake. We passed close to Mr Lance, and the second mate did not stir from his position.

"You'll miss it," the mate said.

Mr. Lance did not reply. He kept his eyes fastened upon the approaching whale, and saw that it did not swerve from the course which the mate's boat was taking. He spoke a word to his crew, and, to my surprise, the men pulled a stroke which brought the boat nearer the whale.

"He's mad," muttered the mate.

But Mr. Lance was not mad. He was anxious for honors, and was determined to gain some, even at the risk of his life. As the whale approached, it raised its head out of the water, and the second mate saw his advantage. He let fly his lance, and the sharp weapon entered the side of the fish, just behind a fin, and buried itself to the socket.

"Starn, all!" he shouted; and in an instant the boat was fathoms from the whale, which breached high into the air, and then sounded as though to collect its ideas under water.

For fifteen minutes we waited for the rascal to show himself. At last, without warning, the whale reached the surface of the water, and a jet of blood, thick, clotted blood, was puffed into the air, and dyed the ocean for many fathoms around.

"Hurrah!" yelled the men; "old ugly has got a bellyful at last."

"By thunder!" exclaimed the mate, "he's spouting blood as sure as I'm a live man. Pull for the ship, men, and let me get rid of the sojers," — meaning those whom he had picked up when the boat was stoven.

The men pulled towards the ship, but kept their eyes upon the whale, and smiled every time the wounded monster spouted blood. We arrived alongside, and I was not sorry to get on board again. After I had changed my clothes I went on deck. I found that the captain had not recovered his temper, for he stood at the galley door, with the cook's wool in one hand, and pounding him with the other. At length the skipper desisted, and as he drew off his forces he muttered, —

"I'll teach you to send me muddy coffee agin."

"So help me God, cap'n —" the cook said; but he was cut short.

"Don't bandy words with me, you black rascal, or I'll tie you up and take the skin off of ye."

The cook returned to his galley, and wiped the blood from his face, and the skipper went aft.

"Good Heaven!" I thought; "is it possible that a man can so misuse another just on account of a little muddy coffee?"

"That's nothin', Pepper," Jack said, as though in reply to my thoughts. "He's got the old boy in him, and it will cum out afore the vige is up, you may believe."

"Jack," I said, drawing him one side, "the Sally is to touch at the Sandwich Islands. Why can't we run away there?"

"How does you know that?" he asked.

"Because, the other day, when it was my trick at the wheel, I heard the captain tell the mate that after doubling Cape Horn, he should shape his course for the Sandwich Islands, and stop at one of them."

"Pepper," said my friend, "I'll think of this 'ere matter, and see what is best."

The whale was spouting blood, and seemed to be growing weaker every moment; but his head was raised from the water quite often, and his terrible lower jaw was worked as rapidly as ever.

"If he don't stop spouting blood in five minutes, that 'ere whale is a goner," I heard the third mate say.

He had hardly ceased speaking when the whale suddenly raised its head from the water, and commenced swimming around in circles.

"Hurrah! he's in his flurry," shouted the men.

"What's his flurry?" I asked of an old man.

"Dying, you fool," was the reply.

"Well; why couldn't you say so?"

"'Cos, tain't ship-shape," was the answer; and he seemed to think the reply was a clincher.

Around in circles the whale went, gradually contracting them, until a circle could no longer be formed; and then a thick column of blood was thrown up, and with one mighty effort the fish threw its whole body from the water, rolled over and over some two or three times, and then remained stationary on its side, and with one fin exposed to view.

"Hurrah!" yelled the men; "he's dead as a Dutchman."

"Brace forward the main yard," cried the skipper, who felt a little more pleasant, when he saw an eighty-barrel sperm whale "turned up," after all hope of its capture was given over.

We run to the windward of the whale, backed our main and mizzen top-sails, and let the Sally drift to the leeward. As we neared the prize, one of the boats brought us a line secured to the flukes, and in a few minutes the whale was alongside, the fluke chain in its place, and I had an opportunity to glance at the animal which had frightened so many men that day. I must confess that I was a little disappointed, for the whale did not come up to my expectations in point of size.

It was about seventy feet long, but how large in circumference I had no means of knowing; but while I was forming a calculation, based on scientific principles the mate caught a glimpse of me.

"What are you doing there?" he roared.

"Measuring the whale," I answered.

He caught up a rope and rushed towards me.

"I'll measure your back," he yelled; but I had no idea of standing still and letting him do so. I made a bolt forward, and the mate after me. As I dodged around the foremast, he caught his foot in the bight of a rope, and over he went upon the deck; and when he gained his feet he heard the skipper call from the quarter-deck; so was compelled to forego his vengeance.

"I say, Charley, it was fun to see old Bilious sprawl on the deck," whispered my friend Will, trying to suppress his laughter. "His shoulders are so high that they struck afore his head. He's mad 'cos the second mate killed the whale."

We got up our "cutting-in" gear, slung our stages for the mates to stand on, and went to work rolling in the blubber, huge blanket pieces, four feet wide and ten feet long, which were stowed away between decks for future use. By sundown, the last blanket piece was on board, and the head and case were secured, and then the carcass was cut adrift.

As the carcass drifted astern, the water was alive with sharks, which were shoving their blunt noses out of their natural element, in vain attempts to secure more eligible positions.

The day after the capture our try-pots were in full blast, and

I was initiated into the mysteries of holding "horse pieces" while my friend Jack "minced" them. The blubber, as it is received on board as related before, comes in the shape of blanket pieces. They are lowered between decks, and after the whale is "cut in," two men are detailed for the very dirty work of cutting the blubber into small strips, called "horse-pieces," and pitching them on deck, where they are thrown into tubs, and are ready for the "mincer." The "mincer" is armed with a weapon that resembles a drawing-knife, only much larger, and his duty is confined to slicing the "horse pieces" into thin leaves, so that every drop of oil will exude when subject to boiling. To enable the "mincer" to do his part with fidelity, it is necessary that some one should hold the blubber while it is sliced; and as the latter work is light, the youngest hand on board is generally detailed for the business. The holder is armed with a small hook, with which he fishes out the "horse pieces" from a tub that stands at his side, and places them upon a bench, ready for the "mincer;" and after they are sliced they are ready for the try-pots.

The position to which I was promoted was not a clean one or an easy one. There was grease on my hands, face, hair, and at last I could almost taste it; and when the last piece was "minced" I was as thankful as though I had received a discharge at one of the islands of the Pacific.

Then came the stowing down of the oil, and the clearing up of the deck; but at last all that was accomplished, and we once more resumed our mast-heads, and the regular routine of ship-duty. Our whale had yielded some eighty barrels of oil.

We crossed the line after the usual number of calms and rain squalls, and the old Sally continued to drift slowly towards Cape Horn. This was a pleasant part of the voyage; but the treatment of the crew was not humane, and it happened quite often that some of the men were knocked down by the captain and mate, and kicked after they were down most brutally.

One morning, when it was my watch on deck, the skipper made his appearance just as we were swabbing down, after washing the deck. A Portuguese, named Henry, happened to flirt a few drops of water upon the skipper's feet.

"You careless dog," roared Bunker, "what do you mean?"

"Me no mean to do dat," replied the man, somewhat frightened.

"No mean to do dat," cried the captain, in a mocking tone; "but you did do it;" and with one blow he struck the Portuguese to the deck, and then kicked him, while down, until the man's face was covered with blood.

"Up with you," roared the skipper; "don't you lay there grunting when you ain't hurt."

"Me hurt," responded the poor fellow, slowly rising from the deck.

"Then I'll hurt you more, and give you somethin' to whine about," the bully responded, and down went the Portuguese a second time; and the captain jumped upon his prostrate body, and then took the end of the main-topsail halyards, and beat the man until his cries could be heard all over the ship.

I looked at the Portuguese members of our watch, and I saw more than one face flush with suppressed rage; and if we had been united, the Americans, English, and Portuguese, that hour would have been the skipper's last in this world.

The sailor got upon his feet and crawled forward. His countrymen crowded around him and washed his wounds; but they did not speak a loud word all the time.

"There's murder in them fellers' hearts," Jack said to me, as I was regarding the scene.

"I wish that they had the spunk to have it in their hands," I answered, indignantly.

"Come here, you Pepper, and swab the deck," the mate cried, interrupting my reflections.

I went aft and performed the work, but I felt how sweet revenge would be to me as I wiped up the Portuguese blood. That day, while I was giving Jack his usual lesson in reading and writing, the conversation turned upon the abuse which the men were receiving at the hands of the captain and the mate.

"Is there no redress?" I asked.

"None, unless we mutiny, but that is a serious thing for the men. I've seen it tried twice in English ships, and the crew got the worst of it after reaching port. Consuls won't take a sailor's word, even if backed with an oath, and the skipper gets the best of 'em, 'cos he has the rocks, and consuls know it."

We went on with our lessons, but while I was directing Jack how to make a few capital letters, a man named Sam joined us, a good seaman, but a great grumbler, and cared more for a glass of liquor than a dinner. He sat watching the slow movements of Jack's huge fist for a few minutes, with an expression of disgust upon his coarse face, and then gave vent to his feelings.

"What's the use of all that 'ere? Your hand is better fitted for a marlinspike and a sarvin' mallet than a pen. It's no use for one like us to larn, 'cos it won't do any good. Now drop that 'ere thing, and listen to me. Do you want some rum?"

"Try me;" and Jack's eyes sparkled.

"Wal, there's two bottles in the forecastle, in the cook's chest. They belongs to Joe Frank, the Portuguese."

"What's it doing in the cook's chest!" asked Jack, his eyes wandering in that direction.

"'Cos Joe Frank fears that the other Portuguese will steal it from him."

"Heave ahead," said Jack.

"To-night, during the first watch, I'll get a key to the chest, and the rum is ours. Of course we must share with the darky."

"Count me in," cried Jack.

"It's not right," I said.

"You be blowed," my friend remarked.

"Ef he blows on us —" muttered Sam.

"Avast there!" said my friend. "I know that Pepper is true as steel."

"You know that I tell no tales; but in this matter you are acting wrong, and I'll have no hand in it."

"The more for us —" grunted Sam.

"Recollect I'm to know nothing of the matter," I continued.

"Ef you'll only hold your tongue, we don't want you to," was the answer.

I left the men plotting, and turned in; but that night about five bells in the first watch, I saw Jack and Sam rise from the vicinity of the try-pots, and steal lightly towards the forecastle. I went to the scuttle and waited. They extinguished the light, which hung at the foot of the steps. Intently, as I listened, I could hear the movements of the two thieves, for they were doing a job which they had often done before, on board of other ships; and let me state here, that the stealing of liquor from a shipmate is not considered a serious offence at sea with those who obtain a share.

After Jack and Sam had been in the forecastle about five minutes, I heard a sudden click, as though two bottles had touched each other, and then the men commenced their retreat up the steps. I stepped aside as they passed me and made for the galley, where they concealed themselves and the liquor.

At four o'clock we again went on deck, and about that time the doctor was called to start a fire in his galley. I kept watch, and presently I saw Jack and Sam in the galley, and the weather door shut, and in a few minutes both men left, wiping their mouths with the backs of their hands. Half a dozen times they repeated their visit, and it began to tell on them. As for the cook, he commenced shouting, —

"De Lord am my Shepherd, and I am his sheep,"

until the noise aroused the mate, who came forward.

"What are you making all that row for?" Mr. Spadem grunted.

"Why, bless de Lord, Mr. Mate," cried the cook, "I feels dis mornin' as dough I was goin' to de land of Canaan."

"You black rascal, ef you don't hurry up my coffee, I'll see if I can't make you sing another tune;" and the Christian-like mate walked aft, not suspecting that the doctor was drunk.

While washing down the decks I kept one eye upon the cook, for I saw that the liquor was getting the better of him. Just as the captain came on deck, the doctor left the galley with a huge copper, the water in which he wished to empty over the side.

"I'se bound to hab de glory,
I'se bound to hab de glory,"

he sang in a loud voice, which attracted the attention of the skipper. He glanced at the poor fellow, who was unconscious of the attention which he attracted, and while looking the doctor reached the rail and raised the boiler. Just at that instant the ship gave a lurch, and over went the boiler into the ocean, and the cock was compelled to cling to the monkey-rail to prevent going too.

"It has gone to glory,
It has gone to glory,"

sang the cook, looking somewhat surprised, and scratching his head with decided vigor.

The skipper jumped for the unfortunate man, and caught him

by his neck, and brought him to the deck; but as he struck on his head, it did not hurt him much.

"You black rascal," roared Bunker, "what do you mean by throwing that biler overboard for?"

"I'll hab a little glory, I'll —" began the doctor; but the skipper choked him so hard that he could not finish the stanza.

"O, don't do dat," cried the darky; "it hurts."

"I'll hurt you, you black rascal," said the captain; and he lifted the negro's head by the aid of the wool, and dashed it upon the deck.

"I'll hab a little —"

"You have had a little rum this mornin'; that's what you've had," interrupted the captain: "and I'll find out where you got it;" and seizing the doctor by the wool, he dragged him aft.

Jack and Sam, the two who were instrumental in inducing the doctor to drink, skulked near the foremast, and looked rather foolish.

"Now, you black rascal, tell me where you got your rum," said the Christian Captain Bunker, with sundry kicks at the doctor.

The prostrate man commenced singing, "Glory," but the skipper interrupted him.

"The rum — where did you get it?" was the fierce question.

"Wal, cap'n, you jist luf alone my throat, and I'll tell you."

"Tell, you black rascal;" and down went the head upon the deck with a crash.

"Golly! don't do dat," cried the negro, as though he felt a little uncomfortable under such treatment.

"Don't tell me what to do," said the enraged captain, with an oath. "I'm the cap'n of this 'ere ship. I'll make you into a hash if I please."

"I's too tough, cap'n," cried the negro, who, in spite of his position, could not help showing a specimen of humor.

"I'll see how tough you are," roared the skipper; and down upon the deck went the poor man's head with a bump.

"Dat hurt," he said.

"Then tell me where you got that rum. I want to know, and I will know."

"Dat rum was Joe Frank's; but I —"

The Christian captain did not stop to hear more. He gave the negro's head a thump upon the deck, and shouted to the mate, —

"Bring that 'ere Portuguese aft."

Joe Frank was asleep in the forecastle, and dreaming of the little plot of land which he expected to own some day. He was awakened by a rough hand taking him by the nape of the neck, and dragging him out of his berth, and from thence on deck.

"What dis for?" asked the man, a little wildly.

"Never you mind what it is for," was the unsatisfactory answer which the mate returned.

Joe Frank was hurried aft, and by the time he was confronted with the skipper, the cook had gained his feet.

"What is dis all for?" asked Joe Frank.

"Silence, you Portuguese rascal," the captain replied. "Don't you go for to speak till I tells yer to. What did you give that nigger rum for?" he asked.

"Me no gib 'em rum, sar," the man replied, with a look of astonishment.

"Don't you tell me you didn't, when I know you did."

"Me no gib 'em — "

The captain did not wait for the man to finish. He gave a jump, and caught the Portuguese by the neck, and shook him for a moment, and then, finding that such work was fatiguing, knocked him down and jumped upon him, landing heavily upon the man's breast; and I thought had crushed his bones in.

"Now get up," roared this Christian New Bedford skipper.

"Me can't," whined the poor fellow.

"Get up, I tell you;" and the boots were once more applied to the man's ribs.

The Portuguese arose with some difficulty, and stood trembling before the quarter-deck tyrant.

"There, didn't I tell you you could?" the captain cried, triumphantly; and then drew back his arm, and let his fist fall upon the unprotected face of the Portuguese, and he fell to the deck as though struck by lightning, and he didn't move, either, for some minutes.

"Take this brute forward," roared the captain, bestowing a kick upon the bleeding man; and two of the men took the Portuguese in their arms, and carried him to the forecastle, and poured buckets of water upon his head to revive him.

"Now, you black rascal, do you go into the galley, and don't let me hear of you agin, or of your getting drunk. I can sing all the hymns that's wanted on board this 'ere vessel."

The darky limped into his galley, and finished getting breakfast, but he was lame for two weeks.

CHAPTER V.

A LIGHT OFF OUR WEATHER BOW, AND WHAT CAME OF IT.

ONE night, when it was my first watch on deck, and while I was pacing back and forth with Jack, I saw the sudden flash of a light about a point off our weather bow. The Sally was then close-hauled on the wind, and was making a prodigious attempt to move through the water; but it was all froth, and no substance.

"Jack," I said, "there's a light off our weather bow."

He looked in the direction indicated.

"That's no light from the try-works," he said. "It's too much of a glim for that. I'll give the mate a hint, or he may swear that we don't keep a lookout;" and going aft he informed Mr. Spadem of the fact.

"Eh," he grunted; "it's some old craft on fire;" and then he put his hands in his pockets, and commenced walking the decks as as though nothing more was to be done.

"Paps there may be humans on board," Jack said.

"Well, what of it?" Mr. Spadem asked.

"Wal, paps they'd like to be saved," my friend continued.

"Well, who's to prevent 'em," the mate inquired.

"I don't know who's to prevent 'em, sir," replied Jack; "but I should like to have a hand in saving 'em, sir."

"And bring a parcel of folks on board what will eat us out of house and home," sneered the mate.

"I'll give up part of my rations for 'em," said the sailor.

"Well, *I* won't, and I don't want to hear any more about it," cried the mate; and as that was a hint for Jack to move forward, he was about to do so, when the captain came on deck.

"What's the matter?" the skipper asked.

"A light off the weather bow, sir," returned the mate, who suddenly grew wonderful obsequious in the presence of the captain.

"What is it?"

"A vessel burning, sir."

"And why didn't you let me know of it afore? Jist as like as not we can pick up some sails and rigging aboard. We are not more than two miles from the fellow," said the captain, "and I think I'll send a boat and see what there is on board."

"What boat shall I send?" asked the mate.

"Let Mr. Lance and his boat go," said the captain, after a pause.

The second mate was on deck in an instant, dressed and ready for duty.

"Clear away the waist boat," was the order; and as half the crew belonging to that boat were below, and it was not desirable to disturb them, Jack and I sprang to obey the command.

We cast off the gripes and falls, and then sang out to lower away, Jack at the bow tackle, and I at the after one. No sooner had the boat struck the water than half a dozen men threw themselves over the rail for the purpose of manning it.

"Come out of that," roared the mate. "I only want five hands."

"And there's six here, sir," Jack answered.

"Then the last man come out," was the order.

"That means Rooney, sir, for he's the last at everything excepting the kid," some one cried; and there was a low laugh.

"Then come up here, Rooney," said the second mate; and Rooney went.

"Shove off!" was the order.

"Wait one moment," cried the skipper, poking his head over the rail. "If you find anything worth saving, make a raft, if you can, to put the things on. I'll hist a light for yer to know where I am."

We dipped our oars into the water, and sent the boat flying over the long swells; and in a few minutes the Sally was lost to our sight in the darkness of the night.

We glanced over our shoulders, and saw ahead of us a large ship, with fire raging forward, but with the after part uninjured.

The sight inspired us with renewed exertions; we bent to our oars until the perspiration streamed down our faces in large drops; and almost before we were prepared for it, the light of the burning vessel fell upon the boat, and at the instant Mr. Lance exclaimed, —

"Give way, lads; there's some one on board. I can hear them call us."

Two more strokes of the oars, and we were alongside of a ship with painted ports, and a run as clean as a Baltimore schooner's. The second mate climbed up the main chains, and I followed him. As we reached the monkey-rail, I saw that the crew of the ship were making efforts to hoist the launch from midships. Mr. Lance jumped on deck, and I followed him.

"In the name of God, where do you come from?" asked an elderly gentleman.

"We came from a ship a short distance from here," I answered; for the second mate, with the feelings of a tar, had rushed to render what assistance he could to those who were working so hard with the boat.

"My dear boy!" exclaimed the old gentleman; and he laid his hand most affectionately on my neck, as though to embrace me; "your presence is most welcome here, for now we shall be saved, and my child will not suffer the horrors of thirst and hunger in the boats."

"O, no fear of that, sir," I answered. "We can find room for you on board the Sally, where you will be well taken care of."

He embraced me most affectionately, and then seized my hand.

"Come," he said, "let us go and comfort my child with the joyful news of your arrival."

He led me towards the quarter-deck, and on the poop I found a young lady whose attention had been so much attracted by the fire, that she had not seen the boat which I came in.

"Julia," he said, "assistance has arrived, and most unexpectedly. This gentleman has come with a boat from a ship but a short distance off."

As the father was speaking I took a survey of the lady, and I thought that she was nearly as pretty as my loved Jenny. She was about fourteen years of age, with dark hair and eyes, and a face that was so pleasant in its expression, that I wished she would give me the same reception that her father had, and put her arms around my neck; but she didn't, for she arose and took one of my hard, black paws in her delicate little hands, and pressed it so kindly, and looked at me so sweetly and sadly from those dark eyes of hers, that I am fearful I forgot Jenny, the old Sally, and everything except the lady before me.

"O, sir," she said, "you are an angel, and will have your reward for thus coming to our rescue."

"I, for one, want no reward, except the consciousness of having assisted so beautiful a lady in distress," I replied, removing my cap and bowing low before her, for the purpose of showing that I knew what politeness was.

"Surely, sir, you must be the captain of the ship which has hastened to our assistance," the lady remarked.

Just my luck. I had made an impression, and now it was to be effaced, if I told her that I was but a boy on board the Sally.

"No, marm, he ain't the skipper; but ef he lives long 'nough he will be one," said a deep voice at my side, and Jack shoved his oar in.

"Yes, marm," continued Jack, with a scrape of his foot, "this youngster is my friend. He and me is chums, marm, and I am larnin' him a seaman's duty, and in return he is larnin' me how to write and read. We belongs to a bloody old blubber hunter, and how two sich likely chaps as I and Pepper come to be aboard of her, I don't know."

The lady smiled at the earnestness of Jack, but her father had given me a keen look while Jack was speaking. He seemed to read my thoughts, for he said quickly, —

"To know how to command a ship, it is necessary to learn all the duties of a sailor's life, and those duties can only be acquired by serving in the forecastle."

"Bully for you," cried Jack. "That's what I tells Pepper every dog-watch. But, then, what does sich a feller want to go to sea for, when he has got a daddy that could afford to feed him on plum duff every day in the week?"

I did not wait to hear more. I ran towards the men who were at work on the long-boat, and left Jack to talk as he pleased.

"You know the young man's father, then?" asked the old gentleman, as soon as I was gone.

"Lord bless you, sir, I don't know him; but then I can read,

On the Burning Ship. Page 68.

and if Pepper didn't run away from home, and a good home, too, I'm a sinner."

"Pepper! what a singular name," said the lady.

"Wal, that ain't Pepper's name; but we call him Pepper, 'cos it's short."

Just at this instant the launch, which had been hoisted clear of the chocks, fell upon the monkey-rail with a crash, and the boat rolled over upon the deck, bottom up. The fire, which was running up the foremast, had burned the tackles which were fastened to the fore-yard-arm.

"We must use the quarter-boats," said the captain of the ship; and he ordered them hauled alongside, for they had been towing astern.

"Let one of your boats start for the Sally with as many people as it can contain," said Mr. Lance, addressing the captain. "I will also send my boat with passengers, and in a few minutes it can return with the rest of the Sally's boats."

"It shall be done," the captain said, promptly. "I will remain until every one leaves the ship."

"And I will stay with you," Mr. Lance replied. "I may be of some use. Pepper!" he cried.

"Here I am, sir," I answered.

"Get the boat alongside, and take the lady and gentleman and their baggage on board; and tell Captain Bunker that more boats are wanted to save the rest of the people. Stay," he continued, and lowering his voice, "tell him that the ship is loaded with a rich cargo, and bound for the Sandwich Islands; and that much of the stuff can be saved. Be lively now."

"Anything more, sir?" I asked.

"No. If the captain should ask where I am, say that I am collecting what valuables I can."

In a few minutes I had the boat alongside, and then I lowered two or three trunks over the rail, and went to inform the old gentleman that we were ready.

"Come, Julia," the father said; "we must not keep these good men waiting."

"But how am I to get into the boat?" the lady asked.

"I have slung a pair of steps at the gangway," I said. "I will assist you."

"I have no doubt of it, my lad," the father remarked; and he gave his arm to the child, and led her to the gangway, where the master of the ship was standing, giving orders.

"Captain Starboard, I hope we will meet again on board the stranger. I would remain with you, were it not for my Julia."

"Your place is not here, Mr. Cherington," answered the master, calmly. "Look after your child. She is of more value than ship and cargo."

"But not of so much value as the life of Captain Starboard, who has a wife and family," the young girl said.

Captain Starboard drew his hand across his eyes, and his lips quivered.

"God bless them," he said. "It will be a hard blow when they hear of this disaster."

"But not when they know that you did all that human being could do to check the fire, and that you are safe," Julia remarked.

The father assisted his child over the gangway, and then passed down the steps before her, holding on to the man-ropes, so that she could not fall. The instant they gained the boat I joined them, and we shoved off and pulled for the Sally; the quarter-boats belonging to the burning ship following in our wake, loaded with men and their clothes. We pulled slowly towards the Sally, for the purpose of allowing the quarter-boats to keep up with us, and while on our way, Mr. Cherington told me how the fire on board the Sea Hawk caught, as near as he could imagine.

"We left Boston," he said, "some six weeks since, bound for the Sandwich Islands, where I have passed some fifteen years of my life in trade, having settled at Honolulu, first in the capacity of a clerk, and afterwards commenced business on my own account. This morning smoke was seen to issue from the fore hatch. The hatches were removed, but such a dense volume of smoke burst forth, that they were put on again, and secured, and we then commenced making preparations for extinguishing the fire by boring holes in the deck. At first we thought that we were likely to succeed; but towards night the fire spread forward, and I saw that all hope was lost. Not so with Captain Starboard, however. He determined never to give up until the masts were on fire; and that is the reason why the launch was not hoisted out in the early part of the evening, as I advised and requested.

The captain feared that the men would neglect their duty, and leave the ship in the boats, if they were launched, although I did finally succeed in persuading him to put a few provisions in the quarter boats, and keep them astern, ready for use. The captain did not relax his exertions all day and all the evening; but they were useless, as you see; and now that noble ship must find a resting-place for her timbers on the bed of the ocean."

"'Tis what we must all expect," said Jack. "I don't want anything better, arter I die, than a ten-pound shot at my feet, a roll in a hammock, and to sleep at the bottom of the ocean."

"Ah, that has been your education, my man," Mr. Cherington said. "But most people have a dread of such a burial, and I, for one, don't like to think of it."

"Don't talk of such subjects, father," the lady said, gently.

"I will not, my child," he replied; and then he turned to look at the burning ship. The flames were crawling up the foremast, and leaping from stay to lift, from brace to halyard, like serpents sporting on a tree; and while we looked, the mast swayed to and fro, and then fell with a crash that sent the sparks flying heavenward, and then all was dark for a moment, and but for a moment, for we could see flames on the mainmast, which grew brighter as they were fed by the tarry and greasy topmast stays. We saw no time was to be lost in hastening back to the wreck.

"There's the Sally, right ahead," said Jack; and in a few minutes we were alongside.

As the men shipped their oars the face of Captain Bunker was visible peering over the rail.

"What you got?" he asked. "Anything valuable?"

"Yes, sir, two human lives," I answered.

"Where's Mr. Lance?" the captain asked.

"He sent me on board with two passengers, sir, and wanted you to despatch the other boats as soon as possible."

I heard the skipper utter a growl, but the men managed to get a pair of steps over the side, and by their aid the lady was landed on the deck, followed by her father; and as they reached the deck the Sea Hawk's quarter-boats came alongside with eight or ten men and their baggage. This was not calculated to raise the spirits of the captain.

"We shall be eaten up," he muttered, "and our vige ruined. Darn such luck."

Mr. Cherington must have supposed that the captain was alluding to the burning ship, for he replied, —

"We have indeed had hard luck, but I trust that we shall bring good fortune to you and your ship. For the trouble which we put you to, I will pay handsomely, as I am well able to."

"O, don't mention it," cried the captain. "I am sure I'm glad I'm here to assist you;" and then, fearful that he had committed himself, he added, "To be sure, I don't know how my owners will feel about the matter. They are close men, and might want something."

"They shall be satisfied, sir," Mr. Cherington said, with dignity.

"That's enough betwixt friends, sir," the captain cried. "Please to walk into the cabin, sir, where the lady can find a seat. And perhaps she'd like something to eat and drink. Steward, make a pot of *switchel*, and put a plate of bread on the table."

I think that the fair Julia did not know what switchel was, for she made no objection to the suggestion of the captain, and all three were about to enter the cabin, when Mr. Cherington spoke.

"There are many things which might be saved, on board the Sea Hawk, if you would send your boats, captain."

"They shall be lowered immediately, sir," the skipper said. "Clear them away, Mr. Spadem, and tell the second mate, who is on board, to be sure and get hold of some running rigging and a few spare sails. Be lively, or they may burn up."

"Does he mean the crew, or the sails?" whispered Jack.

"You Pepper," cried the mate, "go back to the ship with the boat, and tell Mr. Lance to keep his eyes open for stores. Start yourself."

The boat's crew did not wait for a second order. We pulled with a will, for we saw that no time was to be lost, and when we arrived alongside I saw Mr. Lance standing on the rail, as though he had been looking for us.

"What kept you so long, Pepper?" he asked. "Didn't you know that the fire overhead was trying our brains out?"

"The skipper don't care for brains, sir," answered Jack, who was spokesman on all occasions. "He only wants rigging and sails."

"In God's name give him what we have on deck," exclaimed Captain Starboard. "They are of no use to us."

"Let us first save your effects and the dunnage of the men," Mr. Lance said, dryly. "I don't think they should be lost for the sake of a few yards of canvas or a few fathoms of rope."

"The skipper is all ready for you," said Jack, mounting to the deck. "He has ordered a gallon of switchel to be made, and the bread barge to be filled. His heart has expanded like a grain of rice after a long soak in water."

"Silence, sir," cried Mr. Lance, sternly. "Your tongue runs too fast."

"I'll clap a stopper on it, sir," answered Jack.

"And keep it stoppered for the rest of the night. Now, then, Captain Starboard, let me have your chests and valuables passed down, for we have not much time to lose."

The captain would have remonstrated; but as the chests of the master and mates were on deck, Mr. Lance seized upon them, and calling some men to his aid, commenced lowering them into the boat, and by the time the first one was landed the rest of the Sally's boats were alongside. The men worked with a will. The fire was creeping down the masts and stays, and there was no telling how soon the spars would fall, and crush us in their ruin. We had got all the chests into the boats, and some valuable articles, when the second mate gave the order to embark.

"Whar's the captain's sails and rigging?" asked Jack.

"We have no time for them; my life is more valuable than a coil of rope," the second mate answered.

"The skipper won't think so," muttered Jack.

"Shove off, lads, and pull ahead," shouted Mr. Lance. "Be lively, for there is no time to lose."

Our boat was just moving, when a shrill yelp was heard upon the deck of the burning vessel.

"Hello! what is that?" the second mate asked.

"It is the girl's dog. It is too late, poor brute," Captain Starboard said.

"No time for dogs now," Mr. Lance exclaimed. "Pull ahead, and get your oars out;" for the men had paused for a moment, when they heard that a living animal was on deck.

That moment's pause decided my course. I thought how the fair Julia would mourn for her lost pet. As the boat was drawing ahead, I made a spring at the fore chains, and reached the channel before Mr. Lance could open his mouth.

"Come back, you Pepper," he roared.

I did not stop, but jumped on deck, and ran aft to the cabin, and at the door I saw a King Charles spaniel, which was howling for its mistress most pitifully, and yet, owing to the fire, did not dare venture upon deck. As I advanced, the brute retreated into the cabin, which was now full of smoke, so that I could not see him; yet a low whine which it uttered guided me, and I at last laid hands upon the animal, and rushed to the fore chains through a sheet of falling fire.

"Pepper!" I heard the second mate roar, just as I reached the rail.

"Ay, ay, sir; here I am,' I answered. "Shove off. All right. The dog is safe."

"You're a fool," the second mate said, as the boat was pushed clear of the side.

"I suppose I am, sir, and for proof of it, I'm here," I answered calmly.

"I think if the dog had belonged to me, the youngster would not have gone for it," said Captain Starboard. "Is it not so?"

"I love a dog," I answered.

"But you love a pretty girl more. Hey! how's that?" the captain asked.

I was silent, and was fondling the dog.

"There goes the mainmast," cried the second mate.

"It almost breaks my heart to see the ship thus destroyed," muttered the captain, drawing his hand across his eyes, as though fearful of showing some signs of weakness.

"Give way, men," Mr. Lance cried; and we pulled for the Sally.

As the boat started, the flames burst through the deck of the Sea Hawk, and raged more fiercely than ever; and a sad sight it was to every one in the boat, to see so gallant a ship consumed by such a powerful foe. We pulled alongside in silence, and found that Captain Bunker was on deck with Mr. Cherington and his daughter. They had been watching the destruction of the Sea Hawk with such deep feelings of regret, that no words escaped them to show their grief. Bunker hastened towards the unfortunate captain, as I thought, to welcome him. I was mistaken. He had more selfish ideas than that.

"I'm sorry for you," he said; "but I hope you saved your chronometer, 'cos mine is not a reliable one."

Captain Starboard looked at the man as though somewhat astonished.

"One of the men is holding it in the boat," he said, at length.

Captain Bunker rushed to the gangway in a hurry.

"Don't jar that chronometer," he shouted; "I want to use it."

Just at that moment I was coming up the steps, with the dog under one arm, and the skipper thought I had the instrument.

"Here, Pepper, let me have it," he said; and he reached out his hands.

I handed the animal towards him; but the spaniel did not like such a transfer, and growled fiercely.

"What in the d——'s name is that?" he asked, starting back in alarm.

"A dog, sir."

"Pitch it overboard. I want no dogs here."

"O, no; don't do that," cried the young lady, hastening towards us. "It's my pet — my Romey. I would not have lost him for anything. O, how glad I am that you saved him!"

"O, if the dog belongs to you, I've no more to say," the captain growled. "I don't like dogs, unless they is big ones, and bites the men when they won't work."

"O, Romey won't bite any one," the lady said.

The captain turned away to question Mr. Lance respecting the amount of plunder which he had secured, and the lady and her pet were moving aft, when Mr. Cherington laid his hand softly upon his daughter's arm.

"One moment, my child. Captain Starboard tells me that this young man perilled his life for the sake of the dog; and he should be thanked for it."

She turned towards me, but I could not stand there and be thanked by a lady, when I felt that I was inferior to her in position, just at that time. I dodged around the mainmast, and went forward just as Jack was coming to find me.

In the morning, the captain and Mr. Cherington made their appearance upon deck, and the father greeted his child most affectionately, and mutual inquiries were made respecting the manner in which the night had been passed, and then the skipper and the merchant walked aft.

"I don't know what I shall do with all the folks on board," Captain Bunker said, after a pause. "I'm afeard my grub will give out afore I can land all of 'em."

"There certainly should be no fear of starving on board of a whaleship," replied Mr. Cherington, "and as far as the crew of the Sea Hawk is concerned, you can land them at St. Catherine's, or speak some ship homeward bound. They don't want to double Cape Horn for nothing, and I'm certain that Captain Starboard would like to return to Boston as soon as possible."

"And what do you propose to do?" asked the captain.

"If I can make a bargain with you to land my child and myself at one of the Sandwich Islands, I will do so," was the answer. "I'm willing to pay a round sum to be set on shore at Honolulu."

"How much?" and the red eyes of the captain flashed.

"I will give you five hundred dollars."

"It's a bargain;" and Captain Bunker mentally calculated how much of the sum would come into his pocket.

I must confess that the instant the bargain was closed I felt so elated, that I gave the wheel a turn, and up into the wind came the Sally, and her sails were nearly taken aback. Joy, I thought, is mine, for little Julia will remain on board until I am ready to leave the ship.

"You Pepper," roared the captain, "where are you going with the ship? Mind your eye, or I'll jump at yer."

About a week after we had saved the crew of the Sea Hawk, a sail was raised off our lee bow, standing to the north'ard. We supposed that it was some craft bound for the States, from Brazil, and so we edged away to speak to her, and see if we could put Captain Starboard and his men on board. While we were keeping off a couple of points, Mr. Lance came forward.

"Come, men," he said, "who wants to send letters home?"

No one answered, excepting Will, and he dove into the forecastle to scribble a letter to his mother.

"Come, Pepper," the second mate said, in his usual friendly manner, "your folks want to know what you are doing, and you had better write."

I was silent, although I felt a choking sensation in my throat.

"Come, boy, go below and write a good long letter to mother, who loves you, I have no doubt."

I made no answer; but I was about to turn away, when I looked up and saw that Mr. Cherington was regarding me most attentively.

"I am trying to get the youngster to write home to his friends," said Mr. Lance; "but he seems to think that he has been ill used in some way, and don't want to."

"I hope the young man has no such feeling as that. If he has, I am much mistaken in his face, for it does not look as though capable of neglecting a mother's love," Mr. Cherington replied.

"And you are not mistaken, sir, in that," I answered. "I love my mother dearly, and my father also, although we did part in anger."

"And don't your parents know where you are?" Mr. Cherington asked.

"I think not," I answered.

"This is not the proper way of treating them, my lad," he said, with a grave shake of his head. "Go, my boy, and write them an affectionate letter; and tell them that, with the blessing of God, you will return to them some day with a better heart."

"My heart is good enough now," I replied.

"Then the head is at fault, and I like that better. But go. You have no time to lose."

I went towards the forecastle, and as I did so, I heard Mr. Lance say, —

"He shouldn't have tried his luck on board a whale ship. He's a good boy, and I like him, but he don't make a clean breast of his troubles."

I sat down by my chest, and wrote a letter to my father and mother, telling them where I was, and what I had done, and the reason for my course. I also told them of the few incidents that had transpired since I had shipped on board the Sally. I said that I was well, and almost contented, but that if I was at home I would no longer object to entering the counting-room of my father, and doing all that I could to promote his prosperity. Of my mother I asked a thousand pardons for the course which I had taken, and hoped that a few months would restore me to her arms. I folded my letter just as I heard the watch on deck backing the main-topsail.

"Where's your letter, Pepper?" cried the second mate from the deck.

"One moment," I answered; and then directing it to my father, I ran up the steps, and found that we were lying within a cable's length of the ship Brandon, bound for Boston, from Rio, and that the captain of the vessel had agreed to take Captain Starboard and the crew of the Sea Hawk as passengers to Boston, the more willingly as the Brandon was short of men.

"Go and give your letter to the captain, Pepper," the mate said. "He is just about to close the mail-bag. Be lively."

"Where is he?"

"In the cabin."

"Perhaps he wouldn't care to see me there," I said.

"O, don't bother with your 'haps."

I entered the cabin with the letter in my hand. Around the table were seated the captain, Mr. Cherington, Mr. Starboard, and Julia. They were busy over some papers, and a letter-bag was lying before them.

"Well, Pepper, what is it?" asked Captain Bunker, glancing up from his letters.

"I would like to send this letter home," I answered.

"Home! Have you got a home?" he asked. "Why, home is a fool to this place. Pitch the letter down here."

I laid the letter upon the table, and Mr. Cherington took it up, and looked at the subscription, and then at me, in surprise.

"What relation are you to Samuel Allspice?" he asked.

"I am his son, sir," I answered.

"Is it possible? Julia, my dear, you recollect we spent several days at Mr. Allspice's house, just after this young gentleman left home, and you remember what a search was made for him."

"Why, surely, papa, this can't be Charles?"

"That is my name," I said, with a burning face.

"Why, your poor mother nearly went insane at your disappearance. You wild boy, what did induce you to leave such a pleasant home?"

"I hardly know," I answered, lowering my eyes under the earnest gaze of Miss Julia.

"Well, who is the fellow?" asked Captain Bunker.

"Why, he is the only son of Mr. Samuel Allspice, one of the most successful merchants of Boston."

"O, indeed," grunted Captain Bunker. "Take a seat, Pepper."

"Why, what makes you call him Pepper?" asked Julia, with a smile.

"'Cos 'tis short, and I thought it was his name," replied the master.

I did not take the seat that was proffered me, but stood near the cabin door.

"Allspice," cried Captain Starboard; "why, I know Allspice. He's a friend of mine. He's one of the salts of the earth. That youngster is his only child. This is no place for him. Come, Bunker, let him go home with me. You shan't lose by it, I'll warrant you."

Had it not been for Julia, how my heart would have leaped at such a suggestion, and how I should have prayed for deliverance from the Sally and the bondage under which I suffered. But my doubts were soon removed, for Captain Bunker spoke.

"I can't spare any of my crew," he said. "I'd do a favor for Allspice as quick as I would for another man, but you see I must look after my owner's interest."

The old fox was waiting for an offer for my release.

"Come, let the boy go home with me," said Starboard. "I'll see that you are paid for it when you get back."

"If my voice has any influence," said Mr. Cherington, "I should certainly say, let him go by all means. He is an only child. Think of that, Captain Bunker."

I don't know how they would have decided the question, but I thought that Julia looked a little sober at the prospect of a separation, and that made me firm and determined to remain.

"I have shipped for the voyage," I said, "and I think that I will stay on board. I want to see the world, and I don't suppose that I shall have a better chance."

I thought that Captain Bunker's face lengthened, and that Julia's face brightened.

"O, Romey," cried the enthusiastic girl, "you are not to lose your friend, after all;" and she pressed the dog's head to her bosom, and rewarded me with a smile which made my heart beat most wildly.

"Julia!" said the father, in a tone of reproof.

Captain Starboard smiled. The old salt read my heart as though it were an open book.

"After all," he said, "I think that it will be best to let the youngster remain. He may as well sow his wild oats on board a whale ship as to sow them on land. You'd better take him aft,

Bunker, and let him have what clothes he wants from the slop-chest, and send the bill to his father. If he don't pay it, I will."

This was a proposition that suited me, for if I lived in the cabin, I could see and speak with Julia every day. But if I left the forecastle, the crew would no longer respect me, and I should have to give up the company of Jack, Jake, and Will. I confess that I liked the lady more than all three, but I wanted to stand well with the crew.

"I s'pose I might take the lad aft," Captain Bunker remarked, after a pause.

"But I don't want to come," I said; "I had rather stay where I am for the present."

Julia's eyes looked a little reproachful, as I thought.

"Perhaps the lad is right, after all," said Mr. Cherington. "He wants to be independent and free in the forecastle, and he could not be in the cabin."

"Why, papa! And stay in that place, where they smoke pipes all day, and night, too?" cried Julia.

"There are worse things in the world than a pipe, my dear, and I should not be surprised if Allspice used one himself sometimes."

The old gentleman had caught me, one morning, smoking a pipe on the forecastle, and enjoying it also.

"I don't believe that Mr. Allspice would do such a thing," Julia said.

"The boats are all ready, sir," said Mr. Spadem, entering the cabin. "We have got the traps on board, and now they are waiting for the passengers."

"We will be ready in a moment," replied Captain Starboard, and the mate, after looking at me in astonishment, not knowing why I was detained in the cabin, went on deck.

"I shall take charge of your letter, Allspice," Captain Starboard said, "and hand it to your father as soon as I arrive. Be a good boy, and you will find that salt water won't hurt you any."

This seemed to close the conference, and I went on deck; but I almost regretted my resolution to remain, when I saw the neat merchant ship lying within a cable's length of us, freshly painted, and looking as trim as a man-of-war. Presently the party came from the cabin and walked to the gangway, and Miss Julia with them. Captain Starboard started to enter the boat, but stopped and looked around.

"Come here, Allspice," he said; "I must shake hands with you before I go."

The crew looked and wondered, while I went up to the captain.

"There is time for you yet to think of going home," he cried. "Will you come?"

I looked at Julia, and shook my head.

"It is all right, my boy," he said in a whisper. "I don't blame your choice, but I shouldn't care about staying here if I could help it. Take care of yourself, and I hope that your father will have a daughter-in-law before he knows it."

He squeezed my hand, smiled, and was gone.

Some of our men jumped into the rigging and cheered, and the crew of the merchant ship answered it, and then our boats returned and were hoisted up, and the two ships kept on their separate courses.

"Send Pepper aft," I heard the mate cry from amidships.

I went aft, and there I found Captain Bunker, who received me with a sweet smile.

"Pepper," he said, "I don't think that you've got clothes enough. I've opened the slop-chest, and you can take what you like by just giving me a bill on your father."

I followed Bunker into the cabin, and selected such stuff as I really needed, and then gave a bill upon my father for some forty or fifty dollars. I carried my purchases forward, and was envied by those whose credit was not so good; but all wondered how it was that I had so suddenly grown into favor, and the wonder was still more increased when the mate called out to me in the afternoon,—

"You Pepper, go and slush down the main-topmast, and do it well, or I'll take the skin off your back."

"Mr. Spadem," said the captain, with an air of dignity, "don't put Pepper to such jobs as that 'ere. Let some one else do 'em."

"O, very well, sir," was the answer; and the mate looked a little curious.

"Mr. Spadem," said the captain, "Pepper's father is one of the richest men in Boston. He's worth a million. We discovered it by accident."

"Thunder!" cried the mate. "I allers thought Pepper was a little better than the general run of boys, he is so smart and bright."

"I offered to take him aft, and he won't come," continued the master.

"Ah, that lad wants to be a sailor. I can see it in him," cried the mate, who only that morning had called me a "swab," because I had not performed a piece of work to suit him.

"I shall look arter him, and see that he wants for nothing, and you had better keep an eye on him, Spadem, and don't be hard on him, if you please."

"O, no, sir. I took a shine to the lad the fust day he came on board."

The mate told the second mate, the second mate told the third, the third told the boat-steerers, and the boat-steerers told the men. I instantly became a lad of importance on board, and instead of being called to slush down the masts, or tar down the backstays, was allowed the most dainty of jobs, and could stand leaning against the foremast with my hands in my pockets, an hour at a time, and there was no one to haze me for it. To be sure, Mr. Lance treated me just as he always had done, in a kind, fatherly manner, and made no allusion to my position at home. He was too much of a man to do that; and, faith, when he wanted a job done, and I was on deck, he would call on me to do it just the same as ever.

My old friends, Jack, Jake, and Will, stuck as close to me as ever. They were not in the least envious of my good fortune in escaping from the dirty work on board a whaler, and when they heard that I had refused to leave the forecastle for the cabin, they chronicled it as a triumph of my good sense.

CHAPTER VI.

ROLLING DOWN TO HONOLULU. — A PROPOSITION AND THE RESULT.

After many days of battling with fierce gales and terrible cold and sleet, we passed Cape Horn and its dangers, and at length, to our joy, caught the trade-winds, and they blew us towards Honolulu, at a rate of six knots per hour, which was fair sailing for the

Sally. We raised several school of sperm whale, and managed to secure one fish; but as I have already shown how whales are captured when they fight hard, there would be no pleasure in describing the taking of a whale that submitted to its fate without a single struggle. At the time the boats were lowered, when we were fortunate in securing a prize, Miss Julia was on deck, and manifested some signs of uneasiness; and as I happened to be near her when the order was given to clear away the boats, she spoke to me.

"I hope you are not going," she said.

"O, but I am," I answered.

"You will get killed, and then what will your mother say?" she continued.

"O, there is not much danger," I answered.

"O, but there is; and you ought not to go. There's enough without you."

"But they have mothers also," I answered.

"Yes, I suppose so; but then you know you are different from them;" and Julia looked as though she meant what she said.

As we neared the Sandwich Islands she grew more friendly, and even expressed a hope that I would receive my discharge and be allowed to reside at Honolulu, a place which she had not seen for five years, as when a mere child, she had been sent to Mr. Cherington's friends, in Massachusetts, for the purpose of receiving a thorough education, or such a one as young ladies generally receive.

The evening before we made land I had a conversation with Mr. Cherington on the subject that interested me so much.

"I have bad news for you, Charles," he said. "Captain Bunker is firm in his refusal to allow you to leave the ship, unless his terms are agreed to. I have offered him two hundred dollars, to be paid in supplying the ship with refreshments; but he rejects it. It is hard, and far from just; but I am powerless to help you unless you feel willing to sign an order on your father for five hundred dollars. I do not advise you to, but you can act as you please."

"I will not sign the order," I said, firmly; "not if Captain Bunker was starving for the money. Make no more offers. I would not give him one hundred dollars to release me."

"You know your own mind best," was the reply. "In all your undertakings I wish you success for your sake and your father's."

He pressed my hand in a fatherly manner, and left me, and I returned to the forecastle.

The next morning at daylight we found ourselves close in land, and very pleasant it looked, covered as it was with rich verdure and stately cocoa-nut trees; and in each valley that we sailed past, a cluster of huts could be seen, with children sporting in front of them, and the male portion of the community lolling under trees, or else bathing in the surf, which rolled and tumbled on the beach, leaving a white line of foam as far as the eye could extend.

At length we rounded a point of land, and braced up our yards; and then we felt the breeze more sensibly, and the Sally laid over to it with her head pointing for Honolulu, which looked to me like some of our southern cities during the summer months.

"Are we to anchor?" I asked of Mr. Lance.

"No; we are to lay off and on for a few days, and get a few supplies, and then for a long cruise for sperm whale."

Here was another hard blow, which made me feel as though fate was against me. If we did not come to anchor, I knew that Captain Bunker would not permit me to go on shore, for fear I should leave the ship in a hurry. While I was thinking of these things, Mr. Cherington, whose chests and trunks were all on deck, called me aft.

"Charles," he said, "in a few minutes we shall bid you farewell. I have asked Captain Bunker to let you go on shore with us; but he has refused, as I feared he would. I shall keep him on shore to-night, and endeavor to soften him. I will send you a few things on board when the boat returns, and if we never meet again, think of me sometimes."

He pressed my hand, and then led me to Julia, who was standing near the mainmast, waiting to speak with me.

"I am almost ready to cry with vexation," she said, "at the thought of your not being able to go on shore with us. I have been planning such delightful times that I can't bear to think of disappointment."

I could only express by my looks how bad I really felt. I did not dare to trust my voice, for I knew that it would fail me.

"I'll tell you what to do," Julia whispered, putting her head close to mine; "if I was you, I would run off. I would not stay here. Captain Bunker is a selfish, unfeeling man, and I have a good mind to tell him so. There!"

I was about to turn away and go forward, and hide myself

where I could shed tears in solitude, when Julia laid her hand upon my arm, and asked, —

"You will run away — won't you, Charley?"

"Hush, child," said her father; "you must not talk that way to him. It is wrong to advise any one to desert from a vessel. There is disgrace attached to it."

"But you know that you did the same thing, many years ago, father," Julia said with a smile.

The father looked annoyed, and commenced an examination of his baggage. My eyes fell upon a case of liquor which he had brought from the Sea Hawk, and it struck me that I could make use of it most advantageously.

"Will you give me that?" I asked.

"Why, you don't drink liquor — do you?" the young lady cried.

"No. I want it for a particular object."

Mr. Cherington looked at me for a moment, and then he said in a low tone, —

"Take it, but make good use of it; and I think you will."

I seized the case, and watching my opportunity, deposited it in the forecastle, where no one could find it readily. Then I returned to the deck just as the order was given to back the maintopsail, for we were within a mile of the snug harbor of Honolulu, and could see the stars and stripes flying from the peaks and masts of vessels at anchor; while numerous canoes, with Sandwich Islanders in them, were paddling around the shipping, and some of them started towards the Sally.

"We don't want any canoes alongside," cried Captain Bunker to the mate; and that worthy officer said, —

"Ay, ay, sir," but looked disappointed, nevertheless.

The captain's boat was lowered; but a crew of Portuguese were selected, for the skipper supposed that they would not desert as long as there was oil on board; and in this he was correct.

Mr. Cherington's baggage was lowered into the boat, and then Miss Julia shook hands with me, dried her eyes with her handkerchief, attempted to speak, but failed, and was then handed in the boat.

"Good by," said Mr. Cherington; and he shook hands with me, with a moistened eye.

"You'd better go with us, Pepper," said Captain Bunker, as he went over the rail.

"I should be pleased to, sir."

"It remains with you."

"I know it, sir; but I don't wish to embarrass my father. It would be wrong."

The captain did not say another word. He went over the side with a frown upon his brow, and the boat shoved off, Julia waving her handkerchief and applying it to her eyes alternately.

Even the men felt sorry to see her leave the ship, and some of them sprang upon the rail, and gave three hearty cheers, for which they were sworn at by Mr. Spadem, who had no feeling, and thought that others were like himself.

At length our boat was seen returning from the shore, filled with vegetables and fruit; and we speculated whether the captain had opened his heart, or Mr. Cherington had made us a gift. The doubt was soon solved, for the men handed the mate a letter from our passenger, and in it he said he desired all hands should share in what he had sent on board. I also received a note from Mr. Cherington, and in it was some curious advice. He wrote: —

"I don't approve of your contemplated expedition; but I will suppose that you have started. If you should land at Honolulu, the government would feel bound to return you to the ship. If you should manage to reach the south part of the island, you would find plenty of villages and a simple people, who would make no objections to your landing and living in their midst; but your life would be one of idleness for many weeks. So I cannot recommend such a course, for Idleness is the mother of Sin. Whatever you do, think well beforehand, and be sure and destroy this letter. Julia sends her love. The poor child feels really homesick at leaving the ship. I wish that you were here to dine with us. Captain Bunker will stop all night, and will sail for the sperm whaling ground to-morrow. I send you a few articles of fruit, and to-morrow will send more."

I tore the letter into a thousand pieces, and threw them overboard. The fruit consisted of baskets of oranges, bunches of bananas, some tomatoes, a box of grapes, and a lot of eggs.

"Well, Pepper, your friends don't forget you," said Mr. Spadem, when my presents were paraded on deck; and I must confess that I felt a little proud of them.

"No, sir; and I trust you will take a portion."

"No objections to that, Pepper;" and I gave him a fair share of the fruit, and carried the rest forward, and made a dividend with the crew.

About eight o'clock I commenced my preparations for an escape, although I had not said one word to those whom I was anxious should accompany me. I took two flasks of brandy from the case Mr. Cherington had given me, and carried them aft, where I met Mr. Spadem, who was just thinking of "turning in."

"Well, Pepper, what is it?" he asked.

"I've got a little present for you and the rest of the officers," I said. "I didn't know but you would like to drink to 'sweethearts and wives' to-night; so I've brought you a couple of bottles of brandy."

"You have!" and he reached out his hand for them eagerly, as I knew that he would, for Mr. Spadem was rather fond of a glass, when it didn't cost him anything.

He took the liquor and went into the cabin, and in a few minutes I heard the mates seated around the table and drinking with refreshing rapidity.

Then I went forward, and found Jack and Jake on the topgallant forecastle, whispering together.

"What's going on, Pepper?" Jack asked.

"I'll tell you," I answered; "I'm going to leave the ship to-night."

"I go too, sure," said Jake. "Dat what we just talk about."

"Silence, you snow-ball," cried the white man. "Let's hear his plans afore we say anything about what we'll do."

"Go ahead, Pepper. Let's hear 'em," said Jake.

"At eight bells, or after, when it's our watch on deck, we'll lower the third mate's boat, and start for the shore. By daylight we can be out of sight."

"But what's to be done with the boat-steerer, and the rest of the watch?"

"Dose them with brandy until they are quiet."

"I likes the idea," said Jack.

It may not be generally known to landsmen that in every whaleboat, when equipped for service, is a can of water, and a can containing bread, a lantern, candle, and matches, and we thought that with a few additional articles, we should have enough to last us for some days, even if we could get no food at the numerous villages on the south part of the island. We deemed it best to be on the safe side, however, and we collected a second can of water, a kid of beef, a bag of bread, the sail belonging to the boat, and then "turned in," knowing that we should be called, at eight bells, to stand our watch on deck.

My excitement, however, was too great to permit me to sleep; and I lay and listened to the striking of the bell until twelve o'clock, when I was called and went on deck, where Jack and Jake joined me, and in a few minutes Sam and a Portuguese made their appearance, and then the boat-steerer, "Bushy," who had charge of the watch, came on deck, yawning and rubbing his eyes.

"What do you want up here?" asked Jack of the Portuguese. "Go below and turn in. No one wants you. There's nothing to do."

The Portuguese hardly knew what to do; but Jack made a playful kick at him, and he went down the steps in a hurry, and we saw no more of him.

"Heave ahead," whispered Jack. "Bait Sam with a stiff horn, and then give Bushy a dose."

I went below and got a bottle from the case, and poured into a tin pot about half a pint of raw brandy, and then called Sam into the forecastle.

"I don't want Jack to know that I've got the liquor," I said, "for he would want some. If I give you a drink, will you turn in, and not come on deck, so that he can smell your breath?"

"Sartin. Here goes."

He put the tin pot to his lips; and, as I expected, he did not take it away until its contents were nearly gone. He smacked his lips, and then retreated to his bunk; and that was the last we saw of him that night.

After seeing Sam disposed of, I took my bottle and went on deck, and at the scuttle I found Jack and Jake, both listening to hear how I succeeded.

"Now try Bushy," whispered Jack. "He'll take a pint at one swig, and never wink at it."

I went aft, and found the boat-steerer leaning over the rail, gazing at the land, which was astern, and lighted up by numerous fires on the sides of the mountains. He looked up and saw who was near him, and then resumed his easy position.

"You must be dry," I said. "The officers in the cabin had some punch, and why shouldn't you?"

"'Cos I ain't got it; that is the reason why, Pepper," Bushy said; and he laughed a little.

I held up the case bottle and shook it, and Bushy's eyes opened to their fullest extent.

"Taste it;" I said.

He put the bottle to his lips, and before he drew breath about half a pint of liquor was lost to this world forever.

"Ah, that is the best that I've had since I left New Bedford," Bushy said.

"Try some more," I replied; and I handed him the bottle a second time, after making a faint show of drinking myself.

"Well, I will. Now, this is kind of you, Pepper. I didn't expect it. You and me will be chums hereafter; and if you wants anything, come to me."

Once more the bottle was put to his mouth, and the fluid disappeared rapidly; and then I induced him to take a seat on the hen-coop, and in a quarter of an hour he was inclined to go to sleep, yet continued talking and struggling against the feeling. I gave him one more dose, and that settled him. I stole to the cabin door, and listened. Every sleeper in the cabin seemed to be snoring.

"Put the sail in the boat," I said.

"It's in, and the grub with it. We fixed it while you was yarning with Bushy," Jack said.

"Then you and Jake lower the boat, while I get in to unhook the tackles. An inch at a time, remember; for we must not make any noise."

Two or three times Jack and Jake held on to the falls and ceased lowering for the purpose of listening, but no one seemed disturbed or awakened. At length the boat touched the water, and I unhooked the tackles; and as I did so I heard Will's voice on deck, and then my friend's head was thrust over the rail.

"Charley," he said in a whisper, "I don't think this is fair. You might have told me what you were going to do. I wouldn't have peached."

"We can't yarn here all night," Jack said. "Go below, and don't show your head on deck till morning. We is off; so no more noise."

"Well, then, let me go with you," pleaded Will. "I ain't happy here, and I don't want to stay."

I hesitated, for I knew that Will was the support and hope of a widowed mother; but before I could say a word, the boy was in the boat, and Jack and Jake followed him.

"Shove off," I said, in a whisper; and the boat dropped astern, and the ship slowly forged ahead, and left us in her wake.

"Out with the paddles," whispered Jack.

We had five paddles in the boat, for the purpose of paddling upon whales during calm weather, when the use of oars would have galled the animals. These we got out; and keeping in the wake of the ship, we stole quietly towards the shore. For fifteen minutes we worked hard, without speaking; and then the hull of the Sally grew dim, and we stopped a moment to rest and get out our oars.

"There, they can't see us now, or hear us," said Jack. "What's the next move?"

He looked to me for advice.

"We will head in shore, and then pull along the land till daylight. If we can find a good place to beach the boat, we'll do so; and keep quiet until night, when we can continue our journey until we reach the extreme south part of the island, where we shall be safe until the Sally leaves the coast."

"Why not keep moving all day?" asked Will.

"Simply because the captain will inform the authorities at Honolulu that four of his men have escaped, and he will offer a reward for our capture."

"Well, I's for Pepper's plan; so out oars," said Jack; and each of us took one and commenced pulling.

"I have suspected something of this for some time," Will remarked. "I laid in my bunk, Charley, and saw you dose Sam with liquor, and I knew what it was for."

"Did you put any of the stuff in the boat?" asked Jack.

"Not a drop," I answered.

He sighed, and was silent for a moment.

"I'm glad of it," he said, at length. "I shouldn't have been contented unless I had a swig at the bottle, and one swig would have been just ballast enough for a cargo. I'll stick to water, and swear that it's equal to rum."

We pulled on in silence for an hour; and at last got under the land, and out of sight of the Sally. Then we changed our course, and pulled along the coast until daylight, when we began to look about us for a safe place to land and remain during the day.

We pulled in shore, and at length saw a small cove, formed by a reef which extended some few fathoms from the land, and over which the surf broke with mournful murmurs, as though weary of its incessant labor. The beach was covered with white sand, and looked inviting after our long pull. Scarcely a ripple broke upon it, and we determined to land there. As we pulled along we saw quite a number of fish around the rocks, and then Jake grinned, and held up a fish-line which he had in his pocket.

"You don't cotch dis child widout a fish-line," he said; "and ef I don't take a mess of dem beauties, 'tis 'cos I don't know how to get 'em;" and so earnest was he, that he begged we would wait for him one moment, while he tried his luck. Jake baited the hooks with a piece of salt pork, and threw them over the side of the boat. Before they had sunk near the bottom there was a rush towards them, and Jake hauled up two red-colored fish, of the cod species, each one weighing about a pound and a half.

"Told you so," cried Jake. "Dis nigger ain't cotched flounders in New Bedford for nothin';" and over went the hooks again, and with a like result; and Jake grew insane with delight, and wanted to shout in triumph; but we choked him into quietness, and after he caught about a dozen fish we would not wait any longer, and pulled for the shore. As we neared the beach, we saw that there was a narrow creek on the larboard side, which looked as though large enough to hold our boat, and conceal it entirely unless the cove was entered. In went our boat, and was secured to a tree; and then we landed and climbed up the steep banks to see if there were any houses or huts near us. We searched till sunrise, and could find none; but we did discover a small stream of water, as clear and cool as iced Cochituate, and we had a fresh-water wash before we returned to the boat.

Then Jake put his skill into requisition. He produced a frying-pan, which he had stolen from the ship's galley; and while one of us commenced cleaning the fish, the negro built a fire, and soon had some salt pork frying, and after it was finished in went the fish; and the prospect of breakfast was good, when Jack produced a sauce-pan and a box of ground coffee, all stolen from the Sally. Will and myself ran to the spring for fresh water, and while on our way we discovered a banana tree, laden with ripe fruit. After breakfast we took our hatchets and cut down some trees and bushes and covered the boat with them, so that it could not be seen readily, even if any one should enter the cove. Then we lighted our pipes, and retired back into the country a short distance, and went to sleep under the shade of a cocoa-nut tree. I was awaked by hearing voices, speaking in kanaka dialect. I awakened my companions, and we crawled to a point of observation, and saw a canoe, containing half a dozen natives anchored just inside of the surf, fishing; but one thing was certain: they did not haul in piscatorial treasures as fast as Jake had done, and the negro noticed it, and commented on the same.

"What dat fellow know 'bout kotching fish? Look at 'em jerk when 'em get a bite. Dat ain't de way to fish. De boys in New Bedford all laugh if dose black fellows kotch flounders dat way. I like to go and show 'em."

But we refused to allow him to move, and we remained concealed, watching the movements of the natives for two hours, or more, when one of the men pointed in the direction of Honolulu, and said something in a rapid tone, and then seizing their paddles, they started up the coast.

We waited for some few minutes in our place of concealment, then heard the sound of oars; and one of the Sally's boats hove in sight with Captain Bunker in the stern-sheets. How cross he looked! so much so that Will, who was lying by my side, fairly trembled and turned pale with apprehension. The skipper glanced suspiciously at the cove, and ordered his men to stop rowing; and when he spoke I saw that Mr. Spadem was with him, carrying a double-barrelled shot gun in his hand, as though he was out on a hunting excursion, as I had no doubt he was.

"That looks like a place where they would land," said the captain, his voice raised so that we could hear him above the roar of the surf.

Mr Spadem glanced at the cove, and shook his head.

"No, sir, they wouldn't land there, 'cos they'd expose the boat. I don't believe they came this way. They would be more likely to steer for Oahu. If they had come here, the fellers in that canoe would have seen 'em."

The captain remained silent for a moment, and then turned the head of the boat, and pulled towards Honolulu. We climbed a hill, and saw that there was no danger of Captain Bunker turning back, and then cooked our dinner in high glee at our success, thus far, in avoiding our enemies.

At dusk we again embarked in our boat, and as there was a fair wind, we set sail and steered along the coast, keeping well out at sea, to avoid sunken reefs and rocks. At daylight we found that we were at the extreme southern end of the island; so we pulled in shore, and looked for a place to land. We saw no huts, and thought it best to beach the boat, and remain quiet for a few days. We picked out a good place, and landed, and then used our oars for rollers, and hauled the boat up high on the beach. Then we covered her with brushwood, and made it appear as though it was some that had drifted upon the beach. After this, we lighted our fire, and had a substantial breakfast, and then retired into a cocoa-nut grove, where we went to sleep.

We were awakened by voices; and starting up, I saw six females, natives of the island, near the grove, with baskets in their hands, filled with oranges and bananas. They were all young, too, with light-colored faces, long black hair, and bright eyes and white teeth. I went forward, and as their backs were towards me, I was within a few fathoms of them before they heard my steps. Then they looked around, but instead of rushing towards me and giving me a hearty welcome, as I had reason to expect, they uttered shrill screams, and fled like frightened deer, jumping over fallen trees and uneven ground as nimbly as though trained in a gymnasium for the express purpose of showing their agility; and so much did they hurry, that they did not stop to take their baskets with them, and thus all the fruit which they had collected fell into our hands. I rejoined my companions with a mortified air; and the rascals, instead of thanking me for attempting to open communication with the village, openly reviled me for failing to obtain a parley.

"It's jist as I 'spected," said Jack. "You set a boy to do a thing, and he spiles it."

"I should hab been de chile to talk wid 'em," said Jake. "If dey had seen dis nigger comin', dey wouldn't hab run, 'cos I's jist dere color, and dey think me one ob 'em."

"Your hair, Jake, is rather curly for a kanaka," cried Will.

Jake ran his fingers through his wool, and acknowledged that it did kink a little; but he accounted for it on the ground that he had not used a comb for a few days past.

We were at the extreme southerly end of the island, and near some village — that was evident. The question was, would the natives make us prisoners and send us to Honolulu, or keep us? It would take a canoe two days to reach Honolulu, against wind and tide, and we rather thought that the Sally would not wait so long to hear from us. Jack was in favor of launching the boat, and starting for some other island; but to that proposition Will and Jake were opposed, and I did not like it; so we voted that down in short time. Jake proposed that we should go fishing, and fill the boat with fish, and offer them to the natives as a bribe; but as there was only one line, and that Jake wanted to use, the plan was not adopted, to the intense disgust of my colored friend, who retired from the conference, and went to sleep. We were about to do the same thing, and wait for events, when, looking up, I saw some thirty natives, armed with clubs and hatchets, winding round the base of the hill, and advancing towards us; and following them were about fifty women, all dressed alike, but not all young and handsome.

Our first impression upon seeing the natives was to take to our heels; for we could not help remembering that on some of the islands white men had been eaten, and esteemed a luxury. But I assured the men that I thought there was no danger, and that if any one was to be eaten it would be me, on account of my tender years. Therefore we maintained our position, and awaited the approach of the natives, who advanced in solemn silence, an old white-haired man at the head of the delegation; and from the deference which his followers paid him, I supposed that he was a chief.

"Look at dat old woman," said Jake. "She got her eye on dis child, and I tink dat she mean to eat me for sure."

"Be quiet," I said. "The old man is going to speak."

The procession halted about eight fathoms from us.

"*Ouri miti kanaka*," said the chief.

"What in thunder does he mean by that?" Jack cried.

"Speak English," I said, advancing a few steps towards the chief.

The chief consulted with one of his counsellors, and presently a young fellow stepped forward, and the people raised a murmur, as much as to say, "Now you will see something."

"Say," cried the young fellow, with an oratorical flourish of his hands and a smiling face.

The crowd took up the cry, and all shouted, "Say," and then they laughed. People don't laugh when they contemplate eating human beings. My hopes of a peaceable settlement revived.

"Say," shouted the young man, and then he stopped.

"Say," repeated the natives, and crowded closer around us.

"That makes twice you've said it," muttered Jack.

"Say, where come, hey?" the young kanaka continued, and his friends all shouted, "Ha, ha—*houri*, *houri*," and then nodded their heads numerous times.

I pointed in the direction of the water. The women clapped their hands.

"Say, when come?" asked the interpreter.

"This morning," I answered.

I must have said something witty in those two words, for the natives repeated them, with every variety of intonation, and then, forgetful of their fears, crowded around us without much ceremony.

"Say, what do?" said the interpreter.

"Stay here," I answered.

As soon as the young kanaka had repeated the words to the chief, and the latter to the people, there was an immense amount of talking. The old veteran dug his fist into the side of his interpreter, and the latter once more opened fire.

"Say, where boat?" he asked.

I pointed to the beach, and the chief intimated that we would confer a favor if we would lead the way and show where the boat was concealed. I led the party, followed by the young ladies, who seemed to think that they had some claim upon me, in consequence of first discovery. We continued on until we reached the beach, and tore away the brush-wood which we had piled around the boat. Then there was a shout, and the old women howled louder than all the rest.

"Ugh," grunted the chief; and his eyes brightened as they fell upon the hatchets, knives, and harpoons which the boat contained. I took a hatchet and knife, and handed them to the chief, and the old man spoke a few words to the interpreter.

"Say," said the latter, "this him?" pointing to the articles.

"Yes, all for him," I replied.

When this was known there went up a shout, and the young ladies crowded around me. The chief slipped the hatchet in the bosom of his shirt, and put the knife in a belt which he wore around his waist. The rest of the natives looked wishful; so we gave to one a harpoon and to another a lance, until the whole stock was exhausted. One hatchet I kept, and a knife I gave to the interpreter, which pleased him so intensely that he muttered his thanks in such a mixture of broken English and kanaka lingo, that there was no understanding him.

Then the chief pointed in the direction of the village, and the interpreter said, "Come," and we started, the women clustering around us and manifesting many tokens of kindness; and the chief did not evince any desire to rebuke such conduct. A ten minutes' walk brought us to the village, which contained about sixty huts, and were nestled in a valley that was surrounded by cocoa-nut trees, and orange and banana trees, the fruit on them hanging ripe, and large quantities on the ground, having dropped off, and were lying uncared for. Near each hut was a patch of cultivated land, on which were growing yams, potatoes, and other vegetables, and before each door was a brood of chickens and a few ducks. The houses were thatched to keep out the wet, and looked neat and comfortable.

We went directly to the chief's house; the inside of which we found furnished with a raised platform, covered with a bullock's hide, and seemed intended for a bedstead. Around the walls were spears, paddles, and sharks' teeth, and also a few sperm whale teeth; the latter evidently highly prized from the manner in which they were polished. There was no floor, but the earth was beaten smooth, and even polished, with constant use. There were no chairs, but, as a substitute, grass mats were spread in various parts of the room; and to these the chief pointed, and motioned for us to make ourselves at home. We squatted down, and the natives followed suit, in the open air, however, as no one but a young lady, whose attentions I was disposed to suffer without rebuke, followed us into the house. The young girl lounged on the bed, and looked at us, and laughed, and then she said something to the chief, and he laughed, and then we all laughed. Tl. interpreter suddenly made his appearance, and after a short confab with the chief, asked,—

"You eat?"

And he placed his hands upon his stomach, and made his mouth move fearfully.

"By golly," cried Jake, "he mean dat he like to eat us. Dat old man got his eye on me. But I's tough, and he find out dat he better take de younger ones."

"But you'll be first," I suggested. "They always reserve the delicate ones for the last."

Jake's eyes began to grow large. To add to the negro's terrors, the chief, at that moment, laid his hand upon a spear, and looked unusually grave.

"Look ahere," cried the colored sailor; "I don't stand dat. I's a 'Merican sailor, and will fight like de debil afore I let you eat me."

"Be quiet, you fool, and don't cry out till you is roasting," said Jack.

"It's all berry well to say be quiet; but I won't be quiet when dey is calculating how much fat I'se got on my ribs."

If we had any doubts on the subject of cannibalism of the natives, they were happily dissipated by the entrance of two old women, who brought in stewed yams and fish, a boiled chicken, and a large basket of fruit; and as the food was set before us, the chief intimated that we were to make a meal, and the outside barbarians laughed and encouraged us when they saw that we had good appetites; but after we had finished our first course, the young lady — whom I had supposed to be the chief's daughter, and whom I called "Lilly," not on account of her white skin, however, but because she was tall and graceful — seated herself by my side, and pealed an orange for me, and insisted that I should eat it. I was not hungry, but I would have swallowed that orange if it had burst me. Then she stripped the skin from a banana, and offered me that; and I took it, and squeezed her hand while her father was not looking. I think that I should have killed myself if Jack, who was a little jealous on account of my popularity, had not said, —

"They're stuffing Pepper to get him fat. He'll be the fust one they'll eat."

I didn't believe him, but still the remark made an impression upon me, and I refused to eat the next delicate bit of fruit which was offered by Lilly, much to her regret.

She had a most bewitching method of tempting me with oranges, and smiling when I refused. I thought that she appeared to take pride in my acquaintance, and I am sure that I felt proud of her notice; and for a while I forgot Julia, Jenny, home, and everything but the pleasure of leading a sort of vagabond life on the island, doing as I pleased, and accountable to no one. There was no need of wealth to find happiness where I was. The sea yielded up its treasures to supply the natives with food — on the land, fruit was in season through the year without cost or price.

After the chief had seen that we were not inclined to eat more, he motioned for us to rise, and started for the door; but Lilly stopped him, and spoke eagerly for a few seconds. I saw the chief cast his eyes upon me, and therefore I suppose that the conversation was regarding my welfare. He nodded his head, and called the interpreter to explain; which that grinning individual did in a brief manner.

"You, here," he said, and intimated that I was to remain.

My companions were motioned towards the door; and as they went they had some few words of encouragement for me.

"Good by, Pepper," they said. "If the old fellow eats you, we hope you'll lay hard on his stomach, and give him the nightmare."

"The same to you," I responded; and off they went, the chief leading and the crowd following, as before.

I felt a little lonely at thus being separated from my companions, but I rightly imagined that it was only to find them quarters during their stay in the village, and that no harm would come to them or to me while we were apart. My friend Lilly remained behind, and intimated that I might lie on the frame and go to sleep if I wished, and I liked the idea, for the heat began to grow oppressive. I filled my pipe, but before lighting it considered it would only be proper to express my gratitude to the young lady. As I knew no heathen method of doing so, I thought that I would try the civilized. Therefore, while the young lady was watching my motions with much curiosity, I advanced, and put my arm around her waist, and kissed her before she could recover from her supprise; the next moment I got a clip on the ear that rather startled me; and before I could account for it, the young lady ran from the house laughing, as though she had perpetrated a good joke, and knew how to appreciate it. I lay down upon the bench and smoked, and went to sleep; I dreamed that I had been elected chief of the village, that I had married Lilly, and was to be tattooed with all the ceremonies, as soon as a sufficient quantity of ink and fish-bones could be obtained. And upon that I awoke, and found that Lilly was seated by my side, fanning me, and keeping the flies at bay.

"Well, Lilly," I said, taking her hand, and fearing that she would hit me with it every moment, "I'm exceedingly obliged to you for your kindness, and will do the same for you some day."

She did not understand me; but lovers seldom do comprehend each other until married. As I felt much refreshed by my siesta, I arose and walked to the door; but no one was to be seen in the village, excepting two or three old women, who were making matting.

"Where have they all gone, Lilly?" I asked.

She must have understood me, for she pointed inland.

"Come, Lilly, let's go and find them," I said; and I gave her my hand, and like two young lovers we wandered off together, followed by half a dozen dogs. We went through the village, and entered the woods, and followed a path which appeared to have been much used by the natives. It was sheltered from the sun by stately cocoa-nut trees, each one of which was disfigured by notches cut in the trunks to enable the natives to climb them readily, and obtain the fruit when ripe, or while in that pulpy state which resembles ice-cream made of milk. Yet in spite of the mutilation of the tree, they seemed to flourish and look so stately that I stopped to examine them Lilly must have supposed that I was anxious to taste the fruit, for she made signs that she would procure some for me; and then she put her little feet on the notches, and was about to ascend a tree, when I detained her. She pouted a little, and then gave me her hand again, and we walked on, perfectly contented with each other. Suddenly I was startled by hearing the most uproarious laughter, with shrill yells, and an immense amount of splashing. Lilly instantly became excited. Her eyes brightened, and the rich blood mounted to her cheeks as if the small veins would burst. She hurried me along, and in a few minutes we came in sight of a small lake, with sandy shores, and fed by a waterfall, which gushed from between two rocks at the base of a high hill. In the water, and upon the shores of the lake, were all the young people of the village, boys and girls, men and women, diving, and plunging, and splashing around like mermaids, or nymphs. I was so much supprised that I dropped Lilly's hand, and gazed upon the scene before me in astonishment. On one of the rocks, near the falls, was seated the old chief, gently chafing his skin with a cocoa-nut husk, and rinsing off with water which he dipped up in a cocoa-nut shell; and while I was looking at him, the old chap grinned at me, and then rolled from the rock into the lake like a huge turtle from a log; and those standing on the shore also disappeared in the water, and some remained under it so long that I thought they had committed suicide. But I was mistaken. All reappeared. Then I missed Lilly, and while I was wondering what had become of her, I heard a merry laugh, and saw, near where I stood, a light form skimming through the water, with scarce an effort, her long black hair trailing after her, and her arms glistening like burnished copper in the sunshine. It was Lilly, swimming so easy and graceful that I envied her power. I grew interested in the scene, and walked around the lake until I reached the rocks near the waterfall; and there at my feet sported the graceful Lilly, laughing and blowing water at me, and shouting for me to join her. But I refused, and she pouted and spattered me, and then dove and disappeared from sight; and when she came to the surface, she raised her arms towards me imploringly, and her face assumed an aspect of terror.

"Good Heavens," I thought; "perhaps she has got the cramp, and will drown."

No one noticed her, so I shouted to the natives to go to her assistance; but they laughed at me, and continued to spatter each other with water, and in the mean time Lilly seemed to be drowning. She stretched out her arms towards me, and appealed for help. I kicked off my shoes, and off the rock I went, head first; but the instant I laid my hands upon Lilly, she slipped from my grasp, and down she went towards the bottom. I took a long breath and followed her; but, although the water was clear, I could see nothing of her, so was compelled to come to the surface; then I felt a hand laid upon my head, and I had just time to catch a view of Lilly's face, when down I went again, the jade having rewarded my devotion by ducking me. She had shammed that she was drowning for the sake of getting me into the water. I can hardly understand how another person would have felt in my place, surrounded by some forty water nymphs, each one as clamorous to have a hand in ducking me as Lilly herself. I know that I looked upon the matter as a stupendous joke. I turned for the beach, when one of the amiable young ladies seized me by the feet, and down she went under water, and I with her. I kicked and freed myself from her grasp, and rose to the surface, and struck out for the shore. Then two girls ranged alongside, and intimated that I must put my arms around their necks, and that they would help me. As they looked serious, I trusted them, and was willing to encourage their humanity; but I had hardly put my arms around their necks than they suddenly settled, and down I went with them. I must confess that, encumbered as I was with clothes, I began to feel tired, and desired no longer to contend with the swimming girls of the Sandwich Islands, whose power of endurance in the water far exceeded mine. I struck out for the shore, and Lilly followed by my side. I crawled up the beach, and the natives received me with many good-natured grins, and one of them ran and brought my shoes and helped wring the water from my shirt and pants; and then Lilly, whose toilet was soon made, motioned towards the village, and we walked in that direction. We went to Lilly's home, where I changed my clothes, having taken the precaution to carry off with me a bag full of garments when I left the ship. Then I started to look up my shipmates, whose absence I began to miss.

"Lilly," I said, "I want to see my shipmates. Where are they."

She shook her head, and showed her small, white teeth, and looked so wishful at not being able to understand me that I commenced explaining in pantomime what I meant; and my gestures must have been expressive, for she took my hand and led me to the outskirts of the village, and pointed to a house which looked as though it had long been deserted. I walked up to it, and glanced in, and there saw my shipmates lying upon mats and smoking their pipes with an expression of contentment that showed they were suffering no great hardship.

"Hullo, Pepper! they haven't eaten you yet," the men said, when they saw me enter alone, for Lilly remained outside.

"No, but they nearly drowned me," I replied.

I had to explain to them the scenes through which I had passed.

"You see, arter we left you," said Jack, "they conveyed us to this place, and said we musn't leave it till we got orders from some one, I don't know who. They give us plenty of grub, and we have sleep enough, but somehow I should like liberty to go where I pleased, and not be cooped up here all day."

I cheered the boys, as well as I was able, promised to talk with the chief about their condition, and then went home with Lilly, to whom I endeavored to explain what I wanted by signs, and I think that she understood them. We found the chief at home, squatting near his door and smoking a very short pipe, the bowl of which was carved by some native artist with much skill. The old man looked up and grunted when he saw me, but made no other sign of recognition or welcome. I lighted my pipe, and then sat down beside him, and as I did so I forced into his hand a plug of tobacco. As I expected, that made his face brighten, and he patted me on the shoulder, and said, —

"Twood," which I think was intended for *good*.

"Chief," I said, "I want you to give my shipmates liberty. They have no desire to escape. They like your village too well."

"Twood," he repeated, and shook his head; and thereupon I was compelled to explain by signs, and with Lilly's aid he understood me, and intimated that he would think of the matter.

At sundown an old woman, who seemed to act as housekeeper, brought us some supper, and we gathered round a calabash which contained it. It was a mixture of tomatoes, yam, and sweet potatoes, with pieces of fish, not cooked enough to suit my taste. Supper over, we lighted our pipes, and sat down at the door of the house, and smoked until dark, and then my host intimated that it was time to go to bed; and without further ceremony he lay down on a pile of mats, pulled one over his shoulders, gave one or two kicks, one or two grunts, and was asleep in less than five minutes, leaving me to look at Lilly and wonder what I was to do. I took my blankets and spread them upon a mat, and down I went, and lie there, staring at Lilly, until the room was so dark that I could not see her; and then I went to sleep. Shortly after daylight I felt some one pulling the blanket from my shoulders. I started up, and saw that Lilly had made her toilet, which consisted in running her fingers through her hair and loosening the braids, — probably done up the night before after dark, so that I should not see her operate, — and in giving her simple garments a fresh hitch over her shoulders. — And such shoulders as they were! — full, round and polished, with not a bone to be seen to mar the symmetry, or a blemish as large as a mole to grieve the sight of such admirers of female loveliness as myself. The little witch knew that she was charming, and she showed it by every coquettish act, many of which would have done honor to the belle of a ball-room. I sat on the floor for a few minutes looking at Lilly with so much admiration that the girl put her hands to her bosom, as though to veil it from my sight, and then laughed a long, merry peal, which made her father look up from his seat by the doorstep.

"O, Lilly," I said, with a sigh, "I have dreamed of you all night."

And then the little witch laughed, and mocked me, and danced around me, with her scant garments held in one hand, until her gruff old father, who didn't appreciate such an exhibition of personal charms, threw a potato at her head. And Lilly picked up the esculent and hurled it at her daddy, and it struck him on his grizzly head, and bounded off like an india rubber ball. Then the chief smiled, as though Lilly was a pet, and could do no wrong; and I laughed so heartily that the little beauty recommenced her rotary movements; and only stopped when she was nearly breathless; and then she sat beside me, and leaned her head upon my shoulder. The chief looked up, saw the position of his daughter's head, saw my arm stealing around her neck, and her cheek close to mine, in loving embrace, but the old fellow only grunted his satisfaction, or dissatisfaction, and continued smoking.

"Ah, Lilly," I whispered, forgetting that she could not understand me, "do you know that I love you dearly?" and the presure of my arm was increased until her lips were close to mine and I tasted them. And yet the old chief smoked on, and saw no danger in our dalliance. She said something, and then her arm went around my neck, her breath, fragrant as orange blossoms, was upon my cheek, and still the old chief grunted and smoked on, his back towards us. Suddenly I heard a step, and looked up. Standing in the doorway was a native, tattooed upon face and nose, and as ugly a specimen of humanity as could be found in the village, not excepting the old women. I did not recollect seeing him the day before, and he looked as though I would make him a lunch some day.

"*Kamaka!*" cried Lilly, in surprise, starting to her feet, and looking confused.

"Ugh," he grunted, and he gazed at me and then at Lilly, as though wondering which he should kill and eat first.

The chief continued smoking, and did not turn his head.

"Kamaka is a rival," I thought; "he can't help himself, as I am better looking than he is."

The reflection gave me some satisfaction, and while Kamaka was sulking I talked with Lilly in the best kanaka that I could master, and was pleased to see that she responded in a merry tone, and neglected my rival. He sat on a mat looking at us for a few minutes, and then walked off. After a long smoke the chief knocked the ashes from his pipe, arose, and then stalked in the direction of the lake which I had visited the day before.

"*Ami mi*," said Lilly, and held out her hand.

She led me through the village, and we followed the route which her father had taken.

"Are you to have another swim, Lilly?" I asked.

She smiled, and put an arm around my neck.

"Do you love me a little, Lilly?" I asked; and pressed her graceful form until she said something which must have meant "yes." And on we went, the sun shining upon our path, and the birds making music overhead, as though participating in our new-born happiness.

When we reached home the antiquated specimen of womanhood, who appeared to do the house-work for the chief, was just preparing our breakfast, which consisted of a dish similar to that we had for supper. The meal over, the chief lighted his pipe, and commenced smoking at the door with his back to Lilly and me. Then we began our love-making, and were progressing most satisfactorily, when the old fellow gave a grunt, and put away his pipe. First he gravely arose, and took some fishing-lines from a peg, and was about to walk off, when I thought that I would go also. Lilly followed me, and thus we moved through the village, past the place where my shipmates were confined, and who did not seem to be moving, to the beach, where, in a narrow creek, floated the pride of the village, the canoe owned by the chief.

CHAPTER VII.

A FISHING PARTY. — THE OLD SALLY IN SIGHT. — TO THE HILLS.

WE entered the canoe, the chief at the bow and Lilly at the stern, and with a flourish of the paddles, we left the shore and steered for a reef about half a mile from the island. For a few minutes I sat under the awning, and watched Lilly ply her paddle, which she managed so easily and gracefully that I was lost in astonishment at her proficiency.

We paddled to the leeward of the reef, and dropped overboard a stone, secured by a grass rope, which served as an anchor. Here the chief lighted his pipe and threw over his line, and Lilly did the same. I was not much of a fisherman, but I determined to try my luck. We baited our hooks, and with lines made of grass by some native genius, threw them over and waited for a bite, and I had one in an unexpected manner; for Lilly put her face to mine, and nipped me with her sharp teeth, until I cried out.

"*Miki*," said the old chief with a frown, and made motions that I would frighten the fish unless I kept still.

While I was stealing an arm around Lilly's waist, and she was making no objections, I felt a bite (not one of the lady's), and with a jerk I hauled in a noble fish, which weighed about three pounds. The chief uttered a word that must have meant "good," for he hauled up and examined his bait, and then dropped his line overboard again, and waited for luck. I grew excited over my good fortune, and while hoping for another bite, I felt a tremendous one — as though a shark had swallowed hook and sinker. In an instant I was pulling at my line with all the eagerness of an amateur fisherman; but imagine my surprise when my pet Lilly lay down in the bottom of the canoe, and laughed until her eyes shed tears. The jade had jerked my line, and made me suppose that I had hooked a fish. The chief suffered a grim smile to steal over his tattooed face, as he uttered his favorite word "*miki;*" and then he closed his eyes, and waited for a bite.

We fished for an hour or two, and then Lilly tired of it, and I tired of it, and we lay down in the bottom of the canoe; and she pillowed my head in her lap, and ran her fingers through my curls; and before I knew it I was fast asleep. I was awakened by Lilly's calling out and pulling my hair at the same time.

"*Timi — timi!*" she exclaimed; and pointed up the coast.

About a mile to the windward, coming down with square yards, was the old Sally, the most hateful object to me, at that time, that could have appeared. I knew her by the many patches on her sails, by her iron-rusted sides, and the slovenly manner in which her sails were set. I made one bound to the bows of the canoe, and commenced pulling up the stone which anchored us.

"*Miki*," said the chief, opening his eyes, and regarding me with astonishment.

"Miki or no miki," I said, "I'm going on shore."

"*Miki*," he repeated, looking at his daughter with astonishment.

I out with a paddle and commenced making for the nearest point of land. Still the old chief sat in the bow of his canoe, his line trailing in the water, and his eyes fixed upon me, too much astonished to speak.

The ship would have to pass outside of the reef, where we had been fishing, before she could head for the village; so I thought that I had time enough to reach the shore before I was overtaken, and dragged as a prisoner on board of the Sally.

"Lilly," I said, "if you have the slightest love for me, now is the time to show it."

She looked at me with her large black eyes. Then she gazed at the ship, and appeared to comprehend my position.

"*Kim ki!*" she exclaimed, and took a paddle and applied herself to the task of assisting me with all her strength. And I desire my female readers to understand that Lilly, although slight and delicate-looking, was rather muscular in her arms, as I had found out when swimming.

"*Kim ki!*" she exclaimed to her father, who was still lost in astonishment, and did not know what to make of our actions.

"*Miki*," he repeated, mechanically, and then took up a paddle and aided us with his skill.

Over the water we went, much faster than I supposed the canoe could be urged; but still the broadside of the old Sally was fearfully distinct.

A few minutes more and we were on the beach. I left the

chief to secure the canoe, and then retreated to a grove of cocoanut trees with Lilly, for the purpose of watching operations.

The Sally rounded the reef, and headed for the shore, and stood on until I saw that Captain Bunker was determined to land. I ran for the house, and on my way stopped to communicate information to my shipmates, who were all under cover, and stretched upon the floor, smoking and sleeping.

"Run, boys!" I shouted; "for the old Sally is close in shore, and Bunker is after us."

I think that Jake must have jumped at least ten feet, he was so frightened.

"O, golly!" he exclaimed; "dis nigger is a goner. Whar shall I go?"

"To the hills," I cried. "Make for the woods."

The men gathered up their blankets, and a few articles which they would want, and started for the woods. I saw them disappear, and then started for the chief's house, my friend Lilly keeping close to me all the time. Hurriedly I gathered up my blankets, pipe, and tobacco, and filled my pockets with oranges and other fruit, which were abundant. Then Lilly took the lead, and led me towards the lake where we had bathed.

Past the lake we went at a rapid pace, and ascended a hill that commanded a fine view of the ocean. Then I looked back and saw the Sally still lying with her main-topsail to the mast, and a boat pulling for the shore.

"*Ouri*," said Lilly, laying her hand upon my arm and pointing to a higher hill, covered with a growth of timber.

"Ah, Lilly, you don't want to lose me — do you?" I asked; but the little coquette repulsed the arm which I attempted to put around her waist, and with one bound was ten paces from me. I grew a little sulky, and continued my journey without noticing, apparently, the many arts which Lilly resorted to for the purpose of attracting my attention and eliciting a smile from me. Suddenly her large, black eyes, usually so full of fire, met mine, and I saw that there were tears in them.

"*Kimini oh miki*," she murmured; and it meant, if I understood the language of eyes, "What have I done to offend you?"

I put an arm around her waist, and this time there was no resistance. Once more her eyes brightened, and her face was lighted up with smiles. A stately tree, with wide-spreading branches, stood near, and under it we sat down to rest, like weary pilgrims; and then Lilly's tongue commenced working with the rapidity of a windmill. She sang with a sweet voice native songs, full of fire at times, and melting with love and tenderness. Then she wove a chaplet, composed of leaves, for my head, and while I was watching her busy fingers, she started up and listened, as though she heard some one approach. In an instant she was at my side, and motioning for me to fly for safety; and then cautiously she led the way to a thicket, where we concealed ourselves. Hardly had we done so when I heard footsteps, and peering through the bushes, I saw the kanaka, who had called at the chief's house the day before, and had looked upon me with such wicked eyes. It was Kamaka, the tattooed rascal. He passed by us, peering into the bushes and under the trees, and every few paces stopping to listen. But at last he passed out of sight, and that was a relief to me as well as to Lilly.

"*Miki*," she whispered, with a frown upon her pretty brow, motioning in the direction of the native.

I had learned enough of the kanaka language to know that that word meant "bad."

"If that fellow is a bad one, Lilly," I said, "we must keep out of his way until the Sally sails."

She looked earnestly at my face while I was speaking, as though to understand my meaning by the expression of my eyes. Suddenly she started to her feet, and, seizing my hand, made me arise, I confess rather reluctantly.

"Where are we going now?" I asked, a little peevishly, for it was very comfortable under the bushes.

She pointed with her hand in a direction different from that which we came; so up the mountain we commenced our ascent.

After an immense amount of toil, we reached the top; and then I was amply repaid by the view which was spread before me. On one side was the ocean, beating upon the beach. The Sally still lay off and on; but she now looked like a bird reposing upon the water. Inland I could see rich valleys, with cattle feeding in them, and small streams meandering towards the ocean.

For a few minutes I stood and gazed upon the scene before me, lost in admiration. But I was recalled to myself by Lilly, who touched me on the shoulder, and motioned me to follow her. After walking a few steps we came to the entrance of a cave, the mouth of which had been concealed by some bushes, in a very careful manner, for what purpose I did not know.

To show that I had nothing to fear, Lilly bent her head and entered the cave, and I followed her. It was large enough to hold a dozen people. The floor was covered with mats, to prevent dampness, and there were many spare ones rolled up in a corner. I was overjoyed at the sight of my quarters, and I almost wished that my shipmates were with me, for the sake of sharing them.

But while I was thinking, Lilly was acting. She improvisated a broom from the bushes, which were thick near the cave, and then commenced sweeping out my quarters. I assisted as well as I was able, and when we had concluded our labors it was near sundown; but still the Sally lay off the village. I saw that I would have to stop upon the mountain all night, and I prayed that Lilly would remain to keep me company. But as the sun descended I noticed that she made preparations for going home.

"Lilly," I said, "you won't have the heart to leave me here all night?"

But the girl only smiled and held out her hand. I made many significant signs that I did not like the course she was taking; but she was deaf to my prayers. I thought this was desertion with a vengeance; and had I been like some men I should have sworn; but swearing would not bring her back; so I wisely took what fruit I had, and carried it to the point which overlooked the village and the ocean, and there I ate my supper and smoked my pipe, until the sun had disappeared. Then, feeling lonely enough, I retired to the cave and lay down upon the mats, and while I was thinking of Lilly, I fell fast asleep, and when I awoke I heard her voice singing one of her favorite kanaka songs. I started up. It was morning, but not sunrise. I left the cave in a hurry, and saw Lilly climbing up the mountain.

As soon as she saw me she shouted out something in her dialect, and pointed towards the water. I looked, and not a sail was in sight. I clapped my hands with joy, and then rushed towards Lilly to embrace her; but she was in one of her coquettish moods, and avoided me easily, until she saw a frown gathering upon my brow; and then she came up and laid her hand upon my shoulder, and patted my face, as though she knew that I was a spoiled boy, and must sometimes be petted. While I write this, memory carries me back to the time when I was free from care, with no aspirations excepting those of living in a kanaka village all my life, and loving Lilly; and, as I mention that name, all the wrongs which I inflicted upon her rise before me, and stare me in the face, as though warning me that some part of my punishment was yet to come. And perhaps I deserve it; but I can safely say that Lilly had my love, as sincere as any that I ever knew. Christians, or those who call themselves Christians, men with white faces and black hearts, have much to answer for in the world to come, when they settle their Sandwich Island accounts.

"Lilly," I said, "has the ship gone?"

She nodded.

"Did they get any one?" I asked, holding up three fingers, to intimate that I meant my shipmates.

"No," she answered; and then she laughed and danced around me, and muttered some words which I wished to understand for her sake.

I put my arm around her waist for the purpose of steadying her down the mountain; but she broke from me, and skipped along before me. At length we reached the base of the mountain, and then Lilly took my hand, and we started for the house of the chief, where the old man was seated, smoking his short, carved pipe. He looked up when he saw me approach, and a smile ruffled his face.

"No catche ye!"

I looked at him in astonishment, never expecting to hear so much English from his lips.

"So you can speak English?" I asked.

"*Maliki*," was his answer.

"O, hang '*maliki*,'" I said. "Speak English, for I know you can."

But the old chief refused to open his lips, although I asked him a dozen questions.

As soon as we had eaten breakfast I started off to find my shipmates. I was compelled to call upon Lilly, and ask her aid; and after she understood my meaning, she led the way towards the woods once more. We continued on through cocoa-nut groves and over hills for some two miles, and at last Lilly pointed to some smoke which was curling in the air from the base of a hill. On we went, and at length I could hear the voices of my friends.

I listened, while they were discussing whether it was best to return to the village. I suddenly shouted, —

"Here they are — seize the runaways!"

Then I dashed towards the camp, and as I did so, I caught sight of Jack, Jake, and Will, running towards the bushes as though for life.

The sight was a little too ludicrous for me to maintain my gravity, and I laughed; but my shipmates did not stop or turn round at the sound. As I saw them plunge into the bushes, I shouted to them to stop, as there was no one to fear. At length I saw Jake's black face peering at me, and then the darky said, —

"Darn dis nigger ef I didn't tink it was old Bunker. Come back, boys. 'Tain't nobody but Pepper. Ha, ha! how dis child was scared."

In a few minutes Jack and Will came in, and the former grumbled, as a matter of course.

"Where's the Sally?" asked Will.

"Gone, and I hope will never return," I said.

"Good!" cried all three; and then they told me that they had run for half an hour after leaving the village, the day before, and at length brought up where I found them.

We returned to the village, Lilly close by my side.

"Now that the Sally has gone, what do you propose to do?" I asked of my shipmates, as we walked along.

"We'll do what you do," was the answer.

"But I shall remain in the village for the present," I said.

"And so will we," they cried.

"Or a lifetime," suggested Jake. "Jest give dis child plenty fishin', and see ef he don't stay contented."

"Then you had better commence cooking your own food, and not be dependent upon the natives. If you catch more fish than you want, some of the people will exchange vegetables with you for the surplus. In that manner you can live quite well."

"Lord, hear de boy," cried Jake. "Any one tink dat he chief of de village."

"If I am not, I shall be soon," I answered, a little proudly.

"Don't you make a fool of yerself," growled Jack. "Your folks won't be ready to accept a kanaka wife for their son."

"I don't care," I answered, somewhat sullenly.

"Yes, you do care, Pepper. Only think what Miss Julia would say!"

I was silent. Lilly must have known that the conversation was concerning her. She seemed to comprehend that the seaman was attempting to depreciate her, for she looked at him with a frown and a toss of her pretty head that did not betoken much friendship.

"Lord, how quick a woman is with her temper!" muttered the sailor.

I did not care to hear the man's remonstrances; so lingered in the rear, and let my friends pass on to the village. No sooner were they out of sight than Lilly recovered all her gayety.

We sat beneath the shade of a cocoa-nut tree, near a small stream of clear water, and rested and refreshed ourselves with the milk of a newly-plucked cocoa-nut, the bark of which I stripped off with a hatchet, which I carried by my side. Those who have never drank milk from a cocoa-nut just from a tree can form no idea of its goodness. It quenches thirst, gives tone to the stomach, and a pint is almost equal to a hearty meal.

After Lilly and I had abated our thirst, I found the position too pleasant to leave in a hurry. A gentle breeze stirred the air; but there was not a sound to be heard, excepting the murmur of a brook, that ran singing on its way towards the waterfall, which fed the lake where the natives bathed night and morning. At our feet was a soft carpet of green; overhead was an unclouded sky; on each side of us high hills, covered with waving trees, which perfumed the air with an odor like that of sandal-wood. Near us were orange trees bending beneath the weight of golden fruit, and others frosted with flowers, which had just burst from the buds, while the wind was scattering the blossoms over the grass, like pearls from the hands of some prodigal fairy.

I laid my head in Lilly's lap, and she wove a wreath for me; but before she finished it, we were both asleep; and when I awoke it was with a start, for Lilly had uttered a subdued cry of terror. I rubbed my eyes and started up, and standing before us was the tattooed Kamaka, the hideous kanaka, who seemed determined to follow our footsteps and watch our motions.

"What do you want here?" I asked, a little fiercely.

He smiled scornfully.

"Dis no place for sailor-man," the wretch said, speaking English for the first time. "White man go away — no stay here longer. He get hurt."

"You dog, do you dare to threaten me?" I asked, advancing towards him.

"White sailor-man, go away," he answered.

"I shall stay here as long as I please," I replied. "And if you follow me round much more, I'll punch that ugly head of yours."

The New Zealander laughed as though he would like to see me attempt it.

"Go away," he said, "and no come back. S'pose you no go, me make you."

"You will?" I asked; and I went up to him and put a hand upon his throat; but in an instant the tattooed rascal had thrown his arms around me, and with a sudden turn of his foot, thought that he would throw me. But he missed his aim, and the next instant I landed him upon his back, and pressed my hands so close upon his throat that he gasped for breath.

"Will you keep a civil tongue in your head hereafter?" I asked, and I shook the native until his teeth chattered.

"Let me up," he gasped.

"Not until you promise," I said.

He sulked for a moment, and then said, —

"Me do."

Kamaka shook his head, smoothed his long hair, and then said some few words to Lilly; but that amiable young lady must have opened a terrible battery upon him, for her tongue moved rapidly, and her eyes flashed. The native listened in silence, and walked quietly away; but once he stopped and looked back at me, and his face did not seem agreeable.

We strolled back to the village, and found the chief seated at his door, smoking as usual, and into his ears did Lilly pour the tale of her wrongs.

"*Maliki*," he muttered, and smoked on.

At length he knocked the ashes from his pipe, and looked up.

"Kamaka bad," he said, and went to sleep without delay; and left Lilly and I looking at each other.

We did not feel sleepy; so wandered through the groves, and swung in grass hammocks beneath the shade of trees, until it was time to return home and take the usual afternoon bath. As we passed by the house where my shipmates were quartered,

I saw them sitting at the door "laying up" grass threads into fishing-lines.

"Charley," said Will, "the master of the Sally didn't come it — did he? He searched through all the village; but not a native would give him any information. He didn't even find the boat, and it's lying on the beach all right."

"And what are you going to do with it?" I asked.

"Goin' fishin'," responded Jake. "Ef your folks wants any fish, jist let us know. We sells cheap for cash. Yaw, yaw!"

We passed on, and were soon rolling in the clear water of the lake; and I ducked dusky girls instead of being ducked; but in going home I saw that Kamaka had commenced an acquaintance with my shipmates, and was busy talking with them, and assisting them in their tasks. But the New Zealander did not raise his eyes when I passed, or look at me. I marvelled that he should be thus engaged, and wondered what it meant.

We had supper, and the night passed more pleasantly than the one before. Once I was startled by the old chief, who shouted while dreaming, —

"No catche ye," which I supposed referred to me, and I rewarded him by throwing a paddle in the direction of his head. After that pleasant little episode, I went to sleep, and was awakened by Lilly, who pulled my blanket from my shoulders to accomplish it.

While Lilly was tugging at my blanket, I held on to it; but it was no use. She was determined that I should arise and go with her to the bath. We went and returned home for breakfast; and after that important matter, the chief smoked, as usual, for an hour. At last he got upon his feet, and said, —

"Me go."

"Well," I replied, "go along. Don't remain at home on my account, if you please."

He selected a spear, which was leaning against the wall, a stout, serviceable weapon, with a stone head; and after looking at it for a moment, turned to me.

"Ugh," he grunted; "me kill cow."

"Where?" I asked.

He waved his spear in triumph, and pointed in the direction of the hills, and then stalked off. I thought for a moment, and then followed the old chief, first taking a similar weapon from the wall.

Before I had gone ten rods Lilly joined me, also armed with a light spear. She had no idea of being left at home alone. We followed the chief through woods and valleys, and up some high hills; and at last reached the summit of one, so that we could command a fine view of the valley beneath. Then he cast his keen eyes around, and pointed to a dozen head of cattle, which were quietly feeding at our feet, exclaimed, —

"Me want one."

"All right, old fellow," I said. "A taste of fresh beef would be a pleasing variety, for I'm tired of fish."

The old chief continued to scan the herd of cattle in silence. I improved the opportunity to kiss his daughter, to which she made no objection. Her father did not notice it.

"Come," said the chief, turning round so suddenly that he nearly caught me repeating the experiment.

We followed him down the hill; and near a narrow gorge, which led from one valley to another, between high hills, the old chief halted. On each side were trees and bushes, and to these the chief pointed.

"Me wait," he said; and down he sat behind a clump of bushes.

There was nothing for Lilly and me to do but to wait also. We got under the shade of a tree, and sat down and went to sleep. I was awakened by the chief, who was punching me with his spear. The old fellow pointed with his finger in the direction of the valley, and said, —

"Cow come."

"Well, let her come," I said.

"Me kill!" he exclaimed.

"Well, I shan't prevent you;" and I was about to lie down, when I was startled by hearing the bellowing of a bull. I looked up and saw the herd of cattle within a few rods of us, the bull in advance, snuffing the air and pawing the earth.

"No speake," said the chief, in a whisper; and then he crouched behind the bushes, and grasped his spear firmly.

I did the same. The bull came on, his eyes resembling balls of fire. After reaching the gorge, he stopped and glared around; but the cows pressed on, and the bull was compelled to move. Once in the gorge, he quickened his steps, and passed us unmolested. Then he turned, and pawed the earth and bellowed out his defiance. As he did so the old chief rose from his ambush, and with a sudden motion hurled his spear at a young and fat cow which was within a few fathoms of him. The weapon whistled through the air, struck the cow near her fore shoulder, and nearly passed through her body. She gave one groan and one leap, then tumbled upon her head, motionless, if not quite dead.

"Good for you, old man!" I shouted, rising up in my delight and going towards him.

My applause was too sudden, and somewhat out of place, for the bull turned, and came towards me much faster than was desirable on his part.

"Stern, all!" I shouted, recollecting the words most used by whalemen when in a tight place. But the bull was not accustomed to obey such orders. He was shortening the distance between us rapidly, when I heard Lilly scream, and then saw her at my side, as though her arms would ward off all danger. I could not fly after that. But even in the moment of peril I heard the chief shout one word, which he must have meant as good advice.

"Run," he said; and I remember of wondering where he learned that simple yet important monosyllable.

I held in my hand the spear which I had brought with me, and with hardly a hope to accomplish anything, I put it before me, the point towards the bull, and the shaft resting on the ground. The bull came on with a bellow, and with a toss of his head which did not argue much for my safety; but that movement of his head was the very thing that did save me, for the point of the spear entered the neck of the bull, and the animal did not stop until two thirds of the shaft was in his body. Then he staggered, the hot blood gushing from his terrible wound in torrents, and with a last expiring bellow of defiance he fell at my feet.

I turned and looked for Lilly. She was but a few steps from me, on the ground, as though she had fallen from the effect of terror.

"I'm safe, Lilly," I said; and I put my arms around her and raised her up. She looked at me with her large black eyes, as though she did not understand how I could possibly be alive; and then her arms went around my neck, and she commenced crying.

I kissed her cheek and talked to her; and while I was doing so the chief disturbed me by this sage remark: —

"By darn — two kill! Good-y."

I paid but little attention to him, for I was comforting his daughter.

"By-by, chief," he said, and patted me on the shoulder, to intimate that I had done a very good thing.

"Go tell 'em," said the chief; and he waved his hand in the direction of the village, and spoke a few words to his daughter.

She nodded to me, and we started over hills, and in the direction of the village. The natives were eager for the fresh meat, and old and young went for it. Even my shipmates followed in the crowd.

After we had seen every one depart, Lilly and I, satisfied with what we had done, retired to the shade of an orange tree, and ate fruit, and went to sleep. Commend me to a kanaka village for good, wholesome sleeping. Much of it can be done there, for there is nothing else to do, after you have counted eating, swimming, and fishing.

CHAPTER VIII.

A SIMPLE LIFE AND A HAPPY ONE. — A LETTER FROM MR. CHERINGTON. — THE ARRIVAL OF A MISSIONARY.

Weeks passed on, and I found myself so entirely domesticated in the village that I had no thoughts of leaving. My shipmates were of the same opinion. They fished and hunted, and were looked upon by the inhabitants as useful members of the tribe. My love for Lilly did not diminish with time; but of that the chief took no notice. He smoked, and shut his eyes to all that passed within his house. We fished together, and hunted together, and I regarded the old man with much friendly feeling, and I know that he had a warm attachment for me. By attention, and under the direction of Lilly, who was one of the most patient teachers I ever saw, I acquired a sufficient knowledge of the language of the island to make known my wants, and to understand nearly all that was said to me.

Ah, how many times did she ask if I was contented in the

village! Sometimes she was very grave when she asked the question. And after one of her reveries she would redouble her attentions to me, and assume her most fascinating airs. A number of times I found her in tears. But I was thoughtless, and did not suppose that those tears were shed for me. And sometimes I was wicked, for I would steal off and flirt with other girls.

As for my rival, Kamaka, he was so badly beaten in the contest for Lilly, that for the last three weeks he had not been seen in the village; and his disappearance was an occasion of rejoicing among many who disliked the tattooed rascal. One day I was swinging under a tree, in a grass hammock, when Lilly came to find me, her face showing some signs of uneasiness.

"What is the matter?" I asked.

"Bad news," she replied.

"Let me hear it."

"Kamaka is here."

"I was in hopes that he was dead. What does he want?"

"To see you."

"To see me? Confound his impudence."

"He has a paper for you," said Lilly; and then, as though there was something dreadful in that, she commenced crying, and looking as miserable as possible.

The rascal did not appear as though he felt humiliated when he stood before me.

"What do you want of me?" I asked.

He took off his cap, and from the lining removed a letter. It was somewhat soiled by contact with his head; but the superscription was quite legible, and on it I saw, "Charles Allspice."

"Read," said Kamaka.

I saw that it was dated at Honolulu, and that Mr. Cherington's name was at the bottom of it. The letter read as follows: —

"I have heard from you, and I must say that I am surprised at your conduct. Little did I think that the son of my old friend would consider it an honor to remain on the island, isolated from all society, and constant in his attentions upon a native girl, whose uncultivated mind is the only excuse which she can have for leading such a sinful life. Better, a thousand times better, would it have been for you to have remained on board the Sally, than to have landed upon these shores, and indulged in such wickedness as you and your companions are reported to have done. Leave the village and join me, and the past shall be forgotten. If you do not, we must remain hereafter as strangers.

"I need not tell you that Julia is excessively shocked at your conduct. At first she refused to credit it; but when she was compelled to, she shed many tears over your fall. Let me see you within two weeks."

I folded the letter, and then looked at the fellow who had brought it.

"Your revenge is not yet complete," I said to myself. "You have learned from my shipmates that Mr. Cherington was a prominent man at Honolulu, and friendly with me; and your visited the city for the purpose of informing him of my conduct, and took good care to exaggerate as much as possible. But I am not to be driven by threats."

"You go?" asked Kamaka, looking up.

I sprang from the grass hammock in which I was reclining, seized a stick, and rushed for the native, but he turned and ran.

"What is it?" asked Lilly, as soon as I returned.

I told her that a friend wanted me at Honolulu, and that Kamaka had slandered me.

"You will go?" she asked.

"No, I will not go," I said. "I will stay here with Lilly."

I heard no more of the Kamaka for some days. He left the village a few hours after delivering the letter, and then my life was without change for several weeks; but after I had lived with my new friends about six months, and was upon good terms with all the natives, the old chief entered his house, one afternoon, looking unusually excited.

"What is the matter?" I asked.

"Missionary come," he said; and then, lighting his pipe, squatted down by the door.

I lighted my pipe, and placed myself by the side of the chief, while Lilly, trembling, seized some work, and awaited the arrival of the reverend gentleman. In a few minutes he rode up to the door, and dismounted from a fine-looking horse, and a kanaka servant instantly took charge of the animal. I looked at the man's face as he approached the house, and I read there some pride, much resolution, and but little humility. He was a tall, dark-looking man, with a commanding eye, thin lips, and a clean shaven face. He approached the chief, but the latter smoked on without rising.

"Good day, my brother," he said, extending his hand; and the chief took it, held it for a moment, and then dropped it suddenly, as though fearful of being burned.

"Good day, daughter," the missionary continued, speaking in the Hawaii dialect, and addressing Lilly.

And then the tall man turned his eyes upon me.

"Who are you?" he asked.

"A sailor."

"A runaway?"

"Yes."

"I thought so;" and he sighed, as though his thoughts were sinful.

"If you thought so, why did you ask me?" I demanded.

"To be sure of the matter. You are living here in idleness and sin, I suppose."

"I am living here," I answered, "but not in idleness, and with very little sin."

The missionary looked at me with some surprise, and after a pause, said,—

"I suppose you are one of the young men who escaped from the whaleship Sally."

"I had the honor of leaving her," I replied.

"Were you aware that you were violating the laws of the island by remaining on shore without permission of the government?" he asked.

"No."

"Then let me now inform you of the fact, and warn you that it is necessary you should receive permission of the Secretary of State."

"I will obtain it when I see him," I answered.

"Then you had better see him without delay. Time is precious in this sinful world."

The good man sighed and looked at Lilly. The poor girl dropped her eyes. Her vivacity was all gone.

"Is that girl your wife?" the missionary asked.

"She is not," I answered.

"Should she not be?"

"That depends upon circumstances."

The reverend gentleman looked shocked, and kept silent for a moment. Then he sighed and groaned once more.

"I came to the village in search of a young man named Allspice. Can you tell me where he is to be found? I understand that he has respectable connections, and I wish to secure him from a life of sin."

"He does not care to be secured," I answered. "He is quite contented as he is."

"How do you know?"

"Because I am the individual you are in search of."

"Is it possible? Are you the young man whom Mr. Cherington takes such an interest in?"

"I know Mr. Cherington, and he was friendly with me when he left the ship. I do not understand his feelings at the present time."

"They have not changed in spite of your ingratitude. He has heard of the rude manner in which you treated his messenger; but still he loves you for your father's sake."

"I am much obliged to him. I hope I shall never forfeit his respect."

"But, my dear young man," — and the missionary grew confifidential — "you will forfeit it if you remain here in idleness. Leave the village. Go with me to Honolulu, and become a merchant and a respectable member of the church."

I looked at Lilly, but I could not make up my mind to desert her.

"I am contented here, and have no desire to leave," I said, with as much firmness as I could command.

"Consider for one moment, young man. I can have you tabooed, and your best friend in the village would not dare to lend you assistance, or even furnish you with food. What could you do then?"

"Retire into the country, and live on fruit."

"But if you were arrested?"

"I should escape as soon as possible. I only ask to remain here and live in peace. I have no aspirations, nor any desire to leave here."

"There is something fascinating in living in idleness, I will confess," he said; "but just think how much better your time could be employed in civilized society."

"There are no petty jealousies here," I remarked. "All our wants are supplied, and what more can man desire?"

"Have you not Christian wants?" the missionary asked.

I was silent. The reverend gentleman saw that his last broadside had touched me, and he followed it up with a fresh one.

"I saw Miss Cherington a few days since. I was at her father's house, when a native — Kamaka, I think they called him — related the manner in which you treated him after reading Mr. Cherington's letter. He told some sad stories of your life, and the lady denied them with much spirit, and with some indignation. She said that she knew your nature too well to think you would be guilty of such gross immorality as the native charged."

"I bless her for the good thought," I cried, a little warmly. "She only does me justice."

"Shall I return to her and report that you prefer the company of a kanaka girl to that of a sensible, highly educated white lady?"

"No, no. Do not do that," I exclaimed.

"Then what shall I say?"

"Tell her nothing," I answered. "She is too good for me to think of. I know not if she would speak with me should we meet."

"Then make the attempt and see what the result will be. Julia is a girl of Christian principle, and has a forgiving heart."

I looked up and saw that tears were in Lilly's eyes. All my love for her returned, even if it had strayed for a moment. I could not leave her. The missionary saw my resolution.

"What shall I tell Mr. Cherington?" the Rev. Mr. Gangle asked, as he mounted his horse.

"That I thank him for his kindness," I answered.

"You will one day be glad to accept of his offers. Sin carries its own punishment, and yours will soon come."

I felt that his words were true; but sin sometimes takes too firm a root to be plucked out without a struggle.

Mr. Gangle turned his horse's head, and with a cold bow was about to ride off, when I laid a hand upon his bridle.

"One moment," I said, speaking hurriedly. "Tell Miss Cherington that there is not a day passes without my thinking of her. Tell her not to believe me wholly bad, for I am not."

I turned and plunged into the woods, and the missionary left the village. I threw myself under a cocoa-nut tree, and covered my face with my hands, and almost shed tears at the position in which I was placed. While I was thus repenting, I felt a light hand laid upon my head, and looking up I saw that Lilly had stolen to my side.

"The missionary wanted you to leave me," she said.

I did not answer.

"If you think it is for your happiness, I desire you to do so," she continued.

"I am contented, Lilly," I answered. "I shall never leave you."

The next day I went about my work as usual. I had laid out a garden near the house of the chief, and in that I labored some two or three hours each day, assisted by Lilly. I had planted all kinds of vegetables, and by attending to them, they were growing finely. One corner I devoted to roses, and their perfume filled the air night and morning. The natives of the village grew ambitious after witnessing my success, and all commenced gardens precisely like mine, and but little labor was required to make them flourish as well. Even the children took an interest in the undertaking, and they would sit for hours and drive the hens and chickens away from them.

Thus I occupied my time, and I had nearly forgotten the visit of the missionary, when one morning Lilly rushed into the house where I was mending a fish-line, and said, —

"Run, for they have come."

My first thought was, that the Sally had landed a boat's crew, and I prepared to leave the house without a moment's delay; but a glance at Lilly satisfied me that the danger was more imminent.

"What is the matter, Lilly?" I asked.

"Soldiers," she managed to articulate, and around my neck went her arms.

"They are coming here," she cried. "O, run, and don't stop;" but she only clung the tighter to my neck as she spoke.

Just at that moment the chief entered the house.

"Sogers come," he said. "No cotche ye, no hab ye. Run;" and he proceeded to light his pipe with all imaginable coolness.

I ran but a few steps when I caught sight of four kanaka soldiers, advancing in the direction of the chief's house.

"That is he," I heard some one say; and looking up, I saw my tattooed rival, Kamaka.

The soldiers were armed with muskets and bayonets; but whether they would dare to use them against me was a question that I did not ask, for fear that I should find an unfavorable answer. As the men advanced, I receded for a few feet, and then determined to attempt to run the blockade and escape to the mountains.

"Catch him," shouted Kamaka; and as he uttered those words I made a dash at him. He dodged, but was not quick enough. I struck him a running blow as I passed, and he rolled over two or three times before he stopped. A soldier put up his musket, and told me to halt, but I knocked his piece down, and passed all four of them, and thought that I should escape, when I suddenly found myself in the presence of six more, who received me with open arms. The fellows piled on me, and slipped a pair of irons on my hands, and pointed bayonets at my breast while doing so. But still I heard a sergeant, who had charge of the squad, say in a low tone, —

"Carefully, men. No violence."

He spoke in his native tongue, which he thought I did not understand. I had a chance to notice the soldiers while they surrounded me, and I saw that they were light-colored young fellows, wearing blue cotton uniforms, trimmed with red worsted braid, hats of no particular pattern, and shoes which showed a number of toes protruding. Before I had finished my survey, I heard the voices of my shipmates, as they came rushing towards me. Some one had informed them of my arrest. They had armed themselves with clubs, and Jack had a lance, one of those which we stole from the Sally.

"Let him go," roared the English sailor, as he hove in sight. "Drop him, I tell you, or I'll make blubber of you fellers;" and he raised his lance as though to make a dart.

The kanaka soldiers looked their astonishment, but did not offer to raise their muskets to resist the attack.

"If them sojers ain't out of this place in five minutes, I'll dart," shouted Jack; and I believe that he would have kept his word, had I not spoken.

"Put down your lance and throw away your clubs," I said. "Do you want to be lodged in the calaboose for attacking the soldiers?"

"Who put them darbies on your hands?" they asked. "Take 'em off, or we'll lick the sojer what did it."

They turned fiercely upon the kanaka soldiers, and the sergeant was called upon to explain.

"He hitte wid fisty," he said in explanation.

"Well, that's what they were made for. Take 'em off, or you'll get keel-hauled in no time, my hearty."

The kanaka soldier looked at Jack's burly figure, and seemed to have some dread of it.

"You no runny?" he asked, speaking to me."

"I shall not run," I answered.

He removed the irons from my wrists, and my shipmates all crowded around me, edging the soldiers away as though they had no right there. I wondered where Lilly and the chief were. But as we moved off I heard a scream, and the next moment Lilly rushed towards me, her hair streaming in the wind, and her face expressing the agony which she felt. She broke through the ranks of the soldiers, and threw her arms around my neck, and bathed my face with her tears.

"You shall not leave me," she cried.

"I will return, Lilly," I said, and I strove to comfort her.

"You will never come back," she cried. "I shall see you no more. O, let me go with you."

"You must not go with him," the sergeant exclaimed. "We were ordered not to take any one but the sailor."

"But you shall not take him."

"Lilly," I whispered, "have patience and a little courage. We shall meet again. As soon as I am released I will return to you."

"No, no; you never will return to me," she cried, clinging convulsively to my neck.

I strove to disengage her hands, but she resisted my efforts until her father appeared. The crowd fell back before the dignified old chief.

"*Maliki*," he said; and his face looked troubled, and his eyes showed how much he sympathized with me.

He put his arms around his daughter, and whispered some words in her ear; and then she released me after one kiss, and the poor girl was carried in a fainting state towards her home.

For the purpose of getting me beyond the reach of such dangerous men, the soldiers hurried me to the beach, where a whale-boat was lying, in which they had pulled nearly all the way from Honolulu. A hundred natives followed close upon us, and they beat their breasts and filled the air with their lamentations at the prospect of losing me.

"Shove off the boat," said the sergeant, speaking to his men in his native language. "Be quick, or the people will stone us."

This was sufficient to make the soldiers hurry their movements; and I think that a volley of stones would have saluted them if the old chief had not suddenly appeared on the ground, and spoke to his people in such a manner that there was no mistaking his words. Lilly's father came towards me, and motioned me aside.

"When you come back," he said, speaking in his native tongue, which I understood sufficiently to comprehend, "you must marry my daughter and then you can be a chief, and the soldiers can't take you. I love you as a son, and my child thinks of you only. If you should not come back she would die, and then I should be alone in the world."

"Chief," I asked, "why am I taken away?"

"It is the work of the missionaries," he replied. "Kamaka has told them false stories, and they believed him."

I was almost inclined to rush among the crowd and escape to the mountains; but I recollected my word of honor. I looked around in hope of seeing Lilly.

"She is sick," the chief said, guessing whom my eyes sought. "It has gone to her heart. Hasten back, or she will die."

"We must go," cried the sergeant; and I shook hands with my intended father-in-law, and stepped into the boat.

"Shove off," was the order; and the boat had just left the beach when I heard a shriek. The crowd on the shore parted to the right and left, and then I saw Lilly rushing towards me, her arms extended and her long hair streaming in the wind.

"Take me too," she cried. "O, take me, or come back."

"Pull hard," the sergeant cried; and the native soldiers bent to their oars.

I glanced at Lilly to wave her an adieu; but the instant she caught sight of me, she rushed into the water, and then swam for the boat, as though determined to follow us to Honolulu.

"Come back," she cried, and threw her slight form nearly out of the water as she uttered the words; and then from her mouth I saw the blood spirt; but still she continued to swim after us, and uttered many wild shrieks, which pierced my heart and nearly drove me frantic. I made desperate efforts to break from the grasp of the soldiers; but they held on to me so tightly that I could not move. I covered my face with my hands, and groaned with bitterness; and just then the sergeant touched me on the shoulder.

"They will save her," he cried, "and in a few days you will see her."

I looked up, and saw that two thirds of the natives were swimming to Lilly's assistance, and that the poor thing had turned her head towards the shore. I waved an adieu to my friends, who were watching me, and then sank back into the stern of the boat, and remained in a state of stupor until we reached Honolulu. Then they placed me on a bed, and my head fell back.

"The sailor-man is sick," one of the soldiers said. "He should not remain here."

I saw some one lean over me and feel of my pulse, and then place a hand upon my head.

"He is threatened with brain fever," I heard him whisper. "He must be moved from here at once. There is no time to lose."

"We had better send word — had we not?" some one asked the speaker.

"Of course. Our plan is frustrated by this attack of sickness. Poor fellow! he has taken it too hard — much harder than I supposed. I imagined that he would laugh at the joke after it was explained to him."

"I will send word at once, and we can have him moved in half an hour. The daughter will look after him some — will she not?"

"You can rest assured of that, although she is a little grieved just now at his past conduct."

"You saw that kanaka girl while you were making your annual visits — didn't you?" asked the man who still held my hand.

"Yes; and I am not surprised at his infatuation. I never saw a girl on the island that would compare with her in point of beauty, and she is as artless as a child."

"Poor thing! poor thing! God help her. She feels as bad at the separation as this boy, who has allowed his heart to turn his brain. The work has been done most bunglingly, I must say."

"But what were we to do?" asked the man addressed, whose voice sounded like that of the Rev. Mr. Gangle. "His father expects him to follow in his footsteps, and become a good man. If he had remained in that village he would have been a vagabond all his life."

"I doubt that," said the man who was holding my hand, and who, I thought, was a physician. "If you had let them alone they would soon have got tired of each other, and then separation would have ensued quite naturally."

He laid his hand upon my heated forehead, and I suddenly thought it was Lilly's hand, and that she was asking me to go with her to the bath.

"Wait till daylight, Lilly," I said. "I am too sleepy to get up just yet."

"You see how his thoughts run."

"Miss Julia will prove a good nurse," said the other, and then they left the room, but presently returned, and I felt myself lifted up from the mattress on which I was lying, and carried into the cool, pure air. I was placed in a carriage, and laid upon blankets; then the horse was started, but only at a walk, for fear of jarring my head, which began to pain me severely. At last the carriage stopped, and then I heard a voice which I remembered perfectly. It was Mr. Cherington's.

"How is he?" I heard him ask.

"About the same," was the answer. "The fever is slowly increasing."

"A room is all ready for him," Mr. Cherington remarked. "Let us move him ourselves. I don't want to trust the servants."

They took me in their arms and carried me into the house, and then up one flight of stairs, and laid me upon a bed. I heard a low, sweet voice in the room ask, —

"Father, may I look at him?"

"Yes, my child," was the answer.

And then I felt a soft hand laid upon my head, and a sweet breath fan my cheek, and a soft pair of lips touched mine, but very lightly.

"Poor boy," she said; and then I heard no more conversation for many days.

When I awoke — as if from a deep sleep — I tried to recollect where I was, and how it happened that I was lying on a mattress, with clean linen sheets and a white bed-spread. I raised my hands, and, to my surprise, saw that they were white and thin, and that my arms had lost most of their flesh. Then I knew that I had been sick; but for what length of time I could not imagine.

The room in which I was lying was just light enough for me to notice that the floor was covered with straw matting, which looked cool and pleasant, the furniture was of substantial black walnut, and around the walls hung pictures and engravings. The windows, which were open to admit the cool and fragrant air, were covered with blinds, and on the inside hung lace curtains with heavy blue silk tassels. The bedstead on which I was lying was one of the old style, with four tall posts, each one surmounted with a brass ball, and over all a canopy, with a mosquito net. I lay perfectly still and waited, and presently some one opened a door; and then I heard whispering, and I recognized the voices; and how my heart beat as I listened!

"How is he this morning, child?" asked Mr. Cherington.

"There is no change, father," answered Julia, in a low, sad tone.

"Has he wandered as bad as usual?"

"No, I think not. Once or twice he has imagined that he was on board that miserable ship, and sometimes he has spoken as though he was conversing with that poor girl whom he calls Lilly. It is dreadful, father — is it not? — and he so young, and at one time so good!"

"We must not be too hard on him for that, Julia. He is not the first that has fallen after landing on these shores. Consider his youth and inexperience."

"I have, father, and yet I am fearful that I have not charity enough. Only think how good and pure he was on board the ship."

"He has done wrong; but we must forgive him, child."

"I don't feel that I ever can," Julia said, with a gentle sigh, which told me that her heart was not so hard as she would have her father believe.

"For his parents' sake, we must do so," the old gentleman replied.

"For their sake I'll try," the young lady said; and I felt rejoiced at her decision, although I did not think at the time that I had committed much sin.

"Has the doctor been here this morning?" Mr. Cherington asked.

"Yes, and he left some new medicine; but I have not given Charles any, and don't think that I shall. It is horrid smelling stuff."

Blessed girl, how much I thanked her for it! She wanted to spare me some trouble, and let me die a natural death.

"Did the doctor express any opinion?" asked Mr. Cherington.

"None. He said that the fever might take a favorable turn, and that, if it did not by to-morrow night, he should shave his head and put a blister on it. Only think of that!" and Miss Julia expressed in her tones, the horror which she should feel at such an act.

"It should have been done before," was all the consolation the young lady got from her father.

"He would look so odd with his head shaved!" Miss Julia remarked. "Pray don't have it done until all other means fail."

"His life is of more value than a few curls," the unfeeling man said, and left the room; and Julia and I were alone.

Then I thought that it was best to let her know that I was awake.

"Where am I?" I asked, speaking for the first time, and in so weak a tone that it rather startled me.

Miss Julia jumped up and looked astonished, and then she bent over me, her face expressing her anxiety.

"Charles," she said, laying her hand upon mine, and speaking very seriously, "do you know me?"

"O, yes," I answered; "you're an angel, and have come to comfort me."

"No, Charles," she said, with a sweet smile, "I'm not an angel; I am a human being."

"You are handsome enough to be one," I managed to say; and I don't think that remark displeased her.

"You poor boy," she cried, "you must be sensible. You talk quite rational."

"I think that I am," I answered; and I carried her white hand to my lips and kissed it. "Tell me, Miss Cherington," I asked, "how long have I been sick?"

"O, not long. But you must not ask questions. You are too sick."

"I have no pain left in my head, but I am terribly weak."

"Then you must not talk."

"If you command me not to, I won't," I answered.

"Then I do command you not to speak unless you are spoken to;" and she was about to sit down, when a thought struck her.

"Do you feel hungry?" she asked.

"Very," I answered. "See how I have fallen away!" I sighed, as I held up my hand, and then accidentally let it fall upon her own.

"You have grown thin," she said; and I felt my hand pressed ever so slightly, and then, as though frightened, she closed the mosquito bar, and left me to my own reflections.

"What would you like to eat?" she demanded.

"A beefsteak, some dry toast, a few broiled potatoes, and half a dozen boiled eggs," I answered, quite promptly.

She was not much accustomed to domestic matters, and supposed that it was all right when I stated that I desired such substantial fare.

"You shall have all that you ask for," she said. "Now go to sleep, and when you awaken your breakfast shall be ready."

I fell asleep, and must have slept until near night; for when I awoke, I saw Mr. Cherington sitting at my bedside, and a stranger with him. I awoke with a sigh, for I had been dreaming of the kanaka village and Lilly.

"Charles," asked Mr. Cherington, "how do you feel?"

"Hungry," I answered.

The stranger took my hand, and felt of my pulse for a moment in silence.

"Pulse regular," he said; "skin cool and moist. I've brought him round, you see. That last medicine did the business; I was positive it would. No pain in the head, hey?"

"None," I replied.

"I thought so. The powders which I gave would relieve that. How is the mouth?"

"Rusty for the want of use," I answered.

"The effect of the drops. There's iron in them," the doctor cried, quite composedly.

"You think that he is improving fast — do you, doctor?" asked Mr. Cherington.

"I know so, sir. The physician to his majesty, Kamehamaha, is not likely to make a mistake. I said I should save him. I can't perform miracles, but I can cure a man if he will let me, and don't fight against nature."

"But you seem to forget that nature is fighting me, and will soon conquer, unless assistance is rendered. I'm hungry. I asked Miss Cherington for some breakfast a few hours back, and she said that she would have it ready when I awoke."

"Well, you are awake — ain't you?" asked the doctor.

"Why, yes, I believe that I am," I replied.

"Well, you don't see the beefsteak and the broiled potatoes — do you?"

I moved my head, but nothing but phials and powders met my gaze upon the table.

"You don't see the boiled eggs — do you?" the doctor asked.

"No."

"Well, you won't see them, if my orders are obeyed, for two weeks to come."

I sighed and looked towards Mr. Cherington for relief.

"Don't be alarmed, Charles," he said. "You shall not starve as long as you are in my house. The doctor will give you something nourishing, I know."

"Yes, sir, I shall, and I want my directions carried out to the letter. To-night a piece of chicken, large as one of my fingers, and a bowl of gruel. If the king was sick I should serve him in the same manner. And I should be obeyed, or I would know the reason why."

"You shall be obeyed, sir," Mr. Cherington remarked; and then the doctor, after giving me one more punch in the region of the ribs, and one triumphant glance, left the room.

"You have had a hard fit of sickness," Mr. Cherington said; "but thank God, all danger is now passed, I hope."

As he rose to leave the room, Julia came in, followed by a kanaka girl, who bore a tray with the slight refreshments ordered by the doctor. She cleared off the odious-looking bottles, and arranged the tray upon the table by my bedside, and looked so happy while doing so, that I could only follow her movements in silent admiration.

"The idea," she said, "of your ordering a beefsteak for supper! And I should have given it to you if it had not been for father, who laughed at me."

She raised me up, and washed my face and hands, and talked all the time, but would not allow me to answer. But after my scant meal it was imperatively ordered that I should go to sleep again, and I went without the slightest trouble, and waked up to find Mr. Cherington at my bedside.

"Well, how do you feel this morning, Charles?" he asked.

"Quite fresh."

"That is right. Your improvement will be rapid, I have no doubt. I must go to the store; but I shall leave you in the care of Julia. She will read you some extracts from Boston newspapers. Your parents are well, and we have letters for you; but it is not desirable that you should read them at present."

I had Julia for company that day. She read to me and talked to me, and so the hours passed quickly until night, when Dr. Pendergrast, own physician to the king and all his cabinet, called.

"We're improving," he said, "very rapidly improving. I must show you to the king, after you are well, as an evidence of my skill. He'll be pleased at my success. How is your appetite?"

"Ferocious."

"A good sign. You are doing well. I spoke to the king about you, and he will be delighted to see you. Perhaps you are not aware of it, but no other man in the kingdom could have brought you through in the manner I did. It's a great triumph of medical skill."

"Don't you think it would be a greater triumph by allowing me to eat something?"

"All in good time. Miss Cherington, he may discontinue the drops, but take the powders regularly, and increase his food to two pieces of chicken and a piece of dry toast."

Then the doctor punched me once or twice, and left the house.

"Julia," I said, after the lamps were lighted, "how long have I been sick?"

"O, you are a naughty boy, and must not ask questions," was the evasive answer.

"But I am serious in my demand."

"Then I will tell you to-morrow."

"There is another question I want to ask of you," I said. "Why was I arrested?"

Instead of receiving an answer, Miss Julia commenced crying, and left the room quite abruptly, which I thought strange, and I did not see her again until the next morning, when Dr. Pendergrast judged that I could sit up for a while; and after I was up, and reclining in an old-fashioned rocking-chair, with a neat dressing-gown and embroidered slippers, Miss Cherington made her appearance, looking more beautiful than I had ever seen her.

"What shall I do to amuse you?" she asked, as she took a seat by my side.

The window where I sat was open, and I could look out upon the harbor and see the shipping and the boats moving about. At our feet were the houses of foreign residents, substantial white wooden structures, surrounded with trees and gardens, in which bloomed flowers and fruit trees the year round. It was my first near view of Honolulu; and no wonder I was astonished at the paradise which met my gaze, and that I forgot to answer the question which Julia put to me. She laid one of her little white hands upon my arm, and that recalled my wandering thoughts.

"I was wondering why a person should ever wish to leave such a paradise as this," I said.

"Do you think it so very beautiful?" she asked.

"I never saw a spot more lovely," I answered. "What an air of comfort pervades the entire town! Your dwellings are as good as those found in New England, and seem to have every convenience."

"And why should they not?" she laughed. "They were erected by New England mechanics, and designed by New England architects. Everything can be obtained here for the building of a house; not only plain ones, but even those ornamented with carved work.

"The longer I look at the town the more I am delighted with it," I said. "I should never wish to leave it, it seems to me."

"Did you never possess such feelings before?" she asked, with a malicious smile, which quickly gave place to one of gravity.

I blushed, for I recollected that only a short time before I had told the Rev. Mr. Gangle, when I was conversing with him, that I never desired to leave the kanaka village. I looked up, and saw that Miss Cherington's black eyes were fixed upon my face. My own fell; and once more sought the harbor.

"What shall I do to amuse you?" Julia asked at length, after punishing me sufficiently.

"I leave it to your own invention. Only don't wound me with such cruel remarks as you just made."

"You poor boy, I did not intend to hurt your feelings. I meant to show you that you did not yet know your own mind. You are so fickle that I believe you would be contented in most any spot for a while, and then risk your life to escape from it. You are impulsive, but I don't think you really mean to be bad."

"A thousand thanks for your good opinion," I cried. "I asked you last night how long I had been sick.

"O, a long time," she answered. "But do you think you are strong enough to talk of the matter?"

"I feel very comfortable," I answered.

"And happy?" she whispered.

"No, not quite happy," I replied.

"What do you desire?"

"Health, wealth, and your respect."

"Health you soon will have; wealth will depend upon yourself; and my respect upon your future actions."

"And you are willing to forgive the past?" I whispered.

"I forgive nothing, for I have nothing to forgive. You must learn wisdom and self-respect before you can expect your friends to love you."

Before I could frame a reply, Mr. Cherington entered the room.

"Good morning, Charles," he said, shaking my hand with gentle warmth. "You are getting along bravely, my lad. In a week's time you can be out."

"You must not hurry him, father," the young lady remarked. "He is doing very well under my treatment."

"I have no doubt but that he will soon tire of it. Now I have come to talk with him, and thus relieve you. You can soon return," her father said, as the door closed upon her.

Mr. Cherington took a seat by my side, and produced a package of letters, which he handed me.

"These are from your parents," he said. "Your father is not very complimentary, but you can read for yourself."

I broke the seal of my father's letter, and read as follows: —

"MY DEAR CHARLES: You're a fool. What did you want to leave home for? And what in the name of thunder made you ship on board of a whaler? We supposed that you were drowned, and I offered a reward for your body. I had the whole police force after you. I don't understand it yet. A boy who has had the advantages you have had should not have left home so suddenly. My old friend, Mr. Cherington, speaks highly of you, and thinks that you will be contented at the Sandwich Islands. I know better. You can't be contented unless you have a mother looking after you. If you want to remain at Honolulu for a while, I havé no objection; or if you can go into business there and make a good thing of it, I will let you have the money, say from five thousand to ten thousand dollars; but I want Mr. Cherington's approval, and if he is satisfied, draw on me. I have done pretty well, lately. I was elected an alderman on the 10th, and I've just sold some of my land for five times the amount I paid for it. I made a cool forty thousand dollars by the operation, and I shall do as well by the other lot on Washington Street, near the Neck. The city wants it for a square; but the city has got to come down squarely with the cash before it gets it. Old Fairchild asked after you the other day, and said that it would not be a bad idea for us to unite houses by marriage. He has got a pretty daughter, and my son used to be a decent-looking boy. I asked him what he would give the girl, and he said, as much as I would you. I thought that I would let him know that the grocery business is as profitable as the hide and leather; so I said, kinder carelessly, that when you married, I should give you fifty thousand dollars to start with. That made him stare; and after a moment's hesitation, he said that he would do the same. So, you see, if you want to come home and settle down, here is a chance. I'll take you in partnership, and get you nominated for the common council, where you can get a very good thing if you are smart; and in course of time you can run for alderman, and if elected, your fortune is made. I long to see you, you young rascal, for I feel that I love you much better than I supposed I did. If you remain at the Islands, I shall consign to you a number of articles, and you may sell them on commission. I shall write by the next ship."

I read the letter over carefully.

"Your father is prospering, he tells me," said Mr. Cherington.

"Yes," I answered, and I placed my letter in his hand. "There is nothing in it which I need keep secret from you."

He read the letter very deliberately, and then handed it back.

"Your father's letters to me speak about your engaging in business here; but on that subject we can talk after you have grown stronger. You have a bright prospect ahead, if you will only try to improve it."

"I shall need a little money," I hinted, "to purchase clothing for my new position."

"I will advance what is necessary. Give yourself no uneasiness on that score. My house is your home as long as you remain in Honolulu."

I expressed my thanks, and then the old gentleman was about to leave me, when I detained him.

"Can you tell me on what ground I was arrested by the soldiers, and whether I am still regarded as a prisoner?"

"I have seen the Secretary of State," he said, "and have secured your release and permission to remain on the island as long as you may be disposed to."

"But why was I arrested?" I asked, more earnestly.

"I think that the Secretary was informed that you were not leading a moral life at the village of Kammaira, and that it was better for you to be removed. He will, probably, explain all some day."

"Does Miss Cherington believe the slanders which were circulated respecting me?" I asked, after a moment's hesitation.

"She is young, and has seen but little of life. She has confidence in human nature and in man's honesty. After she has resided on the island as long as I have, she will not be so credulous. Men change wonderfully after leaving Cape Horn. You have not acted worse than others, and —".

"I thank Heaven for that!" I exclaimed.

"And no better," the old gentleman continued, which rather took me aback.

My cautious friend left me, and I was alone to read my mother's letter. It was a long and affectionate epistle, blaming me for not confiding my grief to her, and for my cruel conduct in leaving home. The reading of the letter made me melancholy; and I found that I would have to retire to the bed and rest, unless I ran the risk of over-exerting my strength. I touched a bell, and a kanaka servant — a young and willing fellow — waited upon me, and by his aid I was soon comfortable.

"Miss Julia gone out, sir," the man said, after he had darkened the room. "She will be back by noon."

I was so fatigued that I fell asleep, and did not awaken until afternoon; and then I found upon the table, at my elbow, a bouquet of fragrant flowers and half a dozen large golden-hued oranges.

I felt refreshed and strengthened by my rest, and was anxious once more to try the virtues of an easy-chair. I touched the bell that stood upon the table, and the kanaka was promptly at my side.

"The family are just eating dinner," he said, "and will be with you as soon as they have finished. What can I serve you with?"

"Help me to that chair first, and some dinner afterwards," I answered.

The smiling kanaka, who could speak better English than I could the language of his country, assisted me to rise, dressed me with what clothes were necessary, opened the windows, and drew back the curtains, and left me to enjoy the glorious view which I had looked upon in the morning.

Presently in came Mr. Cherington and Julia.

"Did you notice the beautiful flowers which I placed by your bedside while you slept?" she asked.

"I did, and thanked you in my heart for the gift," I remarked.

"Julia is very skilful in arranging bouquets," Mr. Cherington said. "I wish that she would exercise her talent a little oftener, and decorate my room."

"So I will when you are sick."

"Well, I don't care to be sick, even for the flowers. But while we are talking, Charles is starving. What is he to dine on?"

"O, I have some delicious broth for him. The doctor says that it is strengthening. And for dessert I have a nice orange and some splendid jelly."

"I am ready to meet it face to face," I said; and I soon had an opportunity.

From that time my recovery was rapid, and in a week I was able to ride out and view the town. I rode out with Julia every day, for Mr. Cherington not only kept his horses and carriage, but he was very particular that they should be as showy as could be found on the island. Sometimes the old gentleman joined us of an afternoon; but we generally went alone, and I willingly dispensed with his company. It was dangerous work for a young man of nineteen to sit by the side of a young lady of seventeen, day after day; and as my health became established, I found that I was gradually forgetting my passion for Lilly, and thinking more and more of the bright eyes and clear skin of Julia, and hoping that I was not indifferent to her. I ordered linen shirts by the dozen, and grumbled terribly if my washerwoman did not polish them until they shone like a mirror. I affected tight shoes and white stockings, and changed the latter three times a day if I had visits to make in the evening in company with Julia. I wore the whitest of linen coats, and the neatest of linen pants, and the most delicate of vests, and sported a Panama hat that was a marvel of workmanship and purity. I purchased a chronometer watch from a reduced sea captain, and then bought a chain to match; but still Mr. Cherington made no complaint, but honored my drafts without a murmur. A month passed on, and still Mr. Cherington had said not one word of business. I visited his store every day, and found that he dealt in most everything which a ship would want, or a landsman require. He traded with whalemen, merchant ships, and men-of-war; and I judged that his profits were large. One day I was seated in his counting-room, reading the last number of the Honolulu Advertiser, when he came in and took a seat by my side.

"You feel quite well," he said, after scanning my neat appearance with a calm smile.

"Never felt better," I answered.

"And you have no desire to go back to kanaka life?" my friend asked.

"None," I answered with a sigh, for I thought of Lilly.

"I am glad to hear it. I suppose you are anxious for something to occupy your time."

"I am doing very well at present."

"But you must have something to occupy your mind. You wish to remain on the island for a few years, I understand."

"For a lifetime," I answered, warmly.

"We will make arrangements for a few years, and see if you don't get restless. Do you wish to enter my employment as a clerk? I can give you a position as such as long as you desire."

"I should prefer some other position," I remarked, after a moment's reflection.

"What other position would you like? Speak freely."

"My father spoke of advancing money in case I was disposed to enter into business arangements here," I said, after a lengthy pause.

"I know that he did, and I am willing to second you in any manner in my power."

"Then," I replied, "I should like to become a partner in your house. I will work cheerfully, and in a few months hope to be able to take much care and labor from your shoulders."

The old gentleman did not answer me for some time. At last he took from his safe a ledger and opened it.

"My business," he said, "is much more extensive than you suppose, and the profits are large. I have no desire for a partner, yet as I am growing old and I have taken a fancy to you, I will allow you one third of the concern, at a fair valuation, and you may select any business man on the island to be the judge."

"My dear friend," I cried, "I will leave that matter entirely to you. I am not acquainted with trade, and it will take me some time to learn it thoroughly."

"The profits of my business the past year," said Mr. Cherington, calling my attention to a page of the ledger, "were a trifle over twenty thousand dollars; the year before, eighteen thousand; the year previous, sixteen thousand. The losses have been trifling. Now, to admit you to share one third of such a business, I shall charge you the sum of eight thousand dollars."

"Before I accept or reject the proposition," I cried, "tell me how much money you will allow me to draw out of the concern for current expenses."

"How much do you think you will need?" my friend asked, with a calm smile.

"I want to make a good appearance," I said, "and I can't do that unless I have a good wardrobe and money in my pocket to pay my stable bills."

"My horses and carriages are at your service any time you wish to ride," my friend remarked.

"How can I thank you for such kindness?" I cried, with some emotion.

"By taking Julia with you on some of your excursions," he answered.

"Take her with me!" I cried with warmth; "why, I should not want to go unless she was with me."

"Ah, is that the case?" the old gentleman exclaimed, dryly; "then I don't see that we need quarrel about that. Julia is eager to go, and you anxious for her company. There is no occasion for a dispute on that score, unless you and the girl spat it a little for variety."

"I cannot quarrel with Miss Cherington," I said.

"That is what I used to think, before I was married;" and the good man sighed.

"Then I have a board bill to pay," I continued, enumerating my expenses.

"Are you contented where you are?" Mr. Cherington asked.

"Indeed I am," I answered, most promptly.

"Then you shall stay there until you tire of our company; and to save your independence, your board shall commence on the day that we sign articles of copartnership. Until then I consider you my guest. Does that suit you?"

I could only press his hand.

"What say you, Charles, of the propositions?" asked my friend, with a calm smile.

"That I accept them with much pleasure, and will strive to merit your commendations as a partner."

"Well, then, let us go to dinner; I see it is time. Give me your arm, and walk slow."

CHAPTER IX.

A NEW FIRM.

In a few days the necessary papers were made out, and I was introduced to the foreign residents of Honolulu as the junior partner of the great house of Cherington & Co. In a few weeks I was able to take charge of the books of the concern, and was very proud of my penmanship, as I recorded the various transactions of the firm upon the white pages. During my leisure hours I made many acquaintances and received many invitations to bachelor quarters; but as I was in love, I preferred to spend my evenings at home, hearing Julia sing, or else chat with her upon the events of the day.

One day, as I was going home, some one brushed past me, and then stopped directly in my path. I thought the man intoxicated, and inclined to assert his right to the whole of the side-sidewalk, so stepped to the wall, and was passing on without a word, when a familiar voice saluted me.

"Blast my eyes, but doesn't you know a shipmate when you sees him?"

"Jack," I cried, overjoyed to see the man, and shaking hands most heartily, "where did you come from?"

"Same old place where you left me when the sojers carried you off. I haven't been in town but an hour or two."

"And Will and Jake — where are they?" I asked.

"They is down to the boat waiting for me."

"I am glad to see you, and shall be happy to shake hands with the rest of my shipmates. But I have not time to go to the dock now."

"All right, maty. It's just as well. We didn't come here to interfere with your business, 'cos now you is a gentleman, and can walk the quarter-deck, and we is fore'stle men, and knows our place."

"But I want to see you and talk with you," I cried, feeling a little hurt at his remarks. "I have not forgotten you and your kindness, and I never shall."

"That may be, Pepper, but it would not do for us to be seen on equal terms here. Your partner wouldn't like that, you know."

"How do you know about my partner?" I asked.

"O, Kamaka visits us sometimes, and yarns off the news."

So it seemed that Kamaka was well aware of my movements, although I knew nothing of him. There was one question that I wanted to ask, yet feared to, and I tremblingly awaited Jack's communication on the subject. He saw by my looks that I was uneasy, and said:

"What is it, Pepper?"

"You know what I would be informed of. Is she alive?"

"O, Lilly," he cried. "Ah, I recollect. She is not so well as she used to be. She took your sailing to heart, and for two months she didn't show her face outside of her father's house.

The natives thought she would die, 'cos she busted a blood-vessel; but the old women give her some roots and yarbs, and she come round arter a while; but she don't sing now."

"Does she know that I am here?" I asked.

"O, yes; Kamaka told her all about it, and a good deal that wasn't true, I think, 'cos I saw 'em talking, and she was crying."

"The rascal! Why don't you drive him from the village?"

"So we did, arter you was gone a little while; but then the sneak come back, and give us the news about you, and as we had no other way of hearing of you, we let him come."

"And Lilly's father; is he well?"

"The old fellow smokes and bathes as much as ever, but he don't seem lively since you left us."

I felt a pang of remorse as I recollected how I promised to return and marry Lilly, and be a chief in the village.

"We is quite contented at the town," Jack continued, not noticing my internal struggles. "We has each of us got a wife, and they takes care of our clothes, and we supplies 'em with fish; and if we only had a little tobacco to smoke, we should have no cause to complain."

"You don't mean to tell me that Will has a wife."

"No, we wouldn't let the boy take one; but he grumbled some at us 'cos we refused our consent. Boys don't know much — do they?"

"Is Will contented at the village?" I asked.

"Well, sometimes he is, and then agin he ain't. I come to see you on his account."

"Indeed!"

"Yes; you know that Will has got an old mother to support, and I don't think it right for the boy to sojer his time away doing nothing, like me and Jake. We don't care, you know. A day or a year is no object to us, but 'tis to Will. Now you can give him something to do here in town."

"I am glad you spoke of the matter," I said, for I had often thought of some way to relieve Will, and yet did not know how to go to work to do it. "If he will remain here with me, he shall have a salary and something to do."

"I knew you would help Will," Jack cried, seizing my hand and wringing it most heartily. "You jest talk to him to-morrow, and he'll stop here. You tell him it's all for the best."

I promised that I would, and then Jack looked me all over, and shaded his eyes as he did so, pretending that my appearance dazzled him.

"You is all rigged out like a new frigate jest from the dock," he said. "You don't look as though you had slushed down masts and tarred down ropes. Let's see your hands, if it ain't too much work to peel them things off of 'em."

He meant a pair of white silk gloves which I wore for the purpose of shielding my hands from the hot sun, and preserving their whiteness. It will be seen that I was fast merging into the habits of a dandy. I was not ashamed to show my hand, for all the stains contracted on board the whaler were removed. Jack lifted it up in a dainty manner, and examined my palm, and then dropped it with a sigh.

"It looks cleaner than it used to," he said, "but is it as honest a paw as it was when I showed it how to use a marlinspike and a sarvin' mallet?"

"It is a hand that is at your service at any time, friend Jack," I replied.

"Ah, boy, time changes men's hearts as well as their hair. You is fresh and green to-day, and to-morrow you is — well, blast me if I know what you is to-morrow."

"Then you mean that I am green to-day?" I asked, laughing.

"That's 'em;" and the old salt shut his larboard eye and winked. "All boys is green," he continued, "and don't know much till they has been afloat a dozen viges or so."

"I must leave you now," I said, "but will see you to-morrow forenoon. Call at the store. Ask any one where we keep, and you will be directed right. Now, where do you propose to spend the night?"

"In the boat," he answered, promptly.

"No, that won't do. Here is money. Go to the hotel, and all have supper and breakfast, and I will see you in the morning. Remember, no liquor, Jack. It will get you into trouble."

"Not a drop," he answered; and then we shook hands and parted.

The next morning one of the clerks entered the counting-room, and said, —

There are three sailors in the front store who wish to speak with you."

I went out, and saw, surrounded by boxes of tobacco, pipes, and bales of goods, my friends Jack, Will, and Jake.

"Good Lord, is dat Mr. Pepper?" Jake asked, surveying my personal appearance with looks of astonishment.

"Blast yer eyes, can't you see it is?" said Jack. "I knowed him the minute I seed him."

"I am glad to see you," I cried. "Now take seats, and tell me all the news."

"I kotched fifty fish day afore yesterday," Jake said. "Golly, didn't I snake 'em in."

"What do you 'spose Pepper cares about that?" Jack growled. "Tell him some news. My wife says you must come and see us one of these days."

"Who married you, Jack?" I asked.

"Well, we jumped over the broomstick, I s'pect. That's about all the marriage I had. It answers just as well as any other, I s'pose. My wife obeys me, and 'tain't every wife that does, you know."

"I am glad to hear," I remarked, addressing Will, and speaking very gravely, "that you have no thoughts of taking a wife."

"O, but I did want one," answered the young rascal, promptly. "Jack said I shouldn't have one, and the old chief backed him up; so no young girl dared to accept of me."

"Think how it would have grieved your mother had she heard of such actions," I remarked.

"I don't think that you've got much to boast of," Will said, a little inclined to be sulky. "I s'pose I've got a right to have a wife as well as you."

I sighed at such depravity, and thought what I should say in reply.

"I had no wife, and have none at the present time," I said.

"O, that's all gammon, you know; I've got two eyes, and can see things as well as any one."

I looked at the young rascal, and concluded that I would not argue with him until I could show a fair record.

"When do you propose to return to the village?" I asked of Jack.

"O, we want to be off just as quick as we can. You said something about some tobacco yesterday, and if you can afford to give us a few pounds, we shouldn't take it amiss."

"You shall have a keg," I said; "but I want you to supply the chief as long as it lasts. He was kind to me, and I have not forgotten him."

"Or his daughter," cried Will, with a laugh; but I frowned the boy into silence.

I called a clerk, and told him to put up a number of pipes, a box of tobacco, a piece of bright calico for Lilly, a looking-glass for the same person, — for I knew she was woman enough to like a glimpse of her face once in a while, — and then I walked towards the beach, where their boat was hauled up.

"You haven't said one word about Will," whispered Jack, as we neared the boat.

I had not said one word about him, I very well knew. The reason was, he appeared a little too knowing for me. Perhaps Jack suspected what I thought, for he suddenly seized Will by the collar of his shirt, and shook him as though just recollecting an old grudge.

"What is that for?" asked Will. "What have I been doing now?"

"Are you going to tell me whether you mean to go back with us, or stay here?"

"How can I stay here when no one has axed me?" responded the boy.

"Will you keep a quiet tongue in your head if you does stay? Answer me that."

"Of course I can keep quiet, but I won't be shook like that and say nothing, now I tell you;" and Will looked his indignation.

"Don't talk to me, you boy," cried Jack. "You comes here, and is entertained in good style, and yet you must open your jaws and reel off yarns — must you?"

"I ain't reeled off any yarns."

"Don't you go for to answer back. Now, if Mr. Pepper will take charge of you, and look arter you, will you keep secret-like, and say nothing to nobody?"

"In course I will," was the cry. "Does you think I is leaky?"

Jack looked at me to know if that was satisfactory. I nodded.

"You can remain here, Will," I said, "and I will find something for you to do; but keep a still tongue in your head."

"I understand, sir. You don't want me to say one word about your old flame, Lilly."

Jack caught the boy, and once more shook him.

"There you go agin, in spite of my warnin'. Won't you keep still?"

"Let me alone, or I'll knock thunder out of you," said the lad.

I made Jack release the boy, and by the time we reached the water, the articles which I had ordered were on the beach and put into the boat, the same one we had stolen from the Sally. I saw that my shipmates had everything that they needed for the short trip which they were going, and after a hearty hand-shaking they shoved off.

We walked back to the store. Mr. Cherington was in the counting-room, and looked at my shipmate with some surprise.

"Don't you recollect this lad?" I asked of my partner. "He was on board the Sally with me, and showed me many acts of kindness."

"O, I recollect him now. He appears to be a bright boy, Charles, and I think that we can give him something to do, and at a fair salary."

"We want some one in the store to check off goods as they are received and leave the premises," I said. "When not thus employed he could visit vessels, and be very useful on account of his knowledge of seamanship."

"So he could. We have long wanted such an intelligent boy."

I introduced Will to the clerks, and set him at work, and he seemed quite contented when he found that he could make a good living.

That day the dinner was not enlivened with conversation, and I was glad when it was finished, for one of the young men of Honolulu had told me a strange story, and I was anxious to know if it was true. I followed Julia to the sitting-room.

"Julia, may I not congratulate you upon your engagement?" I remarked.

I saw her face flush and the work drop to her lap, as though too much astonished to say a word. But she rallied and made sail, although I could see that she made considerable leeway while getting under way.

"Why, Charles, what do you mean?" she asked.

"Just what I said," I replied. "I have been told that you were engaged to a naval officer, and I congratulate you; but I am sorry that you did not hint something of the kind to me."

"Who told you such a story?" she asked.

"O, I cannot tell you."

"You need not, sir; I know. It was that odious Hatch. It sounds just like him."

"And do you mean to tell me, Julia," I asked, moving my chair a little nearer her own, "that the report is untrue?"

"Of course I do, sir. What could possess you to believe such a story?"

"Ah," I said, "it was mostly on account of that report that I have been miserable to-day. I felt as though I had not shared your confidence. I thought that you might have told me if that was the case. I am sure you have been to me as a sister."

"A sister?"

She started as she repeated the word. I saw her dark eyes raised as though reproachfully, and I thought that there were tears in them.

"You will be a sister to me — won't you, Julia?" I asked.

There was no response.

"I am sure," I continued, "I should be glad to know that you had a good husband, and one that would love you as you deserve to be loved."

Still there was no response.

"Do you feel offended at my words?" I asked, after a pause.

"O, no. Why should I?" she replied. "You have been kind to me, and I thought at one time that you —"

She ceased speaking, and once more resumed her work.

"Will you not finish your remarks, and tell me what you think?"

"Why should I? You only want a sister's confidence."

I gently removed the work from her hands, and then she looked up.

"How can I ask for any other kind until I know whether the reports which I have heard are true or false."

"Then I will tell you. They are false. Does that satisfy you?"

"No."

She looked up surprised and grieved. I took possession of one of her hands.

"Julia," I whispered, gaining courage very fast.

"Charles," was the answer.

"Do you know that I have more than a brother's love for you?"

"I thought so at one time."

"Do you not think so now?"

"How can I tell?"

I moved a little nearer, and accidentally dropped one hand over the back of her chair, and let it circle her waist.

"Julia," I said, "since the night we met on board the whale-ship, I have loved you."

"O, Charles, think before you speak. Consider the events of the past few months, and then confess that at one time I had nearly faded from your mind."

"No, I will think of nothing but my love for you. Time cannot change that."

She looked at me with those dear bright eyes of hers, and I fancied that I saw hope expressed in them.

"Can you love me a little, Julia, if you should try very hard?"

"Yes, I think that I could if I should try very hard," she answered, and her eyes began to grow light with mischief.

"Will you try?"

"I will think of it."

My happiness was so complete that I did not care to move; so I sat there encircling her waist and holding one of her hands.

"You think that you like me well enough for a husband?" I asked at length.

"I think that I shall, after you have grown a little more stable in mind," was her answer.

"Can you believe me fickle?" I asked.

"I do think so, Charles. I may as well speak plain."

"I never loved but you," I murmured; and then before me rose memories of Jenny Fairchild, whom I had worshipped, and poor Lilly, whom I had been forced to part from.

"We are both too young to think of marriage for many years," she said. "There is time enough for us to talk of such matters."

"But I don't think so," I cried, "and you will break my heart with your proposals of delay."

"I should be sorry to do that; but at least you will consent to wait until you are twenty-one."

"You don't love me," I said, a little pettishly.

"Yes, I do; but it is your happiness and mine that I am striving to secure. Only think, if we were married, and you should see some one you liked better than myself."

"But I never shall," I answered, kissing her so rapturously that for five minutes she could not answer me; and while I was thus engaged, the door opened softly, and into the room walked Mr. Cherington.

I think that Julia managed to leave my arms about as quick as a distressed female could tear herself from such a pleasant position. I arose from my seat and confronted my partner, and appeared as cool as possible under the circumstances.

"I don't understand the meaning of this scene," Mr. Cherington said. "Will you, sir, be kind enough to explain?"

"I thought the scene explained itself," I answered. "I was kissing Julia."

"By what right?"

"Love's attraction," I answered, although not quite so bold as before.

"I am still in the dark," he said.

While I was thinking what excuse I should render, Julia came to my rescue in her calm, sensible manner.

"Tell him all, Charles," she said.

"And I should like to be told all," was the reply of her matter-of-fact parent.

"Well, sir, you shall know all. I had just told Julia that I should like to make her my wife — that I loved her dearly — and she had answered that although she rather fancied me, she was too young to think of being married."

"Humph," grunted my partner; "what do you suppose your parents would say to such an arrangement?"

"They would say that I was sensible in marrying such a charming creature."

"I don't know about that;" and then the old gentleman looked thoughtful.

"I hope you don't disapprove of my suit?" I said.

"Too young, too young," he muttered.

"I know we are young, but we are growing older every day. If you will give your consent now, I will wait as long as you please."

"If I give my consent you must promise to wait with patience for two years."

"Two years!" I cried, horrified at the length of time proposed.

"Two years," repeated Mr. Cherington.

"I consent," answered Julia.

"And you will also consent, Charles? It is for your welfare and that of my child that I make the proposition; but now I must return to business. Charles, you and Julia had better ride out. The air is delightfully cool."

"Perhaps I should return with you," I said, demurely.

"No, no; I'll see to everything. Enjoy yourselves while you can. Life is short, and sometimes not over pleasant. Be home in time for tea, and don't drive the horses as though they could be made to trot in less than three minutes;" and off went the old gentleman.

We had a pleasant ride, and then returned to town, stopping for Mr. Cherington. I entered the counting-room to tell him that we were waiting for him; but saw that he was holding a conversation with a rough-looking man, dressed like a sailor. They were conversing in whispers, but stopped when they saw me, as though I intruded upon them. At the same time the sailor hastily thrust something into his pocket, and then sat gazing at my partner as though anxious to know what he should do.

"The carriage is ready," I said, looking at Mr. Cherington and the sailor with astonishment.

"I shall not go home with you. I am not quite ready. You need not wait for me," my partner said.

"Very well," I answered, and turned to leave.

"O! tell Julia that she may prepare the west room for company, and also have a good supper for one or two guests."

"Somethin' fresh, with a glass of grog to top off with," said the sailor. "I feels as though I could eat double rations, I've been kept short so long."

"Whom, in the name of common sense, has my partner picked up?" I asked myself; and as I left the two, their heads went together, and they re-commenced whispering.

"Where is papa?" asked Julia.

"He is in the counting-room, holding a close conversation with a sailor;" and then I delivered to her Mr. Cherington's orders, and she wondered as much as myself.

"It must be one of my father's old shipmates," Julia remarked. "He meets with one sometimes, and then he has to talk for a week about old matters."

I considered that might be a proper solution of the affair, and thought no more of it until after dark, when Mr. Cherington brought the sailor home, and entertained him at supper, afterwards gave him a large glass of punch, and then attempted to get him to bed; but the seaman refused to move until he had emptied a bottle of brandy, when he began to sing songs and act in rather an independent manner, as though he was at home.

"Why don't you send the fellow to the guard-house?" I asked, disgusted with his conduct, and sympathizing with the alarm which Julia manifested.

"Hush, my dear boy," cried my partner, with a look of dismay. "Don't say one word to offend him. He will retire to rest in a few minutes."

"Not by a d—— sight," retorted the bold mariner. "I'm on shore, and I'm going to drink as much as I please. I can pay for it, and I don't care for any of you. Send me to the guard-house!" cried the fellow, after a moment's pause; "I'd like to see you do it. I'd blow the yarn to every one I met, and then how would you like it?"

I saw that Mr. Cherington was really agitated, and anxious for me to leave. What could be the meaning of the secrecy between them? Had my partner at one time committed some shocking crime, and was the sailor acquainted with the mystery? I returned to the drawing-room, where I found Julia pale and agitated; for the sailor had made considerable noise in the house, and frightened her, as well as the kanaka servants.

"What is the meaning of this?" the dear girl asked.

"I have not the slightest idea," I answered.

"It is the first time such a scene has occurred in the house, and I trust that it will be the last."

"I trust so, too; but I have every confidence in your father, and no doubt he will explain the matter when disposed."

About eight o'clock, one of the servants informed me that Will was desirous of seeing me on business, and I went to him immediately. The few weeks that Will had been in our employ had produced quite a change in his deportment. He was fast improving in his duties, and had reached a position which he was proud of.

"I am sorry to disturb you, Mr. Allspice," he said; "but while putting away the books this evening, I found on the floor this leather bag, filled with some kind of yellow metal. I didn't know but you would like to hear of it; so I brought it to the house."

"It would have kept until morning," I remarked, with a smile, and took the bag, but was astonished to find that its contents were very heavy.

When I reached the drawing-room, I saw Mr. Cherington conversing with his daughter.

"Who wanted to see you?" he asked, nervously.

"Will. He found this bag on the floor of the counting-room, and he thought you or the sailor might have dropped it."

"Did Will mention the subject to any one?" Mr. Cherington asked.

"No, I think not."

"Then, my dear boy, run after the lad, and charge him not to say one word of the matter to any one."

"Why, father, what is the meaning of this mystery?" asked Julia.

"No matter — don't ask me any questions. I cannot explain, and I will not. Go, Charles, and delay not a moment. If the lad has mentioned what he found, or is disposed to, lock him up, so that not a soul can see him until to-morrow. Delay not, my boy."

I overtook Will just as he was entering his boarding-house.

"Will," I asked, "have you mentioned to a single person that you found that bag on the floor of the counting-room?"

"No, sir. Every one had left the store before me."

"All right. Keep a close tongue in your head, and say nothing until I tell you to. There is some mystery connected with the bag, and it will be investigated."

"I hope that you don't suspect me of anything," the boy said, with a tremor in his tone, which showed how honest he was.

"You would be the last one, Will," I remarked, as I turned to walk home. "We have known each other too well for that."

"I mean to be honest, at any rate," he answered; and then I left him and went home, where I found Mr. Cherington in company with the sailor, and still allowing him to drink as much as he pleased. The mariner, however, was in the room allotted to him for the night, and was too drunk to make much noise, excepting to roar out for brandy every ten minutes.

As soon as Mr. Cherington saw me, he left the sailor's company.

"Well, well," he asked, "what is the news? Did you see him?"

"Of course I did."

"And he has been silent—has he?"

"He has not spoken a word about finding the bag."

"Thank Heaven! Then we are safe."

"You mean that you are safe," I replied.

"No, sir, I mean that we are safe."

"I confess that I do not understand you," I remarked, a little coldly.

"I know that you do not," was the unsatisfactory answer.

Suddenly a suspicion crossed my mind—a cruel suspicion—and I was determined to have my doubts satisfied.

"Mr. Cherington," I said, as my partner was turning from me, "tell me one thing; answer me one question."

"I cannot now, Charles. To-morrow you shall know all."

"Let me know to-night this one thing: Is the firm in danger of failing, through some bad speculation of which I have been kept in ignorance?"

"My dear boy, the house never stood in a better position than it does to-day."

"Are you in any danger from the threats or exposure of that drunken ruffian?"

The old gentleman smiled.

"The only danger that I run is hearing some very vile language; but that I must submit to for the sake of the firm."

"I cannot understand you, or your meaning," I remarked.

"I suppose not. You will, however, in good time."

I looked hard at the old gentleman, but he was quite cool now, and his eyes were as keen as ever.

"You think me mad," he said. "I don't blame you. But leave me. Go and comfort poor Julia."

And I left in search of Julia, whom I found in the drawing-room, anxious for me to report.

CHAPTER X.

ASTONISHING NEWS OF THE GOLD MINES OF CALIFORNIA — WE BUY TO THE RIGHT AND LEFT, AND MAKE PLANS FOR A FORTUNE.

The next morning, when I awoke, I found that it was sunrise, and that Mr. Cherington was standing by the side of the bed. I looked at my partner, and saw that his face was pale, as though he had passed a sleepless night and was tired.

"Where is the sailor?" I asked. "I hope that he has left the house."

"Heaven forbid, after all the trouble that I've had with him. The fellow is sleeping off his drunken debauch, and will not awaken until afternoon — at least I hope that he won't. He has proved a tough customer, for his head is as hard as iron."

I looked at my partner, and saw that even if he did appear tired, he was quite cool and collected, and I marvelled at it.

"Come, get up," he said. "We have work before us, and much to accomplish before night."

I was soon dressed and at the table. It was just six o'clock as we sat down, and twenty minutes afterwards we were on our way to business.

"How many barrels of flour have we in the store?" my partner asked, as we walked along.

"Not more than fifty."

"And ship-bread? How many pipes?"

"Ten."

"And how much pork have we?"

"Not more than a dozen barrels. Hatch wanted to sell me some yesterday, taken from the condemned ship Betsy Baker, of New London. He offered it cheaper than we sell it by a dollar a barrel."

"How many barrels did he say that he had?" asked my partner.

"About one hundred, or more."

"It is all mess, I suppose," Mr. Cherington remarked.

"No, one half is clear and of good quality. I saw some of it unheaded, to show as a sample."

"Does the firm want ready money?" my partner asked.

"I believe that it does. It bought the stores of the Betsy Baker for cash at a low rate, and the money is wanted to pay for them."

"That is good. I am glad to hear that. In a business point of view, you know," my partner added, hastily.

We reached the store and found Will already there. He was hard at work arranging goods, which provoked a smile from Mr. Cherington.

"Smart boy," he said. "Make a good man for us;" and then we passed into the counting-room, and my partner commenced an examination of the books. Then he made some memorandum on a piece of paper and closed the books.

"I'm going to trust you with very important business," he said, "and you must show yourself worthy of the firm."

I pricked up my ears. He was going to confide the secret to me at last.

"I want you to go to the firm of Vida & Hatch, and buy all the flour, bread, pork, tobacco and pipes which they have on hand. Get everything at a low figure for cash. Here is a memorandum that will guide you. Don't pay more than the figures I have set opposite each article, and get them as much lower as possible. You will understand all in the course of the day. If you hear of any one having provisions to sell at our prices, buy them without hesitation — buy all you can get."

I started to leave the counting-room, but Mr. Cherington called me back.

"Let me see, — you are in the habit of smoking, are you not?"

He knew I was; but seldom at the house.

"I think that you had better visit the store with a cigar in your mouth. It will look as though you were not in a hurry."

I sauntered along until I came to Vida & Hatch's store, and by good luck found Hatch standing at the door smoking.

"Hallo!" he cried; "come in and talk a little while. I have just come on shore. We had a good time on board the Constellation last night. Wish that you had been there. But come in."

I hesitated, and then followed Hatch to his counting-room, where the senior member of the firm was smoking, and looking, as I thought, a little dull.

"How is business over at your place?" asked Mr. Vida, who was a short, dark-eyed man, a Chilian by birth, and fond of a paper cigar and a glass of champagne.

"Nothing doing since the whalers left. It is the dull season, I suppose."

"Yes, dull enough; and here we have got a large stock on hand, and can't sell it," remarked Mr. Vida.

"You don't offer it low enough," I said, with a laugh. "We sold out pretty close, and might be induced to buy."

"Catch Cherington at that," Hatch cried. "He is too smart for such nonsense. I offered you pork, yesterday, at a dollar less per barrel than you can buy it in the city."

"If you had taken off fifty cents more per barrel, I might have traded with you, and been willing to wait for a rise."

"I'll do it now," he cried, hastily.

"How many barrels have you?"

"Two hundred."

"I'll take them for cash. Send them over to our warehouse as soon as you can, for we want to store them."

"Are you in earnest?" asked Hatch and Vida, in a breath.

"Yes, I mean what I say. I don't believe that pork can go any lower; so I will buy it on speculation. I'll buy anything cheap, and wait for a rise. That is better than letting money remain idle."

"Then take our flour and bread on the same principle. The fact of it is, we need the money just at the present time."

"We'll buy anything if you only put it low enough."

Vida and Hatch consulted together, and the result of their conference was an offer of their stock, far below what Mr. Cherington had instructed me to give.

"But, understand us," the senior member of the firm said. "We don't want to take any advantage of you, for the reason that Mr. Cherington might not like to ratify the contract. We will sell at such a price for cash, the goods to be delivered to-day. If that proposal suits your firm, the bargain is closed."

"Confidence begets confidence," I said. "I will convince you that I am acting with the consent of my partner, who is anxious to buy on speculation."

The firm once more put their heads together, and talked long and earnestly.

"You can have the articles at the sum named," they said, after the conference was closed; and they immediately made out a bill of sale, so that I found I had purchased some six thousand dollars' worth of bread, flour, pork, tobacco, pipes, and ready-made clothing, and just as the bills were made out, a man by the name of Russell entered the store.

"I have called," he said, "to see if you wanted to purchase any flour."

"We have just sold the last barrel that we had in store," Mr. Vida answered. "What do you ask for good flour?"

Russell named a figure, which was a little higher than the sum Vida asked.

"Can't buy at that price," the firm said.

"What will you give?" Russell asked, turning to me.

"The same that I paid Mr. Vida. We buy for cash, and may have to keep it for a long time."

"You can have it," he answered promptly.

I went back to the store, and found Mr. Cherington there, wiping his face, which bore marks of heat.

"Well," he said, "what success? Did you trade?"

"I bought all they had, for less than what you told me to give."

"That is good. Now we are all right. I have bought the schooner Helen at a bargain, and all the fresh provisions which Gangle owned. Now we can afford to let the public hear the news."

"But you forget that I do not know what the news is," I said.

"I know — there is time enough. But close the door, sit down, and I'll tell you."

I did as I was ordered.

"Did you ever hear of such a country as California?" Mr. Cherington asked.

"Why, yes. It was ceded to the United States by Mexico at the conclusion of the war. I don't know its value, although I think that many hides have been exported from California to Boston. That is all I know of it."

"And that is quite enough for my purpose. Well, what will you think when I tell you that gold has been discovered in California? mines of immense richness! In fact, that it can be picked up on the surface of the earth, and cut from rocks with jack-knives."

"I should evince my astonishment by saying that I don't believe it," I answered.

"So I supposed. But nevertheless it is true, as I state to you, and at the present time there are only three persons in Honolulu who have any knowledge of the matter."

"And those are you and myself, and who else?"

"The sailor I carried home last night, and who probably has not yet awakened."

I was astonished, and did not answer.

"I see that you think me dreaming or crazy, but such is not the case. The sailor brought to the island two thousand dollars' worth of gold dust, all collected in the short space of two weeks, on the banks of a river called the North Fork, about one hundred miles in a direct line from San Francisco."

"If gold is so plenty, why did the sailor leave until he had collected more?" I asked.

"Why do sailors always remain poor? Simply because he thought he was worth a fortune. He went to San Francisco, engaged a passage in a vessel bound to Canton, and paid three hundred dollars to be set on shore here."

"And how did you get hold of him?"

"Ah, that is the most singular part of my story. I was on board a whaleship yesterday afternoon, when I saw a vessel heading for the harbor with a signal flag flying for a boat. I took my boat, and was pulled on board. I had but a short time to talk with the master of the vessel, for he was anxious to square away for Canton. But he gave me the glorious news, and handed me a San Francisco paper with long accounts of the mines. The people of California are crazy over the discoveries, and all kinds of business have been neglected to seek for gold. Men are running away from ships, and even the United States vessels are short-handed on account of desertion. I took the sailor in my boat and brought him to the shore; but I made him promise that he would not say one word regarding the gold discoveries, until I gave my consent."

"Didn't your kanakas hear of it?" I asked.

"Not a word. They were in the boat all the time I was on board, and did not hear a lisp."

"Have you seen the gold?" I asked. "Is it not possible that it may be some mineral that closely resembles gold?"

Mr. Cherington opened the safe, and took out two small buckskin bags.

"Here are two bags full of the dust. The third one the sailor must have dropped last night, for he insisted on keeping one shot in the locker for immediate use."

He poured the gold into a plate and stirred it with his fingers. Some of it was so fine that it seemed a mystery how it could have been collected, while scattered through the glittering mass were several nuggets, some of them nearly as large as a horse-chestnut.

"If you still doubt the truth of the sailor's report, read the accounts in the California paper, for it seems that one has already been established at San Francisco."

I opened the paper, — a small one, some ten inches long and twenty wide,—and found that the whole inside was filled with letters from the mines, recounting the lucky strikes which miners had made, and how new mines were discovered every day by prospecting parties. From the correspondence I glanced to the editorial columns, and found a short leader, which read as follows: —

"At the present time we know not what to think. San Francisco is deserted, and no business is transacted. Dust is received from the mines by every boat or vessel that reaches us from Sacramento. Our printers have left us to take part in the struggle for sudden wealth, and we have a letter from one in which he says that he dug one hundred dollars worth of gold the first day he reached the mines. If such is the case, we shall have to leave our paper and commence turning up the earth in search of riches; for at the present time we have to do our own composing, press-work, and the 'devil's' work in the bargain. Of course all kinds of provisions have risen to enormous prices, and we fear much suffering, and even starvation, the coming winter. We have large numbers of cattle on the ranches, but men cannot live on meat alone, and in this emergency we must look to the Sandwich Islands for our pork, flour, coffee, and other articles. A vessel loaded with such provisions would reap a rich harvest at the present time."

"What do you think of that?" Mr. Cherington asked.

"I think that I now see the reason why you have purchased the schooner Helen."

"The vessel must be despatched without loss of time. I have a gang of men at work on board of her, bending sails, and to-morrow we will commence loading."

"Let us commence to-day," I said. "We have men enough."

"Good! Cargo shall go on board at once. But there is one thing I have forgotten to speak about. You or I will have to go with the vessel, to sell the provisions. Which shall it be?"

"I, of course," I answered. "You can attend to our business at home better than I can."

"But Julia? What will she say?"

"That I am anxious to make a fortune for her sake."

"I don't think she will," said the old gentleman, dryly. "But you can go. Now, where can we find a navigator?"

That puzzled me; but an idea entered my mind just at that moment, that we could give some master or mate a passage to California for the sake of navigating the Helen there, and during the trip I could apply myself to the task, and learn all that was necessary of the science.

The Helen was about two hundred tons' burden, flat bottom, and intended for carrying a large cargo, and drawing but little water. Of course she could not be classed as a first-rate sailer, excepting before the wind; but we did not look so much for speed as capacity. Even with a full cargo, the schooner did not draw but five feet of water. This was a great disadvantage for sea navigation, but was just the thing for river sailing, as we afterwards found. I made a minute examination of the vessel, and on the whole was quite satisfied with her. We set men at work painting, and another gang to receive cargo, and by night much progress had been made with our arrangements.

"I think," I said, as we walked to the store, "that I will send for my two shipmates who are still at Kammaira."

"They will leave you at San Francisco," Mr. Cherington said. "Not a vessel can drop anchor at that port without losing every man."

"I think that we can make it for the interest of the men to remain with us," I said. "Suppose I should take my three shipmates, and we should tell them to stick to the vessel, and that in addition to their monthly pay, they should have a certain percentage on the profits. Will you let me try it?"

"Certainly."

We reached the store, and I went in search of Will, whom I found taking an account of some goods which were going into the warehouse."

"Will," I said, "we have purchased a schooner, and I am going a short voyage in her. Do you want to go with me?"

"Yes, sir, I am ready for that at any time. Who is going captain?"

"I am."

"That's good. I'll be one of the crew."

"No; I want you for second mate, with the same pay that you now receive, and a chance for dividends in case we are successful."

"Who's going first mate?" asked Will, with a stare of astonishment.

"Who do you suppose?"

The boy looked thoughtful.

"I don't know," he said, "unless you send for Jack. But then he don't know much about navigation."

"Would you like him for a shipmate?"

"I just should."

"And Jake — do you think that he would like to go with us?"

"The darky would jump at the chance. But where are we going."

"No matter about that. I want Jack and Jake to know of my intentions. Will you take a canoe, with two kanakas, and go to Kammaira?"

"I should like to very much."

"Then take any two kanakas in our employ, and go. Tell the men that they shall have twenty dollars per month and a commission on the profits of the voyage if we are successful."

"That will bring them, sure," was the answer.

"Tell them that they must stay by me and the vessel after we reach port, or they will receive nothing."

"You are joking," said Will. "You couldn't get them to leave you. There is not money enough in the world to buy them. At least I think so."

Will selected two of the natives who were accustomed to the harbor, and attended to our boating matters, and in a short time he was off for the village of Kammaira. I returned to the counting-room, where I found the sailor who had passed the night in Mr. Cherington's house. He had slept until noon, and then got up and left the premises, and by the aid of one of the servants, found the store.

"I want my money," he said, just as I entered. "I am going to have a time with it."

Mr. Cherington took the bags from the safe, and placed them in the sailor's hands. The man untied them and examined the dust, and found that it was correct.

"I don't want all this money with me," he said.

We did not answer him. If we had said that we would take charge of it, he would have thought that we meant to cheat him. But as we did not volunteer, he obtained confidence in a wonderful degree, and throwing the bags upon the desk, muttered, —

"S'pose I take this 'ere dust, some one will steal it from me. I don't want it. I don't know what to do with it. Will you keep it for me?"

This was an appeal that we could not resist; and Mr. Cherington promised to take charge of all three bags, first advancing the man fifty dollars for spending money. My partner offered the man some good advice, but while he listened to it with respectful attention, he did not seem inclined to follow it.

"I never had so much money afore," he said, "and now I'm bound to have a time with it. I'll make Honolulu howl afore I've done. I've worked hard, and after all the money is gone I knows where I can get more. Californy is the land for me. What's the use of my saving when I can get more?"

"It will be known all over Honolulu before night," said Mr. Cherington, as we walked home for dinner.

We had too much work before us to remain at the table any length of time, and I had barely opportunity to hint to Julia that her father's conduct had been explained in a very satisfactory manner. I said nothing of my contemplated visit to California, and on that subject Mr. Cherington remained mute also. After reaching the store, the bills for the goods which we had purchased came in, and we were kept quite busy for two hours paying out gold and settling accounts; and just as we had finished, Hatch entered the counting-room.

"Look ahere," he cried, "we sold shorter than we intended. Can't you let us have a hundred barrels of pork and flour at the same price that we paid for them? We have got an order, you know, and we don't like to disappoint our customers."

"Can't do it," said Mr. Cherington. "It is all stowed in the warehouse. We have raised ten dollars a barrel on pork and the same on flour, and we don't want to sell at that price."

"Blast it, I suppose you have heard the news," muttered Hatch, throwing himself into a chair.

"What news?"

"Why, about California. O, it's no use to look grave. I know it. It's all over town. Men are acting as though they were mad. There's a sailor who brought the news. He tells thundering big stories. If one half is true, gold must be plenty there, and grub scarce. What is the lowest you will sell us a hundred barrels of pork for? Be liberal, and give us a chance."

"Ten dollars per barrel advance, and rather you would not buy at that. I tell you, Hatch, gold is plenty in California, and provisions dear," my partner said.

"What can you ship in?" asked Hatch. "There is only one vessel in port excepting whalers, and the latter won't dare to go within fifty miles of the coast. The skippers are half crazy already for fear they will lose their men by desertion. Come, let's make a trade for one hundred barrels of flour and one hundred barrels of pork. Be liberal. You have got the best of us; I acknowledge that."

"Sit down, Mr. Hatch," said Mr. Cherington, with a calm smile. "Charles, haven't we a few of those Havanas left?"

I found the box, and we lighted our cigars in solemn silence, and after Mr. Cherington had adjusted his weed, he said, —

"We bought on speculation, and we shall sell on speculation. We have some five hundred barrels of pork, and the same number of flour. We can sell a portion, and still have enough on hand to freight the vessel which we have purchased."

"What vessel?" asked Hatch, eagerly.

"The schooner Helen."

"O, damn!" shouted Hatch. "If Vida hasn't just gone to buy her, then I'm a sinner."

"He's rather late. She is paid for, and the papers are in my safe."

"Just our darned luck. The old tub has been for sale the last three months, and no one would buy her. Well, I don't blame you. But let us share a little. Give me what I want at a fair advance."

"At what I said. Not a dime less. The market is still going up. To-morrow I shall advance on the price. I don't want to sell; but I will to oblige you. In half an hour others will want to buy. We will sell for cash, you know. Money down."

"Then count me in for two hundred barrels, and send them over at once."

I went with him, taking a kanaka along to assist in bringing the specie to the store.

"You have made a strike, and I envy you," Hatch said as we walked along. "Hallo! here is Vida. Did you buy the vessel?"

Mr. Vida growled out an answer that could not be understood very readily.

"O, it is no use to sulk. They've got the start of us, and we can't catch up. We must follow on behind, and do the best we can. Who in the devil's name supposed that California was going to shed its hides and reveal gold? But I've done something. I've made a trade with Cherington. Took two hundred at an advance. Just the sum we agreed to give."

"That's something, for pork has gone up two dollars per barrel since I saw you," answered Mr. Vida, eagerly.

I received my money for the articles, and returned to the store.

"What was your object in selling?" I asked of my partner.

"Simply because we had exhausted our ready money in buying, and what is due us will not come in for two or three months. We need money just at this period, and I bought with the understanding that we should have to sell in a few days; but I intended to do so at an advance, and for cash. We have made two thousand dollars on one sale. That has placed ready money at our disposal, to meet current expenses, until we can get returns from California. Now we are fortified against every attack. We can lose nothing, and we have paid for everything. There is, therefore, no chance for us to fail, even if the mines should not turn out as rich as we expect."

I saw the force of his argument, and after the day's work was accomplished, returned to the house quite satisfied with what we had done.

During the next forenoon I visited the schooner, and found that the cargo was most on board, and that the vessel was rapidly getting ready for sea. At the rate the work was going on, I calculated that we could leave for California in the course of three days. In the afternoon, while I was at work on board, a little, fat, red-faced man, with a bald head, a moist eye, a pleasant voice, and a jolly smile, came over the rail and rolled towards me.

"Good day, sir," he said, touching his hat, which was a nautical one, and looked a little the worse for wear. "Allow me to introduce myself, sir. My name is Myers, sir—James Myers. I belong in New London, Connecticut. Of course you have heard of that place, sir. A great town for handsome girls and whalemen. It is five years since I was there. Great changes since then. I left there master of a ship; and now I couldn't get a vessel to save my life, I suppose."

"For what reason?" I asked.

"Various," he answered; "various. In the first place, I did not take as many whales as I did nippers of gin; and so, after cruising two years, I went off on a voyage of discovery, thinking that I could find whales near islands, in places where ships never cruised before. I was not successful, and consequently the owners took away my craft; although, to tell the truth, they had a long search before they found me. Since that period I have commanded everything in the shape of a vessel, and now find myself at Honolulu, without funds, without friends, but with a desire to go to California, where I think I can make money enough to cover up my sins. To you I apply. I want to work my passage to the land of gold. I don't care in what capacity."

"How long have you been in Honolulu?" I asked.

"About two weeks. I had a passage given me from the Friendly Islands; so I ran over here to see what I could do."

"I am in want of a navigator," I remarked; "and if you are competent to take charge of that department, and teach me the science while on the passage, you can go with the vessel."

"Give me the tools to work with, and I'll not turn my back to any man in the whaling fleet," was the confident answer. "I'll learn you all that I know in two weeks' time. If you don't learn, it shan't be my fault."

"And if you serve me faithfully you shall be paid for your trouble," I remarked.

"Don't speak of pay, sir," said the jolly man. "Put me in California, and I'll find gold enough to pay me. But you have passed your word, mind you, and I'm engaged."

"Don't be alarmed. You shall take up your quarters in the cabin to-day."

We had at the store an excellent chronometer, and charts enough to fit out a line-of-battle ship, besides quadrants and books which we kept on hand to supply the demand that was constantly made by whalers. From the lot Mr. James Myers, late master of a New London whale-ship, made a selection to suit him, and then left me to send his luggage to the schooner. But he soon returned, and his face looked more jolly than ever.

"This is a great town," he said, wiping his heated brow, and shaking his rather large stomach. "I never met such treatment before, in all my wanderings."

"What is the matter?"

"Why, the blasted marine who keeps the house where I boarded — But you won't believe the statement. It seems incredible — in what is popularly called a heathen country, too. Good Heaven, how remiss the missionaries have been in their duties!"

I suspected the captain's troubles, but said nothing.

"It is but little," he said, in a musing tone. "Ten dollars for board and two for drinks. A trifling sum compared to the immense value of my chest and contents. And he means to hold it, too. That's a joke."

"I suppose you mean that your landlord won't release your clothes until you have paid your board?" I remarked.

"And the extras," cried the little man, with an attempt to blush.

"Well, come with me and I'll pay the bill," I said.

"God bless you," exclaimed the ex-whaling captain, seizing my hand and giving it several violent shakes, as though it was a pump, and he was bound to keep me afloat. "You are a Connecticut man, I know," the captain continued, as we turned the corner of Queen and Kaahumanu (the reader can pronounce the latter name to suit himself) Streets, and headed for a sailor boarding-house, kept by one Terry, formerly from New York.

We reached Terry's, where we found that gentleman with his shirt sleeves rolled up, and his tongue hard at work, damning two kanaka servants, because they did not labor quick enough to suit him, in washing the tobacco juice from the floor. Mr. Terry, on seeing the captain, frowned darkly, and swore with increased violence; but on looking up and finding whom he had for a visitor, stopped his harsh words, and suffered the scowl to pass from his brow.

"What is the matter, Terry?" I asked; "the captain says you won't let his clothes go."

"Now, look ahere, Mr. Allspice," cried Terry, with the air of an injured man; "this feller comes to my house and wants board for a few weeks, till he can get a skipper's chance, or a chief mate's birth. I takes him in and gives him the best that I has in the house. For that I expects money. He hasn't got any, and there's no shipping in the harbor. Then he comes and wants his clothes, and leaves me minus the dosh for his grub and drinks. I don't stand that from no one, I don't."

"But I intended to pay up like a man," cried the captain, rubbing his red nose, and seeming to care but little for his peculiar position.

"Yes, I s'pose you do mean to, but you see I wants the dosh now, to carry on my house and meet my payments. I don't trust, I don't. You can have your duds on paying your bill, and not afore."

"It is extremely unpleasant, this is," muttered the whaler. "But few men from Connecticut care to be placed in such a position."

"No, I s'pose not," sneered Terry; "but I tells you that a Yorker isn't taken in by a wooden-nutmeg fellow, no how you can fix it."

"How much is the bill?" I asked.

After an immense amount of labor the bill was produced, and I paid it, and left the establishment with the heartiest wish of the landlord for my future success in life.

"I see, Mr. Myers," I said, as we walked along, "that a large portion of your bill is for drink. Of course you do not expect me to furnish you with liquor. If you do you will be disappointed."

"O, no," he said; but the response was quite feeble, and the face, so red and fat, did not look quite so jolly as it did a few moments before.

I sent the captain to the schooner, with orders to take his meals at Terry's, until the vessel was in proper trim for sea, and then I went back to the store, and found Mr. Cherington and the clerks hard at work packing up boxes, which I was to take to California on a venture.

"I have been thinking," said Mr. Cherington, "that we can make a good profit on some spades and pickaxes which we have on hand, and have held for some months. At the time I imported them I thought the kanakas could be induced to use them; but they prefer to stick to lighter tools. Shall we send them to California on a venture?"

I said yes; and the same afternoon five hundred spades and five hundred pickaxes were stowed away on board the Helen, and valuable articles we found them. After dinner I was on board, looking after matters, when a boat pulled alongside, and my shipmates tumbled on deck.

"We didn't stop long arter we got the news," said Jack. "We jist packed up our dunnage and left. We promised our wives to return, and they is satisfied. Now we is ready to go to work. The only question is, what shall we do with Jake? Make him cook or steward?"

"I's for de steward's place; be over de cook. I'll butt de feller if he don't hurry up de grub."

So I gave him the position of steward.

Just at that moment Will came out of the boat, and following him was a slight-built kanaka boy, light-colored, and with such a handsome face that he would have attracted attention anywhere. He appeared to be much confused, and I thought trembled as though frightened.

"I gave the lad a passage to Honolulu," said Jack; and then Will and the kanaka went on shore, and disappeared from sight; and in a few minutes the incident had entirely passed from my mind.

CHAPTER XI.

OFF FOR CALIFORNIA. — A SURPRISE AND A PASSAGE. — CALIFORNIA AND OUR CARGO. — HOW WE SOLD IT AT A PROFIT.

The next day we got our stores all on board, and the cargo stowed, and were ready for sea. Then we commenced picking our crew, and in that we found no difficulty. Hundreds of kanakas were eager to ship, and work their passage to California; and many white men would watch an opportunity, and pounce upon me whenever I left the store or the vessel, all eager to urge their claims for a chance. After some trouble I obtained six kanakas and a good cook. Two of them I bound to return to the vessel, and the balance to be discharged after the schooner was unloaded. They swore by all the wooden idols of their forefathers that they would stick to me until I told them they might go. At sundown the crew were on board, and the schooner was hauled outside and anchored. I bade my officers good night, and was passing over the side, when Myers, my sailing-master, detained me.

"You've forgotten one thing," he said, in a whisper.

"What is it?"

"In case of sickness, you know. I've tried all kinds, but I think that brandy is the best. Strange climate we are going to, Mr. Allspice. Bad water, perhaps. I think it would be best to have a little on board. Not on my account, you know, but your own."

I had a keg of brandy on board, but Myers did not know it; and I didn't intend that he should, until I was in a position to look after it. So I shook my head, and talked about the bad effect of liquor, and the master retired, looking far from jolly.

On entering the counting-room, I was astonished to see Mr. Hatch and his partner, and several other gentlemen of Honolulu.

"Glad to see you, old fellow," Hatch said. "I'm just negotiating for a passage with you to California. I'm going to start a branch of our house, if there's an opening. We'll have a good time on the passage, hey? I'll have my things all on board in half an hour. Ain't you glad I'm going?"

Of course I was, for he was a lively, rattling fellow, and would be good company on the passage. He paid the money demanded, and went off to collect his baggage, and then Mr. Cherington and myself finished up the balance of our business and went home to tea. I can't say that I really felt very joyous, for the thought of leaving such a pleasant home was far from agreeable. I knew that I should be lonely and miss the society of Julia; but I strove hard to keep up my spirits, and manifested but little of the gloom that was gathering around my heart. Mr. Cherington was far from lively, also.

Our tea-table was, consequently, a dull one. Mr. Cherington was thoughtful, Julia extremely unhappy, and I anxious and nervous. I feared that something was about to happen that would destroy the understanding which existed between Julia and myself, and therefore I was glad when we retired to the sitting-room, and the lady seated herself at the piano, and played and sang until nine o'clock; and then Mr. Cherington, like a considerate father, declared he felt tired, and must retire, and left us alone to talk as long as we pleased, and I think I availed myself of the privilege, for twelve o'clock struck before we thought of separating.

I was up the next morning, at daylight, and the first thing I did was to glance at the harbor. There lay the Helen, with smoke ascending from the galley stove-pipe, and men busy washing down the decks. A short distance from her was the Constellation, her tops alive with men, employed at some work which I could not make out, owing to the distance.

The family were already stirring, for the day was an important one. Mr. Cherington looked as though he had been cheated of his sleep, and Julia was very pale, and therefore extremely interesting. We could only drink our coffee in silence. Appetites were out of the question; so, after making a farce of eating, we rose and prepared to separate. Then came the most trying scene.

Just then I caught sight of one of the servants with several packages upon a wheelbarrow in front of the house, and he appeared to be waiting my movements. Julia saw the direction of my eyes, and blushed.

"A few things I have put up for your comfort," she whispered. "There's preserves, and a few cans of meats, and some fruits."

How quick a man's heart can be touched by such delicate attentions! Eating is not very romantic, but it is very important; and there would be but precious little love without it. Julia put out her hand, then, like a well-bred woman, commenced crying as though I was her only friend in the world, and she was about to lose me forever. Her father turned his head, and appeared to be intensely interested at something in the harbor; and thus I had a chance to whisper a few words in her ear, and to console her with a kiss, the report of which caused her father to turn his head and mutter, —

"Come, come! I thought you finished all such nonsense last night. You sat up late, I believe."

"I know I did; but you see I am far from feeling anxious to leave."

"And I don't want you to go," sighed Julia.

"But he must go; and it is no time to detain him," said Mr. Cherington. "Time and tide wait for no one."

I snatched a kiss and left the house so hurriedly that my partner was compelled to run a few steps to overtake me.

"God bless me," he said, "if the old schooner could only sail as fast as you run, California would be reached in a short time. Gracious! what an impetuous fellow you are! Give me your arm, and let me talk with you as we walk along."

I slackened my pace, and the old gentleman clung to me, and talked as we moved on.

"Don't trust those sharpers of California," he said. "You will find plenty of them ready to take advantage of you; but you must be smart, and look after them. If you can sell for cash, do so; but be sure that the cash is forthcoming when the goods are delivered. I hope things will look bright after you get there."

"As bright as Julia's eyes," I murmured.

Mr. Cherington sighed, and didn't say any more about business. We reached the dock, and I found the schooner's boat waiting for me.

"Mr. Hatch is on boaad," said Will. "We have hove short, and are all ready for sea."

"And here we part," cried Mr. Cherington. "I would go on board, but the pain of separation would only be prolonged. God bless you, Charles, and may you return to us in safety."

He grasped my hand, held it for a moment, and then I shoved off, and was soon alongside the schooner, on the quarter-deck of which I found Hatch, sipping a cup of coffee, and looking jolly.

"Turn up the side, boys," he shouted. "Here comes the captain and gig."

Mr. Topmall — who was represented in the person of my friend Jack, but as he was doing duty as an officer, it was necessary to have a handle to his name, and for the first time for years the family cognomen was introduced — came aft, and was extremely gracious at the prospect of leaving port.

"We is hove short, sir," he cried, "and only wait the word to trip the anchor."

"Up with it at once," I said; and then I looked at the house where I had spent so many pleasant days, and saw, from the window of the room which I had occupied, a white handkerchief waving in the breeze, and by the aid of a good glass I made out to catch one glimpse of Julia's face; and I answered the signal by displaying a small piece of bunting which had been made by

Miss Cherington, and presented to me for the vessel. On it were some mysterious letters, known only to her and myself; but they represented —

LOVE TILL DEATH.

Up fluttered the signal to the mast head, and its appearance was rewarded by a renewed waving of the handkerchief, and then the anchor was reported clear of the bottom, and the schooner commenced paying off under the jib; and in a few minutes we were before the wind, and moving slowly towards the Constellation.

"Now, sir, if you will commence your lessons, I'm ready to begin," said the ex-whaling captain, who had made himself generally useful during the morning, and had eaten a powerful breakfast to pay for it.

I had learned the use of the quadrant while on board the Sally, and could find the latitude readily, so I was not so green a pupil as Myers had expected; and at twelve o'clock he acknowledged that I was making rapid progress in the science, and should get along handsomely.

The high lands of the islands began to look blue as we left them astern. Down into the ocean they sank, till at last the only mountain that we could see was the peak of Mauna Loa. I turned from the fast-fading view with a sigh, and thought of poor Julia, who was mourning for my absence, and as I did so, I saw the young kanaka, whom I have already mentioned, standing by my side; but he, too, was sighing, and tears were in his large almond-shaped eyes, as though his tender heart was severely tried at thus leaving home for the first time.

"Well, boy, are you sorry that you have left home?" I asked of the kanaka.

"No, sir," he answered. "I am not sorry at present. I don't know how soon I shall be;" and he was turning away to leave the quarter-deck when I stopped him, for his voice sounded very familiar, and I was thinking where I had heard it.

"I have seen you before, somewhere," I said. "Can you tell me where?"

He hesitated for a moment before he answered, —

"At Honolulu, I think;" and then left the quarter-deck, as though desirous of escaping further questions.

"It is singular," I thought; "but that boy reminds me of some one, and I can't tell who."

"Dinner all ready, sar," cried Jake at this moment; and the vexed question left my mind.

By sundown the land was out of sight, and we found that we had made some fifty miles on our course, and were doing very well, although the north-west trades had not set in strong, as we expected.

Our decks were cleared up for the night; the kanakas were seated on the forecastle, chatting and singing, and smoking their short pipes, the mate and the whaling captain were spinning yarns near the mainmast; Hatch was smoking on the quarter-deck, and wondering how he should mix a bowl of punch for the evening entertainment; and I was looking at the private signal, made by Julia's fair hands, which fluttered from the mainmast, and wondered if she was thinking of me, as I was of her, when Jake came from the cabin, his black face looking uncommonly sedate, as though he was puzzled what to get for breakfast.

"Will you come in de cabin, one moment, sar?" he asked.

I followed him into the cabin, and there saw the young kanaka boy, who looked as though he had been crying; and, in fact, he could not entirely stifle his sobs when I entered.

"What is the matter with the boy?" I asked of Jake.

"Wal, sar, dat is jist what I call you in for, sar. He ben crying, and won't listen to my advice a bit. I want you to talk wid 'em, sar, and see what 'em says."

I supposed the lad was homesick, and said so; but the kindness which the natives had shown me, I determined to repay, in some portion, to this poor boy.

"Don't cry, my lad," I said, laying a hand softly upon his head, and speaking in his native language. "We shall be in port in two or three weeks, and then you can remain by the vessel if you don't want to go on shore, and you may return with me if you don't desire to stay in California. Don't cry, for while shedding tears you remind me of one whom I used to love very much."

"And you forgot her — did you not?" the lad replied, attempting to stifle his sobs.

"No, I did not. I have often thought of her, and wondered if she had forgotten me," I replied, without stopping to think of the extraordinary question of the lad.

In an instant the boy was on his knees before me, my hand grasped in his, and his handsome head resting on my knees.

"You still love me! you still love me!" he cried, through his tears and sobs.

His cap fell off, and in spite of the close-cut hair, I discovered the face of one who had been very dear to me.

"You know me. I'm Lilly. Poor Lilly! Don't scold her. She loves you. She can never love but you. Her heart was almost broken when you left her, forced from her side by the cruel soldiers. She was very sick for many weeks, and only the thought of once more seeing you made her live. Now, if you don't love her and speak pleasant to her, she will die. Let her be near you — your slave — your servant; only smile upon her sometimes."

The poor girl's strength failed her; and her hands relaxed their grasp. I saw that she had fainted. What to do I did not know. I had had no experience with fainting women, although I had read that it was always customary to cut their stay-lacings. But the poor thing at my feet had never seen a pair of corsets, and would not have worn a pair if she had. In my agitation I raised her in my arms, and carried her to my state-room, and laid her on a mattress; and then, getting a tumbler of water, I bathed her face, almost white now, and forced a few drops of wine down her throat. The latter revived her. She opened her large black eyes, and smiled faintly when she saw how attentive I was, and then raised her head, and put up her thin lips for me to kiss.

How could I help myself? I had struggled as hard as it is possible for man to struggle; and yet I found myself pressing her lips, and looking with pitying eyes at her handsome face; and this child of nature smiled when she found that I was not cold and stern as I should have been.

"You will not send me away from you? You will let me remain with you — will you not?" she asked; and put her arms about my neck and held me fast.

"I must think of the matter," I answered, striving to withdraw her arms from my neck; but she resisted.

"No," she said, "you shall decide now, or I shall die. For many days I have thought of but you, and now that I hold you in my arms, my heart will surely break if you leave me."

Was ever man placed in a more uncomfortable position? Whichever way I turned there was disaster and ruin to my hopes. If Julia should hear that Lilly was on board, how could I convince her that the kanaka girl was not there from connivance? My protestations of innocence would not be believed. I knew enough of Julia's mind to understand that without the slightest doubt. If I was cold to Lilly, and kept her at a distance, the result would be the same if the fact of the girl's being on board was known. But suppose it was not known? The question suddenly presented itself to my mind with startling distinctness, and I thought of the matter. If Julia should never hear of Lilly's imprudence, of course there would be no trouble, and I should have plain sailing. The kanaka girl would be happy — Julia would be happy, believing me good and true, as I hoped I should be. On the whole, I began to look upon the bright side of the picture; and while I was thinking, I suffered Lilly's arms to remain around my neck.

"Ah, you don't know how I managed to get here," the girl said, in a triumphant tone.

I confessed my ignorance with a smile, for I was fast softening.

"Your friends told me you were going as master of the vessel, and I determined to go with you, and said so. They refused to let me; but I pleaded so hard, and promised not to make myself known, that they consented. They gave me a suit of boys' clothes, and I left the village with them. But I nearly died the first time I saw you. I wanted to run into your arms and kiss you, as I used to. Did you not see me tremble? I then knew I should have to tell you who I was, and longed for the time. You are not angry!"

Of course I could not say that I was, and then I went on deck, and over me was floating the flag which Julia made; and I sighed as I ordered it down; and while it was on its way to the deck, Julia was on her knees, in her chamber, praying for her absent lover. God help us, for fate has played a cruel trick, and one which I would have avoided.

As I walked the quarter-deck of the schooner that evening, my thoughts were far from being enviable. My well-laid plans were disarranged, and I saw disappointment and much misery in store for us, unless I could keep the whole matter secret from Julia. This was what my conscience did not approve; but I saw no other plan, and would therefore turn my thoughts towards enforcing upon my shipmates the great necessity for secrecy; and when I reached this conclusion, I looked up and and saw Mr. Topmall within a few feet of me, waiting as though he was desirous of speaking.

"Do you want to see me?" I asked.

"Yes, sir, I wants to say something about that gal. You've found it out, Jake tells me."

"I have, and I wish that I had done so before. You did very wrong to let her come. It will injure me."

"I hope not," answered the mate. "I would have sooner cut my own hand off than do you an injury. The gal cried and cried, and had fits, and rolled up her eyes, and kicked like a thirty-two-pound gun when she heard you was going, and that we were going with you. She said she would go, and we couldn't help ourselves; and she scratched my face when I said she couldn't. What could I do with such a gal? We thought it was best to take her along, and she promised to keep quiet, and not let you know who she was."

"Still, it is likely to involve me in trouble," I remarked. "I am engaged to an amiable young lady, and if she should hear of it there would be a tempest."

"Then don't let her hear of it," was the sagacious remark. "There's only me, Will, and Jake, what knows it, and we ain't going to say nothing, not if we knows it. I don't think that it's much of a hardship to have a pretty gal on board of a vessel, not if that pretty gal has a fancy for yer."

"It is not right," I remarked.

"It may not be right," replied the matter-of-fact mate, "but I know it is quite human; and I allers supposed sailors had a good deal of humanity in their buzums. At any rate, they shows it when they comes alongside a pretty gal."

"Well, well," I answered, with an air of resignation, "just keep the affair quiet and tell Will and Jake to do the same. The rest of the men know nothing about it, and they need not. Lilly can remain in the cabin, and I'll let her make up a bed in my state-room for the present."

"Yes, sir, I s'posed you would," was the reply; and the mate looked serious, as though no joke was intended.

"I'll take care that nothing is said," he continued, after a moment's pause. "Only don't you pet the gal afore all hands, 'cos they might suspect that she wasn't a boy;" and after perpetrating such a bull, the mate went forward to smoke his pipe, and Hatch came on deck.

"Say, All-pice, do you know that kanaka boy is lying in your berth, as though he had a right there?" Hatch remarked.

12

"Yes; I put him there for the present. He was sick, and I took pity on him."

"That's more than I would do. You don't begin right for a master of a vessel. Go down and rouse the fellow out, and make him move."

"No; I think I will let him remain."

"Ah, well, I have no more to say. He's a good-looking youngster, and has more of a girl's ways than any boy I ever saw;" and Hatch, entirely unconscious how near he had shot, walked aft, and enjoyed the evening air and his cigar at the same time.

I felt a hand laid upon mine in a timid manner, as though the owner was uncertain of its reception. I turned and saw Lilly standing by my side, her dark eyes raised to my face in such an imploring manner, that I could not help re-assuring her by putting an arm around her waist and patting her cheek.

"You are not angry now?" she asked.

"No; I am determined to do the best that I can by you, but it will be the last time that you sail with me. It is wrong."

"Was it wrong for us to love when you were at my father's village?" she asked.

"Yes, I think that it was."

"Then why did you tell me, at that time, that it was right?" Lilly asked; and there was more sternness in her voice than I had ever heard her use before.

"We will not discuss the matter now," I remarked. "You are here, and I'll protect you, as you protected me when I first saw you. No one need know that you are a woman, and, in fact, I don't desire that they shall."

She promised to retain her boy's clothes, and not expose her sex, and said that in all things she would obey me, and the only reward she desired was a smile and a kind word, and the privilege of being near me; and how could I refuse her the little that she asked?

I sent the poor child — she seemed like a child to me — below, and then walked the deck for a long time, thinking of my singular fortunes, and wondering how they would terminate. At last I gave up all hope of seeing my way clear, and then left the deck in charge of the mate, and went below.

I was awakened the next morning at six bells by hearing the morning watch wash down the deck, and by the pitching of the schooner, as though a fresh breeze was blowing.

At eight o'clock we had breakfast, and my select company mustered around the table with excellent appetites, and quite happy. I longed to give Lilly a chance at the same table with me; but I did not dare to, for fear some questions would be asked and some suspicions excited. The poor girl made a show of assisting Jake to wait upon us, but it was all show; and when Hatch asked her for something, Jake was quickly on hand to supply whatever was wanted.

Days passed on quite pleasantly. My secret was kept, and I don't think that any one suspected it, unless it was Hatch, and he was too much of a man of the world to make a remark unless his opinion was asked. In the mean time we drifted on towards California, sometimes with favorable winds, and at others pounding against stiff north-west trades.

At last we made the land, and by an observation found that we were about twenty miles to the north of the Golden Gate; and with a free wind we ran along the rocky coast, upon which we could see the surf rolling and tumbling, having the full sweep of the Pacific. Then the men commenced preparations for entering port by donning clean shirts and trousers; and Hatch shaved, and appeared upon the quarter-deck with a starched white shirt and black pants, with boots polished as though he were to appear in the presence of ladies with a critical turn of mind.

With a fair wind and tide, we at length reached the entrance of the noble harbor, and pointed the nose of the Helen for Bird Island, over which place thousands of gulls and other sea-fowls were flying, as though never disturbed by man. But we saw no signs of humanity, excepting the Stars and Stripes, which were flying on the starboard side of the entrance.

Very beautiful did the mountains and valleys look, covered with their quilts of green, spotted with flowers, which raised their heads and emitted perfumes, as though proud of their mission. The air was so delicious and pure that it seemed to act on the brain like a glass of wine taken by a person unaccustomed to the juice of the grape; and so enchanted was I with the scene, that it was not until the ex-whaling captain spoke to me that I was aroused to a sense of my responsibility.

"Better douse some of the sail, sir," he said. "We don't want it all."

"In with the foresail and flying-jib," I replied. "I was admiring the scenery so much that I forgot I was in command," I continued, by way of apology to Hatch and Myers, who stood on the quarter-deck.

"Where's the city?" asked the former. "Show me the city. I don't believe that there is one. It's all a blasted lie, and we've come here for nothing."

At that instant we luffed a little, and rounded Telegraph Hill; and then we caught sight of famed San Francisco, and the shipping in front of it. I must confess to a feeling of intense disappointment and disgust. I could see but a dozen or more houses, scattered far apart, and apparently built in a hurry, excepting some six or seven which seemed to have been planted many years, and to have been ill used, and therefore stunted in their growth. Between the buildings were tents, and scattered on the hill-sides were tents of all sizes and shapes — tents of India rubber cloth, and tents nearly as dark, made of stout canvas — tents made of cotton cloth, so very dirty that it seemed a mystery how they managed to stand erect under the heavy weight which pressed them down — tents improvised from rough pine boards and pieces of old sails, with the blocks and ropes still attached to them, and stretched to anchors in the shape of wooden pegs, as though the owners were fearful of returning home some night and finding their houses in the bay. And then along the beach were more tents. In that part of the city which was afterwards known as "Happy Valley" were tents of mammoth dimensions, with rusty stove-pipes protruding from them, as though the owners were perfectly reckless of fire, and cared but little if their castles were burned to ashes.

In front of the town were about twenty vessels, ships, and craft of smaller size, and apparently deserted, with the exception of one man who looked over the rail, and seemed anxious to take flight, and probably wondered why he remained there, when everybody else had fled. The ship-keeper gazed for a moment at our flag, representative of the Sandwich Islands, and then lighting his pipe, paced the deck with rapid strides, as, though suffering under some excitement.

As we slowly drifted past a large ship, I hailed a man I saw on the quarter-deck for information.

"How near can I run in shore?" I asked.

"You can stand in a cable's length further before you touch

the flats," was the answer, "unless you draw over eight feet of water. But you may as well beach the craft as to anchor;" and the speaker tore out a handful of his hair and stamped upon it, expressive of his rage.

"For what reason?" I asked.

"You'll know soon enough. Before your mud-hook is let go, your crew will be on shore, and asking two hundred dollars a month for wages. The men run like sheep. I've been waiting here two months for a crew, and I may wait until the ship sinks before I can get one."

"Gold is plenty, I suppose," I remarked.

"Don't say gold to me!" cried the master. "I'm tired of hearing of nothing but gold and lucky strikes. Luff a little, and you will forge ahead enough to reach good anchorage. What are you loaded with?"

"Provisions," I answered.

"Thank God. They are needed enough. When you sell to the rascals on shore, make 'em agree to land cargo. You will find an advantage in it. Of all the places to discharge ship, I think this is the worst that I ever saw or heard of."

"Won't you come on board?" I asked. "We have some fruit and a good glass of punch for you," I continued.

"Fruit!" repeated the captain with a second pull at his hair. "I don't think I should know an orange if I should see it; and I should faint at the sight of a potato."

"Come and try it," I responded. "I have something that will bring you to, if you should faint."

The captain waved his hand in token of accepting the invitation; and in a few moments, just as we dropped anchor in eight feet of water, with mud for holding-ground, I saw the gentleman leave the side of his ship, and skull a small boat towards us.

He was a thin, nervous-looking man, with stiff, gray hair, and a dark, resolute eye, and introduced himself as Samuel Crosstrees, of the ship Iowa, of New York.

"I loaded with sojers and stores for this place," he said, as soon as we had shaken hands; "and a pretty mess I've made of it. By the time I had discharged cargo, news of the gold mines arrived, and they told such outrageous stories that the town was in an uproar at once. The sojers left their muskets, and run for it. The sailors dropped their marline-spikes, and they run for it also, taking boats and everything they could steal. My men came aft, and asked for their discharges, mates and all. I told them they couldn't have them; and the next morning, when I turned out, two of the boats were missing, and all hands had left in them for the gold mines up the Sacramento River. I applied to the commander of the United States forces on shore, and he said that his men were leaving in the same way, and that if he should send sojers after the sailors, the former would never come back."

I invited the captain into the cabin, where Jake had spread a collation of fruit, and filled a bowl with punch.

"God bless me, are these oranges?" he asked. "I never expected to sée one again. Have you many on board?"

"About ten thousand," I answered.

"Do you know what they will sell for here by the hundred?" Captain Crosstrees asked.

"I have not the slightest idea."

"I should be safe in offering you fifty dollars a hundred, and I'd make a profit at that price."

The sum was so large that I thought the sight of the fruit and punch had turned his brain. But no; the man was serious, and meant what he said. I had yet to take a lesson in California prices.

The captain took hold of the fruit and punch as though he liked them.

"Let me give you a word of advice," he said, while sipping his grog. "When you sell cargo, make an express bargain that the purchasers shall receive it alongside. That will save you an enormous expense and much trouble. By the way, what a handsome boy that is!" and the captain pointed to Lilly, who blushed under his ardent gaze. "He's handsome enough to be a girl. I wish I had such a lad on board the Iowa. He's just what I want to wait upon the table."

Poor Lilly retired from the cabin in a hurry, for she feared the sharp eyes of the captain.

"What prospect is there of starting a commission house on shore?" asked Hatch, who was drinking punch, like the rest of us.

"If you have money to commence with, you can start anything and make it pay. I know that speculators are as busy as the devil in a gale of wind. Money is worth ten per cent. per month, and land is jumping up in value every day. Fortunes will be made and lost in a month's time; and the men who will succeed best are the sharp ones, who will know when they have got enough."

"If it would not be too much trouble, I should like to have you go on shore with me," I said.

"I'll do it. I've got nothing else to do. I'll introduce you to the custom-house folks, and put in an oar on your behalf."

"And then come back and dine with me," I said.

"Not the slightest objections. It is so long since I have had a dinner that I am afraid a good one will make me sick."

I took the schooner's boat and manned it with three kanakas and Will. Hatch went on shore with us. We reached the land with some difficulty, for the flats extended for many fathoms in front of the town, and consequently the water was very shoal. But as our boat grounded, the kanakas jumped overboard, and hauled the pinnace to the beach, and we landed upon the golden shores of California, although, to tell the truth, they did not look very golden, for I saw nothing but mud, dust, broken bottles, discarded shirts, old boots, and much rubbish. Yet every person we met seemed busy, eager, and anxious. Captain Crosstrees called my attention to some lumps of gold in a window, one of which was as large as my fist, and must have weighed several pounds.

"The large lump that you see," the captain said, "was found by a sailor. As soon as he picked it from the dirt, he threw away his tools, and came to this place to have a time. He sold the nugget at the rate of fourteen dollars an ounce, and it's well worth nineteen or twenty dollars. Of course the money was spent for rum, and I recently saw the fellow on his way back to the mines."

We passed along, and encountered an Indian, bareheaded, with only a blanket thrown around his person. Barefooted and barelegged, he moved along, swinging a large buckskin bag, which seemed heavy and full.

"He has just come in from some of the mines," the captain said, "and will buy a barrel of rum and some other articles, and return to his companions. They will have a feast, and a grand drunk, and after getting sober, will once more commence work. But here we are at the custom-house; come in and let's see what the collector says."

CHAPTER XII.

A MODEL COLLECTOR. — DISCHARGING CARGO. — CALIFORIA PRICES. — GOLD AND PROFITS. — MY EXPERIENCE.

THE custom-house did not creafe a profound impression on my mind. It was situated on what was called the Plaza, and opposite to it was a building just under way, which was intended for *the* hotel of San Francisco. The door leading to the collector's room was open, and we pushed in, and saw the officer, with his feet upon a table, a pipe in his mouth, and his hat upon the back of his head.

"Well," asked the collector, "what can I do for you?"

I told him of my arrival, and my desire to discharge cargo as soon as possible, and that I wanted the duties assessed at a reasonable rate if it was in his power to do so.

"I'll do the best I can for you," answered the collector. "I've only two inspectors attached to the office, and they are on board of Chilian ships. Let me see your manifest, and I'll tell you what I'll do."

I showed him the paper, and he looked it over.

"All these articles, excepting the fruit, came from the States originally, I suppose."

"You can be certain of that," I remarked.

"Well, I don't see why you should pay heavy duties, when your cargo is really needed here. To be sure, you will get prices for everything you have; but I don't object to that. Suppose I say five hundred dollars, and settle the matter."

Captain Crosstrees punched me to accept the offer, and I did; for it was less than what we had calculated on by one half.

"Well, then, I'll make you out a permit, and you can discharge as soon as you please; and if you are inclined, you may send a dozen oranges to the office."

"I'll send a hundred," I said.

"Ah, will you? Well, I shan't object."

"While he is in the humor, get a coasting permit," whispered Crosstrees. "You will find it useful in case you want to run up the rivers."

I asked for the permit, but the collector hesitated for a moment.

"Well, you may as well have one, I suppose. It won't do you any harm. I'll make it out, and send it to you when you deliver the oranges."

I received my permit, and we left the collector, and returned to the boats; but to my surprise I found only Will by it.

"Where are the kanakas?" I asked.

"They've gone to look for some friends," was the answer.

"They have run away," cried the captain. "It is no use to stop for them. Such is California. You may see them in the course of a day or two. and you may not."

We pushed off the boat, and reached the schooner, where I was agreeably surprised to find that all hands had not left.

Mr. Topmall uttered a few vigorous curses, directed against kanakas and runaways in particular; forgetting, for the moment, that he had run away twice during his career as a seaman. It was now three o'clock, and Jake announced that dinner was ready. We had hardly sat down to the table, when my friend Hatch entered the cabin, his face manifesting many tokens of rage.

"How much do you suppose I had to pay for a passage on board?" he asked.

We pretended that we didn't know.

"A dollar, as I'm a sinner; and the boatman was as independent as a hog on ice. What do you think of that?"

"I think," said Crosstrees, "that you had better feel thankful for being on board, and not count the cost."

"Perhaps I had," Hatch said; and he seated himself at the table, and fell to with an appetite.

"What luck on shore?" I asked.

"Nothing to boast of," was the reply. "I saw a fellow, and asked him what he would sell his tent for. He said five hundred dollars, and didn't want to sell at that. I laughed at him, and passed on; but I found that the farther I went the higher the prices. No, I shan't buy, but I will build. I have bargained for a lot of land on Montgomery Street, and as soon as I get the boards, up goes a store, and a commission house is opened."

We congratulated our friend on his success, and he rattled on until Jake told me that some men were on deck, and desired to see me. I left my friends, and went to see the visitors.

I found four men, rough looking and roughly dressed, on the quarter deck.

"What cargo have you to sell?" they asked.

I mentioned some of the articles.

"I'll give you five dollars apiece for your shovels and pick-axes," said one.

I was slightly astonished, but did not manifest it. The articles had cost us seventy-five cents each, delivered at Honolulu.

"Yes, or no?" cried the rough man, producing a large bag of gold dust. "Talk quick, for time is worth an ounce an hour to me."

"You can have them — delivered alongside," I answered.

"Can't you land them?"

"I haven't got the men to do it."

"It's a bargain. I want the articles to-morrow forenoon. I shall be off after them at ten o'clock. I'll pay for them now."

All this was uttered so rapidly that I hardly knew how to act, but at that moment Captain Crosstrees came up and relieved me.

"Have you got a pair of scales?" he asked of the purchaser of the picks and shovels.

"Yes, on shore. None here. Supposed that every one had scales to weigh gold."

"Hold on a moment," said the captain. "I've got a pair on board the Iowa. Let one of your men go with me, and I'll get them. I shan't be gone more than five minutes."

I invited the men into the cabin, and set some fruit before them, and gave them some nice claret, and my hospitality won their hearts.

"Come," cried one, "let us see if we can't make a trade for some other articles. We have met a gentleman, and can buy of him as cheap as any other person."

"What will you sell potatoes at a pound?" asked one. "I see you have a hundred bushels."

"What is the price on shore?" I answered.

"There you have us. There are none on shore, and scurvy is making its appearance for the want of vegetables. I'll give you fifty cents a pound, and take the lot; but I want them this afternoon."

"Delivered alongside," I added.

"Well, yes, I'll come off after them."

"I take the offer. Cash on delivery."

"Of course. The man who gives credit here is a fool. You mark that, for you are a stranger here."

By this time the captain of the Iowa arrived with the scales.

"Sixteen dollars per ounce," cried the rough man, as he untied the mouth of the bag, and poured the glittering dust into the scales.

"Of course," I said; and in went the dust until the weight was complete, and I found that I was master of five thousand dollars worth of gold dust, which was worth in the United States or England nineteen dollars per ounce.

"What do you say to fifty dollars per barrel for your mess pork, and sixty for the clear?" asked one of the buyers.

I saw that the captain of the Iowa nodded as though advising me to take up with the offer; so I said that I thought favorably of it.

"Then we'll take it, and have the lighters alongside in the morning. That will do for one day. Come along."

They left the schooner, but in one hour's time a ship's launch came alongside, and the man who had bought the potatoes came with it, accompanied by a platform balance and sacks for bagging the esculents.

I took off the hatches, and set the men to work filling the sacks and weighing them, and before night all the potatoes were in the launch, with the exception of some saved for the use of my crew, and a bushel I sent on board the Iowa in return for the master's valuable aid.

That transaction brought me in the snug little sum of three thousand dollars, and then I sold what oranges I had left for two thousand dollars, and the purchaser thought he had got a great bargain, and I believe the fellow did sell some of the fruit at the rate of a dollar apiece, but I had no cause to complain.

My friend, the ex-whaling captain, as I expected he would, left me early in the day for the shore, in company with Hatch. I was now independent of him, as I had learned enough of navigation to pick my way most anywhere. Mr. Myers did not return on board again until dark, and then he came after his chest of clothes.

"I've got a chance," he said, as he dragged his box over the deck to the gangway.

"At what business?" I asked.

"Well, rather in the pasteboard line," he answered, after a moment's hesitation.

I wondered what that was, but did not ask, as the captain seemed in a hurry.

But to return to our discharging. We got out the pork and shovels during the day, and did not have to work very hard, after all, but while laboring I had any quantity of visitors. The Helen was the only vessel in port that had provisions to sell, and of course the speculators flocked to her in crowds. All day long a stream of gold poured in upon me, and at the end of three days I found that the cargo was almost cleared out, and that I was the possessor of seventy-five thousand dollars, having cleared over sixty thousand dollars by the venture.

I retired to rest the night that the schooner was clear of cargo, impressed with the responsibility of my position, and fearful that I had too much gold on board to feel quite as secure as I desired. It was well known that there were many ruffians in California, who had hastened to San Francisco from ports in the Pacific, and were determined to live by gambling and robbing, and not by honest labor. Many of them were Mexicans and Chilians discharged from chain gangs, and capable of any crimes if gold was to be obtained by committing them.

So firmly was I impressed with this idea, that I arose and struck a light, and went on deck. There was no anchor watch, for the men were tired, and had gone to sleep. The night was quiet, but I could hear music in the gambling saloons on shore, and occasionally the loud blast of a trumpet, as though calling upon every one to come forward and risk their money, and win or lose a fortune.

The night air cooled my brain, and I began to think that my fancies were foolish. I went back to the cabin, and by accident my eyes fell upon a revolver, which I had taken from a chest the day before. I examined it, and found that it was unloaded. I don't know what prompted me, but I commenced charging the pistol, and while I was doing so, the mate poked his head from his state-room.

"What's the matter, sir?" he asked.

"I am loading a revolver," I answered, "I have been thinking it is rather unsafe to remain here in the stream without some means of defence in case we are attacked."

"Well," replied Mr. Topmall, with a puzzled look, "I never thought of the matter afore. but I think no one will trouble us unless they wants their heads broke."

And then the mate went back to his berth, and went to sleep. I finished charging my pistol, and also retired, but I did not go to sleep. I remained awake until nearly two o'clock, thinking of various things, and, just as I was about to close my eyes, I felt something strike the counter of the schooner. It seemed to me that the noise was occasioned by a boat which struck us stem on, and I waited to hear the noise of oars, if any person was coming alongside. I listened, but there was no sound, and I had about concluded that a plank, drifted by the tide, had touched the vessel, when I heard a low whispering under the schooner's stern. I slipped out of my berth in a quiet manner, and went to the cabin windows, and looked out carefully, so that those in the boat should not notice me. The night was starlight, so that I could see quite well, and I counted seven men in a boat, with black beards and dark faces, and they whispered in Spanish, a language that I had not heard since I left school, consequently knew but little of it. It must not be supposed that my nocturnal visitors were in the least imprudent. They made use of gestures, and talked very low; and while they were thus engaged I saw the flash of steel, as the starlight fell upon it. Every man in the boat had a knife in his belt around his waist, so as to have it handy, but I saw no pistols. The latter weapons were too noisy for the ruffians, who trusted to quick and sudden blows for effect.

I remained at the cabin window for fifteen minutes, watching the Chilians; and during that time they seemed half inclined to abandon the expedition. While they were thus hesitating, I went to the berth of Mr. Topmall, and rather startled him by laying a hand upon his mouth before I spoke. He jumped up, and was ready with a blow and an oath, but my voice quieted him.

"Turn out," I said. "Be quiet, and make no noise. There is a boat-load of thieves alongside, and they mean mischief."

"I'll smash 'em to thunder!" replied the mate, with a hoarse growl, which I had some difficulty in checking.

"We will make all sure, and let them commence the attack," I said. "Get a handspike or a heaver, and if they offer to enter the cabin windows, we'll make their heads ache."

Without stopping to put on his shoes, the mate slipped on deck, and returned with two handspikes, and laid them on the transom. Then he called Will.

The Chilians were hauling the boat under the counter, and had evidently made up their minds that they would send one of their number on board for the purpose of reconnoitring, and perhaps making short work of those who were sleeping. The ruffian who was selected for the task, was a tall, thin fellow, with movements like a cat. In his mouth he carried a knife, and for fear that he should lose it, had a second one in his sash. We drew back from the window for the purpose of giving the ruffian a chance to put his head in the trap which we had set, and then awaited events; but while we were watching, Will left us, and went on deck, promising to return in case we needed him. The rascal did not make the least noise in his movements. First his head appeared, and then his shoulders; and while he was crawling through, he suddenly stopped, as though suspicious that something was wrong. A movement on deck had alarmed him. We had heard it also, but knew that it was Will. The Chilian paused, or rather attempted to, but those in the boat continued to press upward, and he was compelled to move forward, like a snake, on his belly. We could see him wiggle as though he was attempting to kick his kind friends in the boat, and thus free his legs, but his companions misunderstood the signal, and "boosted" him harder than ever, and with some little noise the long Chilian reached the transom, and as he did so Jack's handspike fell with a crash upon his head, and a groan was the only reply.

As the handspike which Jack wielded so successfully fell upon the head of the Chilian, I sprang to the window, and just in time to encounter the dark face of another robber. As soon as he saw me he started back, and would have retreated; but that was not easy, as his companions were shoving him upward at the time. I stretched out my hand and grasped the Chilian by the thick hair of his head, and then brought his face down against the hard wood with such force that the rascal uttered a howl and kicked over one or two of his friends. I held on, though, and shouted for the mate, and he came and placed one of his brawny hands amid the rough hair of the rogue, and then we held him between us, and a pretty hard hold it was, and rather rough on our arms; but if we suffered, the Chilian did not come off entirely harmless, if we were to judge by his howls and oaths, and the manner in which he called upon his companions for help. But those he implored to assist him were not able to, just then, for suddenly there was heard a rushing sound, a crash, and by the cries of the robbers I imagined what had happened. Will had thrown two or three large stones into the boat, and knocked its bottom out, and the water was rushing in at a fearful rate, causing the rascals to struggle for their lives, and to shout to all the saints in the calendar for help.

But while the Chilians were thus engaged, Will was not idle. He had carried to the quarter-deck a basket of stones, taken from the ballast, and while the scamps were floundering about, he rained upon their heads a shower of rocks, some of which caused serious wounds; and as the Chilians could not stand that, they dropped from the sinking boat, and drifted far astern, shouting for help, and with but little prospect of receiving it.

"I can't hold this fellow much longer," I said. "What shall we do with him?"

"Let me give him one or two settlers, and let him drop," the mate answered.

"Don't kill him," I said.

"I don't intend to, 'cos I think he was born to be drown*ded*. He'll make a meal for the fish, sure;" and then with one blow of his heavy fist he struck the Chilian upon his face, and with a quick push sent the body out of the window.

We left the transom and lighted a lamp.

The Chilian whose skull Mr. Topmall had fractured was lying upon the cabin floor, almost dead, the blood flowing from his head and staining the deck. The sight was so disagreeable that I went on deck, where, to my surprise, I found Will and Jake, the latter standing on his head, as an appropriate manner of expressing his joy at the defeat of the robbers.

"By golly, cap'n, I hit one of 'em, and he tumbled in de water like a log," cried Jake, suddenly recovering his feet. "You should have seed him drap."

"I did. I was watching the boat from the cabin windows."

"Thank de Lord for dat. I feared you wouldn't see 'em drap. I sleep in de galley, when de second mate come and say to me dat he want me to seed de fun. We got up lots of stones from de hold, and den we let 'em rip."

The joy of the negro was so great that I feared he would commit some extravagant act; so I sent him into the cabin to assist the mate in taking care of the injured Chilian.

The boat was still under the counter, the rogues having fastened the painter to an eye-bolt, and when the stones descended they were too much occupied with their escape to cut the rope. I sent Will down, and he cut the painter, and the boat drifted astern. I then went below, and found that the Chilian had died while being moved from the cabin floor, and the mate was examining the body. He had searched the pockets, but found nothing excepting a head of garlic and a bunch of paper cigars, a flint and steel, and some loose tobacco; and he was about relinquishing the examination when his hand struck a money belt which the dead man had around his waist. He removed it, and we heard the clink of gold. An examination followed, and we counted out one hundred doubloons, which were undoubtedly the fruit of his crimes. We found nothing else of importance, and then the question arose as to what we should do with the body. That was soon disposed of, however, by launching it out of the cabin window. I divided the money among those who were instrumental in beating off the robbers, and we agreed to keep the matter a profound secret, and not even allude to it before the men who were in the forecastle, for it seemed that they had not awakened during the battle. After that arrangement Jake washed the cabin floor and removed all signs of the affray, and then we retired to our berths, but I was glad when daylight appeared, for it seemed refreshing to once more see each other's faces without the aid of the dim lamp which threw its uncertain light over the cabin. At sunrise a boat came alongside from the shore, and relieved us of the few articles which we could dispose of, and then I had a visit from the master of the Iowa, whom I was really pleased to see, and who stopped for breakfast.

"Did you hear a cry on the water this morning?" asked Captain Crosstrees, as we took our seats at the table.

"At what time?" I asked.

"Between one and two o'clock. It came from this direction, and if I had had a crew on board I should have manned a boat and made an investigation."

"It seems to me that I did hear something of a row. Some drunken men, I suppose, going on board of their vessel."

"Yes, I guess so;" and no more remarks were made.

"Now, what do you intend to do?" asked Captain Crosstrees, after a moment's silence.

"Leave port as soon as possible, and return again."

"That is a good idea; but one word of advice. Don't load with flour and pork."

"Why?"

"Simply because the market will be glutted before you can return. Hundreds of vessels are on their way at the present time to this port. They will commence arriving next month, advices having reached the States that food is wanted in this country. Everything will go down excepting fresh provisions, for those will be scarce, and many will die with the scurvy unless they have fruit and vegetables to eat. Do you see the point which I am driving at?"

"I do, and shall improve on the advice; at the same time I thank you."

"When do you leave port?" my guest asked.

"Just as soon as I can get water on board — to-morrow, I hope."

"Have you been on shore evenings?"

"No."

"Then let us make a trip on shore to-night, and see the sights. If you want to see how gambling is conducted, now is your time. Will you go with me?"

"Yes. What time shall we start?"

"Say at eight o'clock. Take your revolver with you, and a bowie knife would not come amiss in a quarrel."

"If you expect a fight I won't go. My life is precious."

"The only way not to expect one is to go prepared. There is not much fear if we don't play."

"Then I shall go, for I will not play."

After breakfast two men who had shipped at Honolulu, and had stuck by the schooner until the last portion of the cargo was out, came aft and wanted to see me.

"We have kept our word, sir," they said. "We told you that we would stick by you till the cargo was discharged, and now we are ready to go on shore, if you don't want us any longer."

"What wages can you get on shore?" I asked.

"Five dollars a day," was the answer.

13

"Well, I will hire you for two days, and pay you six dollars each per day, if you will remain until I get some water on board."

They accepted the proposition joyfully, for they were anxious to show me that they were not ungrateful. I sent them off with Will and a kanaka to fill half a dozen barrels of water.

About dusk Captain Crosstrees pulled on board. He had on a blue flannel shirt, a rough monkey jacket, and a stout pair of boots with his trousers in the tops.

"Take off that white shirt," he said. "Only gamblers wear them nowadays. Put on a flannel shirt and the poorest pair of trousers you own. We don't want to attract attention by appearing too well dressed. Don't forget to put your revolver and a knife in your pockets, for, although California is the most honest place in the world, and has the most civil people in San Francisco that can be found on the globe, yet still it is best to go armed, as other folks make a practice of so doing."

I changed my clothes as requested, and did not forget to arm myself as advised.

It was nearly dark when we landed on the beach at "Happy Valley," and hauled our boat up high and dry.

The first place we sought was the Parker House, which had just been dedicated, and was the largest hotel or building in the town. A crowd was ever in front of it, night and day, for there every one went who was desirous of seeing the new arrivals, and learning the latest news from the mines, the quotations for provisions, and the market rates. This crowd we joined, and talked and laughed with those we knew. From our friends we learned the latest bit of scandal — how a man had arrived with another man's wife, and how many young fellows were after the woman, in the hope that she would run away with them. In those days a woman was something of a curiosity, and was rather highly prized — much more so than at the present time. At nine o'clock the first notes of a post horn, the only instrument of music in San Francisco, with the exception of harps, guitars, and banjos, informed the crowd that the ball was in motion, and that those disposed to bet their money and lose it, could have a chance. In flocked the crowd, and surrounded the tables, and planked their money, dollars, eagles, and gold ounces. For a few minutes we watched the throng, and then Captain Crosstrees nudged me with his elbow.

"Come," he said, "we will visit the other saloons, and see what is going on, and come back here after the games are under way."

"I should think they were started now," I remarked.

"They haven't begun to get warmed up," was the answer. "By one o'clock, or as soon as the liquor commences working, the gamblers will begin to bet. They are only testing their luck now."

As we passed out of the saloon, a man entered whose features bore traces of hard usage, for one of his eyes was closed, and the flesh around it was blackened and swollen. I thought his face, or rather that part of it uninjured, looked familiar, and I attempted to recollect where I had seen the fellow. I stopped to look at him, and as I paused the stranger did the same to speak to an acquaintance. He spoke in Spanish, and raised his hat, and the sight of that thick, black hair, and the sound of his voice, recalled to me the face of the Chilian, whose entrance into the cabin window of the Helen was frustrated by my seizing him by the hair of his head, and by the mate's vigorous blows upon his unprotected face. I was glad that the fellow did not know me, for his acquaintance might have proved troublesome. I saw the Chilian go to a table and take the place of a man who was dealing monte, and I rightly guessed that he was the proprietor of the table, and feared to trust his assistant when the heavy bets came around. If such had not been the case, the fellow would not have made his appearance with his face so badly battered.

"Come along," cried Captain Crosstrees, who was not aware of the interest which I had in the man. "Don't block the gangway, but move on."

I followed the captain, and we wandered into some of the other saloons, where the sound of a violin or a post horn was sure to attract a crowd. At length, while passing along what is now called Montgomery Street, our attention was attracted by a sign on which we read, "Connecticut Astor House. All nations welcome. Drinks twenty-five cents. The best liquors in San Francisco."

"Let us go in and see who keeps here," I said; and in we went, and found a dozen or twenty men smoking and drinking, and in one corner a pine table ornamented with two tallow candles stuck in blocks of wood, and also quite a large collection of silver dollars, and some few gold pieces. To my intense surprise, behind the table, handling the cards with as much grace as though accustomed to the use of them all his life, was my friend, Joseph Myers, the ex-whaling captain, and sailing-master of the Helen. He did not see us; so I stood watching him for a few moments.

"Here is a chance, gents, to make your fortune," cried the jolly whaleman, shuffling the cards. "I'm not in luck to-night, and am foolish to play, but the passion is strong. Who will put down a dollar, and win two. I can't deal cards to-night. I don't pretend to. I shall lose. I know I shall."

He shuffled the cards and threw down three, in a careless way, as though desirous of meeting with reverses. A rough-looking miner stepped up and laid down a dollar on a card. No one else followed his example. Myers dealt the cards, and the miner won and pocketed the silver.

"I told you so, gents," cried the whaleman. "I can't play to-night. I lose every time. Now then, who will bet?"

Some one put a five-dollar piece on a card, and the miner staked a dollar on a different one. There were no other bets. Myers dealt the cards, and the gold piece fell to his lot, and the miner won, as usual.

"Now is your time to make your fortunes, gents," shouted Myers; but the betters were rather shy.

"I go a dollar," I said, laying a piece of silver on a card.

The whaler looked up and saw me, and the next instant had dashed his cards on the table, and, seizing the dollar, forced it into my hands, as though desirous of hiding it from his sight, and thus removing temptation.

"Just you put that 'ere dollar in your pocket," cried Myers. "I don't want to lose my money to a shipmate, and I don't want to win money from one. Put it out of sight, if you please."

I did as he requested, and some of the crowd, the rough-looking fellow among the rest, murmured that "Jim Myers had got a big heart — too big for his own interest."

"I don't care if I have," retorted the whaler; "I don't take money out of a shipmate's pocket."

"Come and take a drink with me," he said, in a whisper. "This is my bar, and I can afford to stand a treat."

Captain Crosstrees and myself followed the whaler to the bar.

"What shall it be?" asked Myers, setting two black bottles before us. "One contains whiskey, the other rum. No great choice, but both are good;" and then, sinking his voice, he muttered, "but I have tasted better."

I poured out a thimbleful of whiskey and tasted and it burned like fire. I emptied the rest upon the floor, taking advantage of Myers when his back was turned.

"How does it happen that you are here?" I asked of the whaler. "Are you in business on your own account?"

"Yes," he said, "this is my castle — my home. I have paid for all that you see. My business is good, and I'm on the high road to fortune, if some cuss don't come along and bust me betting on monte. But I shall try and prevent that."

"Yet your luck is not over good," I remarked. "I saw you lose several dollars to-night in single bets."

"I don't recollect it," was the answer.

"Why, you must recollect paying to that rough-looking fellow several dollars on bets which you lost."

He dropped his loud tones as he whispered: —

"That's my roper-in."

"Your what?" we both asked.

"My roper-in."

"And what is that?"

"The fellow I've hired to do my fighting and betting when business is dull. For instance, to illustrate: a crowd collects within these spacious walls, and all look upon me as I handle the cards. The green ones are suspicious, and don't bet. They want to be encouraged. My roper-in throws down a dollar, and wins — another one, and wins. The green ones stare, and think they should like to do the same. They commence betting, and then I win. Then they bet more to get back what they have lost. But it don't go back, somehow, and I clean 'em out. Perhaps one or two of 'em show fight. Then my roper-in takes a hand, displays two revolvers and a bowie knife, and swears that I'm the only honest dealer of monte in San Francisco, and that he knows, 'cos he has won lots of money from me. The crowd believe him, as he is well armed, and so, you see, I escape."

"But how did you get a start in the world?" I asked.

"Well, you gave me twenty dollars, and yet I had no right to expect anything. I come on shore and commenced betting on monte. I couldn't help it. I didn't mean to. I won five hundred dollars the first evening, and five hundred the next night. I bought this place, took possession, and opened on my own account. I have made money. I sleep all day and play all night. This is my home. It is a palace compared to some places. Who the land belongs to, I don't know; but I'm on it, and I intend to stay here until the shanty burns up. Now take another drink and excuse me."

We declined the drinks. He went to his table, piled the gold and silver on it, and snuffed the candles. We remained for a few minutes to see the play. Myers threw down the cards, and then raised them in a careless way, shuffling them all the time in such a scientific manner that I was astonished at his dexterity.

"Come," he cried; "all who want to make fortunes will begin to bet. I shouldn't wonder if you busted this bank. I ain't lucky to-night, and I hadn't ought to play, but I can't help it. Now, then, here's three cards. Who bets on 'em? Don't all come forward, 'cos I don't want to lose too much at once."

Half a dozen returned miners crowded up, and threw down their gold and silver. There was a moment's breathless silence, and then the card which decided the bet was thrown down, and I saw the whaler rake in some twenty dollars and pay out about six.

"Another bet, gentlemen;" and down went the cards again, and the same thing was repeated.

It was eleven o'clock when we left our friend, yet all around us we could hear the blasts of the horns, and the twanging of guitars and banjos. The streets were still crowded, the people surging back and forth, uncertain where to direct their steps. Many were fresh from the mines, with dust in their pockets, and anxious to spend it, yet not knowing how to do so. There was nothing for them to buy but rum and tobacco; there was no amusement for them excepting the gambling saloons, and hence many men staked their money who would not have done so under other circumstances.

"Where shall we go now?" I asked the captain.

"Well, suppose we look into the Parker House once more. They must be putting up the dust quite lively there by this time."

As usual, there was a crowd of cigar and pipe-smoking bipeds in front of the house, some of them discussing the late news from the North Fork, and others relating wonderful discoveries on the Yuba, where the gold was fine, but of great richness, and found in numerous "pockets," some yielding dust to the amount of ten thousand dollars. Then there was one man, one of the positive kind, who spoke in a loud and determined tone, which carried conviction with it. He laughed at the Yuba mines — he had been there, he had, and he knew all about them. There was not gold enough there to pay more than twenty cents to the pan, and who would work for that?

"I've bin all over this country," the positive man said. "I've prospected everywhere. I've found gold in every panful of dirt. But some of it won't pay, and others will. Up on Feather River, forty miles above the Yuba, where the Injuns is wild and cross, you can find gold by the pailful. I know it. I've bin thar, I have."

"But how can a feller work, if the Injuns are cross?" asked a timid man.

The positive man cast a look of contempt upon the questioner. "A man what ain't reddy to fight the Injuns with one hand, and dig gold with the other, ain't the man to go to the mines of Feather River," was the answer.

"S'posing the Injuns should kill you while you was digging gold?" asked the timid man.

"Look ahere, my friend," said the positive man, amid a breathless silence; "you ain't the kind of feller to go to the mines whar Injuns is plenty. You had better stay at home, you had."

"I want to go to some place where the gold is plenty, and Injuns scarce. That is the reason I make the inquiries."

"Then don't you go to Feather River, 'cos 'tain't safe for a feller like you. Your har would be lost in no time.. I've seen fifty Injuns around my tent of a night; but they knowed I had a rifle and revolver, and that I was a good shot, and they didn't dare to draw on me. I'd sent 'em to kingdom come in short order if they had."

"S'pose," said the timid man, after a moment's thought, "that a large company of fellers should go up there, all of 'em well armed; would there be any danger then?"

"Not if they kept their eyes peeled, and looked out for their har. I'm going back jist as soon as I can get some provisions, and then, if the Injuns want a fight, they can have it jist as well as not. I am stopping here, and any one what wants information can get it. In a few days I shall be off. I brought down five thousand dollars worth of dust with me, and every dime is going to be spent for grub, and to freight it up. That's what I'm going to do."

Half a dozen men rushed up to the speaker, and engaged him in conversation, and gradually drew him one side, as though desirous of gaining further information respecting the wonderful mines of Feather River.

"That fellow is determined to make a good thing out of his yarn," remarked Captain Crosstrees.

"How so?" I asked.

"Because he is about to start a store at the mines which he mentions, and he wants to draw a large crowd of miners there, so that he can make ready sales and large profits."

"But he wouldn't have represented the Indians as fierce and cruel if such had been the case," I remarked.

"Didn't you notice that he represented the mines as being rich?"

"Yes."

"And that large parties would stand a better chance than small ones?"

"I noticed that also."

"Well, that is a convincing sign that the fellow can make more money selling provisions than digging gold. A large crowd leave for the region he speaks of. They take only enough provisions to last them to the mines, and perhaps a few days over. After those are exhausted they must have recourse to the store, and pay such price as the keeper pleases; sometimes two and three hundred per cent. advance upon San Francisco rates. You can see what a gold mine they open when they once start a store where trade is brisk. It is as good as finding a pocket."

"But there must be gold there," I remarked.

"Of course there is, and on the banks of every river in the state; but it cannot be picked up in the manner that fellow describes."

Crosstrees and myself worked our way towards the gamblers' tables to see what was going on in that direction. On all sides of us resounded the words, —

"Walk up and make your game, gents." "Who bets on these

cards?" "Red has won, and black has lost." "Now is your chance to bet — money is made here." "I go an ounce on the king." "Shuffle the cards well," &c., &c.

At length, after much labor, we were enabled to reach a table; and then, on looking at the face of the keeper, I was surprised to find that we were opposite the Chilian who was so badly treated by Jack and myself the night before, while the rascal was attempting to enter the cabin window of the Helen. His eye was shockingly swollen, but the one that was uninjured glared around upon the company most spitefully, as though seeking to find the one who had done him so much damage. I watched the fellow and his play for a few minutes, and saw many a poor man retire dead broke, cursing his luck and the good fortune of the Chilian.

"Do you know anything of monte?" I asked of Crosstrees.

"I've seen it played often enough to tell when a man deals fair."

"Then watch this fellow while I make a few bets."

"For God's sake, what are you doing?" gasped the captain. "Don't touch a card to-night. Promise me you won't."

"Don't be alarmed," I said. "I shan't lose much. I only want to try my luck. Just stand by me, and see fair play."

The captain groaned, and swore that he would leave me; but he finally consented to stay and see me through, though he begged that I would not be so foolish. I cannot account for my infatuation. It was a sudden one, and incomprehensible to me. Something seemed to urge me to stake money upon a game of chance, and I felt powerless to resist. I stepped to the table, just as the Chilian had thrown down three cards, and put ten ounces on the centre one. The dealer looked astonished, for the bet was a heavy one for him. Those in the vicinity of the table seemed surprised, and immediately placed their dollars on the other two cards, thinking, very properly, that the dealer would win the large amount and lose the small ones.

The Chilian dealt the cards, and threw them down upon the table with eager haste, and at last the right card made its appearance; but I could not tell, excepting by the black look of the Chilian's face, whether I had won or lost.

"Draw your money," whispered Crosstrees. "Blame me if you ain't won, and no mistake."

"You try 'em agin," cried the Chilian,

I made no reply. I thought that it was safer to watch the game for a minute or two. The Chilian dealt the cards and threw them down, and half a dozen miners were eager to cover them, to see if they could not emulate my luck. Unfortunately they did not, for the gambler swept the money to his pile, and then looked around for more victims. His eyes fell upon me, and he seemed to dare me to make another bet.

"You one lucky man," he said, with a sneer. "S'pose you bet agin, hey?"

"Down with the cards," I answered, "and I will tell you."

"Don't you do it," cried Crosstrees. "Take my advice, and don't play any more. Let's weigh anchor with what we have got."

"I s'pose de senor is a man and no boy, and can play wid 'em own money," sneered the Chilian.

"Don't you sauce me, you black-faced rascal!" cried the captain, indignantly; and the Chilian thought it best not to, for those who surrounded us were Americans, and of the rough-and-tumble sort, and it would have been a word and a blow with them.

"You bet?" asked the Chilian; and he grinned as if he thought I would not.

I put down twenty ounces upon a card, and awaited the deal. The crowd watched the movements of the Chilian's hands, and if he was disposed to cheat, he found it rather difficult to do so. There was a moment's suspense, and then the miners exclaimed, drawing long breaths, —

"He's won!"

At the same instant Captain Crosstrees slapped me upon the back, and shouted:

"You're a lucky dog!"

Then I knew that I had won, although how it was done I could not tell.

"*Diable*," muttered the Chilian; and his hand trembled as he counted out some ounces from his pile, and handed them to me.

I took the precaution to count them after the gambler, and found but nineteen ounces.

"How is this?" I asked.

"Ah, pardon, senor, one mistake;" and the missing ounce was handed over to me.

"Blast him, he'd cheat if he could," one miner said, and I had no doubt of it.

"Come, don't play any more to-night," cried Crosstrees; but I had got a little interested in the game, and wanted to win some more. I did not feel satisfied.

I resisted the importunities of Crosstrees, but waited for a few minutes, until others had bet and lost, and then I laid down ten ounces upon a card, and once more won, not only to my own surprise, but to that of the crowd.

"I say, you black cuss, 'tain't no use to look ugly arter that," cried one of the crowd; and the man's companions laughed at the sally.

"I win yet," cried the Chilian. "*Caramba*, a man no do dat tree times more."

He flung down the cards with nervous haste, and once more I bet ten ounces and won.

"By thunder!" roared the crowd, "here's a miner what wins every time at monte."

"Where is he?" cried a voice that sounded familiar, and a man left one of the other tables and came towards me.

"The d—l! what are you doing here?" cried Hatch. "Breaking the bank?"

"I'm trying to," I answered; and we shook hands as though we had not met before for months.

"Go ahead — I'll see fair play;" and Hatch placed himself near the head of the table to observe the movements of the dealer, who required watching more than ever, now that his gold was decreasing so rapidly.

CHAPTER XIII.

BREAKING THE BANK. — ALL LUCK ON MY SIDE. — A FORTUNATE THROW. — AN ATTACK ON THE BEACH.

SUCH a run of luck as I experienced in my first attempt at gambling, was so unusual that it attracted much attention in the saloon of the Parker House, and numerous well-disposed persons crowded around me to see how the game finally terminated.

"Go in, old feller, and break the bank," cried several of the crowd. "Now you've got your hand in, don't leave off."

"Play cautiously," whispered Hatch. "Don't make any large bets now."

"Come, leave this place," cried Crosstrees. "You have won enough. Don't be tempted to bet again."

"Don't be alarmed," I said. "If I lose what I have made, I shan't feel it. I am going to bet once more, and see how it comes out."

"Promise me that it shall be the last time," whispered Crosstrees.

"For to-night, yes."

"Does the senor bet again?" asked the Chilian.

"Yes."

"I am ready, senor;" and the gambler shuffled his cards and looked impatient.

"How many ounces have you on the table?" I asked.

The Chilian counted up, and by the aid of silver, managed to find enough to represent one hundred ounces, or sixteen hundred dollars.

"All on one bet?" asked the Chilian, laying down his cards, which he had shuffled carefully, and turning to consult with a confederate on the expediency of such a bet.

"All on one card," I answered.

Just at that moment, while the gambler's back was turned, Hatch leaned over the table, and changed the position of the cards, placing the upper one beneath. It was done so quick that not more than half a dozen persons saw it, and they did not say a word. The Chilian returned to the table, and took up the cards, but he did not change them or shuffle them.

"Me take de bet," he said. "Put down de money."

I counted out one hundred ounces, and laid them on the table.

"Ready?" asked the Chilian.

"All ready," I answered.

He threw down three cards rapidly, but I saw at once that he had made some mistake, or thought he had. They were not the cards that he expected to deal, for I could tell by his uninjured eye the disappointment which he experienced. I placed an ounce upon the middle card, and said, —

"On this card I stake one hundred ounces. Let there be no mistake. Do you understand me?"

The Chilian did not speak, but he nodded his head and drew a long breath.

"Deal away," shouted the crowd; but the noise confused the Chilian still more. He threw down a card, and then there was a death-like stillness.

Down went the cards, one after the other, and many a neck was stretched out to see the result. There was a minute's painful suspense, and then the Chilian dashed the cards on the table, and by one hearty shout I knew that I was the winner.

"Rake it down," cried Hatch. "You've busted the bank."

"I am one cheated man," yelled the Chilian, and with a quick motion he drew a revolver from his breast and pointed it at me.

For one moment I was in peril, but suddenly something whizzed past my head and struck the gambler full upon the face, and he fell as though knocked over by a bullet. The missile that performed such good service was a young sturgeon, which a fisherman had seined that afternoon, and had sold on the sidewalk. He had entered the saloon, fish in hand, to deliver it to a customer; but the instant he saw the revolver drawn, he had taken aim and fired. The crowd yelled with delight.

"Pocket the money," cried Crosstrees; and the gallant captain commenced stowing it away in his pockets, and Hatch imitated him.

"We'll make it all right on board," they said. "You shan't lose a dollar."

In a few minutes the gold and silver were secured, the crowd surging around us to see the operation.

"I say, mister, ain't you goin' to pay me for that sturgin?" asked the fisherman.

"What is the fish worth?" I asked.

"Wal, you know best. I think it did good sarvice about the time it jumped out of my fingers."

I put two ounces in his hand, and they were enough to satisfy his most exalted ideas of liberality.

"Treat the crowd," whispered Hatch. "They expect it."

I had no objections, although liquor was twenty-five cents a glass.

"Come, friends, let's take a drink," I cried. "I can afford to treat after such a night's work."

It was astonishing how unanimous that crowd were on the

subject of patronizing the bar; and what awful horns some of them imbibed, which made the bar-keeper look as savage as a grizzly bear with a litter of hungry cubs.

"Here's to the cove that broke the bank," cried one fellow, who meant well, but his speech did not seem to convey it.

The rest of the crowd repeated the toast, and shouted over it as though it was something worth yelling for.

"I will go on board with you to-night," Hatch said. "You have won too much money to make it safe for you to go alone."

"I don't think there's much danger," I remarked. "That fish appeared to settle the Chilian's coffee."

"As far as appearances are concerned, it did. But don't you put your trust in such uncertain things. The black rascal don't feel any too well satisfied with the night's work."

"Or last night's either," I remarked.

"What do you mean?" my friend asked.

I told them of the visit which I had received, and the manner in which we had treated the robbers. We were talking on the subject as we walked along the beach, and had no more thought of danger than I have at the present moment; but just before we reached the boat four men sprang at us from behind a tent, and were upon us before we had time to think of defence. One of the assailants struck at me with something. I suppose that it was a knife, but it was too dark to see it. At any rate, the fellow miscalculated the distance between us, and the force of the blow which he aimed at me was the means of causing him to lose his footing and balance, and he fell forward, his head striking my chest and knocking me down upon the sand, bottles, and old boots. As I fell my hand came in contact with a bottle, the bottom of which was broken off, leaving the end jagged. I caught sight of the face of my assailant, and saw that I had to contend with the Chilian whose money I had won. I felt the man's hand grasp my throat as though the other was to be used in an entirely different manner; so there was no time to lose if I was desirous of saving my life. I made a sudden movement, and the body of the Chilian was thrown from my breast, but his hand did not release my throat, and while struggling, my fingers came in contact with the bottle above mentioned. I seized the neck of it, and with all the force of my right arm I struck the robber full upon his face. Blood followed the blow. I felt it trickling upon my breast and face, and it seemed to burn my flesh, so hot was it. I once more raised the bottle, and struck with all my might full upon the blackened eye of the Chilian, and I could see the ragged glass cut deep gashes upon his face. The last blow was too much for his endurance. His head reeled and fell over one side, and then the body followed. The grasp upon my throat was relaxed, and I was safe from his knife, so far. I got upon my feet as soon as possible, and then saw that my friends were busily engaged with the other Chilians; but why they did not use their revolvers was a question. Instead of doing so, they were keeping the rascals at bay with them, and the black scamps were circling around them, as though looking for a weak place in which to strike.

"Kill the rascals," I shouted, rushing forward; and with the blow of my friendly bottle I brought one man to his knees, and a second blow stretched him at full length, bleeding like a lanced whale. "Kill the rascals," I repeated, and made a dash at another one; but the fellow dodged me, and in so doing got within reach of Hatch's foot. Up went the latter, and down went the Chilian.

"Heave ahead," shouted the captain. "I'll stave your top lights for you."

The gallant captain made a lurch at the man, but the blow fell short, and then the Chilian turned and ran.

"Clap on all sail in chase," roared Crosstrees, and he started to follow the fellow; but he might as well have thought of pursuing a greyhound.

The captain came back, after a run of a few seconds, breathless and excited.

"He gave me the slip," he said, "while I was crowding sail. He is clipper-built, and I'm on the old style, bluff and square. I can't run with such a feller."

"Why didn't you shoot him?" I demanded. "Both of you have revolvers, and yet you did not use them."

"Bah!" cried the captain, quite composedly; "they couldn't hurt us. We were not afraid of them."

"Yes, but they might have hurt me. Did you not see that I was rolling in the sand with that black rascal on top? And he had a knife in his hand, too."

"O, we knew you was equal to him, so let you fight it out," was the consoling reply.

"To tell you the truth," said Hatch, "we didn't fire because we knew that the noise would arouse the whole of "Happy Valley," and then we should have been surrounded by a crowd of wild Mexicans and Chilians."

This explanation was more satisfactory, and I began to think there might be some reason in it. But the Chilian, whose face I had cut open, now commenced stirring and groaning, as though he found his position far from being pleasant.

"You feel bad — do you?" I asked.

"Yes; me hurted much in me head. Me no do so agin."

"You supposed you were likely to get back your money, but you see you have failed. I have it safe, and I intend to keep it."

"Come, let us go on board, unless you mean to drown or hang this fellow," said Crosstrees.

"Pardon, senor," groaned the injured man. "Me no do so more."

As we were not disposed to be revengeful, we left the fellow, and found our boat. But just as we commenced launching it, — for it was high on the beach, — we heard a shrill whistle; and in a few seconds it was repeated, and then answered from half a dozen tents on shore.

"That means something," cried Hatch. "Into the water with the boat, for I've had fighting enough for one night."

The boat touched the water, and we jumped in. As we did so, a dozen men came towards us, some of them running as though to prevent our moving. We pushed the boat through the mud, and were a few fathoms from the beach before the men got opposite to us.

"Say, you," cried one; "stop a little. We want to speak you. We no hurt you."

We paid no attention to the cries, but pushed from the shore as fast as possible. Four or five rushed into the water as though to overtake us, but at that instant we were enabled to work our oars in the rowlocks without touching bottom. We gave one or two vigorous strokes, and then waited to see what was wanted. The Chilians waded in until the water was up to their waists.

"Say," they cried; "s'pose you come on shore? We no hurt you."

"See you blasted first, and then we won't," replied Hatch, who was seated in the stern-sheets of the boat.

This reply seemed to have exasperated the ruffians, and one of them drew a pistol and suddenly fired. The ball whizzed so near our heads that we involuntarily ducked them, as though that movement would have saved them. We dipped our oars into the water after this salute, but before we had taken more than one stroke, Hatch drew his revolver, and, aiming at the men in the water, fired. One of the Chilians gave a sudden jump and a yell, and fell full length into the mud; while the rest, not stopping to render assistance to the wounded man, rushed for the shore and disappeared behind the tents. In sixty seconds' time there were none in sight, with the exception of the fellow who was floundering in the mud, and yelling when he could get his head above it.

"Let us return and assist him," I cried.

"Yes, and be shot for our pains," said my companions. "We don't believe in such doctrine. We are not angels of mercy, although you may think we are."

We dipped our oars into the water and shot ahead, and as we left the shore we could see the Chilians steal from behind the tents, and wade into the mud, and assist the wounded man to *terra firma.*

"A narrow escape for my old head," remarked Crosstrees, as we neared the Helen.

"Yes, but I ran the greatest risk," cried Hatch, who wanted the most praise for what he had done.

We did not contradict him, for he would have insisted that he was right in spite of facts.

It was near three o'clock when we stepped on the deck of my vessel; yet I found the mate and Jake on the alert, and waiting to receive me.

"All right on board?" I asked.

"Yes, sir; but a boat-load of them ferriners has been round us for an hour or more, and seemed to like the looks of us; but I jist hailed 'em, and they put for the shore. I jist heard two shots, and didn't know but the cusses might have tried their luck somewhere else."

"I's got some hot coffee in de cabin for de company," said Jake. "I s'posed you would need it."

We all adjourned to the cabin on this announcement, and on the transom we found Lilly fast asleep. She looked very handsome as she lay there, with one arm under her head, and her thick hair brushed from her brow. I laid my hand upon her arm, and the poor thing sprang up at the touch. As soon as she saw me, she threw her arms around my neck, and commenced crying; and then, when she saw blood upon my bosom, she nearly fainted as she exclaimed, —

"Ah, darling, you are wounded — you bleed!"

"O, what a cussed fool I've been all along!" cried Hatch. "Hereafter I'll confess that I don't know a man from a woman. I always thought I did until to-night."

Lilly's fears for my safety had betrayed her sex, and Hatch and Crosstrees for the first time knew that the bright-looking being, whom they had praised for gentleness and good looks, was a kanaka girl.

"Devilish lucky fellow," muttered Crosstrees. "He wins in love and he wins in play. He was born under a lucky star."

"I should think so," remarked Hatch, dryly; and then he poured upon the table a stream of gold, which he had assisted me to gather from the bank in the Parker House saloon. The captain also emptied his pockets.

We had a nice dish of coffee, and a pleasant repast. We talked of the adventures of the night, and Hatch explained how it happened that he was present in the saloon while I was gambling.

"I just dropped in," he said, "because, you see, there is no society for me in San Francisco — no ladies, no home, no comfort; and the only excitement is in speculating, or in risking a dollar or two on the wheel of fortune. I don't play for large stakes, you know; but I do win and lose a few small ones."

"Be careful and not let the passion overmaster you," I remarked. "Better quit the dangerous evil while there is time."

"You are a good one to preach," he cried, with a laugh; and as I thought that my words were not likely to effect much, I held my peace.

At length my guests left me; one for the shore to superintend the fitting of his store, and the other to look after his ship. Then I commenced preparations to leave port, for we had taken water on board the day before. I told the mate to keep a sharp watch while I went on shore to close up my business, and get ready to sail the next morning. I did not return to the schooner until late in the afternoon, for I found a number of men who wanted to charter the Helen to bring a cargo of fruit and fresh provisions from Honolulu, and at one time I thought we should agree about the price; but a few hundred dollars divided us, and the subject was dropped. Then I went to Hatch's store, for he had a desk or two, and wrote letters to my parents, telling them how I had succeeded, and relating all the incidents that had befallen me since I had entered into partnership with Mr. Cherington. I dined with Hatch at a late hour, and took charge of the letters which he desired to send to Honolulu; and then we shook hands and parted, not to meet again for many weeks.

As soon as I reached the vessel I hurried to the cabin, for I felt a little remorse at the manner in which I had treated Lilly during the past few days. But the poor girl seemed to have forgotten my neglect, for she came towards me as though delighted at my return. The next morning we got under way, and steered for Honolulu.

CHAPTER XIV.

RETURN TO HONOLULU. — THE GREETING BETWEEN FATHER AND DAUGHTER. — MY PARTNER AND HIS DAUGHTER. — COMMENDATION FOR BUSINESS.

One morning, after a pleasant voyage, we sighted the islands, and I shaped my course for Honolulu, having made a good run for a navigator with no more experience than myself. The breeze was light, but fair; and as we ran along the coast, I thought, with a beating heart, of the moment when I should meet Julia and clasp her to my heart. For two months I had been absent from her side. For two months I had thought of her day and night; and as I paced the quarter-deck, and whistled for the wind, it seemed as though I could not control my impatience, so eager was I to land.

In sailing along the coast we saw the village of Kammaira, not more than two miles distant; and the sight of the town was greeted with a shout of joy from the kanakas on board. Even Lilly gazed at the place with a pleased expression on her face.

"Is not that your father's canoe, Lilly?" I asked, looking

through the glass at a large boat which was at anchor half a mile or so from us.

"It is, it is!" she cried, clapping her hands; "and I can see the chief fishing. Do go near him; and perhaps it is best that I should leave you here."

I caught at the idea. "Do you desire to go?" I asked.

"You know that I do not; but is it not for the best?"

"It is."

"And if I go," — and here her voice trembled, — "will you promise to come and see me sometimes?"

"I will."

I altered the course of the vessel, and headed for the chief's canoe. Lilly commenced weeping at the idea of separating.

"Is she going ashore, cap'n?" asked Jack.

"Yes; she thinks it for the best."

"Then I'd like to send a few things to my wife — some bread and tobacco, if you have no objection."

I had none. Jake preferred the same request, and I granted it. They commenced making up small packages for their wives, while Lilly and I stood silent upon the quarter-deck. We neared the canoe and saw the old chief sitting in the stern-sheets, fishing as patiently as when I used to go out with him and make love to his daughter. We luffed up and hailed him, but he did not know me.

"Come on board," I said; "I want to buy some fish. Give you tobacco for them."

"*Miti*," he said, as he came on board, not recognizing me at first.

"Speak English — you can do so," I answered.

The old man looked at me for a moment, and then sprang towards me, and threw his arms around my neck.

"O, my son," he said, "how glad I am to see you! I never expected this."

"Father," said a soft voice; and Lilly laid her hand upon her father's shoulder.

The chief started back and looked surprised. Lilly threw her arms around his neck, and pressed her head against his bosom. The old chief looked astonished, staggered back, and it was some moments before he could speak.

"O, my child," he said, "I thought that you were lost to me forever."

She only sobbed — she could not answer him.

"Why did you leave me, child? I am old, and you were my only joy."

"She wishes to go on shore with you," I said. "Take her and treat her kindly."

The old chief nodded and smiled. He shook my hand. We were still warm friends. He was too delighted to see me and his daughter to say much, or to upbraid me for what she had done. I whispered to Will, and the second mate got on deck a barrel of bread, some tobacco, a lot of pipes, twine, sail-cloth, and many articles which I knew the chief would like. But when I ordered them put into his canoe, his admiration was excessive. He gave us half a dozen fish and some oranges which he had brought from the shore, and then readily consented to take charge of any articles that the mate and Jake were disposed to send to their wives, whom he declared to be in perfect health, and anxious for their husband's return.

I took leave of Lilly in the cabin, where no one could witness the girl's agitation or demonstration of affection.

"We part," she said, "but not forever. I have your promise that we shall meet again."

"Yes, and before many weeks. Before I leave for California, on my next trip, I will see you."

I kissed her; and, pulling her cap over her eyes, she went on deck, and entered her father's canoe.

"Is there anything you want, Lilly?" I asked.

A sob was the only answer. She did not look up. The old chief smiled an adieu, and waved his hand.

"*Ouri miti*," he said, and his canoe dropped astern.

As we passed the reef, Jake sighed and muttered, —

"O, golly, didn't I snake 'em in dare? Takes dis child to fish. I must find a day, some time, and go back dare."

At length the long-wished-for Honolulu was in sight; and up went my private signal, manufactured by Miss Cherington expressly for my use, but which had not been hoisted since the day that Lilly was discovered on board. By the aid of a glass I could distinguish the barge that belonged to the firm; and then I took a look towards the window, where I had seen a white handkerchief waved on the morning that I sailed. Ah, how my heart fluttered as I recognized the same signal! and I almost fancied that I could make out the handsome face of Julia, with her black eyes and white teeth. I returned the salute, and was then compelled to pay some attention to the schooner, for we were nearing the inner harbor rapidly. We lowered the flying jib and foresail, and then luffed up a little, and hauled aft the main and jib sheets, and pointed the bluff bow of the Helen for the inner harbor, where several whaleships were lying, the crew of which were all on deck, and watching our approach with much interest.

"Here comes Mr. Cherington, sir," shouted Will, almost wild with joy at the thought of returning to port.

The next instant my partner was alongside, and on deck, his face beaming with pleasure, and his dark eyes sparkling with excitement.

"Charles, my dear boy," he said, coming aft with open arms, "welcome, welcome home."

For a moment we held each other's hands, unable to speak.

"Julia," I managed to say, "is she well?"

"Ah, well and happy at your safe return. She has watched for you every day for a week past; and every day, for the past two weeks, she has asked me when you might be expected. See — there she is at the window of your room, waving her handkerchief, and crying at the same time, I have no doubt. But, tell me, have you been well?"

"Quite well. But you do not ask what success I have met with."

"There is time enough for that, my boy. I am satisfied at your safe return, even if the speculation has not paid. You must go on no more such expeditions. I am too lonely without you; and there is somebody else who will complain if you leave Honolulu again."

How I wished that I really deserved such love and affection, and how my conscience smote me to think that I was not worthy of it! But as Mr. Cherington was not a confessor, I did not think that it was worth while for me to recount my misdeeds.

We dropped anchor in nine feet of water, and not more than a stone's throw from the shore.

Mr. Cherington urged me to go home, assuring me that there was some one there who was most anxious to see me.

"Had we not better first remove the treasure which we have on board?" I asked.

"I guess we can take all you brought," he said. "I am quite strong in my hands, and can carry a heavy load."

"How much gold and silver do you suppose I have on board?" I asked.

"Well, perhaps ten thousand dollars' worth," he answered, after a moment's reflection. "I make such a guess on the ground that you have been successful; and I suppose that you have, for I see that the schooner is flying light."

"You must guess again."

"More, or less?"

"A trifle more."

"My dear boy," cried the old gentleman, "is it possible that you have done so well with the cargo?"

"What should you say if I stated that the cargo sold for near eighty thousand dollars?"

"That I was dreaming, or that you were seeking to hoax me."

"You are not dreaming, and I am serious. I found a ready market for every article that I carried to California, and at prices that paid wonderfully well."

"And there were losses?"

"I did not lose a cent. Everything was paid for on delivery, in gold or gold dust."

"And you have seventy thousand dollars on board the schooner at the present time?"

"Yes; in addition, ten thousand dollars which I sent to my father for money he advanced me to enter into business arrangements with you. Or, rather, he did not furnish the money, but gave me credit for goods to that amount."

"And you mean to say that that debt is paid?" asked Mr. Cherington, still wondering.

"I think it is; and I should not be surprised if I had a credit of a few thousand dollars with my father at the present time."

"I am lost in wonder and astonishment. Why, my dear boy, you have excelled me in business arrangements."

"Ah, but you forget that you planned the whole thing, and that I had only to follow your ideas. Think of that before you praise me too much."

"No matter, my boy; I will leave another to tell you how well pleased we are with your conduct. You have nothing to reproach yourself with now."

Ah, had I not? How little he knew my heart, and the heavy load which weighed it down! I thought how his daughter would grieve if she was aware that Lilly had made the passage with me to California, and she might hear of it any day. I now began to realize how peculiar was my situation, and how liable I was to exposure. My partner noticed my embarrassment; but before he could speak to encourage me, thinking that it was on account of Julia, I had rallied, and seemed as gay as ever. He said, —

"If you have so much treasure on board, it must be removed on shore at once, and placed in the safe. I will speak to the boatmen to be ready to take it."

The mate first passed up a bag containing two thousand dollars, in silver dollars. It was a good lift for him, and made him groan. Then a bag containing five hundred dollars in halves was handed up. Then a bag of gold dust, and a sack of gold coins, until at last a keg was emptied. Mr. Cherington looked on in silent wonder.

"Charles," he said, at length, "there must be more than what you mentioned in these lots."

I could not help smiling.

"How many thousand dollars here in all?" my partner asked, in a serious tone.

"My dear sir," I answered, "I found a market and a price for every article that I had on board, and I could have sold the schooner, if I had wanted to, at a large advance on cost. We made over a thousand per cent. upon our venture. I thought that I would prepare for you an agreeable surprise, and I believe that I have astonished you somewhat."

"You have overpowered me, my boy. I can't begin to express my gratitude. And to think that two more such voyages will make us independent — the richest men on the island. Only two more short trips, and then you and Julia can marry and settle down to perfect happiness."

This was a crusher to the hopes which I had cherished, that Mr. Cherington would consent to an immediate marriage between Julia and myself. I dropped the bag of gold which I held, and my face expressed so much disappointment that even Mr. Cherington, absorbed as he was in his schemes for wealth, could not fail to notice it.

"Come, come, Charles; don't manifest signs of disappointment. Consider that you are barely twenty years of age, and that Julia is only seventeen. See what we have made in two months' time.

You are now a rich man, free from debt and independent. Your father must be proud of you — I am proud of you — Julia will be proud of you; but let me beg of you not to speak to Julia of marriage until you are richer than you are now by a hundred thousand dollars. Come, say that you won't."

"Let us go," I said. "I cannot answer now. We will talk of this matter some other time."

"That is right — that is right, my boy. A little reflection will convince you of the truth of my statements. Don't be in such haste to marry. Money first, and happiness afterwards."

"But suppose, while I am thus working for wealth, that Julia should meet with one she liked better than myself. Of what use would my wealth be?"

"Ah, but there is no danger of that. She is yours, my boy; her heart entirely belongs to you, and I think that only some foolish act on your part could take it from you. Let us get riches first, and then have a glorious wedding. The more money, the more respect and importance."

Alas! the wealth which I had brought from California did not satisfy the kind-hearted man, whom I had always looked up to with so much respect.

We deposited the money in the boat, and, after giving Mr. Topmall a few directions, pulled for the shore, my partner talking quite rapidly, as though to prevent me from thinking of the great happiness which I saw receding every moment from my grasp.

"Only think," Mr. Cherington said, while we were on our way to the shore, "we invested some eight thousand dollars in vessel and provisions. We have the vessel, which is worth two thousand dollars more than I paid for her, and between sixty and seventy thousand dollars in cash, not counting the ten thousand dollars which you sent to your father. What a fortunate speculation — only think of the amount of money which we have made in a little over two months' time. This will please Julia."

"Is she so ambitious for wealth?" I asked.

"All women like power, and money is power, my boy. They say they prefer a cottage and all such nonsense, but they mean a cottage with rich carpets and handsome furniture, and half a dozen servants. Such is their idea of love in a cottage. Wait until you are as old as I am, and you will see that I am right. With money goes love, all the world over."

"No, no, I do not believe that, for when I landed at Kammaira, without a dollar in my pocket, I — "

"Tut, tut! don't mention the half savage natives of this island, in connection with people of our own class. The native girls don't know any better than to love a stranger without wealth or station."

"But I care more for Julia than I do for gold," I said, with commendable frankness.

"That is natural. I am glad that you do. It speaks well for your heart. But just consider for a moment. After you were married, you would think that wealth was but a natural lever to show your affections; consequently you would neglect your family to obtain it. No, no; gold first, and marriage afterwards. You will agree with me after a while."

The idea of a young and ardent lover agreeing with an old man on such a point did not seem quite possible.

We sent our boatmen to the store with the gold which we had brought along, and then followed them, some natives bringing up the rear, and shouting and laughing in great glee. It was like a holiday to them. Every few seconds one would run up to me and shout, —

"Say, cap'n, take me next time. Me want to go to California berry much."

We passed on to the office, where the treasure was deposited in the safe, and then Mr. Cherington was anxious to glance at my accounts; but I refused to open them until the next day, and with a sigh my partner did not press me further in regard to business.

"As it is near dinner time, we may as well go home," Mr. Cherington said. "I suppose that Julia will be anxious to see you. But remember, no word about marriage — you must recollect that."

We reached the house, the door was opened, and before me, looking more beautiful than ever, stood Julia. I sprang forward, threw my arms around her, and kissed the red lips which she held up so lovingly. We could not speak for a moment, our happiness was so great. When I released the blushing girl from my fond embrace, I found that her father had very wisely left us together. I led the dear girl into the parlor, and seated myself on a sofa by her side. One arm was thrown around her waist, and one hand held her own.

"You are glad to see me — are you not?" the young lady asked, by the way of commencing a conversation.

"Ah, *so* glad!" I replied, with a slight squeeze, that caused the rich blood to mantle her face and white neck.

"And have you been good while absent?" Julia asked, turning her dark eyes upon my face with a searching glance.

"Very good," I answered, and kissed the sweet face that was close to mine.

"I knew you would be," she replied, in a triumphant manner. "I would stake my life on your constancy."

What a pang shot through my heart at hearing those words!

"Now let me look at you," Julia said, holding me off at arm's length.

I am fearful that my eyes drooped beneath her gaze, it was so pure and innocent.

"You look tired and worried. Your skin is burned by the sun. Still I don't know but I like you better than before you left me for that horrid California."

"But you do not ask me how I have succeeded while absent," I said, after her head was once more nestled on my breast.

"What do I care as long as you are well, and have returned home?" was the answer.

"But you want me to be fortunate in all my undertakings — do you not?"

"O, yes, of course. But then, even if you were not, what does it matter? My father has money enough for us both."

"We have been more successful than we possibly anticipated. I have paid my father what I owed him, and can now claim to be worth twenty-five thousand dollars in my own right, but we may have to wait for some months before I can call you mine. And you will love me just as well?"

"O, yes, of course I will; but I don't see why we should wait."

"We must await your father's pleasure, darling."

"O, yes, I know; but still you have made so much money, and I can buy beautiful laces just now very cheap."

I laughed, for that was a great inducement.

"I don't think it is any laughing matter," Julia pouted.

"Nor I, dear; for while I was on the ocean, my thoughts, day after day, were of you, and the moment when I should call you mine."

Before we could exchange other thoughts we were informed that dinner waited us. The dinner was one of Mr. Cherington's best. It was cooked to perfection, and while we lingered over our coffee and dessert, Julia solicited me to relate some of my experiences in California.

"Ah, yes; let us hear them," cried Mr. Cherington. "Tell us how you traded for the gold which you brought home. A great voyage. Over seventy thousand dollars in two months. That is the way to make money. The richest firm on the island."

The last few sentences were uttered in a low tone.

I commenced my story, and related all the incidents that had happened to me during my absence, excepting the one which connected Lilly with the trip, and my experience in gambling at San Francisco. When I had concluded my yarn, and received warm praise for my management, my partner said, —

"You have had some marvellous risks, and your encountering them only makes you more worthy of other trials. Now you will know how to avoid most of the troubles which surrounded you on the first trip. But, if you feel reluctant to go, why, I will take your place, and you can take mine. To be sure I am old, but I am still active."

I knew what that meant, very well. The old gentleman was aware that I would never consent to such an arrangement.

"I was in hopes," I said, "that I could claim the hand of Julia, on reaching home; but as that cannot be, I am willing to make one more trip, and I trust that it will be such a successful one that no objections to our immediate marriage will be urged on my return. I am anxious for wealth, but more anxious for a wife."

Julia blushed, and Mr. Cherington smiled.

"Just what I expected of you, Charles. I knew your good sense would prompt you to make another voyage. Love is all very well in its way, but wealth is better."

"I don't think so," pouted Julia.

"Nor I; but we must admit your father's argument, for he is the most powerful at present. We must wait, and perhaps you will think it for the best."

"Well done, my boy, well done! To show you that I appreciate your motives, from this day you shall rank as an equal partner with myself in the firm. When the proper time arrives,

I shall be pleased to consign the happiness of this dear child to your care. She is a treasure, and I know you are worthy of her."

I felt a little twinge of conscience as my hand met Julia's. I was receiving praise which did not belong to me, and I feared that some day it would be discovered. But until that time I determined to assume a virtue which I did not really possess.

When we went to the store we found a crowd of natives still besieging the door, anxious to hear more news from California; and they thought that the best way to obtain it would be by squatting in the sand, and waiting until something turned up. They were in no hurry. A day, or even a week, was nothing to them. We forced our way through the crowd, and saw several merchants in the store waiting for us. Among them was Vida, the partner of Hatch, who had taken passage with me for California. He had received the letters which I had brought for him. The counting-room was crowded with prominent men, who were anxious to hear the details of my voyage. So many rumors were in circulation in Honolulu regarding the amount of money which I had brought to the island, that the merchants were frantic to embark in speculations, and make fortunes with the least possible delay. I could see at once that this was likely to affect the price of the very articles which we were anxious to speculate in; for Mr. Cherington, like the prudent man that he was, did not risk too many eggs in one basket. He had bought nothing, and sold nothing of any amount while I was absent from the island.

"Cherington," cried Vida, "it is whispered around town that you have made a hundred thousand dollars by the trip. If that is the case we congratulate you."

"I heard that it was one hundred and fifty thousand," said Brannon, an oil merchant.

"One of my fellows tells me that he saw ten large bags of gold brought ashore," remarked Ludwig, who was in the sugar business.

"Tell us how much you made, Cherington," they all cried, in chorus.

"Upon my word, gentlemen, I don't know what to think of this," remarked my partner, with a smile of extreme good-nature. "I won't say what we have made or lost, it is so recent since the vessel returned."

One by one they retired, until only Brannon remained.

"Cherrington," he said, "I'll give you forty dollars a barrel for that beef of yours."

I nodded to my partner to sell.

"We have got one hundred barrels. You can have all but ten of them for that price."

"Thank you. I'll pay to-morrow;" and off he went.

He had barely left the store when Ludwig entered.

"Got any beef you want to sell cheap?" he asked.

"Just sold the last," was the answer.

The man left the store like a whirlwind.

"A nice speculation they have commenced. Ah, if I had but known that you were successful, what a strike I could have made!" sighed Mr. Cherington. "But what possessed you to signalize me to sell beef at so low a figure?" he continued.

"Because," I replied, "a barrel of salt beef cannot be sold in San Francisco. The miners repudiate it, for they prefer pork. In a few weeks the scurvy will make its appearance in California, and then fresh provisions must be in demand. If we had a load there now, we could make thousands of dollars."

"Then we will have a cargo there in a few weeks," cried Mr. Cherington, cheerily.

I left the store, and went on board the Helen, where I found a number of kanakas, still eager to learn all they could regarding California. Mr. Topmall was quite contented on board. He scorned the idea of leaving the vessel for the shore, but Will was not so nautical. He was pleased to obtain a day or two for himself, and went on shore with me. I reached the counting-room, and found Mr. Cherington hard at work at his accounts.

"Here is one item, Charles, I do not understand," he cried.

"Let me see," I said; and I stepped to the desk, and glanced at the figures.

"You sent ten thousand dollars to your father, and yet I find the total amount received by you to overrun by four thousand dollars. Where did such a sum come from?"

I felt the sharp eyes of my partner full upon my face. I scorned to tell a lie, and so I boldly answered, —

"I made it one night at a gambling table, at San Francisco."

"O, Charles!" cried the old gentleman, throwing down his pen, and clapping his hands in horror at such wickedness.

"My dear intended father-in-law," I said, "I had no intention of playing when I commenced."

"They all say that," groaned the good man.

"But I mean what I say. Now don't groan any more, for it won't do any good. Just listen to my explanation."

He calmly adjusted his glasses, and looked a little more resigned; but still he sighed as though he did not feel quite well. I then told the old gentleman how it happened, that I had risked my money, and won the Chilian's; and after the explanation the frown disappeared from his face.

"Well, I forgive you this time, but don't do so again. It is dangerous. I am glad that you won, of course, but don't attempt it the second time. Only imagine how Julia would mourn if she should hear of it."

"But I trust she won't hear of it."

The good man shook his head.

"You don't mean to tell me that you will inform her?" I asked, in alarm.

"My duty to my child, Charles. Only think of that."

"Nonsense! It is not your duty to make her unhappy, or me miserable. Don't I tell you it was the first time I ever bet?"

"And you say it shall be the last, I believe."

"Of course. Do let the matter drop where it is."

"Well, I think that I will. My daughter's happiness is very dear to me, and so is yours, Charles; but you must not wonder if I am a little astonished at the revelation that has been made. Let it pass. In a few days you will be off on another trip, and during your absence I shall forget what you have told me."

The cunning old fellow was now certain that he had me. And so he had, for I was willing to consent to almost anything rather than have my bad deeds revealed to Julia.

The next morning Mr. Cherington left the house before I got down to breakfast, so that I had a delightful chat with Julia. About ten o'clock I reached the store. My partner was out on business; so I lighted a cigar, and awaited his return. In a few minutes he came in, looking somewhat excited. He threw down his Panama hat, took off his spectacles, and rubbed them before he said a word. I looked at him for a moment in surprise.

"Charles," he said, "what do you think the confounded speculators have done?"

"I am sure I don't know."

"Well, this morning, while you were sleeping, I was up and at work. I thought I would buy a load of fruit before ten o'clock, so that you could sail in a few days for California."

"Your intentions were laudable."

"Don't interrupt me. I went to the largest fruit dealer in town, and attempted to contract with him for two hundred thousand oranges, a lot of cocoa-nuts, bananas, &c. To my surprise, I found that he had sold everything last night, and at prices which would astonish you."

"Nothing astonishes me nowadays," I answered; "not even if you were to give your consent to my immediate marriage with Julia."

"Don't be foolish, Charles. There is time enough for you. Only to think of the rapacity of those speculators!"

"Send to the other islands," I suggested. "There is Lahaina, Kawaihae, Hilo, and Maui. Fruit and fresh provisions are plenty at those places, and they can be bought cheap."

Mr. Cherington uttered a groan of agony. "It is too late," he remarked. "Yesterday afternoon canoes left for all those places, and the agents of the speculators will buy up everything."

"That was a sharp dodge — was it not?" I remarked.

"Yes, I must confess that it was; but still I don't approve of it," and my partner sighed.

Just at that moment the Rev. Mr. Gangle entered the store, and put an end to our conversation.

"O, men, men," said the reverend gentleman, "I have no doubt that you are scheming how to make more money at the expense of your eternal salvation. Cease such work. Give your gold to the church, your thoughts to heaven, and me a cigar. Thank you. Now a match, with brimstone at the end, to remind you, while I am lighting it, of the fate that is in store for you."

Mr. Gangle lighted his cigar, and smoked for a moment in silence.

"Charles," he asked, at length, "how about California? Gold there, hey? Plenty of it, no doubt. Wish that I had a cart-load of the yellow dross. What churches I would build, and what good dinners I would eat! and my friends should help me, too."

"What! eat the dinners, or build the churches? There is a slight difference between the two."

Mr. Gangle looked at me for a moment in sober silence, after I had asked the question. Then he sighed.

"Young man, after you have spent a life attempting to convert heathen, you will know better than to joke with a missionary."

"I was serious," I remarked.

"No doubt of it; but the cloth must not be touched by the profane. But to come to business. The speculators have got the best of you two, and you ought to be ashamed of yourselves for letting them. The islands will be searched for stuff to send to California, and consequently prices will go up at once. Now play a shrewd game, and win the esteem of the natives, and also those who depend upon their labor for support."

"But how shall we do that?" my partner asked.

"I will tell you. Refuse to buy anything of the men who are so anxious to speculate. They think that they can compel you to come up to their prices. If you are firm, they can do no such thing. Tell them that you cannot countenance such transactions — that it will be the means of depriving the natives of their daily fruit, unless at greatly enhanced prices. I will tell all my congregations what patriots you are. The rascals will find themselves in a tight place, and will lose money by their operations."

"How?" I asked.

"Listen, young man, and find out. There is no vessel in port that can be despatched immediately for California. The whalers dare not venture there — their crews would run away."

Mr. Cherington clapped his hands at the new idea. He saw the point, and was disposed to improve it.

"They can purchase as much as they please, but they cannot remove provisions from the island," my partner said.

"Of course they can't. Now, what is to prevent your vessel from slipping off to some port where yams and fruit are cheap, buy at a low figure, and then sail for California? It can be done if you are smart."

I took down from a shelf a map of the Pacific Ocean, and spread it upon the desk before me. I read aloud the names of islands, and while I was so employed the missionary looked over my shoulder, and suddenly stabbed at the map with a penknife with which he had been cleaning his nails.

"There," he cried, leaving the knife quivering in the map, —

"there is where you must go. Everything in the provision line is cheap there."

"The Ladrone Islands!" I exclaimed.

"Ay, the Ladrone Islands," was the remark of our reverend friend. "You will find an abundance there, and at cheap rates. You can run to the island in twelve days, or more, if you are fortunate. No one need know that you have gone there. You can collect a cargo in less than a week's time, and be in San Francisco before the sharp speculators of Honolulu have awakened to the fact that they have been outwitted."

"Bravo!" cried my partner, with glee upon his good-natured face. "That suggestion is worth a thousand dollars to us."

"Better say ten thousand, sir," the missionary remarked. "I will wager that you make as much as that."

"I will go," I said; but it cost me a sigh to say so, for I thought of Julia.

"That is brave. Now let us see when you can start;" and Mr. Cherington rubbed his hands, and began to make his calculations.

"In three days we can sail, if nothing happens to detain us. We have wood and water to get on board, and some men to ship. Some of my people want liberty for a day or two, and if they did not get it they would go to sea dissatisfied."

"Ah, the sinful wretches!" sighed the missionary. "They are not married men, and therefore have no business on the land."

I made no reply, but hurried out of the counting-room to find Will, and luckily I caught sight of him near the store.

"Come and go on board with me," I said. "You must take charge of the Helen while Jack and Jake make a trip to Kaumaira. We are off in three days."

"Where to, sir?" was the question.

"No matter. You will find out in time."

"I'm satisfied, sir. Money first, and pleasure afterwards."

We went on board, and I imparted the news of our speedy departure to the mate and Jake, and gave them permission to leave the vessel for two days. They were not surprised at the orders, and not dismayed at them.

"You can first go on shore, and get from the store anything you want, and then take the schooner's boat, and visit the village. The money that is due you will all be paid to-day, if you desire it."

"How much am 'em, cap'n?" asked Jake.

"Wages and commissions will give to each of you about five hundred dollars."

"O, de Lordy!" yelled Jake, "what dis nigger goin' to do wid so much money? Whar can I put 'em? Some blamed teefe steal 'em. I nebber hab so much money afore."

"Where can I put my rocks?" asked Jack. "I don't know what to do with so much money."

"You can leave it with us until you are ready to draw it," I said.

"Then you just keep it till we wants it. We can take a few dollars to buy some things, and leave the rest;" and the mate and steward hastily completed their preparations for a visit to their wives.

As soon as the two men were on their way to the village, I shipped four kanakas to act as seamen, they having made one or two voyages in whalers, and answered my purpose very well. The cook, who was devoted to my interests, I also shipped. He asked no questions relative to the voyage, nor appeared to care for the destination of the vessel. After finishing up so much business I went to dinner, and found the worthy missionary at the house, earnestly engaged in conversation with Julia.

"O, dear," said that young lady, as I entered the drawing-room, "what dreadful news is this I hear? You are about to leave us once more, and be gone a long time. I think it is shameful."

"Be resigned, my child, to the changes of this world," murmured the missionary.

"Would you talk of resignation if your wife should leave you for two or three months?" asked Julia.

"Yes, my dear child," returned Mr. Gangle, meekly; "I should submit with much patience to the punishment."

Julia smiled. It was reported in certain circles that the reverend gentleman had not lived on good terms with his wife while in the States, and that he had accepted the position of missionary to the islands for the express purpose of leaving her behind.

We went to dinner, and as it was an unusually good one, the missionary detained us but a few seconds with grace.

"By the way," said Mr. Gangle, turning to me, "do you speak Spanish?"

"A little," I answered, remembering my school lessons.

"Then learn more, or the Ladroners will cheat you out of many a dollar before you know it. No English is spoken at the Ladrones."

I promised compliance with the suggestion, and then we talked of the morals of the people — a favorite topic with some folks — until coffee was introduced, when Julia and I retired to the sitting-room, and left the old men to chat of charity and their younger days.

We sat for an hour talking over our projects, before the gentlemen joined us. I saw that Julia, while willing to bow to the will of her father, felt quite keenly the idea that we were so soon to part. She even expressed as much, but not in such forcible language as I did. She still thought that she was too young to marry; but if there had been no impediment in the way of our union, she would not have shed many tears ere she agreed to change her name for mine. I must confess that I loved Julia most dearly — that I was proud of her beauty and her accomplishments, and, while I was sitting by her side, she alone engrossed all my thoughts; yet I felt that I was too young to really appreciate the treasure which I held in my arms. I knew that I was, at times, a little wild and inconstant; but I did not think that I possessed any vices which could not be entirely eradicated after a certain lapse of time.

From this reverie I was aroused by the entrance of my partner and the missionary. They had just left the table and its pleasures, and consequently felt good-natured and sleepy.

"Charles," said Mr. Cherington, drawing out his white pongee handkerchief, "you and Julia had better take a drive this afternoon. The horses want exercise. Gangle and I intend to talk of the church while you are absent;" and, throwing the handkerchief over his face, he made preparations for a short nap. The missionary followed his example.

CHAPTER XV.

FOR THE LADRONE ISLANDS. — A SURPRISE. — MORE PERPLEXITIES. — AN ENGLISH PILOT. — THE GOVERNOR OF THE LADRONE ISLANDS AND HIS DAUGHTER.

Most partings from those we love are alike; so I shall pass over the scene that took place between Julia and myself on the morning that we sailed. Mr. Cherington accompanied me on board the Helen, and did not leave us until the vessel was some four miles from land.

With a fresh and fair wind I shaped my course for the Ladrone Islands, or Marianne Islands, as some call them. While I was thinking of home and my sailing directions, Will came on the quarter-deck, and asked, —

"Shall I let her out, sir?

"Who out?" I replied, with a stare of astonishment.

"Why, Lilly, sir. I locked her up this morning, and she ain't bin on deck since. I thought you'd forgotten her."

And so I had; and once more I saw that I was in an unfortunate position, but must make the best of it.

"Give me the key," I said; and with it I went into the cabin, and unlocked the door of a state-room.

I heard a low cry, as though of joy, and the next instant I felt a pair of arms around my neck.

"Lilly," I said, attempting to prevent the embrace, but she resisted — for the poor child did not comprehend why she should not display some marks of her platonic affection on the first day from port, — "Lilly," I continued, "let us be friends and —"

"Well, ain't we friends?" she asked; and then she laughed as though she thought it a good joke. I could only hope, with a sigh, that no one at Honolulu would hear of this, but I submitted to my fate with resignation, while at the same time I was confident that it was not right.

It would be tedious to relate all the trivial incidents connected with a voyage to the Ladrones. With a fair wind, and nearly as much of it as we needed, we rolled on our way across the broad Pacific, until at last my observations told me that we were close to Guam; and in an hour from that time we made the island, and saw that it was, apparently, encircled by reefs of coral. But, singular as it may seem, that which looked so formidable at a distance disappeared as we drew near the land. The long lines of surf were to the right and left of us, but the chart denoted an opening free from danger, and through a channel we steered, under easy sail, until at last we were within the outer lines of reefs, with a flag hoisted as a signal for a pilot, and lying to until that important individual should see fit to visit us. Never, in all my wanderings, had I seen such a paradise, and that opinion was shared by every man on board. Even the Sandwich Islands, rich in scenery, could not equal the Island of Guam for beauty.

"Here comes the pilot, sir," said the mate, pointing in-shore, and arousing me from a reverie, in which I was wondering why people desired a more enchanting home, or why they should leave such a one. I thought that in a spot like that a man could end his days without trouble or ambition.

"Stand by to throw a line to the boat," shouted the mate.

I went to the rail, and looked at the approaching craft. It was pulled by two dark-skinned fellows, while the principal person was an individual in the stern-sheets of the boat. He was a stout, red-faced man, with a broad-brimmed straw hat on his large head, white clothes on his person, and shoes of untanned leather on his feet.

"Surely," I thought, "that man cannot be a Spaniard."

My doubts were soon dissipated.

"Blast your lazy eyes," yelled the white man, "why don't you pull? I'll pitch you both overboard unless you do better. Now, then, alongside we go. So — that will do."

The large man at last mounted to the deck, and then I saw that he was more than six feet high, broad-shouldered, and looked much like an Englishman.

"Are you the master of this vessel?" he asked, addressing me, after one glance over the deck.

"I am," was my reply.

"Then I am happy to see you, sir. My name is John Wilson

I am the pilot; and if you want your vessel taken to a safe anchorage, I'm the man to do it."

"Will you allow me to see your commission, sir, before I trust the vessel to your care?" I asked.

He took from his trousers' pocket a tobacco box, and on opening it produced a very dirty paper, which he handed to me. The writing was in Spanish, and there was a large seal on one corner of the document, but what it represented I was unable to comprehend. After a hasty glance, I handed the paper to the pilot, and said that I was satisfied.

"I knew you would be. Put the helm up; ease off the main sheet. So — that's well. Keep her as she goes. Steer for that headland, and don't yaw all over God's creation, unless you want to quarrel with me. Now, captain, I am ready to go below for a few minutes."

We entered the cabin, and the steward placed upon the table a bottle of brandy, water, and glasses.

"Help yourself," I said, and pushed the bottle towards my guest.

He did help himself, for I noticed that his tumbler, nearly two thirds full, went to his mouth with a steady hand, and that it was not removed until the last drop was gone.

"That reminds me of 'Old London Dock,'" he exclaimed. "I've not drank such brandy before for twenty years."

I did not invite the pilot to take a second pull at the bottle, for I wanted the schooner looked after.

"Now," said Wilson, as we returned to the deck, "tell me where you are from, and where you are bound, if it is not too much trouble."

I told him that I was from the Sandwich Islands, and was on a cruise to find certain articles, and that I should visit different ports until I found what I wanted, and at prices to suit me. I did not say that I came to Guam expressly to buy, for I feared that would defeat the object of my expedition.

"You have hit the right spot, sir," he said. "You have come just in time. There are no whalers in port, and fruit is plenty. You can buy at your own prices, provided you get permission of the governor. I'll help you. I'm a friend of the governor's. I'm known here much better than in Scotland, although I am cousin to Professor Wilson, whom you may have heard of in the literary world."

I was amazed at the intelligence; and yet, when I took a second look at the pilot, I saw that his face and form resembled the great author.

"Yes, sir; I am a cousin of Professor Wilson, and we attended the same school. He took to literature, and I to the sea. I am contented, for I have a wife and children, and even grandchildren here. But you shall see them. You shall visit my house, and I'll make you welcome."

The Scotchman dashed his hands across his eyes, and then shouted, —

"Lower away the foresail, and be lively, you long-legged kanakas, with bellies like cranes and feet like ducks. Luff a little. Steady as she goes. See the anchor all clear."

"All clear," answered the mate.

The pilot astonished me. He had thrown aside the refined air which he had assumed when conversing with me, and used language which I thought he was a stranger to. The man must have noticed my expression of astonishment, for he said, —

"When I speak to sailors I must use the words which they understand; and, to tell the truth, although I was educated within the shadow of Edinburgh, yet I find that coarse language comes readiest to my lips; and why should I care? I am the only person on the island who speaks English, and sometimes I think that I shall forget it entirely. But here we are, close to the anchorage. Lower away the mainsail, and down with that jib. Put your helm hard down. Steady as you go. Stand by the anchor. Let go the anchor;" and these orders, which the pilot shouted to the extent of his voice, were obeyed, and the Helen was lying at anchor in four fathoms of water, within a quarter of a mile of the shore, in a harbor which was in the form of a crescent.

After the anchor was down the pilot's cares ceased; but still he lingered on board, and as it was near the dinner hour, I invited him to remain and dine with me. When we sat down to dinner, I began to squeeze my guest. I found that the governor of the island was a good-natured man, who loved his glass of wine and cigars, and would not throw any impediment in the way of trade if he received a present, some kind of goods being preferred to gold, for money was not of much use on the Ladrones.

"The governor is a good, hearty old fellow," said Wilson,

"and has the prettiest girl on the island for a daughter. But you will see her, and then agree with me. She is only sixteen years old, and as lively as a lark. Don't fall in love with her, for the governor thinks that she is fit for a hidalgo."

"You think that there is some danger, then, of my falling in love?" I asked, with a smile, as I thought of Julia's bright eyes and handsome face.

"I know of a dozen whaling captains who have offered themselves, and been refused; and their ships have remained here for months in consequence."

"Most of them were married men, I suppose," I said.

"Well, it is quite probable, although I don't know certain whether such was the case. But, at any rate, the owners of the ships did not make much through the susceptibility of their captains. That I do know, and look out that you don't suffer in the same way."

I gave the pilot as much to eat and drink as he could carry, and then he started for the capital in his boat. St. Iguazio de Agana is located on the banks of a river some five miles from the port of entry; and, while I am about it, let me state that the latter place consisted of six huts, thatched with bamboo leaves, and elevated from the ground some four or five feet, for the purpose of remaining dry during the wet seasons, for near the beach the ground was low and marshy.

I waited with patience to hear from my friend, and did not have to wait long. The next forenoon a whale-boat, fitted up with some pretensions to comfort, in the shape of cushioned seats and an awning to screen the person from the hot sun, came alongside, with a crew of four men, one of whom brought me a note from Wilson, saying that the governor, Don Pablo de Oroto, would be pleased to see me if I would honor the village with my presence, and requesting me to use the boat, which belonged to his excellency, for the purpose of transporting my person to the town. The pilot's letter also contained a note from the governor, but as I could not readily read it, I spent but little time over it. I ordered a luncheon for the visitors, and then commenced preparations for departing, intending to be gone for only one night.

Leaving the mate to look after the Helen, I entered the boat and was pulled up the river, which wound its way through a country rich with fruits and vegetables; and on the trees were birds of gaudy plumage, so tame that they refused to move when the boat with splashing oars passed close to them. I must confess that the town looked well at a distance, nestled at the foot of a high hill, with the river sweeping in front, and cocoa-nut and bamboo trees sheltering the houses from the noonday sun. Indeed, so cheering was the spectacle, that the boatmen, with one accord, shouted, —

"St. Ignazio de Agana, senor. *Mucho bueno;*" and then they commenced a song with a chorus, sung in rather a pleasing manner, the burden of which was the delight of living in such a town or city, filled with beautiful women, whose eyes were like the stars, and whose hearts were as warm as the sun, and whose grace was perfection. All of this was explained to me, when they found that I was puzzled at some word; and just as they had finished, with a shout they ran the boat upon the shore, and there at the landing I saw Wilson, the pilot, and half a dozen individuals, one of whom I supposed was the governor of the islands, Don Oroto, for he was better dressed than the others, and looked more distinguished, if such a thing were possible.

While the men were hauling up the boat, I had time to glance at the governor. He was short, fat, and jolly-looking, with a gray mustache, grizzly hair, and a long, peaked beard, after the style of Sir Francis Drake. On the whole, I rather liked the appearance of the gentleman. He looked like a man who would drink his share of a bottle of wine, and consider it no hardship; and, if such was the case, I knew that I had something on board that would please him.

I left the boat and walked towards the governor, who stood a little in advance of his suite. I knew how ceremonious the Spaniards were, and how jealous they were of etiquette, especially on meeting guests; so, when I was within six feet of the Don, finding that no one stirred or advanced to receive me, I stopped, removed my jaunty Panama hat from my head, bowed low, and all the gentlemen in front of me did the same.

"I trust that I have the pleasure of seeing Don Oroto, whose reputation for wisdom and courtesy is well known at the Sandwich Islands. May he live a thousand years;" and, as I spoke in English, I thought I had done very well.

The governor looked towards Wilson for an explanation, and the pilot translated my speech, and I could see that it gratified the man for whom it was intended.

"We are happy to welcome you to the City of St. Ignazio de Agana," said the governor; and we shook hands quite heartily, and then he introduced me to the members of his suite, one of them being his secretary, a second, secretary of state, with nothing to do, and the other the captain of the Spanish troops, the care of whom was intrusted to a sergeant.

A paper cigar was thrust into my hands, the secretary of state gave me fire, and the governor put his arm through mine, and led me through the city, the suite following at our heels, and Wilson, the pilot, bringing up the rear.

All the time that we were marching through the streets, the governor chatted to me in a gay and easy manner; but I must confess that I understood but little that he said, and contented myself with answering at random questions which were put to me. The sun was hot, the streets were dusty, and I was not sorry, at length, to stop before a more substantial looking house than any I had seen, and I was glad to hear Don Oroto proclaim the dwelling as his *casa*.

"My house, senor," said Don Oroto; and there was a look of pride in his face as he pronounced the words.

The polite Spaniard pointed with his cane, and bowed and smiled as invitations to enter, which I could not refuse. I passed up the avenue, and entered the one-story house, the doors of which stood open, and were seldom closed except at night, or when the rain poured down in torrents during the rainy season.

"Senor," said the governor, "this is my house. All in it is at your disposal. May you remain with me a thousand years."

This was only to express that I was welcome, and I understood it as such; but the governor showed his sincerity by passing around paper cigars, and shouting in a loud tone for fire. A boy,—a little fellow not more than eight years of age,—with nothing in the shape of clothing but a very scanty shirt, which hardly reached to his knees, came into the room, obedient to the summons, bearing in his hand a smoking brand which had been plucked from the fire for the purpose of serving as a cigar-lighter. For a few moments we smoked on in silence, all waiting for the governor to open the conversation. At last that gentleman said,—

"The senor capitan has visited us, and we are glad to see him. We understand from our friend, the pilot, that he is desirous of purchasing a cargo of vegetables and fruits."

"Such is my intention, if I can make bargains to suit me; otherwise I must seek other islands."

With Wilson's help I managed to say this; but to avoid repetitions I will relate the conversation as though I was a Spanish linguist.

"The saints forbid, senor, that you should leave us for some other place, where you would not be treated as well as we shall treat you."

"At what prices can your excellency supply me?" I asked.

"Name the articles, and then I will answer," the Spaniard replied; and he nodded to his secretary, who gravely moved his seat to the table, and drew a paper from his pocket and prepared to take notes.

"One thousand bushels of yams. Can you name the price?" I asked.

He whispered for a moment with his suite, and even allowed Wilson to join the conference. At length Don Oroto said, —

"I hope that you don't think two rials per bushel too much, senor."

I did not close the bargain immediately, for I feared that the governor would think me too easy in making a trade. But I continued to mention what I wanted, and among the items were one hundred turtles, fifty pigs, one hundred dozen fowls, fifty thousand oranges, ten thousand lemons, five hundred bushels of potatoes of the sweet variety, and one hundred bunches of bananas, all fit for shipment, and not too ripe. The purchase of so many articles caused the utmost astonishment, and an immense amount of calculating on the part of the officials. But at last they gave me their prices, and they were more reasonable than I expected. I hinted at a contract, and that the articles should all be delivered within ten days. It was some time before I could induce my friends to listen to such a proposition. It was something they were not accustomed to. They wanted to take their own course, and not hurry matters; but at last I showed them that time was all-important to me, and they agreed that, with great labor, the cargo could be completed in the specified period.

It was about three o'clock when we entered the dining-room, and there, for the first time, I saw the famed daughter of the governor; and her reputation for beauty had not been too highly extolled. Her eyes were dark and large, and full of fun; her form was perfect, full, and graceful, and her face resembled Raphael's picture of the Madonna. I thought, at the time, that I had rarely seen so lovely a countenance; and had I not been engaged to a lady, I should have fallen in love without delay.

"Constance," said the governor, nodding his head with a satisfied look, "my daughter."

I bowed very low, and I know, for sometime, I did not remove my eyes from the charming face of the lady, and I am certain that Constance examined my appearance with much curiosity, and seemed happily disappointed to find that she was in the presence of a young man who was not badly dressed, and did not have the smell of tar upon his clothes. At any rate the lady, when our eyes met, smiled and bowed, and then extended her hand. I took my seat at the table by her side, and very glad she seemed of the company; for while we were waiting for the soup, she commenced chatting, and a very musical voice she had. How her tongue did run on! She asked me where I was from, and had an idea that most Americans were black, and was therefore quite surprised to find that my skin was whiter than her own, and the little jade actually placed her hand on mine to show the difference. Constance was the daughter of a pure-blooded Spanish woman, and that accounted for her beautiful complexion and clear skin, not a drop of Indian blood running in her veins. She was a child of nature. All that she knew was contained in a few volumes of Spanish romances, which she had read many times. When she was not reading or smoking a paper cigar, she was playing on her guitar and singing; and I must confess that I have heard much worse music and poorer singers. The soup removed, the governor commenced the conversation; but I was so much occupied with his daughter that I did not understand him, and yet I could comprehend nearly every word that Constance uttered, so rapid was my advancement in the Spanish language when aided by pretty lips.

"The governor speaks to you," said Wilson, who had been dumb.

"I am sorry that I did not hear his excellency. Will you apologize for me, and repeat his remark?"

"The governor says," continued Wilson, "that he is sorry he has no wine to offer you. He is expecting a vessel from Manila with a supply."

"If there was a way to reach the schooner I'd send for some," I said. "I should like the privilege of making his excellency a present for his kindness and hospitality."

As Wilson interpreted my good intention, the dark eyes of the governor sparkled, and even the eyes of his daughter expressed pleasure.

"Send for the wine!" cried the governor; "why, we have a dozen lazy varlets who have nothing else to do than run our errands. We don't want to trouble the senor, but if he has wine on board, and is disposed to send for some, we will cheerfully furnish the means for obtaining it."

I tore a scrap of paper from my note-book, and wrote a few lines to the mate, directing him to send me a basket of champagne and two cases of claret. I also wrote him to tell Lilly that I was well and hard at work, so hard that I did not know when I should be able to return to the schooner. I had many things to buy, and the action of the authorities was slow.

"Will that note cause the wine to be sent?" asked the lady.

I told her that it would; that whoever read the note would obey my wishes.

"O," she said, thoughtfully, "I wish that I could write as well. But, then, who could I write to?"

"Bah!" replied her father; "what does a girl care for such trifles? She would only write love-letters and such nonsense, if she understood the use of a pen. Is it not so, senor captain?"

"Yes, but how happy a woman can render a man by sending him a love-letter! Surely that is an extenuating circumstance;" and I bowed to the little beauty at my side, who clapped her hands and laughed.

"Would you like a love-letter from me?" the spoiled child asked.

"I should certainly esteem it an honor," I answered, stealing a look at the governor to see how he would notice such a remark. But his excellency was picking the bone of a chicken, and seemed not to have heard the question.

"Would you?" she laughed, with a flash of her eye that was as dangerous as lightning. "Will you teach me so to write, that I can send you a note? If you will do that I will teach you Spanish."

"If you can obtain your father's permission, I will give you lessons," I answered.

"O, he will consent, I know he will," she answered, carelessly; but the governor said not a word.

Just at that moment a lady entered the room, and took a vacant chair at the governor's right. She was, apparently, about twenty-five years of age, very dark, with snapping black eyes, and rather inclined to be old maidish, I thought.

"We were speaking of love, aunt Dorothea," said the child of nature at my side. "What do you think of it?" and the young lady shot a glance of mischief from her bright eyes, as she asked the question.

"I know nothing of the subject," was the unsatisfactory answer.

"What, aunt," echoed the young lady, with a giggle, "not know what love means, when you were wooed so strongly by the whaling captain? I am sorry that you are so forgetful."

Senorita Dorothea scowled at her niece, and, as she sent her plate away, replied, rather snappishly, —

"Don't mention the brute, if you please."

"But I thought that you liked him. I am sure he had a lovely nose;" and Senorita Constance leaned back, and laughed until her plump neck was the color of scarlet.

Even the governor smiled, but his sister did not show any sign of mirth. She looked as sour as a barrel of lime-juice.

"Even if you laugh at him, you will please to recollect that the whaling captain would have married me, if I had been disposed to accept of him;" and the aunt tossed her head and looked defiance.

"I am sure I don't recollect all the circumstances of the case," cried the young lady, "for I was too young. But some one must, and I should like to hear them;" and then the little witch turned to me and continued: "The whaling captain took a fancy to aunt, and would have eloped with her, had she not scratched his face and pulled his hair. She has never seen him since."

By the time we had finished coffee it was four o'clock. The heat of the day had ceased, and a cool breeze was passing over the town, fresh from the ocean, giving life and vigor to every one. We left the table and entered the sitting-room, or reception-room, as his excellency called it, and lighted cigars, the ladies joining us in that agreeable occupation.

"Senor," said the governor, "would you like to ride, and look at the natural beauties of the island? Animals are at your service if you desire a short excursion."

"I will also go!" exclaimed Constance. "I will show the senor all the noted places within three miles of the town."

With such company I could not refuse. I intimated the pleasure I should feel at taking a short ride, and the governor gave orders to "prepare the animals," while Constance retired to change her dress, and the gentlemen stretched their forms on the lounges, and appeared inclined to doze while smoking. In a few minutes the young lady re-appeared, with a long dress in place of a short one. On her head she had a small straw hat, with long ribbons attached, but as they were of a bright green color, they did not harmonize with her dark complexion.

"Where are the senor's spurs?" asked Constance, glancing at my feet, and seeing they were not armed with steel.

"O, never mind the spurs," I remarked; "I shall not want to ride fast."

"But you will want the animal to walk fast," cried Constance.

"Certainly," I answered.

"Then you must have spurs," was the answer.

I could not comprehend the meaning of this advice, but before many minutes I was enlightened. I heard a low bellow in front of the house, and I was about to step to the window to look out, when some remark that Constance made detained me. I think that she wanted me to adjust some part of her dress; and after I had performed that duty, she made me light a fresh cigar, and then we chatted for a moment, or until a bare-legged native came in and said that the "animals were ready."

"Pleasant ride," said the governor, and went to sleep.

"Don't let him have his head if you meet any animals on the road," cried Wilson; and his eyes were closed in a second.

"Come," cried Constance, seizing my hand.

We gained the street, and then, O, horrors! before me was a small mule, with a lady's saddle on its back, and an ugly-looking bull, with a gentleman's saddle on his back, and the only bridle to guide the animal was a string through his nose.

"The devil!" I exclaimed, in English; "must I ride that brute, instead of a horse?"

Constance looked up and smiled at me as though we were to have such a fine time flirting, while mounted on the back of a blasted bull. I looked at the handsome face of the lady, expecting to see some token of the fun which she must have anticipated, in case I was disposed to remonstrate against mounting such a steed. But no — there was fun enough in her eyes, but it was not on account of the position in which I was placed. She anticipated a delightful time attempting to make me love her as dozens had done before, and whose hearts she did not value as much as one of the coarse rings which she wore upon her finger. When I was considering if it was not best suddenly to be taken ill, with symptoms of fever and ague, the little beauty at my side said, —

"Senor, will you not give me your hand?"

"Certainly I will," I answered. "But, Constance, must I ride this confounded brute?"

"*Si*, senor," she answered, quite composedly. "My father's horse died a year or more ago, and he has not been able to replace it, for there are but few horses on the island. He has sent to Manila for several, but the saints only know when they will arrive. Since the loss of the horse, this animal has been used, and there is no doubt but you will find him very gentle. Keep a light rein, and use your spurs when he is obstinate. But come, I will show you."

Just at this moment a native passed us riding a cow, and I must confess that I watched the man with some curiosity.

"Hold hard by the string," cried Constance; and I followed her advice, until the native and his novel conveyance were out of sight, and then the masculine brute grew more docile.

"Come, senor, the afternoon is fast disappearing. If you are afraid to ride, why, I will return to the house."

Could I stand such a taunt as that?

I lifted the lady to her saddle and adjusted her dress, and then I approached my gay and restive steed, and contemplated him with feelings of remorse; and the animal saluted me with a bellow and a scowl, and commenced pawing the earth. Constance struck her long-eared mule, and shouted, —

"Come, senor; overtake me if you can."

I made a dash for the bull, and reached his back somehow, I don't recollect in what manner, but I know that the brute dashed along the street at a terrible gallop, and that after I had gained my seat I found that one of my long spurs had been goading the animal's side, and caused him to assume a pace that was foreign

16

to his nature. But at last the animal slacked his speed, and seemed inclined to move at as slow a pace as suited his fancy. I rather liked it, but Constance turned her head and saw that I was lagging behind, and the young lady did not seem pleased at my want of gallantry. She turned her mule, and came towards me.

"O, senor," she said, "if you desire to keep up with me you must use your spurs. Don't be afraid."

"Afraid!" I scorned to manifest fear in the presence of such a handsome lady.

"Come on," I cried, and struck the brute I was riding vigorous blows with my armed heels.

With a plunge and a fierce bellow the bull started, and I saw at once that I had made a sad mistake. I retained my seat, but it was only by clinging to the saddle with one hand; and as I live, Constance saw the movement and laughed. This was provoking, and before I was aware of it I hit the bull two more violent digs, and then he was furious. With a roar he kicked with his hind feet, and as he did so I lost all control of him. The string, which was passed through his nose, slipped from my hand, and then I felt that I should soon be shipwrecked. To add to my confusion Constance laughed, and cried, —

"Don't lose the string."

What was the use of her saying that, after she had seen that I had lost it? And while I was debating, as we tore along the road, the propriety of cutting clear of the craft and letting it sail on to its own destruction, the animal suddenly left the road, and charged upon a group of natives. Heavens, how they scattered! But one old fellow, who appeared to be troubled with the rheumatism, did not move quick enough; so the bull caught him and sent him flying through the air, and when he struck the earth, his loose, flowing trousers were badly damaged; but his lameness was cured — for the man sprang to his feet, and ran at a killing pace down the street.

"Hold on by the line," cried Constance, who was riding after me; and I thought I heard her laughing at the same time that she was giving me such excellent advice.

It was very easy to say, "Hold on by the line;" but how was it to be done?

Through the street we went at a fearful rate, the dust flying in

THE RUNAWAY BULL. Page 243.

clouds, and the women in the houses yelling, and the dogs, suddenly waking up to the fun which was going on, followed close to the heels of my steed, and added their voices to the general uproar.

"Stop him," cried one man, waving a blanket, the worst thing he could have done.

The bull caught sight of the man and the blanket. He thought a challenge was intended, and was ready for it. He made a lunge for the native, and the latter dropped as though struck by lightning. We went over him, and I had the satisfaction of seeing the blanket on the horns of the bull; but it was only for a moment. As we neared the governor's house, I had the pleasure of noting that his excellency and suite were standing in the garden, witnessing my movements, and laughing at them. I thought my steed would stop at this point, but he was still fiery, and on he went, in chase of a woman with a red petticoat. I am glad to say that we missed her; but it was a close shave, very close, for one of the brute's horns touched the sacred garment as its owner went over a door-sill in so quick a manner that it seemed to me she turned a front somersault, and struck on her back when she fell. At this moment the native, whom I had seen riding on a cow, came round a corner at a gentle trot, not dreaming of danger. In an instant we were in full chase, and although the native used whip and spur, we gained on him. I heard Constance scream, and caught sight of her, holding by her saddle, and laughing until the tears ran down her handsome face.

"Go it, captain," she shouted; "you will catch him, if you are smart."

The next instant the native was lying in the dust, and using the whole range of Spanish language to damn me and the bull. For a moment there was a pause, and that moment was improved. I bent forward, seized the rope that was attached to the animal's nose, and with a strong jerk I let the beast know that I was once more master.

"O, what a splendid horseman!" laughed Constance, joining me, her eyes expressive of the pleasure she felt. "Come, senor, shall we have another gallop?"

"I don't think we will," was my answer. "To tell you the truth, I imagine we had better walk our animals. They seem somewhat tired."

So she consented to my request, and we walked our gay steeds through the main street, and beyond the village; but we could not go far, as the sun had set, and darkness was rapidly approaching. On rertuning to her father's house, we found the governor and his suite smoking, and discussing matters which I cared nothing about.

"Senor, did you have a pleasant ride?" asked the governor. who was too polite to allude to my misfortunes.

"O, remarkably pleasant," I answered.

"Ah, I thought you would;" and the governor puffed out a volume of smoke, and then said, —

"The wine has arrived, senor. I owe you many thanks for the same."

I bowed, and would have made some fitting answer; but at that moment a woman entered the room, and cried, —

"I want justice at your hands, governor."

"You shall have it. Speak."

"This man and his bull," she said, pointing to me, "were the means of injuring my head. I fear a brain fever."

I recognized the woman as the one who turned a somersault over her door-sill.

"It was not the senor's fault," his excellency said.

"It was, senor. He did it on purpose."

The governor looked a little puzzled.

"How much are you damaged?" I asked.

"Well, senor, about two reals worth, I think."

I gave her a quarter, and off she went, perfectly satisfied; but no sooner had she left the house than a man entered, and to my dismay I recognized him as the fellow who had waved a blanket, and escaped a horn only by the aid of his legs.

"Justice, your excellency," the fellow said.

"Well, speak. What is wanting?"

"My blanket is ruined. This man and his bull injured it. I want pay. I barely escaped with my life."

The governor stroked his mustaches, and looked grave. He did not want to offend his guest, or lose popularity with the people.

"What is the amount of damage?" I asked.

"I think, senor," he said, "that I should have as much as the woman."

"Take it and go;" and the fellow's dark fingers closed upon a piece of silver. "I hope he is the last claimant," I muttered; but hardly had the words escaped my lips, when a tall, dust-covered fellow entered the room, and as soon as I saw his face, I knew there was more trouble for me. The last time I had seen that countenance it was lying in the dust, and a rampant bull was passing over it.

"Justice, senor governor," cried the fellow, who seemed more excited than his predecessors.

"Well, well, what now? Speak. Who has harmed you?"

"The senor who rode the bull, governor. This man;" and the fellow pointed to me, and as he did so I heard Constance laugh.

"*Caramba!*" exclaimed the governor; "will they never cease coming?" and the poor man looked troubled in mind. "What injury did you receive?" the governor asked of the applicant for justice.

"Ah, senor, look at me," was the reply. I believe the fellow did throw dust upon his person expressly for the purpose of appearing as dirty as possible.

"How much do you estimate your damage?" asked the governor.

"Ah, it is not my own feelings, senor, that I care about," replied the man, with a doleful look.

"Whose, then?"

"My cow's," was the answer.

Of course Constance would laugh at that. It was just like her; and even Wilson, the pilot, had to roar, while the governor looked perplexed.

"Is your cow injured?" I asked.

"No, senor, but she was frightened, and I should have damages."

"I think the demand just," cried Constance; and then she laughed, and even had the impudence to lay one of her small hands upon my arm, and press it, as though to impart some portion of her glee to me.

"What is the amount of the joint claim?" I demanded.

"Four reals, senor, are none too much," the applicant said, with a whine.

"Cheap enough," cried Constance.

I thought so, too, and paid the money without a murmur. The sight of the silver brought a smile to the sharp face of the native, and as he prepared to leave the room, he turned to me, and said, —

"If the senor wants to hire my cow for an excursion, or to visit the bay, I can recommend her as a gentle beast, and one that won't run away with the senor."

This was the hardest blow I had yet received.

At nine o'clock we had coffee, bread, and cake, and after having eaten what we desired, the governor opened the basket of champagne, and put two bottles upon the table. I am glad, for my own reputation, to state that the wine was good, and that Constance took her share without a murmur. It only made her more talkative and merry, and even the lips of her prudish aunt were opened, and I found that she could say a few words when there was an opportunity. At eleven o'clock the ladies retired to rest; Wilson went home, the chief of staff stowed himself away somewhere, and the secretary of state stretched his form on a table. I looked around to see where I was to rest for the night, and the governor pointed to the only spare lounge in the room.

"We keep that," he said, "for visitors. May you sleep in peace. Good night;" and Don Oroto left me for his chamber, if he had one.

I looked at the secretary of state, and that officer looked at me, and puffed away at his cigar quite at his leisure. The gentleman had taken off his coat, and loosened the collar of his shirt. Over a pair of very dark feet he had spread a blanket; but his toes were in sight, and continually working as though longing to kick some one. The senor was not a pleasant-looking gentleman for a room-mate, but I saw no way in which I could change him; so I resigned myself to my fate, and took the position assigned me for the night.

"Senor," cried the official, "does snoring disturb you?"

Politeness compelled me to answer that it did not.

"Ah, I am glad of that, for I snore. At least, those who sleep in the same room with me say that I do;" and the Spaniard puffed his cigar with great complacency and satisfaction, as though he felt proud of his accomplishments.

Hardly had I settled my head when I heard a sound like the blast of a trumpet. The secretary had commenced snoring as though he intended to make a night of it. For a while I submitted to it, and then, growing desperate, I hurled one of my shoes at the head of the official; but, unfortunately, my aim was not good, and it struck the light, and over it went, and I was left in darkness.

Finally I dropped to sleep, and when I awoke I found my room-mate sitting up on the table, smoking, and looking at me very placidly. It was daylight, and near at hand were two cups of coffee, which some of the servants had brought us.

"Good morning, senor," cried my room-mate. "Did you rest well?"

"Yes; quite well."

"My snoring did not disturb you, senor?"

"Not much."

"I am glad of it. I think I must be improving. I hope so, for if I should marry, my wife would have but little rest. It is a disease, senor — a disease."

I did not feel much refreshed by my sleep, but I rolled up the blanket which I had spread over me, and then looked around for water to perform my ablutions.

"What is wanting?" asked my room-mate.

"Water," I answered.

The secretary shrugged his shoulders.

"You must go to the river," he said. "I will go with you after we have drank our coffee."

He whistled, and a naked little native came to the door. My room-mate gave some order, and the lad vanished, after one glance at my face, as though it were a curiosity; and I have no doubt that it was. Then we drank the coffee, and left the house for the river. The governor had not arisen from his couch, I judged, for we saw nothing of him; and the ladies were taking their morning nap, for they had not made their appearance when we quitted the reception-room.

The morning was as lovely as a tropical morning could be. The mountains were bathed in dew, and as the sun rose, its beams touched the grass, and gilded each blade until it glittered like diamonds. The air was pure and refreshingly cool; and to enjoy it, the whole population of the village was out on the sidewalks, some smoking, and others disfiguring their mouths and teeth with chewing the betel nut, which appears to act on the system with the same exhilarating effects as tobacco. But it destroys the teeth in the course of time, rendering them black and brittle. Most of the men at the Ladrone Islands use the nut; consequently a good set of teeth is rarely seen.

As we passed through the streets, I saw that we attracted much attention from the people, and I felt quite proud of the notice, until I heard one woman say, —

"That is the man who rode the bull, and nearly killed Maguel."

"Yes," cried another; "but the senor paid like a prince for it. He may run over me for two reals."

I did not walk so proudly after that. I felt that I was a marked man, and that modesty should be my forte until I left the island.

But at length we reached the river, and I think half the population of the village were in it. Men, women, and children were there, swimming, diving, and washing; and a very jolly looking set they were, shouting and laughing, and splashing the water, and sometimes ducking each other, so that for a while it reminded me of the lake at Kammaira. But I missed the fine forms and white teeth of the kanaka girls, and there was not the same grace in swimming. But the women and girls of St. Ignazio de Agana were not to be despised for their water exhibitions, and while I stood upon the banks of the river, I saw some very good specimens of their skill.

"Come," said my companion, "if you want to wash, now is your chance. This is the public bathing-tub. Here you can find water in abundance."

I looked around, and though I liked the idea of having a bath, I did not feel as though I could swim in such a crowd without a proper bathing-dress; and when I intimated as much to the secretary of state, he seemed to comprehend my delicacy at once, and led the way to a small house, where we found a little native boy with his arms full of towels, and two suits of bathing-dresses. The latter we put on, and then plunged into the river, many of the girls swimming near us for the purpose of witnessing the efforts of the American in the water. But, thanks to the lessons which I had received at Honolulu, there was not one who dared to play me a trick, although I was ambitious of a little fun, and swam near several girls in hopes they would attempt some familiarity. But the bright-eyed nymphs only laughed and edged away from me, and refused to commence a battle, although I did spatter them with water until they were compelled to turn their heads and make for the shore.

At last I tired of the sport, when I joined my companion and dressed. Then, refreshed and contented, we returned to the governor's house, where we found Don Oroto sipping coffee, and we soon joined him in that occupation, and while we were chatting of the morning news, the two ladies made their appearance, and, strange to say, both of their toilets seemed to have been neglected. Constance appeared to have just left her bed, and her thick black hair had not been touched by comb or brush. It hung around her plump shoulders in admirable disorder, and after the first glance of astonishment, I could not help confessing that the young lady looked as pretty, if not prettier, than when her toilet was complete. She wore a different dress from the one in which she had appeared at dinner table the day before. It was shorter, and showed — O, gracious! — two of the smallest, most perfect formed feet that I had ever seen. And they were naked, too, the soles of the feet being protected by sandals, with coverings at the ends just large enough to contain two toes. How she managed to keep them on while walking was a puzzle to me; yet she did do it, and moved about the room in a free, swinging, graceful manner, that was quite fascinating.

"Senor," asked Constance, as she lighted a paper cigar, and brushed the hair from her eyes, "do you feel like riding to-day?"

"The saints forbid!" I exclaimed. "I have no desire to pay damages to half the inhabitants of the town. I had much rather have an excursion on the water."

Just at this moment, whom should I see rolling towards the house, piloted by two natives, but Jack Topmall, the mate of the Helen. "What brought him to town," I asked myself. "Something unusual has happened;" and leaving the ladies to quarrel, I went out to Jack.

"What brings you here?" I asked. "You have news of importance for me."

"Hang me if I hain't," was the answer, "and blasted bad news, too."

"What is it? Speak, man, and let me know the worst. Is Lilly —"

"The gal is well enough, although a little moping. 'Tain't her, but the —"

"What, man? Out with it."

"Well, sir, the cussed old whaling tub Sally is in port, and anchored within a cable's length of us."

The very whaler we had escaped from! This was news of importance, and for a moment I was stunned by it.

CHAPTER XIII.

AN AWKWARD POSITION. — THE OLD SALLY. — A PLAN TO ESCAPE DETECTION.

WHAT should I do? If the Sally was in port I could not avoid meeting Captain Bunker, and of course he would know me, and claim me as a deserter. I could not get under way and sail for some other port, for I had made a contract, and in a day or two the articles which I had bargained for would be alongside, and in a week's time I must be off for San Francisco. Even while these thoughts were passing through my mind, Jack asked, —

"What shall we do, sir? Must we slip cable, and run for it?"

"No, I think not. At least not at present. But before I decide, answer me one question. Has any one on board the Sally seen you, or Will, or Jake?"

"No, sir. We laid low just as soon as the Sally anchored. We didn't show a hand, and if a boat had boarded us, we should have stowed away, and left the kanakas to take care of the schooner."

"Excellent!" I exclaimed. "I have formed my plan, and will carry it out."

"That's the talk," cried the mate, his face manifesting some pleasure, for he had great reliance in me. "I knowed you would fix 'em — I told Will and Jake so."

"Thank you for your confidence in my ability, but recollect that much will depend upon you and Will. You must remain in your state-rooms until we sail. On no account will you be seen on deck, unless it is in the night time."

This information made the mate look doleful.

"That's hard," he said.

"Not so hard as to be compelled to do duty on board the Sally — recollect that, and profit by it. You must lock yourself up in your state-room, and keep quiet all day, but you can stay on deck all night if you please."

"But that Jake — what's to be done with him?" asked Jack, after a moment's reflection.

"We must disguise him," I answered.

"But how, sir? He's a darky, and we can't paint him white, you know."

"I'll attend to him when I go on board. We must make a kanaka of him."

The mate grinned, and shook his head in a doubtful manner. "That wool of his is too kinky for a kanaka, sir," the mate remarked. "But I wish you was on board, sir; I should feel safer."

Mr. Topmall had arrived in the schooner's boat, manned by four of the kanakas, and in an hour's time I could be on board. I left the mate, and entered the reception-room to take leave of the governor and his family, and to beg that they would excuse me for a day or two.

"Leave us?" cried Constance; "we shall not let you go."

"I am fearful that your visit has not been pleasant," the governor remarked. "We have but few pleasures here, but we should have attempted to make your stay agreeable."

"O, don't go!" pleaded Constance, flashing her beautiful black eyes upon me; and I must confess they rather staggered me in my intention.

"Business alone calls me to the vessel," I remarked. "I shall soon return, however. But, in consideration of your hospitality, I invite you all to visit my vessel to-morrow, and dine with me."

"O, that will be pleasant," cried Constance, clapping her hands. "We will go — will we not, padre?"

The governor pondered for a moment, but as I urged my invitation, he consented, and promised to visit me, with his family, the next day; and then, after a general shaking of hands, and an ardent look from the young lady, I left the house and hurried to the boat.

I had just ordered the men to "shove off," when four or five natives, with large hampers on their heads, were seen running towards us, and shouting to attract our attention. I waited until the men reached the landing, and found that they carried packages of oranges, bananas, and a basket of eggs, all of which, the natives informed me, were sent by the senorita Constance, with her best wishes for my health and prosperity. I sent back a kind message, and then we started down the river, but had not proceeded more than a mile, when I saw one of the Sally's boats coming towards us. The mate grew agitated immediately, and I could see that he meditated jumping overboard, and testing the efficacy of swimming and running.

"What shall I do, sir?" he asked. "The rascals will know me."

"Lie down in the bottom of the boat, and don't show your head over the gunwale. Now, then — down you go."

My kanakas looked their surprise and grinned, but they said not a word. In a few minutes the Sally's boat was so near that I could see Captain Bunker in the stern-sheets, working at the steering-oar; and the sight of the tyrant caused me to feel a thrill at my heart as I thought of the cruelties which the man had practised on board his ship while I was a member of his crew. But with a powerful effort I recovered my presence of mind. As our boats neared each other I touched my hat — an act of politeness not noticed, for Bunker suddenly shouted, —

"Way enough! Hold water!"

The men obeyed him.

"Thunder!" the captain shouted, glaring at me in astonishment, "if there ain't Pepper, may I be blasted."

"Did you speak to me, sir?" I asked, as calm as a summer morning, to all outward appearances.

"Pepper, by all that's merciful!" the captain yelled; and I thought that the words would strangle him, and I wished they had.

My boat was slowly passing the whaler, and I hoped that I should proceed without more words; but Bunker was not disposed to let me off in that manner.

"Back water," he said to his crew; and as he spoke I cast a glance over the men, and saw that four of them were sailors who knew me when I was on board the Sally.

"Did you desire to see me, sir?" I asked.

"See you?" roared Bunker. "Well, I'm blasted!"

"Hadn't I better go overboard, sir?" asked Jack, who was lying at my feet, almost smothered in oranges and bananas. The sound of Bunker's voice caused the strong man to tremble, and to seek for an opportunity to escape.

"Keep quiet," I whispered, "or you will spoil all my plans."

In the mean time Bunker was glaring at me, and uncertain what to do, and undecided what to say.

"Do you belong to the ship in the harbor?" I asked.

"Well, I swear, this beats all;" and Bunker made a clutch at his hair, and tore some of it out of his head, and then stamped upon it.

"I asked you a civil question, and you are not disposed to answer it," I said, quite coldly. "Good day, sir."

"Stop!" roared Bunker. "Back water," he cried to his men; and the whale-boat dropped down the stream, side by side with my boat, only separated by the oars.

"Hadn't I better jump and cut for it?" whispered the mate. from amidst the hampers.

I kicked him gently, to remind him that it was necessary he should keep quiet, and then I turned my attention to Captain Bunker.

"Have you a message for me?" I asked. "You seem to be somewhat excited, but I hope no harm has befallen my vessel."

O, how the man did roar and stamp! and I expected every moment that he would run alongside of my boat and attempt to make me prisoner; but if he had, it would have cost him dear, for I had my revolver in my breast pocket, and the six chambers were loaded.

"One question;" asked the captain: "is your name Charles Allspice?"

"I should think not," I answered, with a look of such indifference that the whaler was staggered.

"What is your name?" Bunker roared.

"None of your business, sir," was my reply. "When you ask me my name in a proper manner, I will answer you. Not until then."

"Draw it mild," whispered Jack. "You know what a man he is for tearing things."

"Do you mean to say that you never shipped on board the Sally?" roared Bunker.

"Look you, sir," I answered; "I have endured this questioning as long as possible, thinking that you might have some news to communicate. I find that your object is to insult me, and I'm not inclined to submit to it without first asking if you are disposed to grant me such satisfaction as one gentleman can ask from another."

"My God, it can't be Pepper!" Bunker exclaimed, in a hoarse tone. "Pepper would not dare to talk to me in that manner. Pepper was a civil boy, and polite to his superior officers."

Bunker passed his hand over his eyes, and then looked at me and at his boat's crew.

"Is that Pepper?" he asked, appealing to his men, and pointing to me.

"I think it is," one of them answered.

"He looks some like Pepper, sir; but Pepper wasn't so good looking, and his hair didn't curl like this man's," answered Bushey, the boat-steerer.

"If you have finished your examination, I will proceed," I remarked.

"One moment, sir," Bunker cried. "Don't you know me?"

"I should think not. Who are you, and what is your name?"

"O, my God, this is too much!" roared the frantic captain.

"Gently with him when he pitches," whispered Jack, who was nearly smothered under the weight of oranges and other fruit.

"Good day, sir," I cried. "If you wish to see me, call on board the Helen. She is lying in the harbor."

"I'll have you on board the Sally, in double irons, in less than forty-eight hours," Bunker howled. "You see if I don't."

"You must be insane," I answered. "Go and have your head shaved, and a mustard poultice put on your neck. Such men as you are dangerous to the community."

"Easy with him," cried Jack. "Remember how he'd work our old iron up, if we was on board his blubber-hunter."

I gave a signal to the men, and they dipped their oars in the water, and we commenced moving down the river at a rapid rate, while Bunker, mad with rage, and undecided what to do, tore his hair, and swore at a terrible rate. Jack, as soon as we were out of sight of the whale-boat, raised his head and looked around.

"I'd sooner cut one of my hands off, than go on board of that tub agin," the mate said.

At the mouth of the river, the mate once more sought the bottom of the boat, for fear that prying eyes on board the Sally should obtain a glimpse of his well-known face, and it was well that he did so, for I saw a dozen people on the deck of the ship, gazing at the boat and those in it. As I passed under the bows of the Sally, I saw many familiar faces, and marked the looks of astonishment with which they regarded me. I gave no sign that I had seen the ship or men before, and in a few minutes was alongside the Helen, and on deck, where I met Lilly, who could hardly be persuaded that it was not her duty to throw her arms around my neck, and kiss me in the presence of all the kanakas, none of whom suspected that Lilly was a female, or, if they did, they were careful not to express their thoughts in words or looks.

"O, I am so glad that you have returned!" Lilly said; "I have been so lonely without you!"

I had no doubt of it, for the look of the girl was sufficient to convince me that she spoke the truth.

"Where are Will and Jake?" I asked.

"In the hold," Lilly answered.

"What are they doing there?"

"They are afraid of the ship. They said they were."

I went to the hatch, and called Will and Jake, but I was compelled to speak several times before I made myself heard. At last a miserable-looking negro came to the scuttle and answered.

"Glory to God," Jake cried, as soon as he saw me. "De cap'n come on board agin. Now we is safe, sure enuf."

"What is the matter with you?" I asked, as Will and Jake came on deck, looking pale and anxious.

"O, golly! ain't dat enough, sir? Jist you look at dat blubber-hunter, and s'pose de skipper come arter me. Must I go?"

"Of course," I replied, for the purpose of noting the man's fright.

"O, golly! don't you talk dat way, cap'n. It breaks my heart to hear you," moaned Jake. "I can't leave you. It am no use. I'd die away from you."

"I'd hang myself afore I'd go," cried Will. "I might as well die one way as another;" and the lad did look desperate.

"There is but one way that I can save you," I said to Jake.

"Name 'em, cap'n; I takes dat chance;" and the negro's eyes expressed hope.

"And what am I to do?" asked Will.

"Listen, and I will tell you. You must confine yourself to a state-room, and on no account show yourself while we are in port."

"Golly! I can't do dat, cap'n," cried Jake. "You starve to death. I must hab de air and de light. Who take care of de cabin, if I don't work?"

"But I intend that you shall work, Jake. I can't spare you. But to enable you to appear on deck, you must pretend to be a kanaka."

"Can't do dat," cried Jake. "My lips too thick for dat. Color too brack for kanaka."

"Then you must pass as a New Zealander; and if any one speaks to you, don't understand."

"But de New Zealander's all tattooed on de face. How about dat?"

"Well, we must tattoo you."

"O, golly! don't do dat. Don't spoil de beauty of dis face. See my skin, all fair and sleek; and if it all marked up, who admire dis nigger den?"

"You must either lose your beauty or your liberty. Which do you prefer?"

Jake hesitated for a moment, and then he thought that it would be better if his face was marked a little — "berry leetle." I called one of the kanakas, — a fellow celebrated for his skill in tattooing, — and told him to bring up his instruments, and commence operations on Jake's face. The negro groaned, and vowed that no man was ever treated so badly; and after I had frightened him a little, I let him into the secret of my plans. The kanaka was to draw some fierce-looking lines upon the face of the negro, and after they were dry, they would resemble genuine tattoo marks. I calculated that none but a close observer of the human race could detect the difference between the negro and a New Zealander, especially if the former kept his tongue still, or else muttered a few words in the kanaka lingo. My idea pleased Jake immensely, and his mouth expanded from ear to ear, as he thought of the fierce aspect which he should assume.

"But, cap'n," cried Jake, "ef I wash my face de marks all go."

"Then, for a few days, you must use water only on your hands. But be sure and wash them."

"Of course, cap'n; I allers does dat."

The kanaka commenced operations, and laid out his work, drawing some heavy lines on the face of the negro, extending from his ears to his mouth, and then downward to his chin. From the nose to the cheeks the marks were carried upward, and a more ferocious looking negro I never saw in my life, after the painting was finished. I could not help laughing; and while indulging in my mirth, Will reported that a boat from the Sally, containing the chief mate, Mr. Spadem, was pulling towards us. Upon receiving this news, Jack and Will entered their staterooms, and Jake dove for the galley, where he pretended to be very busy, while I walked the quarter-deck, quite calm and collected.

The boat came alongside, and the mate reached the deck, with a gaming smile upon his face, which instantly changed to one of the most intense astonishment, after he had obtained a fair view of my countenance. He looked at my feet as though desirous of seeing if they were clubbed — then he looked at my face, and at last he spoke to me: —

"Pepper, you devil, what brought you here?"

"Sir!" I exclaimed, with amazement, "what do you mean by speaking in this manner to a stranger? I am master of this vessel, and will not be insulted on its quarter-deck."

"What? The devil! Don't you know me, Pepper?"

"You will excuse me, sir, from holding any conversation with a man who calls me by a name which I do not recognize."

For a moment the mate did not know whether to leave the vessel or remain and explain. The love of "gaming" prevailed. He came aft, and with a smile upon his homely face, said, —

"I hope you will excuse me, Pep— that is, cap'n. You look so much like a boy what cut from us one night, that I thought it was him."

"It is very singular, but I met a man this morning, while coming down the river, who said the same thing."

"It must have been Captain Bunker," the mate said. "He went to town this morning. I s'pose he was struck, the same as me, with your resemblance to Pepper. But the more I hear you talk, the more I am satisfied that you ain't Pepper. He was a modest sort of boy, and didn't dare to wink at me."

"And you mean to say that I am not modest?" I asked, with a careless laugh.

"O, no, cap'n; none of that. I knows what manners is, I does."

"What is the name of your ship?" I asked, after a moment's pause.

"The Sally, sir. And a good ship she is, too. Plenty to eat, and good treatment."

"Have you made a successful voyage?"

"Well, no, I can't say that we have. We've taken some ile, but we ain't made our fortunes."

Just at this moment Jake left the cabin, and passed within a few feet of us.

"What is that fellow?" asked the mate. "A New Zealander?"

"Yes, I think so," I answered, carelessly.

"Singular," muttered the man, "but that man looks like a nigger we had on board the Sally. Have you any objection to my speaking to him?"

"Not in the least. But he don't understand English."

Mr. Spadem walked forward to the galley, and I accompanied him. Jake was sitting in the galley, cooking some mess for the cabin, and did not look up until we stopped opposite to him. I saw that the negro's eyes were full of trouble, but he endeavored to appear composed.

"Well, old feller, how do you like cooking?" asked the whaleman.

Jake looked up, grinned, and then shook his head. He didn't understand English.

"Darned if he ain't got the same kind of head that Jake had. But I guess it ain't him. Ah, you sarvey whaleman?" Spadem asked.

"*Kamiti mimi tamste*," muttered Jake, shaking his head, and then continued his work.

"He says that he does not understand you," I remarked, pretending that I could comprehend the meaning of the steward's lingo.

"Yes, I s'pose he don't," answered the mate; and after one long gaze at the negro, he walked aft with me, but still in a thoughtful mood, as though he did not know what to make of it.

"Have you had any sickness on board the Sally?" I asked.

"No, not much. Why?"

"Because, I should think that there was a mania on board your vessel for recognizing people, or thinking that you had met them before. I can't account for it, and I wish that you would give me an explanation."

But Mr. Spadem was not competent for the task. He could

only ponder on the subject, and wonder how it happened; and after drinking a large dose of gin, his favorite liquor, he left the schooner and went on board of his own ship. But I knew that our danger was not past, and in this calculation I was not mistaken, for I saw Captain Bunker's boat pulling down the river, and by the aid of a glass, I made out that Bunker was in it. I instantly commenced making preparations for defence, in case it was necessary. I gave to each of the kanakas a loaded revolver and a cutlass, and showed how they were to be used. Jake, Will, and the mate were similarly armed, but the two latter were not to interfere in the fight, if we had one, unless they were really needed. We had dinner, and still there was no sign of life on board the Sally. I began to think that Bunker would not pay me a visit, and I had just set Jake and the cook at work to prepare the next day's repast, in anticipation of the arrival of the governor and family, when a boat left the side of the whaler, and pulled towards us. In a few minutes my men were prepared, although no weapons were visible on deck. I saw that Bunker was in the stern-sheets of the boat, and that he looked dangerous. I knew that he was determined on some bold stroke, and I suspected what it was. As he reached the deck he came towards me with a most savage frown upon his brow. I think that I never saw him look more ugly. At one time I should have wilted before that gaze, but now I met his eyes without flinching.

"Do you mean to tell me that your name isn't Pepper?" roared the skipper, shaking his fist at me, and turning red in the face.

"It is none of your business what my name is," I retorted.

"I say it is."

"And I repeat that it is not."

"D—n it, boy, I'll knock you down, if you give me a word of sass;" and Captain Bunker came towards me as though to carry into effect his threat; but when he saw that I manifested no signs of alarm, he paused, and seemed a little undecided. "Will you go on board the Sally?" he asked. "You ran away from my ship, and I want you. If you don't go you must pay me for your services."

"I shall not go on board your old tub, and I shall not pay you a dollar. You have made a mistake in the person, if you think so."

Bunker walked to the gangway, and called to his boat's crew. The men came on deck, but with no degree of alacrity. I knew most of them, and was aware that they would have run away if they had had a chance.

"Put that fellow in the boat," Bunker said; and pointed to me.

"Be careful what orders you issue here," I cried. "Remember, I command this vessel, and if you commit an outrage, I shall resent it."

"You go on board the Sally, or I'll never eat agin," roared Bunker; and I saw that he was in earnest.

"I shall not go on board the Sally, and I warn you against committing an outrage."

"Put him in the boat," cried Bunker, pointing to me.

The men advanced a few steps, and then paused rather unexpectedly, for I had quietly drawn a revolver from my pocket and cocked it.

"Men," I said, "I don't want your blood upon my head. If I am compelled to shoot two or three of you, Captain Bunker included, don't blame me. I shall do so, if you make a movement to lay a hand upon me."

"Do you mean to say that you would shoot me?" demanded Bunker.

"The first man that I shall aim at will be you. Recollect it, and know that my aim never fails."

"Good Lord, this can't be Pepper," remarked the skipper. "Pepper wasn't so bloodthirsty as this man. But do you really mean what you say?"

"Certainly I do;" and then I whistled, and the kanakas sprung to their feet, each of them armed with a revolver and cutlass, and Bunker commenced backing towards the gangway, exclaiming, —

"Don't shoot — we will leave. Get into the boat, boys, or the d—d heathen will eat us. We'll come again, we will, and we'll come armed, we will, and we'll take you, you see if we don't;" and with this shout of defiance Bunker quitted the deck. The boat left the schooner, and Bunker shook his fist at me as he passed under the stern. "I'll have you," he said. "You can't lie to me; I know too much."

I raised my pistol, as though I was about to take aim, and the brave whaler dodged instantly, and shouted to his men to "pull hard;" and they did, and were soon beyond the reach of a bullet.

I supposed that an attempt would be made to board the vessel during the night, and, for the purpose of defeating the plan, the mate and Will agreed to keep watch, and give me warning of the approach of those hostile to us. I "turned in" about ten o'clock, somewhat tired, and soon fell asleep; but about two bells in the morning, or one o'clock, the mate aroused me, with the information that two boats were approaching the schooner. In a few minutes I had dressed and was on deck, where I found my crew all armed, and ready for action. The two boats were within a hundred fathoms of us, pulling with muffled oars, and the one who had charge of the expedition evidently thought that he would surprise us; but in this he was mistaken, for I suddenly hailed the boats, and the instant my voice was heard, the rowing ceased.

"Boat, ahoy!" I cried: "if you pull nearer to the schooner, I shall fire at you."

I could hear the officers who had charge of the expedition whisper, and then Captain Bunker answered, —

"We are going ashore for wood and water."

"Then give my vessel a wider berth. Pull in some other direction. There is room enough for you and me."

Hardly had I ceased speaking when I saw a flash, and then heard the report of a musket. A ball whizzed within ten feet of my head, and struck the water a few fathoms beyond the vessel.

"All ready for a broadside," I cried, speaking so that those in the boat could hear me; and then I whispered to Jack and Will, "Don't fire to hit. Only frighten them."

I did not think it necessary to caution the kanakas, for I did not believe they could hit a boat at so great a distance.

"Fire!" I yelled, and aimed so that the bullet from my pistol would pass close to Bunker's head.

There was a rattling discharge of pistols, and to my surprise I heard some one utter an exclamation of pain, and drop his oar. One of the kanakas had aimed with commendable precision, obeying orders, and perhaps killing a man.

"Hold water," roared Bunker. "Blast 'em, they is firing bullets, and one passed within a few inches of my head."

As the boat lost headway, the skipper again cried, —

"Starn, all — hard;" and the boat commenced receding from

the schooner. While I was wondering if the attack would be renewed, Bunker, in a voice of rage, shouted, —

"Cuss you, Pepper, you have nearly killed one of my men."

I was sorry for it, but I did not say so. I only replied, —

"I'll kill more, if you don't keep away from my vessel. I told you what to expect."

My answer so exasperated the whaler that he again fired at me with his musket; but the ball fell short, striking the water some distance from the vessel. My men answered the shot with a shout of defiance, and dared the whalemen to renew the attack. But the latter had had enough for one night, so they sullenly retired to their ship, and we to our berths, satisfied that no other attack would be made.

At daylight the next morning we commenced preparations for receiving the governor and family. We hoisted flags, washed and scrubbed the decks, spread an awning over the quarter-deck to protect the heads of our company from the hot sun; and after breakfast the crew dressed themselves in their best, and awaited the appearance of our expected company. We did not have to wait long. Two boats hove in sight, and in one of them I saw the sweet face of Constance, and the stern countenance of Dorothea. The governor and suite arrived first, and I received his excellency with such marks of dignified attention that he was delighted, and felt at home at once. The members of his suite were also pleased with their reception. They were all ushered into the cabin, where they found a cold collation upon the table, with a large bowl of claret punch, and coffee for those who preferred that beverage. I left my company in the cabin, and hastened to receive Constance, who reached the deck with a hop, skip, and a jump, and squeezed my hand in the most friendly manner, while her eyes danced with fun, as she thought of the ride which we had taken through the streets of her native village. While I was chatting with the ladies, forgetful of everything but present enjoyment, I heard a deep sigh near me; and turning, I saw poor, patient Lilly, who was regarding me with sorrowful eyes and a heavy heart. But at that moment the look and sigh made me angry, and I spoke quick — much quicker than I intended.

"Boy," I asked, "what do you desire?"

"Nothing, sir," Lilly answered, and walked forward; but I saw the tears gather in her eyes as she passed me.

I forgot the sacrifices she had made on my account — I no longer recollected the love which she felt for me — her past services were forgotten, and all on account of the new face which was beaming on me, and lighted by a pair of very bright eyes.

"What a handsome boy!" cried the Spanish maiden, her look following the form of Lilly. "Do call him, so that I can see his face and eyes."

I imagined the kanaka girl's indignant refusal had I made such a request, and to prevent trouble I declined, on the ground that discipline would not permit me to talk with the boy. With this explanation Constance was satisfied, or seemed so, and with a gallant bow I conducted her into the cabin, where her father and friends were awaiting an invitation to attack the collation. While we were at the table, Will came into the cabin, and informed me that Captain Bunker and two boats' crews were pulling towards the Helen, and he desired information respecting them.

"Arm the men, and have them in readiness to act," I said, and continued to entertain my visitors.

In a short time I heard Bunker's voice on deck, and it was raised in a threatening manner. My guests looked a little surprised; but I re-assured them with a smile, and passed around the table some choice paper cigars. But Bunker's voice did not grow quiet. He grew braver every moment, seeing that there was no opposition to his gaining the deck. I saw that an explosion was about to take place; so I thought it time to say a few words, and prepare the governor's mind.

"Are the whalemen who enter this port troublesome?" I asked of Don Oroto.

"Troublesome!" he repeated; "they are always in trouble. May the saints curse some of them, for it requires my army to keep the drunkards in subjection. But they buy our provisions, and that is the only consolation we have."

"And make love to our ladies, padre," cried Constance, with a sharp look at her aunt.

"Yes, they do bother our women," was his excellency's reply, as though it was one of the natural consequences of a whaler's being in port.

"Confound them for a dirty set," I said, with a look of disgust. "They have already annoyed me."

"Can it be possible?" asked the governor; "it shall be stopped.

I assure you that it shall. My friends shall not be annoyed. The commander of the forces shall see to it."

"Fill your glasses, ladies and gentlemen," I said, "and then I will tell you something that will make you smile. The whaler labors under a strange delusion. He imagines that he has seen me before, and even declares that I formerly belonged to his ship. I have attempted to reason with the man, but he won't listen to reason. Last night he attempted to board my vessel for the purpose of making me a prisoner; but I was prepared, and drove him and his men off. I don't like to be annoyed by the fellow, but really I shall be glad to escape from it."

"Let me talk with this man," cried the governor, with awful dignity. "I will see what he means. He must be rebuked."

We left the table, and went on deck, and saw Bunker and his men looking as though they meant mischief. But at sight of the governor and ladies the whalemen fell back, and some of them walked forward. The captain shook his fist at me, and that attention I repaid with a contemptuous smile.

"Do you know who I am?" asked the governor of the whaler, speaking in Spanish, which the latter could not comprehend.

"I don't want to hear any of your lingo," roared Bunker; "I want Pepper, and I'll have him, or I'll know the reason why."

The governor looked to me for an interpretation.

"He says that he don't care for you or your power," I exclaimed.

The governor raised both hands in astonishment, and turned to his suite for advice.

"We must make ourselves respected," he said. "Even if I have to call upon the whole military force of the island, I will have my authority enforced."

"Look ahere, you Pepper," cried Bunker; "it ain't no kind of use to play 'possum with me. Jist you come on board the Sally, and then if you want to make a bargain I'll talk with you."

"What does he say?" asked the governor.

"That he don't care about your army. He thinks that he could annihilate it in a short time."

The military captain seemed somewhat interested at this stage. Constance raised her eyes in wonder and indignation.

"What do you say?" demanded Bunker.

"That I shall not go with you. You have made a mistake.

You are laboring under some delusion. Go on board of your vessel, and keep quiet for a few days. You may recover by using proper medicines."

The rage of the man was terrible. The military gentleman thought of retreating to the cabin, but Dorothea blocked the way, and he could not do so. Don Oroto turned pale, and looked to me for advice.

"You are governor of the island," I said. "Show this pirate that you are master by using your authority."

"I will," he answered. "Tell him from me that, unless he returns to his ship, I will command the fort to fire upon his vessel."

I interpreted the words to Bunker. He was somewhat astonished, but luckily did not know the actual force at the fort — a six-pounder and one soldier.

"Pepper," he said, "give me a hundred dollars, and I'll call it square. Make it a bargain, and I won't say one word about your running away."

I shook my head.

"You must leave the vessel," I said. "I cannot talk with a man who presumes to dictate to me."

"Cuss your impudence," he yelled. "You beat a Portuguese all holler. I've a good mind to take you at any rate — and that nigger, too. In spite of his tattoo I think he is my Jake."

The governor, who supposed that his authority was still defied, waved his hand in token of a wish to terminate the interview, and Bunker, after a moment's consultation with Spadem, left the vessel; but he grumbled terribly, and swore that he would write to his government.

Of course I commended the governor for the energy which he had exhibited, and complimented his suite for their courage. Such a course was well calculated to win their favor, and we all adjourned to the cabin and finished the bowl of punch, and then repaired to the deck to chat until dinner-time.

At four o'clock we had dinner, and an excellent one it was. The land and the sea contributed their stores to supply the table. We had turtle and fish, fresh from the brine, fruits plucked from the trees that morning, fowls which we brought from the Sandwich Islands, ducks from the shore, and sweetmeats from the East Indies; while for liquids we had coffee, claret, and champagne; and, in justice to my company, I must state that they relished the latter much more than the former, which I considered an evidence of refined taste on their part. At six o'clock my guests left the table, all satisfied, and all congratulating me upon the successful manner in which the dinner had passed off. Even Constance's eyes beamed with extra brilliancy upon the occasion, and her smile was more saucy than ever. She put her arm through mine, and walked the deck, smoking her cigarette, and chatting in a most lovable manner.

"Senor," said the governor, as the boats were coming alongside to take the company home, "I will protect you and your vessel."

I thanked his excellency for his kindness, but did not intimate that I was able to protect myself.

"I shall issue orders to the men" (one man he meant) "in the fort to open fire upon the whaleship if the master molests you; and to still further secure you from attack, the commander of the forces will remain on board until you feel perfectly safe."

The gallant gentleman thus alluded to did not seem to relish the position.

"Will there be any fighting?" he asked.

"Perhaps there will be. It is impossible to tell what the whaler will resort to," I answered.

"Then I should have some of my soldiers on board to assist me," pleaded the captain.

"Your presence is sufficient to defeat any schemes of attack," was the governor's answer. "You must remain and see that the rights of neutrals are respected. We must have order in our harbor. We are under too deep a debt of gratitude to the senor captain not to afford him all the protection in our power."

The military gentleman would have said something in remonstrance, but the governor cut him short by entering his boat, while I assisted Constance over the rail.

"You will come and see me to-morrow, or the next day," she whispered, and pressed my hand.

I returned the pressure and promised, and the next instant the boats had left, leaving the military man to be entertained by me, and to wish that whalers were sunk in the ocean with their own oil poured upon their heads.

"I trust that we shall have a quiet night," the captain said.

"The whaler will not dare to attack us after the warning which the governor gave him."

"They are desperate men," I answered, and will not scruple to commit desperate deeds. If we have a fight, it will be a hard one. But I have no doubt we shall be able to beat them."

The Spaniard shuddered, and looked at me with some surprise. He thought I must be a wonderful man for courage, and I did not think it necessary to undeceive him.

At an early hour my guest retired to bed, and then I let the mate and Will out of their state-room, much to their joy, for the poor fellows had heard the fun which I had had all day, and were unable to participate in it. They cursed their fate, and were in favor of defying Bunker and all on board the Sally.

I cooled them down after a while, and they became reconciled to their lot; and then I turned to speak to Lilly, who I had hardly noticed all day, having so much business to attend to. I felt guilty when my eyes met hers, for they looked so mildly reproachful, and I recollected how kind she had been to me in adversity and prosperity.

"Do you think that you have treated me justly?" she asked.

"Why have I not?" I said.

"Ask your own fickle heart why you have acted so coldly," Lilly cried.

"I have, and I can obtain no answer."

"There goes the answer!" the girl exclaimed, pointing with her hand in the direction which the boats had taken. "The Spanish lady has driven from your head all thoughts of Lilly, and yet I love you better than she does, or ever can."

"And do you suppose that I doubt it, Lilly? Have I not proved to you how highly I estimate your friendship?"

"You have proved nothing," she exclaimed, passionately, "except your fickleness."

Tears, which she no longer could restrain, rolled down her cheeks, but she dashed them off as though ashamed of showing so much feeling.

"Lilly," I said, "listen to me for a moment. The ladies who were on board were my guests, and I could not help showing them some attention. If I had neglected them they would have supposed me impolite, and not anxious for their company."

"But why did you not devote your attention as much to one as the other?" she asked, with flashing eyes.

"Did I not?"

"No; you know you did not. I saw you attempt to kiss the girl with the fresh face, and you looked foolish when she would not let you. Do not deny it."

Of course I did not deny it, for the truth was not to be denied at such a moment; but candor compelled me to state that at the time I attempted to steal a kiss, I had no idea that Lilly was watching me. But a man should be careful in his love affairs — for a woman is Argus-eyed.

"Lilly," I asked, "would you have had me kiss the elder female?"

"You should have attempted to kiss neither," was the answer, accompanied with a stamp of the foot.

I could not help smiling at the passionate little thing, and my smile so excited the girl that she turned her back upon me, and walked aft. I did not say a word. I lighted a cigar, and sat down, taking no notice of Lilly, for I thought that she would soon come to terms. My predictions were verified. In a few minutes I heard a soft breathing near me, and then I felt some one's warm breath upon my neck. I smoked on in silence, not even turning my head. Presently a pair of soft arms were thrown around my neck, and a smooth cheek was pressed to mine.

"Do you forgive me?" whispered Lilly. "I was angry, and I had no right to be. I did not mean to reproach you; but O, I have been very miserable to-day."

Poor child! I could tell by her face that she had suffered, and her tender pleading touched my heart. I threw away my cigar, and put an arm around her waist, and then she laid her head on my shoulder, and sobbed as though her heart would break. For a few minutes I allowed her tears to flow without restraint, for I knew that she would recover her usual gayety after she had given vent to her grief, and my anticipations proved correct, for she raised her head, and asked, —

"Do you forgive me?"

"For what?"

"For doubting you — for speaking as I did?"

"Certainly I do; but let us have no more doubts, Lilly. You must trust in me, and make no complaints if you see me paying attention to a lady. You will remember — will you not?"

"Yes," she said; but the word came forth with an effort, as

though she would strive to obey the request, heartless as it was. Then she left me and entered the cabin, while I remained on deck until near ten o'clock; and then, seeing no sign of an attack, I "turned in," and slept until morning without being disturbed.

About eight o'clock several boats came alongside with yams, and we commenced receiving cargo on board. This kept me busy until nearly sundown, and then, leaving the mate in charge, I entered a shore boat, and was pulled up the river, intending to pay a visit to the governor and his pretty daughter, whose sweet face had made more of an impression upon me than I was willing to allow.

Upon arriving at the governor's house the first person I met was the senorita Constance, who, seated in the sitting-room, was sweeping the strings of her guitar in a thoughtful manner, as though her mind was not on her music. I advanced a step, and the sound awakened her from her reverie. She turned her head, saw her visitor, and with a look of glad surprise arose and came towards me with extended hands.

"Ah, senor, I am so glad you have come, for I was very lonely."

I took her hands and pressed them, and then kissed them, which act only caused her to blush; but she did not look offended or displeased.

"Remember our compact — no love making," she said, with a laugh.

"I have forgotten it," I answered. "I forget everything but you, when in your presence."

"It is not on my account that I caution you," Constance said, after a moment's thought. "It is for your sake. I did not command you to avoid loving me — remember that. I do not forbid you to worship, only you must not expect me to return it."

"Have matters your own way," I said. "I shall admire you, but still not love you. My heart has passed beyond my control."

My companion looked up, and a shade passed over her face, but it was soon dispelled.

"Are you married?" she whispered, and her hand was withdrawn from mine.

"O, no; but I hope to be, some day."

She replaced her little hand in mine, and I thought that I noted a glow of satisfaction upon her face; and while I was admiring her eyes I heard a step in the hall, and on looking up who should stand in the doorway but my ancient enemy, Captain Jonathan Bunker, of the whaleship Sally, of New Bedford.

"Wal, you feller is cuttin' it fat, I should think," the skipper remarked, as his little red eyes rested upon my hand, which held Constance's; and, as he spoke, he entered the room, and landed on a lounge, from which position he gazed at us with most provoking coolness. "I say, you boy," continued Bunker, "that is a mighty pootty gal you is talkin' to, and huggin'."

"Sir," I demanded, with pretended astonishment, "who do you take me for?"

"I takes you for Pepper, and darned if you ain't Pepper, and its no use to say that it ain't your name."

"I shall not renew an argument with you," I said. "You can think as you please. If you suppose I belonged to your vessel, why don't you take me?"

"And so I would, if it wan't for them blasted revolvers. But you give me an equal chance, and see if I won't do somethin'."

"I will give you an equal chance," I said. "You may take a revolver, and I will take one, and let us see if we cannot settle the matter."

"I have a darned good mind to try you," the old fellow said. "I'd clip your wings, I would, 'cos I can shoot. I can hit things as well as you."

"Don't spoil a good mind," I cried. "I have a revolver in my pocket. We can toss up for the first fire."

"Wal, I guess I couldn't get square in a better way. But where's the old cock what has charge of these mole-hills?"

"Do you mean the governor?"

"Wal, yes; I 'spect I do. But 'tain't much honor to be governor of these islands."

I turned to Constance, who had listened to our conversation in silence, and inquired for her father. She informed me that he and the rest of the family were visiting in the town, and might be expected home in a few minutes. I had hardly explained this to the skipper when I heard the governor's voice in the entry. Don Oroto was glad to see me, and said so; but he did not manifest the same pleasure at meeting Bunker.

"O, you needn't put on airs to me," cried Bunker, who noted the coolness. "I'm goin' to pay for all I take on board. My money is as good as another man's, I guess. I'm a Yankee, and know what's what"

Luckily the governor did not understand what was said, and I did not care to make more trouble between the captain and Don Oroto by interpreting the exact expressions used.

The evening passed rapidly away. The governor produced some claret and coffee, and did the honors of his house with his usual politeness. But Bunker was neglected in the general arrangement, and this he bore with commendable fortitude, until Dorothea, who seemed to have taken pity on the man's isolation, commenced a conversation with him; and this so enlivened him that I believe they managed to understand about one word in every forty which were uttered.

When we separated for the night, the secretary was sent out of the house, as his lounge was needed for the skipper; and then I found that Bunker and I were to occupy the same room, which was far from agreeable to me. I took leave of Constance with a warm pressure of her hand, and I noted that the whaler was unusually affectionate to Dorothea; and, faith, the elderly maiden seemed to like it, for her face was wreathed in smiles, and she even let the captain squeeze her hand, as though he was desirous of extracting tar from her long, lean fingers.

I went to sleep, and when I awoke, it was with a start, for I heard voices in the apartment. The lamp had gone out, and the room was pitchy dark. For a few minutes I lay perfectly still, trying to recollect where I was, and while in this state I heard a vigorous smack, which sounded like the report of a pistol; and then, before the sound died away, I was further disturbed by a scuffle which seemed to take place in the direction of Bunker's lounge. For a few seconds I listened in silent amazement, and then I heard Bunker say, —

"O, 'tain't any kind of use to try to get away from me, my little duck. I knows you love me, and I love you. Ask Pepper if I don't."

"You brute!" exclaimed the shrill-voiced Dorothea, "will you let me go? I'll scratch you unless you do."

The captain, I am glad to say, did not understand one word that she said. For a few minutes the struggle went on without a word; and then Dorothea must have lost patience, for she suddenly struck at the skipper's face. At least I judged so from what Bunker said, for he exclaimed, with some show of anger, —

"Darn it, don't scratch like an old cat!"

Before he could obtain an answer there was a renewal of the struggle, and then followed a crash, which shook the house. The lounge had capsized, and Bunker had rolled over on the floor, and in his fall had dragged down Dorothea, and the lady, in attempting to save herself, had caught at the table. The latter was overturned; consequently there was crash upon crash, and the heaviest sleeper must have been awakened by the noise. As the fight had nothing to do with me, I kept still, and heard the struggle renewed upon the floor; and, from the words which Bunker uttered, I thought that he was getting the worst of it.

"Darn it, don't scratch so!" the whaler shouted. "You is tearing my flesh all to pieces. What do you mean by coming to see a man, and acting in this way, hey?"

I heard a movement in another part of the house, and expected to see fun before long. The parties who were mixed up with the lounge, table, and lamp, paid no attention to anything but the fight. At last I saw a gleam of light, and then I thought that it was time for me to move. I left the room, and in the hall encountered the governor, his secretary of state, and Constance, the latter looking charming in her white robes, which I noticed did not reach to her feet.

"In the name of the saints, senor, what is the matter?" gasped the governor. "Are we attacked by ladrones?"

"I know not," I answered; "but there is a struggle going on in the sitting-room. I was just coming in search of you."

"Then stand by us, senor, and we will all advance in a body. Look to Constance, senor, and see that no harm comes to her. Now, then, forward, and may the saints protect us."

We moved forward, the struggle still continuing, and when we gained the door of the sitting-room, what a scene did the lights reveal! Upon the floor were Dorothea and Bunker, and around them were lying the table, lounge, oil from the lamp, books, and Constance's guitar. For one moment Don Oroto gazed at the scene before him, and then, raising his hands, exclaimed, —

"The saints be with us — in their name what is the meaning of this?"

"The brute, the monster!" cried Dorothea; and she made an attempt to rise; but unfortunately her feet touched that part of the floor which was well oiled by the broken lamp. They slipped, attempted to regain a firm hold, failed, and then the lady plunged

A Night Adventure. Page 272.

head first in the direction of Bunker, who was seated amid the ruins coolly wiping the blood from his face. She struck him on his chest, and over he went, as sudden as though shot.

I have no doubt that the captain supposed the lady was about to renew the attack, for he commenced kicking with wonderful vigor, and swearing that she did not fight fair.

"They will kill each other," cried the governor. "O, senor captain, do something. Save them, captain. I'll hold the light."

This was an important office, though not a dangerous one. I could not decline the position assigned me; consequently I moved forward, avoiding the heels of the one and the claws of the other, and soon had the satisfaction of raising Dorothea from the floor; but in her fury she supposed that I was hostile to her; consequently she aimed a blow at my nose, which I narrowly escaped, and before she could repeat it I had pinioned her arms to her side, although she made use of her feet, and kicked at my shins with great good will; and had her feet been covered with shoes, I should have suffered some.

"Coward!" she cried, "release me or I'll scratch your eyes out."

"Hold her," responded the governor. "Don't let her do more mischief."

"Stick to her, Pepper," roared Bunker. "Don't let her loose. Look at my face."

My prisoner, in a short time, came to her senses, and ceased her struggles. She began to realize her position, and to distinguish friends from foes. I must confess that I was glad of this, for holding an insane woman is not an agreeable occupation.

"Let me go," Dorothea cried. "I will keep quiet."

On this promise I released her. She made a rush for the door, but her brother stopped her.

"We want an explanation of this," he said.

"I can give none, excepting that I have been badly treated by that man;" and she pointed to Bunker, who was wiping the blood from his face, and looking far from happy.

"The wretch!" cried the governor. "He shall suffer for this insult."

"I think that he has already suffered," exclaimed Constance. "Look at his face. It is terribly scratched."

"It is," muttered Don Oroto,

"Ask aunt why she came here at this hour of the night?" continued the malicious little Constance, who seemed to enjoy the confusion.

"True, I had forgotten that important question," the governor muttered. He turned to Dorothea with a frown upon his brow. "Why are you here at this hour of the night?"

"I walked in my sleep."

"This shall be investigated," the governor said, with more energy than I had given him credit for.

"Pepper," exclaimed Bunker, who really looked pitiful, with his lacerated face, "what do they say about me?"

"Bunker," I said, "the governor is determined and resolute. He has the power and the will to punish you. He thinks you have insulted his sister. I pity you. You can choose the method of your death, however. That is a great consolation."

"I'm glad you think so," was the dry answer. "I look upon the matter in a different light. Dying ain't so very pleasant. S'pose you try it and see."

"What does the wretch say?" asked the governor. "Will he apologize for the insult that he has offered my family."

"We must first frighten him," I answered. "He is inclined to be stubborn. He says that he merely attempted to kiss the lady."

"I don't know what to do," the governor answered. "Such a thing never occurred before."

"Place a soldier at the door of the room, and keep the captain prisoner for a few days. That will be punishment enough for him," I said.

Don Oroto consented to the suggestion, and, in a few moments, a sleepy-looking soldier was standing guard over the whaleman, whose terrors were magnified by the operation; for he thought that his flirtations were likely to cost him dear.

CHAPTER XVII.

BUNKER PROMISES. — HE ESCAPES. — A REAL COQUETTE. — HE MAKES A PROPOSITION, AND IT IS AN ASTONISHING ONE.

In consequence of the few rooms which the governor's house contained, I found that, to obtain any sleep, it was necessary I should share the quarters of the prisoner; and when Bunker saw that I was about to return to the lounge, which I had occupied during the early part of the night, his delight knew no bounds. He wanted some one to talk to; consequently, no sooner had I lain down than he opened.

"What do you think they will do with me?" Bunker asked.

"It is hard to tell, but I should think you would be shot or hanged."

"Don't you imagine a feller could run for it, Pepper?"

"What do you mean? escape?" I asked.

"Yes, that's it. Can't you help me?"

"Would you leave port as soon as you gained your vessel?" I asked.

"You better believe I would. I know the way out. Let me get clear of this, and you see if I don't cut stick."

I glanced towards the sentinel. He was dozing at the door. A light was burning in our room, but I shied a hat at it and extinguished it.

"What's that for?" asked Bunker.

"Listen to me, and I'll tell you. I intend to assist you to escape, but you must promise that if we meet hereafter, you will no longer pretend that I once belonged on board your vessel. Do you consent?"

"Of course I do. Do you think I'm a fool? All I want is to get clear of this place. Catch me meddlin' with women agin! They always get a man into some scrape."

"But our duel. What is to be done with that?"

"Why, I'll apologize. It's all right. We don't want to fight each other — do we?"

"Not if you are satisfied. Now listen to me. You must

escape, or you are a dead man. The Spaniards will never forgive you. I am certain of that."

"So am I," groaned Bunker.

"You must escape by this window, and make the best of your way to the river. Take a canoe, and paddle to the ship. Get under way, and sail at once. Don't come back again. Go to some other island, and say nothing of what has happened. You understand me?"

"I should think I do," was the answer; and the next moment I saw the form of Bunker steal to the window, and drop softly to the ground. The sentinel still dozed, and took no notice of our movements.

"Good by," whispered Bunker. "I'm off. I shan't forget you in a hurry. I wish we could take a drink together."

He left me. I went to sleep, and did not awake until daylight, when I heard the sentinel utter a number of oaths at the disappearance of his prisoner. Of course I pretended to be as astonished as the soldier, and suggested that Don Oroto be informed of the escape immediately. The sentinel lighted a cigar, and then hunted for the governor. His excellency was not long in making his appearance. He rubbed his eyes, and then asked my opinion of the subject.

"I should be glad that he is gone," I said. "Had he remained, what could you have done with him?"

"True. The saints be praised that matters are no worse. He has gone, and may the devil go with him. Let us have some coffee."

When I reached the Helen I found that the Sally had sailed early in the morning, and gone no one knew where. So we now commenced taking on board cargo in earnest. It came full as fast as we wanted it, and the men worked from daylight until dark without murmuring. At last the hold was filled, and we only wanted our living freight of turtles, fowls, and pigs; and while waiting for them, Don Oroto and his daughter came on board, the former to settle the accounts, and the latter to coquet as usual, much to the disgust of Lilly, who looked upon Constance as an intruder, and one who should be expelled. For an hour or two Don Oroto, his secretary, and myself were engaged in business; but after it was settled to our mutual satisfaction, I had a chance to spend a few moments with Constance.

"I have been dying to see you," she said, as I joined her on deck, leaving the governor to empty a bottle of wine in the cabin. "I thought that you would never finish your figures. You men are so slow and tedious."

I laughed, and she continued, —

"I want to speak to you on a matter of importance."

"I am all attention."

"The fact of it is," the young lady said, casting down her eyes, "I have a strong desire to see California. You have spoken so much about it that I should like to visit it."

I was silent — too astonished to speak. What did the young lady mean? Was it a gentle method of declaring her love for me? It did look like it.

"How do you propose to go?" I asked, after a moment's silence.

"I thought," cried Constance, with a modest blush, "that I would go with you, provided you had no objections."

"But what would your father say?"

"O, he must not know it, and you must swear to me that you will not say one word to him on the subject. He would not like to part with me, I know."

I shook my head.

"I cannot wrong your father in the manner you desire. It would be an act of ingratitude too base for my nature."

"Don't I tell you that I will be responsible for all blame? I will leave word that you had nothing to do with my elopement — that you are not aware that I am on board. Will that suit you?"

"No, I confess that it will not."

The little beauty stamped her foot and paused.

"You do not love me," she said.

I smiled and remained silent.

"You are too mean to give me a passage to California!" she exclaimed. "I did not think it of you."

This touched me.

"Obtain your father's consent, and I shall be happy to give you a passage. Until then —"

"You refuse?" she asked.

"Yes."

She remained silent for a moment, and then laid her hand on

mine, and looked up with such an innocent expression in her eyes, that I felt my resolution shaken.

"Listen to me for a moment!" she exclaimed; and a blush mantled her face as she spoke. "I love you, and will follow you to the ends of the earth. If I do not leave in your vessel, I will in the next one that stops at the island. I will seek for you in California and the Sandwich Islands, and never rest until I find you. Do you think that I am in earnest now?"

I was forced to confess that she was.

"You need not know that I am on board. You may suspect it, but you must not make inquiries until out of sight of land. Do you understand?"

I managed to say "yes," but it was very faint.

"Then say not one word of this. Let me see if you can keep a secret. To show that I am in earnest, you may kiss me."

She put up her red lips, and I touched them, wondering if I was awake or dreaming.

"You love me a little — do you not?" she whispered.

I pressed her hand, but remained silent. I was thinking how I could avoid my embarrassments. She must have read my thoughts by the aid of her sharp eyes, for she said, —

"Do not deceive me. If you do, all my love will turn to hate."

"And suppose you deceive me?" I asked.

"O, there is no danger of that," she answered, with a blush, and turned away.

I had thought of sailing the next day, and wondered if I could not hurry my movements, so that I could leave before the time designated. At least the attempt should be made.

"Remember," whispered Constance, "I insist that you do not speak to me until we are out sight of land. Promise me."

I promised, but hoped that Constance would be prevented from carrying out her intentions; for with my increase of years came sober thoughts of morality and virtue, and how necessary they were to happiness.

"Come and see us again," said the governor, as the boat was ready to shove off. "You shall always be welcome."

"Padre," cried Constance, "may I go to California with the senor?"

She laughed as she spoke, and her father supposed that she was joking.

"O, yes, if he will take you."

"You see," she cried, "I have his consent;" and the boat left the side of the vessel, and pulled towards the mouth of the river.

"It can't be possible," I thought, "that Constance will carry out her threat. It would ruin her reputation and my own. I should have a row with Lilly, and what is of more importance, lose Julia forever."

In the midst of these reflections a canoe paddled alongside, and two men came on deck and walked aft, hats in hand. To my surprise, I saw that one of them was Bushy, a boat-steerer on board the Sally, and the other was Kamaka, the kanaka who had attempted to rival me as a suitor for Lilly's love.

"Beg pardon for disturbing you," cried Bushy, "but we ran away from the old Sally last night. Had enough of her, you know. Poor tub. Hope you will give us a passage somewhere."

"I will take you," I said to the American, "but as for the kanaka, I will not receive him on any account. He knows the reason why."

The tattooed rascal showed his teeth, but did not look disappointed. He was about to turn away, when, as ill luck would have it, Lilly came from the cabin without her cap, thus exposing her face and head. I saw Kamaka start, and then I knew that my secret was exposed. I ordered Lilly to the cabin, but I was too late. Like a man of the world, I should have made the most of the matter, and attempted to win the kanaka by acts of kindness; but I was young and thoughtless, and did not think of such things.

"You no want me, cap'n?" asked the kanaka.

"No."

"O, wal, me go shore. Me no want to stay here. Me find udder ships. Me see you in Honolulu. Me recollect dis."

Bushy saw that I could not be turned from my purpose. He went to the canoe, and removed his clothes; then the kanaka shoved off, and paddled for the shore. He fired a parting shot, however, which rather raked me.

"I say," the rascal cried, "you s'pose de young lady in Honolulu no hear of dis, hey? Can't love two women at the same time."

"Why did you leave the cabin?" I asked, turning to Lilly rather angrily, although the fault was not hers.

"Why did I leave my native village?" she answered, with a sigh. "If ever I return I will remain there."

I made no reply, for her words stung me to the quick. The next day, just at dusk, our live stock came on board and was taken care of, and then I was ready to sail; but unfortunately there was not a breath of wind, and I was compelled to remain at anchor until morning. This I regretted, because I feared that Constance would pay me a visit during the night; and my fears were realized, for about twelve o'clock a canoe arrived alongside, and it contained a woman and a man. The former was veiled so closely with a mantilla, that I could not see her face; and, remembering my promise, I did not try to. I escorted the lady to her state-room, she locked the door, as though fearful of importunities, and I was left in the cabin to meditate upon the foolish position in which I was placed. From my reverie I was aroused by a light hand laid upon my shoulder. I started up, expecting to see Constance; but to my surprise I saw Lilly, whom I supposed asleep.

"What does that woman want on board this vessel?" she asked, rather sternly; and I saw that all the jealousy of her nature was aroused.

"I do not know," was my reply.

"It is false; you do know. She is the young girl with the white face, and you love her."

"What nonsense you talk, Lilly!" I replied, with a forced smile. "The young lady is going to California as a passenger. I do not want to take her, but am compelled to."

The kanaka girl expressed her disgust by a look, and said not another word. I lay down on the transom, and slept until daylight, when I was called by the anchor watch, and informed that a breeze was blowing off shore, and that the pilot was at the mouth of the river, pulling in our direction. In a few minutes I was on deck, and ordered all hands called; and by the time Wilson was alongside, we had hove short.

"Are you all ready?" the pilot asked.

"Yes; say the word and we will be off."

"Sorry to lose you," Wilson cried. "You have given us life and fun. Come again when you can. Got a few things in the boat, which the governor sends you to show his good feeling. He also told me to tell you that whatever happened, you might expect his forgiveness."

I started at this information. It seemed as though he knew of the elopement of his daughter, and took this method of assuring me that I was not blamed for the part I had taken. Did Don Oroto suppose that I was in love with his child, and was he willing to trust to my honor? If such was the case, I would not disappoint him. The presents which the governor sent me consisted of sweetmeats, prepared in the highest style of art, and a few boxes of cake, of home manufacture. In return I directed that some cases of wine should be sent to Don Oroto, also a piece of silk suitable for ladies' dresses. I then made Wilson a present, and in half an hour's time we were over the reef, bounding towards California.

During the afternoon I saw Jake pass into the cabin tea and toast, and surmised whom the articles were for; although, to tell the truth, I had not given my lady passenger that attention which her merits demanded, for I had been very busy during the day.

"Steward," I asked, "how is your patient?"

"Well, cap'n, to tell de bressed truth, de woman am well, I dink, for she keep makin' signs to me to bring her more grub. She eat all de time."

I should have demanded an interview with the lady, if I had not promised that I would not speak with her until the second day out. The next morning, while at breakfast, I saw the steward enter Constance's state-room, with a substantial breakfast, and in a few moments I heard high words, and then a crash of broken dishes. I arose from the table for the purpose of ascertaining the cause of the alarm, but before I could leave it Jake plunged headlong into the cabin, his face streaming with blood, and his eyes distorted with terror.

"I radder wait upon de debil dan dat woman," he said. "Look at my face."

I did look at him, and was unable to say one word, or ask an explanation, for a few moments.

While I stood gazing at Jake, unable to comprehend the meaning of his misfortune, the negro was wiping the blood from his skinned face, and groaning at his humiliating position.

"Could it be possible," I asked myself, "that the gentle Constance would treat a human being in that manner, unless she was provoked by some great indignity?"

"Rascal!" I shouted, "you have insulted the lady in some way, or she would not have scratched you."

"So help me God," whined the steward, "I only take in 'em breakfast; and she look at it, and den at me, and den she say somethin' and fly at me. Dat's all, cap'n, on de honor of a colored gen'man."

I was compelled to believe Jake, for he never deceived me; but, to satisfy my doubts, I walked towards the state-room to ask an explanation at the hands of the lady.

"Don't you go, cap'n," Jake cried. "She treat you in de same way dat she treat me. She perfect debil wid her finger-nails."

I did not notice his remonstrance, but passed on, and was just about to lay my hand on the knob of the door, when the latter was suddenly opened, and the senorita Dorothea stood before me. The surprise was so great that I staggered back; and Jake, thinking that I was attacked, shouted, —

"Look out for de nails, cap'n, 'cos she got sharp ones."

"There is some mistake here," I murmured, speaking in Spanish. "I thought that —"

"Don't tell me what you think," cried Dorothea. "I thought when you offered me a passage on board this vessel, that I was to be treated as a lady; still it was very kind on your part to send a pressing message to me through that giddy flirt, Constance."

I did not understand her, and said so.

"O, don't blush at the generosity you displayed. You know what I mean."

Hang me if I did, but I waited for an explanation. I did not wish to commit myself.

"When Constance first spoke to me on the subject, I was inclined to doubt, for I feared a trick; but she talked fair, and I agreed to accept your terms."

"My terms?" I murmured, in astonishment.

"Of course. Shall I repeat them?"

"If you please."

"Perhaps I had better relate all the particulars. The day before you sailed, Constance informed me that she had had a long and confidential conversation with you; that I was the subject of that conversation. She had pleaded in my behalf, and after some demurring you had agreed to receive me on board as a guest, to seek Captain Myers, — whom I have seen at the governor's, and who you say is now in California, — persuade him to marry me, or, if he refused, to obtain some suitable husband. Of course I accepted such terms — why should I not?"

I groaned at the words.

"What is the matter with you?" she asked. "Are you sick?"

"No, no; go on with your romance;" for I felt that it was a romance she was relating.

"The only conditions which my niece exacted were these. I should not speak after reaching the vessel, and I should remain in my state-room until out of sight of land. She said you were firm on these points, and I consented to abide by them. I did, and here I am."

I saw in an instant the manner in which that arrant coquette, Constance, had cheated and fooled me. She had blinded me with pretensions, and I had not seen the trick. With all my smartness I had allowed a little vain Spanish girl to get the best of me. She had pretended that she was to take passage with me, and exacted certain promises the more effectually to blind me to her designs.

I will not recount in a minute manner all that I underwent at the hands of Dorothea during that dreadful passage to California. I endured much, and the recollection of it still makes me shudder. At one time the lunatic — for I could call her no less — chased me all over the deck for the purpose of clawing my face, simply because I would not allow her a cask of fresh water in which she could take a bath. At another time she threw a cup at my head because I would not praise her beauty; and when she discovered that Lilly was a girl, her rage was ferocious, and she threatened to pitch the kanaka overboard, alleging that her presence was an insult. The steward had no peace, night or day. In the middle of the night he would be called from his bed to make coffee and toast for the amiable passenger, whose appetite was never satisfied. Jake feared her, and so did I, and so did every one on board.

At last I had the satisfaction of sighting the coast mountains of California; and, upon my conscience, as soon as land was discovered, Dorothea commenced dressing, as though she was to meet her beau in a very few hours; and when she came on deck, arrayed in her best garments, she actually looked and appeared amiable, and a smile was on her lips — the first one I had seen since she drank a bottle of champagne at one sitting.

"So, this is California," Dorothea said, pointing to the coast range. "Well, provided I find a husband that will love me, I care not what kind of land it is."

She sat down upon a hen-coop, and looked towards the mountains, and did not remove her eyes from them until dinner-time. She seemed to have lost much of her former fierceness, and when Jake handed her a plate of soup, at the table, instead of scowling at the steward, she actually smiled on him, and intimated that he would be rewarded when she was comfortably settled for life.

We had made the land to the windward of San Francisco, so were compelled to run down the coast some five or ten miles before we sighted the Farrallones Islands. Steering for San Francisco were half a dozen craft; one, a new clipper ship called the Sea Ranger, the best looking specimen of marine architecture that I had ever seen at that time. She hailed from New York, and was an honor to the city. She passed within twenty fathoms of us, and I noticed that her quarter-deck was covered with passengers, most of whom saluted us by touching their caps, while several ladies waved their handkerchiefs, which was responded to by Dorothea and my crew. The ship sailed two feet to our one; so of course she passed us, and we followed in her wake, and she piloted us into the harbor. A great change had taken place since my first visit. There were two or three hundred vessels lying at anchor directly in front of the town, but most of them deserted, with the exception of one man, who acted as ship-keeper. There were crafts of all nations in the bay, but the most numerous displayed the star-spangled banner, and I can safely add that those which hoisted the best and handsomest flag the world ever saw, were the most admirable specimens of marine architecture in port. I took one hasty look at the town, while the schooner was working her way through the shipping, for the purpose of getting an inside berth. Houses had sprung up as if by magic, and extended along the sides of Telegraph Hill. All through Happy Valley were tents and wooden buildings, the latter struggling for the supremacy, but unable to crush out the blackened canvas walls.

"God help that place if a fire ever breaks out," said Bushy, the man who had escaped from the Sally. He was standing near me at the time he gave utterance to his thoughts.

I had not thought of fire, but I could not repress a shudder as I pondered over the damage which the flames would inflict if they once got under way.

We were no sooner at anchor than we were boarded by a custom-house officer, a man who looked as though he was in a hurry, and disliked trouble. When he reached the deck Dorothea rushed towards him.

"Where," she asked, in Spanish, "is Captain Myers?"

"Hullo, old lady, what's the matter with you?" cried the official, somewhat astonished at the question. He thought she was a lunatic.

I led her to the cabin, and calmed her with a few words, and then returned to the custom-house officer, who despatched his duty in a short time, and left me, with two dozen oranges in his pocket handkerchief. I learned from my visitor, however, that no vessel had arrived from the Sandwich Islands loaded with vegetables, and that fruit of all kinds was unknown in the market. This was consoling, for I feared that some of the merchants of Honolulu had got the start of me.

As soon as the sails were furled I went on shore and saw the collector, gave him an invoice of my cargo, and received a permit to land what I pleased, without delay. As soon as I had left the collector I went to the Parker House, and found that it was the same busy place that it was when I first knew it. I saw that the gambling tables had increased, and that they were loaded with coins and bars of gold, and some had silver piled a foot high, but no coin was less than a dollar. I noticed the table at which I had won so much money, but a stranger had charge of it — an American, I thought. The Chilian, he informed me, had gone to the mines some weeks before. I left the house, and walked towards the spot where I had last seen Captain Myers, the jolly whaleman, but the ground which his tent occupied was covered with a large wooden hotel; and, to my surprise, I read on the front of the building, in block letters, these words: "The Connecticut House." While I was wondering at this, I saw a red-faced man, dressed in fancy-colored clothes, saunter out of the hotel, his hat on one side of his head, his hands in his pockets, and such an air of independence in his swagger, that I was awed, and supposed the man was some great merchant, who had made a fortune, and did not care if people knew it. But as he glanced up at the front of the hotel, the hat was disarranged, and I saw his face. To my surprise I found that the flashy dressed man was no other than the one I desired to see above all others, ex-captain Joseph Myers.

It took me but a moment to cross the street and slap my old friend on the back, an act which astonished him so much that he turned round with a jerk, and narrowly escaped pitching his hat into the gutter, while the blood rushed to his face till it blazed like a meteor.

"What in the devil's name do you mean by such familiarity?" roared Myers, who did not recognize me. "Do you know me, sir?"

"I should think I did," I answered, with a smile.

He looked at me for a moment, and then grasped my hand and shook it most heartily.

"Charley Allspice, by all that is lovely! 'Gad, I'm glad to see you. Come in;" and he dragged me into the house, asking a multitude of questions at the same time.

"Dinner in number two," shouted Myers to the men who stood behind the bar, most of them busy serving out drinks to very thirsty customers.

We went up stairs and entered a room that was well furnished, and which overlooked the street.

"Here we can be quiet and undisturbed. I haven't been to dinner, and I suppose that you haven't. No matter if you have; you must dine with me. When did you arrive?" and Myers jerked the bell as though he was in a hurry. "A bottle of wine," he said to the man who answered the call. "Let it be good and cool."

Myers noted my look of astonishment, and laughed.

"I'll explain all presently. But tell me, when did you arrive?"

"Two hours since — not more."

"What have you brought?"

"Fruit and vegetables."

"Good. You are just in time. There is hardly a vegetable in the market. I shall want some of you. and will pay the current rates. If your cargo is in good condition you will make a strike."

"It is in good condition, as far as I know."

"That's right. I'm glad to hear it, for I haven't forgotten your kindness. You see me here in this house — don't you?"

"I should think that I did. Are you boarding here?"

"Yes, I am; but the proprietor never presents his bill;" and Myers laughed.

"How is that?"

"Well, to explain: I own the building, and it is paid for. Everything in the house in the way of furniture and fixings I own, and have paid for. You are surprised — ain't you?"

I confessed that I was, for it seemed strange that the man who a few months before had received a few dollars from me for the purpose of supporting himself until work was found, should now own a hotel, bar-room, gambling saloon, and all the paraphernalia connected with such an establishment. It was strange, and for a moment I thought that the whaler was deceiving me.

"No wonder you look astonished," Myers cried, as the dinner was brought in. "But I have made money the past three months. Would you like to learn the secret?"

I said that I would, and the whaler waited until the servant had left the room, when he continued, —

"I made money when I was under the tent, gambling and selling liquor; but that didn't suit me. I wanted more. I commenced selling land."

"Selling land!" I repeated. "I did not know that you owned any."

"Well, I didn't at one time; but, when I saw men claim house lots and sell them, I thought that I might make a few honest dollars by the operation. I commenced business in that line, and made money. Every house lot that I could find, not claimed, I pretended to own, and sold to the man who would pay the highest price."

"But was there no objection to this?" I asked.

"Of course there was. Sometimes I had a fight over a lot, but I always had a big fellow to assist me, and consequently whipped. Occasionally I would find a man who had a better right to the property than myself, and then I did the fair thing. I compromised, he paying me something for my claim. In this way money came in with a rush, and I was enabled to build this house."

"But you could give no valid title to purchasers," I urged.

"Well, I don't know about that. I gave them papers, and signed them, and I got the money. If that ain't valid, I don't know what is."

"But where are the original owners of the land?" I asked, lost in astonishment at the man's impudence.

"God only knows — I don't," piously exclaimed the whaler. "You wouldn't have me hunt around for them — would you?"

"But there will be trouble at some future time," I urged.

"This is a world of trouble," was the rejoinder. "A man can't go through it without meeting with some disagreeable things. Until that trouble occurs, my deeds are as good as another's."

"But it astonishes me to think that you can find people ready to accept of your deeds," I remarked.

"I'm as much astonished at times as you are," was the laughing answer. "But the people here are insane. They all want to make money in short order, and to do so they are willing to run some risk."

"But suppose you should be prosecuted for selling the land?" I asked.

"I don't think there's much fear of that. Before the courts are established my lots will have changed hands twenty times. I shall rely upon my old Mexican deeds if they touch me."

"Old Mexican deeds?" I asked.

"O, I have half a dozen. They were made for me, and look real ancient. They were smoked to make them appear so. I show them to my customers, and they are satisfied. If they are, I am. I've made money by the operation, and that is all I want. I'm worth over one hundred and fifty thousand dollars. Pretty good for the whaler who couldn't pay his board-bills at Honolulu. What do you think?"

I did not say that I thought his money had been obtained in a dishonest manner, for it would not have reformed Myers, or prevented his gambling.

"By the way," exclaimed Myers, "did you come direct from the Sandwich Islands?"

"No."

"No? Where from, then?"

"From the Ladrone Islands." I pronounced the words with an effort, and watched to see the effect.

"The devil! How's my old flame, Dorothea?

"She is well and handsomer than ever," I remarked. "She often spoke of you, and always with a sigh. She must have loved you very dearly."

"Gammon!" he exclaimed. "She loved nothing unless it was her dinner. You can't play that on me, you know."

It was quite evident that the whaler had an increased idea of his own importance since his acquisition of wealth, and although there were not fifty women in San Francisco, yet I very much doubted if Myers would not prefer to wait for an importation instead of accepting the stock which I had on hand.

"Come," cried the whaler, ringing for a second bottle of wine, "tell me how you passed your time at the Ladrones. You saw Wilson, the governor, and —"

"Dorothea," I added.

The captain laughed. "Is she married?" he asked.

"I don't think that she will ever marry unless you offer her your hand," I said.

The wretch laughed in my face. "I can't go to the Ladrones for a wife. It wouldn't pay. I can't leave my business. My lots must be looked after. It is only yesterday that I seized six on Montgomery Street. They are too valuable to be neglected. No, Dorothea must come to me, if she wants a husband."

"My dear friend," I exclaimed, seizing his hand and pressing it, "I am glad to hear you speak thus. Dorothea is here. She still loves you, and desires to become your wife. Don't speak,"—for I saw that the whaler desired to roar out an oath. "Don't thank me," I continued. "It was on your account that I took the trouble. You don't know how she has thought of a joyous meeting. But you must see her at once."

"I'll be hanged if I do, and that's plump," was the reply. "I don't want her. I didn't tell you to bring her — did I? I ain't going to thank you; not much."

I emptied my wine-glass and arose from the table with a grave face and a sinking heart. I saw that it was necessary I should change my plans.

"I must leave you," I said. "I must return to the Helen, and crush a timid heart with the news which I offer. She will feel the blow keenly, but she will bear up under it, I think. It may kill her; but I trust not."

"O, gammon! you don't mean it, Allspice!" cried the whaler.

"Where does Hatch do business at the present time?" I asked. "I must ask his advice. He can find a home for the lady."

"Damn it, Allspice, apply to a moral man for help," cried Myers. "You know he's the devil among the girls."

"I will see him, at any rate. Since you reject her, I must look in another quarter."

"You are not going, Allspice?"

"Yes; I must. Dorothea will be anxious to hear from you. She is all impatience. But I must crush her hopes. You say that Hatch is on Montgomery Street — do you?"

"Yes; but don't go near him. You know what a loose sort of a fellow he is. Where is the vessel lying?"

"Off Clark's Point. Come on board and see me. I'll give you a dish of fruit and a glass of wine."

"How long before you will be on board?" asked Myers.

"In an hour's time."

"I'll be there."

I left the whaler to search for Hatch, whose commission store was on Montgomery Street. I had no difficulty in finding him. I entered, and saw Hatch looking over his books at the desk, a cigar in his mouth, a black bottle and tumblers near his elbow. He did not notice me till I slapped him on the back. He turned round with an oath upon his lips; but the instant he caught sight of my face, he dropped the pen which he held in his hand, and reached towards the whiskey bottle.

"Charley," he said, "where did you come from?"

I told him in a few words; but long before I had finished he had thrust a glass of whiskey in my hand, and was taking his own share without the slightest difficulty. I related how I had received Dorothea on board, but I did not mention that Constance had tricked me. I told him that it was important she should have a husband, so that I could be relieved of her presence, and concluded by stating that I needed his assistance in convincing Myers that it was wrong on his part to slight such devotion and love. Hatch listened attentively, and comprehended my meaning at once. He closed his books and put them away, and then took another drink.

"I see that I must go on board with you and meet this woman face to face," he said. "I'll bring it about; although, since Myers has made money, he has grown quite pompous."

"And how is your business?" I asked.

"Fair; although I have not yet received a single consignment from Honolulu. Vessels are scarce, I suppose."

"Can you leave your business?" I asked, as we prepared to quit the store.

"O, yes; my man will look out for it. But, see here, you want to sell your cargo — don't you?"

"Certainly; as soon as possible."

"Then come with me to the office of the Alta Californian. You must advertise it. People will know what you have for sale, and where to find you."

After transacting business at the office of the paper, we walked to Clark's Point, where Will was waiting in a boat for my return. We pushed off, and soon reached the Helen, and the first person to welcome my arrival was Dorothea.

"Have you seen him?" she asked, after one sharp glance at Hatch.

"I have."

"And did he seem glad to hear of my arrival?"

"O, yes."

"Who is this man who came on board with you?" she asked.

"A friend of mine."

"Married?"

"No; single."

Dorothea remained silent for a moment, and then she said, —

"I am not particular about the whaler if you know of any other moral man who will treat me kindly. This senor is good looking. Is he a Catholic?"

"No."

I answered her rather short, for I began to think that she would trouble me for life.

"Well, I don't care much. Let me talk with him. The more I see of him the more I like him."

I had to introduce them, but I cautioned Hatch of the danger he was in; the fellow was delighted, and began to appear as fascinating as possible. The hint which I had conveyed to him was sufficient to inflate his vanity, and, man-like, he desired to stand well in the estimation of the first woman he had spoken to for some months. Dorothea could speak a few words in English, and Hatch knew a little Spanish; so they began to converse, and at last I saw that Hatch was holding one of the spinster's hands, to which she made no objection. While I was walking the deck, and wishing that Hatch was compelled to marry the woman as a punishment for his sins, I saw a shore boat approaching, and in it Myers. Instantly I ran to Dorothea, and informed her of the circumstance. She waved her hand, and said, —

"I am engaged, sir, and don't wish to be disturbed."

"But your intended husband is within a few fathoms of the vessel."

"Sir," she exclaimed, rising to her feet, and confronting me with flashing eyes and contracting fingers, "I was not aware that I was pledged in marriage to any one; and, if you insult me again, I shall call upon this gentleman to protect me."

I left the spooning couple, and hurried to meet Myers, who came over the gangway in such a dignified manner that I knew he was determined to refuse the hand of Donna Dorothea.

"Well," he asked, "where is the woman who wants to see me? Where is the woman who is desirous of owning my name? Pass her out, and see if I don't euchre her."

"The lady is busy at the present time," I said. "In a few moments she will be at leisure. Don't be in a hurry. You have all the evening before you."

I pointed to the quarter-deck, where Hatch and Dorothea were seated; and the sight, to my intense delight, seemed to rouse the jealousy of Myers. I could see it in his eyes and face.

"I thought the woman came here to marry me?" he asked.

"And so she did, but you must recollect that you refused her no longer than two hours since. You have lost a prize, Myers, and I don't blame you for feeling as you do. Just look at the lady, and see how handsome she is."

Myers looked long and earnestly at the amiable and gushing female who was talking to Hatch. I saw that she was making an impression on the hard-hearted whaler, and if Hatch had been out of the way, I think that I could have made a bargain without delay.

"This thing must not go on," cried the whaler, with energy. "That woman belongs to me. You brought her for me. I'll pay her passage. Name the price."

"We will talk of that some other time. The man who wins that treasure must pay her passage. I hope you will be the one. But come, I'll present you."

"I'll punch that fellow's head," muttered the whaler, as we walked aft.

"No violence," I whispered. "The lady is opposed to anything of the kind."

By this time we had reached the parties who were playing the agreeable on the quarter-deck. Dorothea looked up, blushed, and then arose and extended her hand, which the whaler pounced upon and kissed with all the ardor of a sailor. Dorothea modestly withdrew her hand from the grasp of Myers, and then looked at Hatch, as though wondering what he thought of the matter.

"Come, Hatch," I said, "I wish to speak to you."

The rascal made a grimace, but accepted the invitation, and entered the cabin with me. Just as we were seated at the table, and Jake was about to place some fruit before us, we heard a shriek, and I knew that Dorothea's lungs were exercised. We hurried on deck to discover the cause. While I tore up the steps, with Sam close to my heels, I am fearful that I uttered several adjectives, and thanked God that all women were not like Dorothea; for usually a woman is perfectly contented if she can have one person of the masculine gender to love.

On reaching the deck I found Dorothea and Myers facing each other, the countenance of the former exhibiting signs of intense passion, while the latter looked extremely foolish, and appeared undecided what to say.

"I have been insulted," cried Dorothea in Spanish. "That man has insulted me."

She pointed to Myers, who actually blushed.

"How happens it that you have insulted this woman?" I asked, turning to Myers, and pretending that I was really angry.

"I only offered to kiss her. Does she call that insulting?"

"I am surprised at your conduct," I remarked. "The lady keeps her lips for her husband."

"Then let her marry me at once. I'm good for it. She knows me. I made love to her before to-day."

"Then wait for a moment, or until I talk with the lady."

I led Dorothea into the cabin, and took a seat near her.

"Now," said I, "here is an opportunity for you to marry. What you have wished for is likely to occur."

To my surprise and consternation, she immediately arose and faced me.

"I will not listen to such language," Dorothea said. "It is insulting."

"Did you not visit California for the sake of procuring a husband?" I asked.

"No, sir; I came to see the country. I am satisfied where I am, at present."

"What will you do?" I asked, after a moment's pause.

"I'll marry the young man," the artless maiden replied. "I like him best."

"But he is not as rich as Myers. He has not as good a house, and he cannot feed you as well."

"Still I love the young man best," she answered, after mature reflection. "I had rather have him."

"He won't have you," I cried, after a desperate pause.

It was lucky for me that I jumped as I did. An instant later and I should have been clawed most unmercifully, for the woman struck with her talons, like an eagle making a swoop for a lamb. She missed me, and then rolled on the floor.

"God help the män who marries you," I thought, as I stood her on her feet.

"You want Mr. Hatch for a husband," I said. "He is not suitable for you. He is too fickle. He would not stay at home nights."

"I'd make him," she said, with a grim smile.

"He would not give you half enough to eat," I continued.

"Then he should starve with me."

As a last resort I exclaimed, —

"The senor Hatch can't marry you, and he won't. Do you understand that? The captain is the only person in California who is anxious to wed. Do you want him? Yes or no."

"Yes," she answered, quite promptly. "I'll take him, under the circumstances. But I'd rather have the other."

I hastened on deck to communicate the good news to Myers, and found to my disgust that the whaler had tired of waiting for me, and gone on shore in company with Hatch. This last blow was too much for me. I instantly retired to the cabin, and drank several cups of tea, and was about to light a cigar for consolation, when Dorothea asked,

"Where is my husband?"

"Gone on shore," I said, almost fiercely, for I was reckless.

"And who sent him there? Did you? Is this one of your tricks for the purpose of keeping me on board? Am I to have no husband, after all?"

Just at this moment, Lilly, who sympathized with me in my terrible misfortunes, placed an arm around my neck, and the act aroused all the fury of the Spanish girl's nature. She flew at the kanaka, tore out a handful of hair, and was about to scratch her face, when I interfered, and on the instant determined to rid the vessel of such a curse.

"In fifteen minutes," I said, addressing Dorothea, "you go on shore, and shall never return. I have seen enough of you to last me a lifetime. Get ready, for go you shall."

To my surprise she made not the least objection. She arrayed herself in her best, and entered the boat with me. We were pulled on shore, and the instant we reached it, I steered for the whaler's establishment. Of course the appearance of a woman in the streets of San Francisco was the signal for an intense excitement, and we were followed to the doors of the hotel by merchants, gamblers, and miners, all eager to see Dorothea's face, and to learn if she was in the market. Of course the lady noticed the crowd.

"What do these people want?" she asked, as I hurried her through Montgomery Street.

"They think you are a Mexican," I replied, "and they dislike the Mexicans."

We entered the hotel and rushed up stairs. I entered the room where I had dined a few hours before, and sent a waiter to find the landlord. In a few minutes Myers stood before me, looking surprised and embarrassed.

"Do you want the lady for your wife, or not? Sharp is the word," I said.

Myers hesitated.

"Then you reject her. Just as you please. Come, Dorothea, you shall find a husband more worthy of you than the captain."

As I moved towards the door, Myers asked, —

"You couldn't let a feller take her on trial — could you?"

"No, sir," I exclaimed, indignantly. "She is too good for such bargaining as that."

"I'll take her," he said. "Don't leave the room. Send for a minister. Send for half a dozen of them. I'll go it blind. We'll be married now."

As soon as the vows were recorded, I breathed a sigh of relief, and congratulated the married couple so heartily that Myers began to think he was a fortunate man, and in a short time the champagne corks commenced to fly, and a jolly crowd soon got uproariously wild at the expense of the captain. With the consciousness of having done a good deed, I retired to my vessel, and dreamed of Julia, who, I thought, was anticipating my return to Honolulu with all the happiness of a pure spirit and a confiding disposition; and while I was making preparations to be married, and was debating about the style of coat I would wear, Will awakened me with the information that it was near sunrise, and that three persons were on deck to see me. I found that two of the men were parties who had purchased provisions of me on my first visit to California. Of course I was glad to see them, and they expressed pleasure at meeting me.

"What have you got to sell?" they asked.

I named over the principal articles, and after I had concluded, I astonished them by an invitation to breakfast.

"We came to trade, not to eat," one of them said.

"And can't you buy after you have eaten, just as well as before?"

"But some other customers may come off while we are eating," they said.

"But I pledge you my word that I will not listen to them until you have made your offers," I replied.

"O," they answered, "that is fair. We will eat on those conditions;" and they followed me to the cabin, and were delighted at the repast set before them.

At the time the firm of Smith, Melvin & Brown traded with me, on the morning of which I write, the house was prosperous, and its word was as good as its bond; therefore I awaited the moment when it was ready to make a bid for my cargo, with some anxiety, for I knew that I should have no trouble respecting payment. As soon, therefore, as breakfast was finished, the notebooks were brought into requisition, and the figuring commenced with much earnestness.

"Let us see a specimen of your yams," said Smith, after a short consultation with his colleagues.

I had a lot on deck, and showed it with some pleasure, for the yams were really good.

"How many bushels have you?" was the next question.

"One thousand, more or less."

"We will give you ten dollars per bushel, and take the lot, delivered alongside," Smith said.

I had paid twenty-five cents per bushel at the island of Gugam.

"How many sweet potatoes have you?" asked Smith, as soon as the first trade had been concluded.

"Five hundred bushels."

"We will take them at five dollars a bushel. Recollect they won't keep like yams."

"They are yours," I answered.

But I will not relate all the transactions of the morning. It will be sufficient if I state that I sold ten thousand lemons at ten dollars per hundred, for which I paid ten cents per hundred; the fifty thousand oranges at twelve dollars per hundred, for which I paid twenty cents per hundred, and a hundred dozen fowls at twelve dollars per dozen. I sold the latter rather cheap because I was anxious to clear the deck and get rid of them; chickens not flourishing well on shipboard. After I had disposed of the chickens, I sold the pigs and the turtles, and I must acknowledge that I did well with the two last ventures. I had one hundred turtles and fifty pigs. I received fifty dollars each for the turtles, and twenty-five dollars each for the pigs; and when the bargains were completed, I found that I had disposed of cargo enough to amount to near thirty thousand dollars, besides having on hand eight barrels of lime juice, and ten thousand limes, and other articles of less amount, but which I knew I could sell at a moment's notice; and as Smith was not disposed to pay me what I considered a fair price, I determined to hold on to them for an advance; and it was well that I did so, for the next day I sold the lime juice at the rate of ten dollars per gallon, and there were thirty-six gallons in each barrel. By eight o'clock launches came alongside, and we commenced discharging cargo without delay. I sent Will on shore to convey my respects to the happy husband, and he returned with the information that Captain Myers was not visible. I laughed, and thought no more of the matter; but about twelve o'clock a boat came alongside, and a man wearing a felt hat drawn over his face, almost concealing it, stepped on deck. The stranger was so muffled with a blanket, worn in the same manner as Mexicans wear their *ponchos*, that I thought my visitor was one of that race. He did not speak, but beckoned me with his hand, and then passed into the cabin, as though he was well acquainted on board.

"Go and see what the man wants," I said to Jake.

The steward followed the man into the cabin, and was gone but a few minutes, and then returned, a grin upon his face, and his mouth stretched from ear to ear.

"What does he want?" I asked.

"He wants to see you, sar," was the answer; and then the negro went forward, laughing as though he had discovered a good joke.

I went into the cabin, and saw the visitor seated at the table, a glass of grog before him; but his hat was still on his head, and the blanket muffled the lower part of his face. It instantly flashed upon me that some treachery was meant, and I placed my hand upon my revolver, and drew it from my breast pocket. But at this sign of defence the visitor did not move.

"What do you want of me?" I asked, after a moment's silence, still keeping my revolver in my hand, to guard against surprise.

The stranger did not answer. He still looked at his liquor, and shook his head, and I heard a deep sigh, as though there was some internal trouble.

"Who are you, and what do you want?" I asked. "Speak, or go to the devil."

The stranger groaned, and sat still for a moment, then slowly arose from the table. He unwound the blanket from his neck, and then removed his slouched hat, and before me stood Captain Myers, his face as raw as though it had been skinned.

I comprehended all in a moment. I dropped my revolver, and sank upon the transom, powerless to utter one word. I could but gaze upon that mangled face, and ask if I was not dreaming. Alas! I feared not. By a desperate effort I was enabled to arouse my scattered senses, I staggered to the table, and mechanically seized the glass of liquor which had so long been untouched. I threw back my head, and the spirit disappeared. This revived me.

"Myers," I said, "speak to me. What is the meaning of this frightful appearance?"

The wretched man arose, and, without a word, walked to my liquor case. He selected a bottle of brandy, and placed it upon the table, and then filled a glass from the bottle and drank its contents without speaking. After that operation he sighed and looked at me, and shook his head in a mysterious manner. While I was watching his motions, his right arm was raised in a threatening manner, and with his fore-finger pointing to his face, he said, —

"Do you see this?"

"Yes; how happened it?"

The wretched man laughed in an hysterical manner as he answered, —

"She."

"Who?"

"The wife of my bosom, and be hanged to you."

He once more clutched the brandy bottle, while I fell back upon the transom, my worst fears realized, and wondering if I should have to take Dorothea back after having warranted her.

CHAPTER XVIII.

POOR MYERS AND HIS WIFE. — HER OBJECTIONS. — RECONCILIATION. — LETTERS FROM HOME. — A SAN FRANCISCO FIRE.

For a few minutes after I had learned the worst, the whaler and I sat glaring at each other, hardly knowing whether we should quarrel, or explain matters. Luckily the brandy, which was good, had a soothing influence upon Myers — so much so that his eyes lost their fierceness, and had not the scratches upon his face been so livid, I should have anticipated a good story, or an attempt at a song.

"What do you think of it?" asked the whaler, at length.

"I don't know. Tell me how it happened."

The whaler smiled in a sarcastic manner.

"She did it," he said.

"For what reason?" I asked.

"She says," continued Myers, slowly and distinctly, "that we're not married strong enough. She wants a priest to marry us. She says I'm spliced, but she's not. What kind of an argument do you call that, hey?"

"Tell me all about the subject, and then I can judge if she is right or wrong."

Myers attempted to blush, but the effort was a failure.

"I guess I won't tell all," he said; "but after you had gone, and my friends had gone, and the house was quiet, I told the old woman that she'd better retire; but she didn't seem to understand me, and at last I took her in my arms, and — Well, it's no matter about all the particulars, but here I am, with a scratched face and —"

"Why didn't you coax her?" I asked.

"Coax the devil!" was the ungallant exclamation.

"What did you do?"

"I didn't do anything. I swore a little, and then she took one room and I took another. What am I to do?"

"We must find a Catholic priest," I said, "and have you married in ship-shape."

"Well," muttered Myers, with some show of resignation, "you got me into the breakers, and now you must get me out. Go and see the woman, and tell her that I'll dress her like a queen, if she'll only keep her finger nails still, and treat me like a husband. Do you understand?"

"Of course I do. I'll go."

"And I'll stay here until you return."

I went on deck, and saw that I could leave the vessel for a short time; so rowed ashore, and paid a visit to Dorothea. I found the lady sulking and looking miserable.

"Your husband is deeply grieved at your conduct," I said, "and will take measures to obtain a divorce. I suppose that you are aware that a divorced woman cannot marry a second time."

"Should I be compelled to live single as long as I remained in the country?" Dorothea asked.

"Of course."

She started up immediately.

"Let me see my husband, and ask his pardon for what has occurred. Take me to him."

"Will you promise to treat him well? Remember he feels grieved at your course."

"He is my husband, and the only one that I can have. Of course I will respect and love him."

"Come with me," I said, delighted at the success of my mission.

"I have interested myself to make you happy, but this shall be the last time. Remember that. You have a husband who has money, and he will dress you like a queen; but he won't stand any more nonsense."

We passed through the streets, and reached the water, and in a few minutes were on board. I led her into the cabin, where Myers was seated.

"Here is your wife," I said. "She is sorry for what has occurred. Forgive her if you can, and love her as much as she deserves."

"O, my husband!" cried the Spanish woman, and rushed towards him.

The whaler opened his arms, and she fell into them. The scene was so affecting that I did not care to remain in the cabin, fearful that I should laugh. Lilly and I went on deck.

"What a fool that woman is!" cried Lilly, as we reached the deck. "She don't deserve a husband."

"Hush, child," I replied. "We must be thankful that she has obtained one. All women are entitled to husbands."

"All but me," was the answer; and the kanaka girl turned from me and walked aft.

We did not disturb the married couple; so they remained in the cabin until dinner time. Then they took their seats at the table, and seemed quite cheerful. Dorothea appeared to manifest some affection for her husband, and actually smiled on him, while Myers, if his face had not been scratched, would have looked happy. Of course I encouraged them to remain so, and when they left the vessel at night for their hotel, they were like two doves, billing and cooing, and acting as silly as most couples just united.

The next day we continued to discharge our cargo, and made good progress; and towards night I went on shore, and paid a visit to the post office, to see if there were any letters for me from my parents; although I did not much expect there were. I found that the office was located in a wooden building on the hill, and that there were but two delivery windows; each of these was besieged by two long lines of men, and a rougher looking set was rarely seen. I saw that I should have to wait for two hours before I could get a sight at the window, and the prospect discouraged me. While I was reflecting as to what I should do, a fellow near the window shouted, —

"Mister, you want to buy my chance?"

"Chance for what?" I asked, seeing that the conversation was directed towards me.

"Why, to get a letter, of course. I'll sell you my position."

"How much do you ask?"

"Five dollars. Speak quick, for I am almost to the window."

A dozen voices cried, "I'll give you one dollar," "Half a dollar," "Two dollars," "Two dollars and a half," &c., &c.; but the fellow was firm, and would not abate a dollar of his charges. As time was an object to me, I gave the man five dollars, and took his place; and, with the remark that he had made "thirty dollars that day," the fellow fell back to the rear for the purpose of once more getting near the window, and selling out before dark. When I had obtained my letters I hurried on board for the purpose of reading them. The first one which I looked at was from my mother, my dear mother, who loved me so well that she never allowed a wish of mine to go ungratified. It was a long letter, four pages, and filled with regrets at the absence of her darling son. But she did not complain. She thought that if I was satisfied, and doing well, I had better remain. She had received letters from Mr. Cherington, my partner, and in them he spoke in the highest terms of my industry, moral character, and all that tends to make a man great and good. She was overjoyed at hearing such nice accounts of me, and Miss Fairchild, who was visiting her when the letters were received, also expressed much gratification at my success, and sent her best wishes for my future prosperity. How the name of Jenny Fairchild thrilled me! I wondered if the little beauty thought of me; and then I began to speculate as to how it happened that she was visiting my family, when I knew that her father was proud and aristocratic, and had always looked upon my father as several degrees removed from his circle. I could not solve the problem; so I laid down my mother's letter, and took up my father's. It commenced, as usual, remarkably blunt. He wrote, —

"MY DEAR BOY: I'm proud of you. You are a chip of the old block. You are making money, and so am I. We are both doing well, and I hope will continue to. Be careful in your speculations. Look well before you leap; I always do. My position as alderman has given me some nice contracts, through a third party, and I shall clear this year one hundred thousand dollars aside from my business in the grocery line. I'm worth fifty thousand dollars more than Fairchild, and this fact makes him quite polite. He and his family now call on us and spend the day. I've bought a house on Beacon Street, and paid fifty thousand dollars for it, all cash, and it is one of the best bargains I ever made. I have furnished it throughout in style, silver plate, and all such kind of nonsense; and I tell you, Charles, we can cut as big a dash as any of them. Your mother don't like it; but I tell her she must be as fashionable as any of her neighbors, and she tries to, but I don't think she's got impudence enough for the position. I have a carriage and span of horses, and your mother and I make calls when I have nothing else to do. I don't like it, though, for it is rather tiresome work. I sold our old house to the city, and got my price; nearly enough to pay for my new residence. The city wanted to cut a street through the court, and of course it needed my land, and it had to pay for it. That is the advantage of being an alderman. I said that it was a homestead, and my feelings must be respected. The board respected them by giving me just twice what the property was worth. So, you see, I'm doing well, and I am pleased to know that you are succeeding. The money you sent arrived safe, and I have invested all of it in your name in real estate, and will look after it until your return. I have been elected president of the Stout Man's Bank, and own a large portion of the stock. You see that I am looking up in the world. I think that next year I shall be elected mayor of the city, although there is one talkative fellow who is trying to get the start of me; he is lecturing for the purpose of bringing himself into public notice. I don't think that he will succeed. I am pleased to know that you and Cherington are making money, and that you have struck the California trade in the right time. Mind and leave it in the *right time*, or you'll burn your fingers. Our folks overdo everything, and they will rush goods to California until the state is flooded. A dozen vessels are fitting out at Boston, and they are loaded with an awful quantity of trash. Some one will lose money. It won't be me, for I don't trust to that trade. Be careful, my dear boy, and mind how you speculate. Any surplus money that you may have, send to me, unless you can invest to better advantage in Honolulu, or San Francisco. If you want to come home before you have made a fortune; don't be ashamed to do so, for you shall be welcomed with open arms. Your mother is a little nervous about you, but I'm not afraid to trust you. You have got some of my common sense and business tact. I can't think of anything else to write at the present time; so I must close. Let me hear from you often. I have written to Cherington about business, and you and he will find it satisfactory. Fairchild sends his regards, and says that Jenny often speaks of you."

It was a long time before I could compose my mind sufficiently to retire and sleep, and then I dreamed of home, of Jenny, Julia, Lilly, and that treacherous rascal, the kanaka, Kamaka, who, I thought, was to cause me some trouble. I was glad when daylight appeared, so that I could finish discharging cargo; and after that was done I received my pay in gold coin and dust, and then felt as though I could rest for a few days, and let my men have a run on shore. For a wonder, none of the crew desired to leave me. Even Bushy, the boat-steerer, said he would like to remain if I would pay him the same wages and percentage that the others received, which I agreed to do, for the man was faithful and honest, and I needed his services. I advanced Will three hundred dollars, which he sent home to his mother in New Bedford; and the delight which the boy experienced by this good act was participated in by me.

The second night after the vessel was discharged, I was awakened by the anchor-watch, and informed that a terrible fire was raging in San Francisco. I dressed and went on deck, and found that the business portion of the town was in flames, and that they threatened to make a clean sweep of every house and store near the edge of the bay. We could hear an immense amount of shouting on the part of some men; but no efforts could save a building after it was once on fire, owing to its inflammable nature. Desirous of rendering such assistance as I was able, I took Will and Bushy and pulled ashore in the boat, landing at Clark's Point.

We stood for a moment upon the bluff to watch the progress of the flames. They were sweeping down Montgomery Street, gathering force every moment, under the influence of a stiff breeze from the north.

"What shall we do, sir?" asked Bushy, who had watched the progress of the flames with impatience, thinking what splendid pickings were to be found in the streets.

"Go and render what help you can, and in what manner you please;" I replied, and the whaleman and Will started for the scene of the fire, and were soon lost in the crowd.

In a few minutes I followed them, but at the corner of Montgomery Street my progress was checked by the fire. I entered the lines and passed water for a short time, but soon saw that it was useless work, and then turned my attention to saving property. I entered several stores, and threw goods into the street, where they were trampled in the mud, or else carried off by those who were not entitled to them. Finally I tired of such business, and stood looking at the flames as they fastened upon a two-story building, which, I judged by the sign, was occupied by a German, as it bore the name of Wismer. There was no hope for the store after the fire reached it, and I was mentally calculating how long it would be in consuming, when I was startled by seeing a man at the upper window, and hearing him shout, —

"For de love of Moshes, save me, shentlemen. I gibs all I's worth if you saves me, good peoples."

"Jump, you fool," roared some of the men, who were inclined to laugh at the unfortunate man.

"Ah, I can't shump, shentlemen," was the answer. "I's lame."

The flames had caught the roof, and the room in which the German stood was filled with smoke, which was pouring out of the windows in volumes, so that I really feared the man would be smothered before help could reach him.

"Save me, shentlemen," he cried; "save me, for de love of Moshes."

"There ain't no Moshes here, old feller," yelled one of the crowd; "and if there was he wouldn't save you."

But the German continued to repeat his cry, and waved his hands in a frantic manner; and when he saw that no efforts were made to save him, he tore his hair and beat his breast; and then was lost to view in the dense smoke which poured out of the windows.

"He's a goner," muttered a fellow who stood near me.

"Well, he's only a Jew, anyhow," was the response of a ruffian who the next instant shouldered a box of tobacco, and walked off with it.

I saw at a glance that the flames would reach the German in a few minutes, even if he was not already suffocated by the smoke. I thought for a moment, and considered that the chances were good for a man to enter the building and make an attempt to save the old fellow, and with the thought came a resolution to attempt the rescue. As I entered the store, I saw a flight of stairs that led to the second story, and up these I ran as fast as possible, encountering smoke at every step, and it grew more dense the higher I ascended. I could hear the flames roar, and I could feel the heat as I reached the second story, and I paused a moment to get a breath of fresh air at the windows. It revived me, and then I crawled on my knees in the direction which I supposed the stairs leading to the story above to be.

When I reached the head of the stairs I found a door; but it was open, and the flames were already at work in the apartment. The roof was nearly consumed, and the fire was hotter than was desirable; but I did not meet with so much smoke, as it had an opportunity to soar heavenward. I heard the roaring of the flames and the shouts of the people, and every second or two a crash, as though heavy beams were falling. Even around my head pieces of timber were tumbling; but I had escaped thus far any serious injuries, although my hands were slightly burned by coming in contact with a board which was like a living coal. I glanced around the room in which I was in, and saw nothing of the German; but on approaching the windows overlooking the street, saw a bed spread on the floor; and upon the bed, which, by the way, was on fire, saw the form of the man I was in search of. His clothes were burned, and his face was blackened by smoke, and his long, white hair was singed, and for a moment I thought that I had arrived too late, and that the man was dead; but as I extinguished the fire upon his breast, saw that he still breathed.

There was no time to lose if I desired to reach the street alive, for the roof of the building was all in flames, and the tin with which it was covered was melting fast and running down in streams, several drops of the fiery liquid touching my clothes and flesh, and burning them so rapidly that the pain made me think of flight without stopping to care for the German. I extinguished the fire which was consuming my clothes, and then caught the man in my arms and rushed down stairs, staggering and struggling with my burden, and fearful, after all my exertions, that I should lose him, for the smoke was dense, and I could not see which way I was moving. Just as I thought I should drop, I felt a breath of fresh air, and found that I was near one of the windows on the second flight. For one moment I rested there; and that brief time enabled me to gather my strength, and carry my burden down the next flight of stairs; and exhausted and nearly suffocated I staggered into the street, but my appearance was greeted with tremendous cheers from the very men who had a few minutes before declined to render aid. After treatment the German opened his eyes and looked around.

"Shentlemen, how comes it dat I is saved? I vos in de store, and de flames roars around me, and I dink dat I am dead; and holy Moshes, how hot it vos!"

"This feller risked his life for yourn," said a man, laying his hand on my shoulder.

The German looked at me with his large black eyes, and seemed to reflect upon the service I had rendered him. He laid his hand softly upon mine, and murmured, —

"I's a poor Jew, and haven't got any money to reward you for dis. My property is all gone; de flames eat 'em up, and de old man is very poor."

"Don't let that distress you," I said, for the old one had meekly kissed my hand, and I felt sorry for his misfortunes.

"Have you any friends in this place?" I asked of the German.

"Vot for you ask dat?" he said, with a suspicious glance, and an attempt to re-arrange his clothes around his waist.

"I ask you because it is necessary that some one should take care of you. You need your wounds dressed, and medicine, and careful attendance."

"Dat vill cost monish," he said.

"Yes."

"Ah, I have no monish. I is a poor man now. De fire take all."

"I will see that you are taken care of," I remarked. "You shall go with me, and I will look after you."

"Vidout pay?"

"Yes, without pay."

"You is a very good young man, and I is much obliged to you. But I has no monish, you know."

Just at that moment I saw Will and Bushy staggering towards the boat under a load of silks, and I called to them.

"We have made a raise, cap'n," said Bushy. "We found a store goin' for it, and the owner told us to go in and get what we wanted; and we did."

"I've got as much as I can carry," cried Will.

"You are sure that you have made no mistake," I remarked.

"Of course not, cap'n. We wouldn't steal."

"Well, take the silk to the boat, and then come back and help me carry this poor man on board. Be lively, for he needs attendance."

The two men staggered off under their loads of silk, and I waited by the side of the German until they returned. Then Bushy took my patient in his arms, and carried him to the boat, and while on the way, the Jew exclaimed, every few moments, "I've no monish, you know!"

"I am aware of it," I answered.

"And you takes me with no monish?"

"Yes."

"Ah, you is one kind shentleman; but I has no monish, you know."

We got the man on board, and I had him carried to the cabin. After preparing a berth in a state-room, I helped the old man in, and closed the door, leaving him to undress at his leisure. No sooner had I left the room than I heard the German lock the door, as though he feared we would intrude upon him while taking off his clothes.

"I tell you what it is, sir," cried Bushy, in a hoarse whisper; "that man is a woman."

"What makes you think so?"

"Shyness, sir," was the answer. "Men don't act in that way."

"And women don't wear beards."

This rather staggered Bushy; but he rallied after a while.

"Some of 'em does, sir. I've seen 'em."

We were interrupted by a groan; and then the cries of the German alarmed us.

"O, Moshes," he said; "I is suffering like de divil. Mine flesh is all burned off. O, vot shall I do?"

"Do you want help?" I asked.

"Yes, I must have some help, young man, for mine flesh is burned off."

"Then open the door."

"You will not look at me?" he said.

"No."

"Den come in."

Busby followed me into the state-room; but the German did not like his looks, for he whispered, —

"Send him away, mine friend. Don't let him stop here."

I humored the old man by telling Busby that he had better go on shore, and bring off a doctor.

It was daylight when Busby and Will returned with a physician, whom they found after much trouble. The man was from the New England States, and, although he had been in San Francisco but a short time, yet was fast making money by his practice. He examined the German's injuries, and prescribed for them, commended what I had done, and then put on his hat, and announced that he was in the habit of being paid every time he visited. It was his only safety, he said. To this the Jew listened with much interest, but said not a word until I asked, —

"How much is your fee, doctor?"

"Two ounces," was the reply.

"Holy Moshes," cried the German; "only dink of dat. I has no monish."

"Then who is to pay me?" demanded the doctor; and he looked black.

"I will. Here is your money;" and I handed him two ounces, which he slipped into his pocket in a hurry.

"A good young man," muttered the German. "Vot a pity I has no monish!"

I followed the doctor on deck.

"What do you think of your patient?" I asked.

The physician shook his head.

"He can't live many days, even with the best of attendance. I will call as often as you want me to, but I can do no good. Good day. Shocking fire. Many people injured, I hear. We should have a hospital, where such cases can be treated. Let the patient drink lemonade;" and with these words the doctor was off.

I returned to the cabin, and looked at the patient. He was awake, and Lilly was sitting by his side. He called me to him, and putting his mouth to my ear, whispered, —

"I shall die, holy Moshes, I shall die; but I have no monish, you know."

I did not reply, for I supposed that the poor fellow spoke the truth.

Lilly promised to look after the old man for a few hours, and with this assurance I lay down, and was soon dreaming of fire and smoke, and ruin and death.

When I awoke it was near ten o'clock in the forenoon. The fire which had raged all night was nearly subdued, thanks to a sudden change of wind. A large portion of San Francisco was gone, and hundreds of its inhabitants had lost all that they were worth. Yet no one seemed dismayed or discouraged, and the mate informed me that he had visited the ruins, and found men at work upon certain parts as though buildings were to be erected immediately. After breakfast I visited the German, and found that he was suffering intense pain in the region of his breast. His voice was husky, and he breathed with difficulty; yet no sooner did he see me than he smiled and held out his burned hand, exclaiming, —

"A nice young man — but I has no monish."

"How has he rested?" I asked of Lilly.

"Very badly. He has moaned, and groaned, and talked in a tongue that I could not understand."

"Let me whisper you," the German said, motioning to me to draw near his berth. I complied with his request. "I vant de safe," he whispered.

I thought that his mind was wandering. He noticed my look, and said, —

"I vant de safe. De safe in my store. You know."

I understood him at once, and said so.

"I have papers in it, but no monish, you know. I is a poor man, but I must have de safe. Can you get 'em for me, and bring 'em on board? See, here is de key."

He took from beneath his pillow a brass key of peculiar workmanship, and handed it to me.

"You get de safe for me, dat is a good young man."

"Is it large or small?"

"Small. What shall I do wid a large safe?"

"As soon as the heat will allow, I will have the safe removed from the ruins," I said.

"I dink dat you can get 'em now. I vant de safe. I have papers in it."

"But the key will not open it. The fire has probably warped the door. It must be cut open with chisels."

"Ah, yes; but bring de safe to me, dat's a good man."

I promised compliance; and giving my patient some medicine, intended to relieve his pains and make him sleep, I went on shore with half a dozen of my men, armed with shovels and a tackle. We proceeded to the spot where the German's store once stood, and found that the flames had entirely consumed the thin boards of which the building was composed; and in the cellar were a few smoking rafters, among which was the safe we were in search of.

How to move it from the cellar was a question that puzzled me. The safe was not a large one, being only about two feet high, and weighing about five or six hundred pounds. It was hot, and in a hot place; and I saw no way in which we could remove it unless we could hook the tackle on to one of the handles, and then hoist it out. But to do that required shears, and a strong rope to support them, all of which was obtained after a short search. Then we threw a piece of timber amidst the burning mass, and Will ran along on it, and managed to reach one of the handles of the safe, and then rejoined us without injury. We bowsed away at the tackle, and in a few minutes the safe was landed in the street. As soon as our success was demonstrated, half a dozen merchants, whose stores were in ruins, came towards us.

"I'll give you two hundred dollars to land my safe so that I can get at it," said one. "My funds are all locked up, and I need them to commence rebuilding."

"And I will give you as much more," cried another man.

"And I," said a third.

I found that I could make a good thing by the operation; so I left the German's safe to cool, and moved the shears to the next cellar, and in an hour's time had made two hundred dollars, and received the money. Then I went to the premises of the next person, and landed his safe, and continued the business until I had made one thousand dollars, which I thought a good day's work; and so did my men, for I gave them each an ounce, with which they professed themselves extremely satisfied.

We then returned to the German's safe, and found that it was still hot. After some consideration we took a number of iron bars, and by their aid rolled it towards the landing. At length we reached the boat, and by pouring water on the iron, were enabled to cool it sufficiently to handle and get it on board, and then I visited Mr. Wismer, and announced to him the success which had crowned our efforts.

There was much sickness in San Francisco, and some of the prominent merchants thought that I could make a good thing of it by taking passengers to Honolulu, where those afflicted with the scurvy could rapidly recover. I considered the matter, and decided to advertise for first and second class passengers, and charge one hundred and fifty dollars for those who preferred the steerage, and two hundred and fifty dollars for those who desired the luxuries of the cabin. I calculated that I could accommodate about fifty persons — ten in the cabin, and forty in the hold. But the latter place needed fitting up with berths and a temporary deck. After some inquiries, I found all that I needed on board a ship that had just arrived from Panama. I purchased the berths and lumber at a bargain, and set my men at work. Bushy, who was something of a carpenter, took charge of the job, and in three days had nearly completed all the plans that I had laid out; so that, when people came off to look at the vessel, they were quite well satisfied with the accommodations, and I had no difficulty in taking my choice from the people who offered themselves.

While I was thus occupied I did not neglect my patient, whose health, I saw with much regret, was failing quite fast; and all the efforts of the doctor, who visited him once a day, were futile to relieve him of the intense pains which racked his frame. I attended him anxiously and carefully, and the poor man seemed grateful for my exertions. He was very calm and quiet now, and no longer complained that he was destitute of money. I told him that I should take him to Honolulu, where he would stand some chance of recovery; but the German smiled grimly, and one afternoon said, —

"My friend, it is useless. I shall die. I feel it here in my breast. It is all parched and burned."

"O, you will live many years," I said.

"No; I is a poor old man, and I has no friends or family, and I shall be better off in de ground."

He rested for a moment, and then said, —

"But you is mine friend. You take care of me, and you dink I has no monish. Dat is so — is it not?"

"Yes."

"Ah, I is a poor man. but I has little monish; and now I die I leaves it all on de earth, and no one to dink of me arter I is gone." It is impossible to convey to the reader the melancholy manner in which the German spoke; and, as he turned away his head, I saw a tear rolling down his wrinkled face, and disappear amid his beard. I did not speak, but allowed him to reflect and conquer his emotion. "You take care of me ven you dink I vos poor," he said, at last. "Now you is a good boy, and I makes you mine heir."

"Heir to what?" I asked, smiling at the old man's earnestness."

"You see by and by. You is a good boy, and I likes you. Go open de safe and bring de contents to me."

"What is in it?" I asked.

"No matter. You go and open 'em, and den we see."

I saw that he was so earnest in the matter, that I went on deck and examined the safe. I found that the door was so warped that it was impossible to open it with a key, and that the heavy iron would resist the blows of a top-mall. As a last resort I sent Will on shore to find a machinist, and after a long search he discovered one in a tent on Telegraph Hill. He brought on board a drilling machine and several chisels. With these the man commenced operations, and in the course of two or three hours' time, was enabled to cut the bolts and open the door. I must confess that I was astonished at the sight that greeted me; for although there were several books and some papers in the safe, yet I saw four buckskin bags filled with gold dust, and I judged that each one contained at least ten thousand dollars' worth of the precious metal.

"Bring de contents to me, my dear boy," he whispered. "You shall have all after I'm gone, but I want 'em now."

I paid the machinist for the job, and carried the four bags of gold dust to the German, and laid them by his side. For a moment his eyes assumed an unnatural lustre, but the emotion quickly passed away, and the poor man uttered a deep sigh.

"Ah, I shall make no more monish in dis world; all my life I work for de gold, and now I must leave it. O, Moshes, it is hard — is it not?" He patted the bags with his thin fingers, and then pushed them from him. "You take 'em, and when I gone you have 'em."

"Have you no relatives to whom you can leave this dust?" I asked; not wishing to accept of the donation if he had lawful heirs.

"No; I is all alone in de vorld. My parents die ven I vos a leetle boy, and I hab no friends left. Hans Smidt vos de only friend I had, and he die too. Ven I leetle boy I work for my bread, in de city of Hamburg. I sells dings in de streets, and ven I makes a stiver I saves 'em. Den I takes a store and sells everyding, and I makes monish very fast. I buys gold and silver and de precious stones; and at last I leave Hamburg for California, 'cos de people tell me dat much gold here, and dat I could sell diamonds for one large price. I buy lots diamonds, and come here one month ago, and now I is a poor old man, and dying."

The German wiped away the tears, which would force themselves from his eyes, and for a long time remained silent. I thought that he desired to sleep, and prepared to leave the state-room; but as I moved he turned his head; and motioned me to remain.

"You is a good young man, and will take care of de monish?" he asked.

"I will try to do good with it," I answered.

"Den call in some vitness. I can't write, 'cos my hands are sore. I makes you my heir. I wants all to know it."

I called the mate, Will, and Bushy into the state-room, and after they had assembled the German said, —

"I makes dis good young man, vot saved my life, mine heir. I gives him all my property. All, every mite of it. He keep 'em all de time, forever, and neber gib 'em up to no one, 'cos I want him to hab 'em, so help me Moshes."

"You understand what he says?" I asked the men.

"Yes, sir. He has made a will, and left you all his dunnage," Bushy said; and the other two nodded as though that coincided with their ideas of the matter.

"Dat vill do," cried the German; "now you may go."

The men left the state-room, and the sick man appeared so exhausted that he did not speak for some moments. He made a movement with his hands, as though he was chafing his breast; and while his breath grew thick and his eyes glassy, he drew from beneath the blanket, which covered his thin form, a wide belt, made of wash-leather, and quilted like a silk petticoat.

"Take it," he gasped. "I give it to you. It contains diamonds vorth forty dousand dollars. I bring 'em here to sell."

As he handed me the belt, which he had guarded with such care, it seemed as though his life departed with it; for the instant his fingers released their clutch, he gasped once or twice, strove to utter some word of friendly warning, and died.

I closed his eyes in sorrow, for the man had endeared himself to me through his patience and generosity. After a long search I found a man who agreed to make a coffin and line it with lead, and then I hired a man to dig a grave near the entrance of the Golden Gate, where I thought the bones would rest in peace until the city was able to lay out and dedicate a cemetery.

The next day the funeral took place, and most of my men followed the remains to their resting-place.

After my return to the vessel I examined the belt which the deceased had worn around his body for so many days. I ripped it apart, and what a rare sight met my gaze! There were diamonds of all sizes — some no larger than a grain of coarse powder, and others as big as peas. I saw that the large ones were very valuable; some of them I estimated worth as much as five hundred dollars each, and one I thought would command at least a thousand. All were stones of the first water, so clear and brilliant that I sat for some time and watched the light as it flashed upon them and was reflected in a thousand different rays. It seemed as though I was dreaming, as I sat in my state-room, wondering what I should do with my treasures, and how protect them from thieves. But in the midst of my perplexity I recollected that I could grace the fingers and neck of Julia on the day that we were married, and I wondered if she would like me any the better for my presents. Yes, I resolved that I would have a necklace manufactured for the lady, and several rings for her fingers; and with this idea I put my treasures aside in a secure place, and turned my attention to receiving passengers, who were offering themselves for Honolulu.

The day before I was ready to sail, I shipped to my father about thirty thousand dollars' worth of gold dust, a part of that which Mr. Wismer had bequeathed me; and I requested my amiable parent to invest the amount in such a way as he thought would pay best. This done I paid a visit to the whaler, for the purpose of taking leave of him and his excitable wife. I had not seen them for several days, and I longed to know how they were progressing.

CHAPTER XIX.

AN UNEXPECTED HONEYMOON. — OFF FOR HONOLULU. — A TERRIBLE ANNOUNCEMENT. — JULIA AND HER ILLNESS. — A PAINFUL MEETING.

I INQUIRED at the bar of the Connecticut House for Captain Myers, and the skilful gentleman who dispensed cocktails and whiskey-skins at the rate of twenty-five cents per drink, informed me, with a knowing grin, that the captain was in number eight, and that I had better "knock at the door before I entered the room," for which information I was duly thankful, and passed up stairs to find my friend and wife. I easily found number eight, but I was compelled to rap twice before the captain's bass voice shouted, "Come in." I opened the door, and was so astonished at the sight which met my view, that I could do nothing but stare in stupid amazement. Seated on a lounge was the amiable Dorothea, and in her lap was the head of the captain, not separated from his shoulders and gory with blood, but reposing with confidence, and looks of intense satisfaction upon his face; while the lady — she who always scratched and snarled at men — looked as though she was contented for the first time in her life, and her features actually appeared handsome. For one moment the whaler started as though about to raise his head; but when he caught sight of my face, he said, —

"Ah, it's you, is it, Allspice? Come in;" and down went his head, and his wife continued to play with his hair, except when the captain interrupted her by seizing her hand and kissing it with rather a boisterous sort of affection, which the lady appeared to relish exceedingly.

"Come in, my dear friend," cried Dorothea, with a sweet smile. "You don't disturb us in the least."

"Well," I said, dropping into a seat, and still staring at the amorous couple, "I'm astonished, and no mistake."

"What at?" asked the whaler.

"The love which I see displayed."

"Well, I do love my little petsy," cried the lady.

"And I love my little chickabiddy," answered the husband, striving to get his arm around her neck.

"For Heaven's sake stop such blasted nonsense!" I exclaimed. "You will drive me crazy. What do you mean?"

"We mean that we love each other dearly; no more rows, no more quarrels. We now understand each other."

"My little petsy is the best man in the world," enthusiastically exclaimed the wife.

"My little chickabiddy is the best *woman* in the world," answered the husband.

And then they recommenced kissing until I thought they would devour each other. I was disgusted. Although rather fond of kissing pretty women, I did not like the manner in which they conducted the business.

"I won't stand this," I said. "If you don't stop such nonsense I'll leave."

"Is it not right for a wife to love her husband?" asked Dorothea.

"Yes, but don't show so much of it in public."

"What do we care for the public?" asked the whaler. "The public may be cussed if it pleases, but I'm determined to love my little chickabiddy."

I saw that the maniac was incurable. A reaction had taken place, and softened his brain. I laughed, held out my hand, wished them well, and left the room; and the last thing that I heard, as I closed the door, was the sound of kisses.

I visited the rest of my acquaintances, and took leave of them, Hatch sending a lot of letters to his friends at Honolulu, and giving me his blessing with much fervor at parting. Then I mailed letters to my parents, and left San Francisco for the Helen. I found my passengers all on board, and anxious for a start. I had nothing to detain me — the wind was fair and fresh, and I had enough of daylight to enable me to pass the entrance of the Golden

Gate. To the delight of all hands I ordered the crew to man the windlass; the anchor left its resting-place with lots of mud upon its stock and shank, and we commenced dodging amidst the vessels which were lying in port, until we were off Goat Island, when we were enabled to make sail, and passed the Golden Gate at a rushing speed, a three-knot current being in our favor. I had no trouble with my passengers, excepting some trifling difference respecting rations. Some of them wanted to live on bread and butter, and others preferred "plum duff;" but when they found that I gave them the best that I had, and enough of it, they were disposed to be rational. I did not lose a passenger. All of them recovered their health, and were landed in safety at Honolulu, where they swore I was the best man that ever lived, and much more to the same purpose.

I will not tire the patience of readers with an account of my passage, but simply inform them that just six months had elapsed from the time I left Honolulu until my return. Ah, how well I recollect the morning when I dropped anchor in the basin of Honolulu! I was happy with the thought of meeting Julia — with clasping her in my arms, and soon calling her my wife. There could be no excuse now offered by her father. I was twenty years of age, rich enough to support a wife, and with love enough to cherish one. How I counted the moments which detained me on board! I was too impatient to hardly notice Lilly, meek and quiet as she was. Poor girl, her lot was indeed a hard one, and she knew it; but she uttered no complaints, and made no sign. She little knew that in a few days I should be married to one who was my equal in wealth and position, and possessing all the virtues which man looks for, yet seldom bring to the married state. Perhaps women do not expect perfection in men. We look for it in women, and are furious if we are deceived. Why should we not be on an equality? How is it that men can indulge in vice, and yet escape the frowns of the opposite sex? I have never yet been able to comprehend it, or to satisfactorily answer the question. I wish that men were more virtuous, and women more exacting when they are asked to marry. We should all live happier, and die with the consciousness of having accomplished some good in this world. I can see no remedy for the evil, for education, while it enlightens, does not make us shun vice. Some of our most intelligent men are the most unprincipled, and so I am afraid that each succeeding generation will follow in the footsteps of its predecessors. But a truce to moralizing, for it will effect no good.

As soon as we dropped anchor, I saw my partner, Mr. Cherington, coming off in the boat which belonged to the house, and I prepared to welcome him, and to ask a hundred questions respecting the lady whom I loved so well. He reached the deck and our hands were clasped, and for a moment we stood facing each other.

"Charles!" the good man exclaimed; and tears moistened his eyes.

"My dear father!" I replied, and then I stopped.

"You are well," he said; "your looks proclaim it."

"Thank Heaven, I am. And Julia — she is well?"

"Yes, she is well," answered my partner; but his looks did not confirm his words, and I saw that his usually cheerful face wore a look which was grave and impressive.

"You are deceiving me," I said; and I felt the blood rush to my heart in icy torrents, leaving me weak and trembling, as though smitten by the ague.

The good man saw my emotion, and a look of pity crossed his face. He laid his hand upon my arm, and led me into the cabin, where we could be alone for a few minutes. I gazed in his face, and whispered, —

"I know it all — Julia is sick or dead. Is it not so? Do not fear to tell me. I am firm and able to hear it;" and at the same time I was trembling so violently that I could hardly raise a glass of water to my lips.

"O, no, not dead," cried Mr. Cherington, who saw my distress. "Julia has been very sick, but she is now convalescent, and able to walk and ride out. She will soon be well, I trust."

"Thank God!" I exclaimed, with heart-felt gratitude. "If she lives I will love her so dearly that the roses of health will soon bloom upon her cheeks. In a few weeks, or perhaps days, we shall be married. Ah, my dear father, more than father, you cannot imagine how I have longed for the hour when I may call Julia mine. Day and night I have thought of her, and all my plans have been laid with this one view."

"Poor boy!" muttered Mr. Cherington; "so enthusiastic and yet so rash!" and my partner's face was gloomy for a moment; but when he saw that I was noting every expression upon his countenance, he attempted to smile, and did manage to call up one; but it fled like a ghost, as though scared at the approaching day. He took my hand and squeezed it for a moment, and said, —

"Well, well; let us talk of something else. Tell me of the voyage. Has it been successful?"

"Yes, quite so. But Julia — was she attacked with fever?"

"Yes, a slow fever. You sold everything at good prices?"

"Yes. When was she taken ill, and how did it happen?"

"Three weeks since. Her illness was sudden. You sold for cash, I suppose."

"Blast the cargo!" I exclaimed, pettishly, irritated at the man's returning from the subject which interested me to the selling of a cargo of vegetables. "What do I care for gold, only as a means of winning Julia's hand?"

"Charles!" exclaimed my partner, in surprise, "you forgot that there is time enough for you to learn all the particulars respecting Julia's health."

"And there is time enough for you to look over my accounts," I retorted. "You may love money, but I love Julia more than I do gold."

"I suppose so, Charles; yet it is a pity that you have acted in so thoughtless a manner."

"What do you mean?" I asked. "There is some mystery connected with your words."

"There is, Charles; I cannot disguise it. We have heard evil reports of you, but I trust that you can refute them."

My head dropped at once. I could no longer meet the calm, earnest eyes of my partner, and I knew they were fastened upon my face, and that he there read guilt which my impudence could not permit me to deny. Ah, who can tell how much I suffered in a few minutes' time, and how much I would have given to have been enabled to repudiate every assertion that reflected upon my name? I knew that my partner pitied me, and would help me; but I did not dare to ask for it, and I did not care to pursue my inquiries any further just at that time.

"You do not speak, Charles," said Mr. Cherington, after an embarrassing pause.

"What can I say, until I know the charges against me?"

"Your old ship, the Sally, touched at this port a month since," my partner continued.

"Did you see Captain Bunker?"

"O, yes. He was very anxious to see me, and one day he called at the house and saw Julia. I should have prevented it if I had known that he contemplated any such thing."

"The old rascal! Did he speak of me?"

"I am sorry to say that he did, and not in such favorable terms as I could have wished."

"Why, the cussed scoundrel!" I blurted out; "I saved him from a thrashing at the Ladrones for insulting a lady."

Mr. Cherington smiled, and played with his watch chain.

"You don't believe me," I said.

"O, yes, I do; but it is singular that he should say that it was you who attempted familiarities with the lady, an elderly one, and that he saved her virtue, and persuaded the governor to forgive you."

"O, my God!" I exclaimed, in the fullness of my heart, "did that rascal have the impudence to say that?"

"Indeed he did, and much more which I shall not relate. There was a young lady, also; the captain said she was an artful girl, the daughter of the governor. She was represented as very handsome, and that your attentions were not thrown away upon her."

"And is it possible that you can believe such a statement?" I asked.

"Well, human nature is weak, my son; but I should not have placed much confidence in the report, if it had not been corroborated."

"By whom?" I demanded, in surprise.

'O, an old enemy of yours. You may not recollect him."

"Yes, I shall."

"Well, it was Kamaka, the kanaka, a revengeful rascal, and one who does not love you; but he did love a native girl whom you took a fancy to, while leading an indolent life at Kammaira."

"And is this all?" I asked, after a long breath, while I attempted to see the way out of the net that had enclosed me in its meshes, and was dragging me into deeper water every moment.

"I think that it will do for the present.

"And so do I."

Just at this moment we heard cheers on deck, and there were loud calls for me. With a heart crushed by the information which I had received, I went on deck, and found that the passengers were all ready to leave the vessel for the shore, several barges lying alongside for the purpose of taking them to the beach.

"We can't go without bidding you farewell, sir," cried half a dozen of the passengers, who, when they came on board, were nearly dead with scurvy, and had improved on the diet which I had served out to them. They came crowding aft, and shook hands with me, many of them shedding tears, as they did so.

"Three cheers for the captain!" some one cried.

They were given with a will, and half a dozen more followed, until the people on shore thought that some great event had happened, and came rushing to the beach to find out what it was.

"A speech!" the men yelled, in true Yankee style.

I addressed them a few words, and told them how I hoped they would save their money after they reached the land, be moral, and preserve their health, and finally return to California, and make their fortunes. The passengers were satisfied, and left the vessel, with bag and baggage; and then Mr. Cherington and I returned to the cabin to talk over matters connected with the voyage. But I found that it was impossible for me to concentrate my mind on business. I thought of the different reception which awaited me at the hands of Julia from what I had anticipated. I saw that all my castles, which I had built and reared so high, were tumbling about my ears, and were likely to crush me in their fall.

What plea could I offer, excepting the folly and impetuosity of youth? Would a young, romantic girl like Julia, who believed the world as pure as her own thoughts, accept of many excuses at my hands? I knew that she was generous, but I was aware that she was just, at the same time; and in no light that I could view the matter, was there hope for me. For the first time, while seated in my state-room, considering these matters, did I fully realize how much I loved Julia. My suit had prospered so well — there was such an absence of opposition to it — that the real strength of my affections had not been brought out; and now, when there was a prospect of losing the lady, I felt as though I was capable of committing some desperate act, although in doing so I should but lessen myself in Julia's estimation, and in the esteem of her father. I saw that the latter sympathized with me, and would stand by me; but Miss Cherington had a mind of her own, when disposed to exert it. It was a favorite plan of my partner's, marrying me to his daughter, and I knew that it would cost him many sighs to relinquish it; but what were his feelings compared to those of an ardent lover, who returns fondly anticipating an affectionate welcome and an early wedding, and finds coldness, and perhaps dislike? I filled a goblet with wine and drank it, and the liquor gave me a forced buoyancy, and raised my spirits to such a degree, that I began to think matters were not so black as they appeared. My partner saw the change, and smiled.

"We can wait until to-morrow, Charles," Mr. Cherington said.

"No, a little attention to business will help me at the present time. My burden is great, but I must try and bear it."

As I spoke I opened the desk where I kept my papers and books. Had I stopped to think for one moment, I should not have done so, for directly before my eyes lay a mantilla, a pair of slippers, and an embroidered waist, which Dorothea — may the saints confound her! — left on board at the time she packed up so hurriedly; and Lilly, out of sport, had placed them in my desk, and I, like a fool, had forgotten to remove them. There they were, staring me in the face, and of course caught the eyes of my sharp-sighted partner.

"Are these business papers, Charles?" asked the old gentleman, with a slight smile.

I gathered the articles in my hand, and threw them under my berth; but Mr. Cherington would not let me alone.

"Curious kind of account books, those, Charles," he said. "They are none too clean, either, I should judge."

I stammered out some excuse, which only increased my confusion; and I was not released from it until I had opened my books and attracted Mr. Cherington's attention by pointing out the large sums which I had received for the cargo. This interested him very much, and he soon forgot waist and slippers while footing up a column of figures. The result was satisfactory in all respects, and when I produced the gold which I had received, not alluding to that bequeathed me by Mr. Wismer, the old gentleman was delighted, and complimented me highly upon my success.

"Come," he said, "we must go on shore. Dinner is ready for us."

"But how shall I appear before Julia?"

"About as usual. Take no notice of her coldness, until you are compelled to. Come, my dear boy, we shall see daylight, I hope, in a short time."

But I knew there was no light for me, for months to come.

It was in vain that Mr. Cherington attempted to converse with me. I could not answer him in a rational manner, and the old gentleman, with a sigh, gave up the task, and in silence we reached his door, and entered the house. How I missed a warm welcome at the hands of Julia — she whom I had so foully wronged! She did not meet me in the entry, as was her custom, and suffer me to throw my arms around her and kiss her lips, and the change was terrible to an impulsive being like myself. For one moment I stopped to collect all my resolution, and then I entered the sitting-room, where I knew I should find the lady. As I opened the door, she was seated on a lounge at the window, looking towards the harbor, and I knew that her eyes were directed towards my vessel. She did not stir until I was close to her. Then she started up, and I saw the change which sickness had produced. Her face had lost none of its wonderful beauty, although it was pale, very pale; but the skin was transparently pure, and the blue veins could be traced from the temple to the cheek, like small streams in a lovely landscape. Her black eyes looked larger than ever, but they were not flashing and full of fun, as on former days. They were more gentle, but perhaps full as attractive.

"Julia," I said, and held out both hands. I could not speak another word if my life had depended upon the effort. My head throbbed as though it would burst, and it was only by an effort that I could keep my tears from falling.

"O, Charles," Julia said; and she touched one of my hands, and then sank upon a lounge, agitated and faint.

For a few minutes neither of us spoke.

"I am sorry, very sorry, that you have been ill, Julia," I said, at last.

"I have been ill, but am much better," was the answer; and the conversation ceased for a time.

Mr. Cherington had not entered the room, so that we could converse at leisure; but I saw that no explanation was likely to ensue, unless I pressed the matter.

"I had looked forward to this meeting with much pleasure," I said, at length. "For many months I have thought only of you, and the joy of seeing you."

She raised her calm, black eyes, and looked me full in the face. Heavens! what a glance was that! Not scornful or malicious, but calm and slightly incredulous, as though my word and virtue were doubted. I could not endure it; so my eyes were lowered to the straw carpeting upon the floor. She did not answer me, but gazed towards the harbor after she had given me such a searching look; but I saw that her face flushed, and her eyes looked humid, as though tears were only kept back by an effort.

"Julia," I whispered, with a slight pressure of her hand, "do you hate me?"

"O, no, Charles; you know that I do not."

"Then why do you receive me in this cold, cruel manner? What faults have I committed that cannot be pardoned by you?"

"Do not distress me by asking, Charles. I have loved you dearly — I still love you, and always shall; but I have heard such strange reports concerning your conduct, that you must not expect me to give you the hand which you now hold."

I felt the struggle coming, and I nerved myself to the task of meeting it, although I feared that it would be helpless, and render me more unhappy than at present.

"Do you mean, Julia," I asked, in a low tone, "that I must no longer look upon you as my affianced wife?"

She bowed her head in token of assent, and then the tears did flow in spite of all control, and she sobbed most bitterly; but during her burst of grief, she did not reject the arm which I placed around her waist, nor did she repulse me when I drew her head to my shoulder, and kissed the tears from her eyes. I thought that I had conquered, and that my faults would be overlooked; but I presumed too much, for, after enjoying a few minutes' taste of heaven, the brave girl withdrew herself from my arms, and made an effort to check her tears.

"O, Charles, how could you conduct in such a manner while absent?" she asked. "If you had no love for me, why did you say that you had? You knew that I loved you, and you alone, and that I would have died ere I had been guilty of wrong in your absence. Not a day has passed but I have prayed for your return; and O, how much I desired it! I have pictured to myself the happiness which we should enjoy. I thought you truthful and honest. Would that I could still labor under that delusion."

"Are you sure, Julia," I asked, "that I am as bad as you have heard? Will you not allow me to explain some of the mysteries which you have been told?"

"I will hear all that you have to say. You shall not be condemned unheard. Tell me in a truthful manner all that a maiden should hear, and then I will judge you justly."

Of course I intended to tell the truth, but in doing so it was not necessary that I should tell the whole truth; for if I had, it would only have distressed the dear girl, and I was desirous of avoiding that as much as possible. For a moment I thought what kind of a story I should invent, for I feared her anger and reproaches, and trembled at her power. But while I was collecting my thoughts I saw that Julia's eyes were upon me, and I knew that she was reading my intentions. This confused me a little, and I feared that I looked guilty. Under that impression I faltered.

"I am ready to hear your excuse, provided you have one," Julia said, after a moment's silence.

Thus urged on, I commenced an account of my voyage to the Ladrones, but I entirely forgot to mention that Lilly accompanied me. I thought that it would be useless to mention such a trifling circumstance, unless Julia alluded to it. I told her of Bunker's flirtation with Dorothea, and had the satisfaction of knowing that it was not believed in all respects. I could see that by her eyes. I lightly alluded to Constance as a pert young miss, unworthy of consideration, and possessing no beauty excepting a pair of bright eyes; and then I explained how it happened that I took Dorothea to San Francisco. She was in search of the man she loved, and who loved her, and I had seen them happily married. I invested the affair with as much romance as possible; for romance touches a woman's heart quicker than any other feeling. I told her how grateful the couple were to me for my trouble, and how enthusiastic they were, when they learned that I was returning to Honolulu in hope of securing a darling little wife. Julia's face did not change at the last words, and, mentally, I was compelled to confess that I had undertaken more than I could carry through. I had tried to excite her mirth, and her love of romance; but I had failed in the most signal manner, and considered that my cause was lost. There was an awkward pause for a few moments. I attempted to catch a glimpse of Julia's face, but she was looking out of the window, and avoided my gaze. Still she suffered me to hold her hand, and to press it; but no pressure was returned. I felt that if she loved me she was struggling hard to prevent it from appearing, and this I regarded as an ominous sign.

"Julia," I whispered, drawing the dear girl nearer to me, "do you still love me?"

"As much as ever — more, perhaps," was the trembling answer.

I attempted to kiss her lips upon the strength of this confession. but she drew back her head.

"No, Charles, no. It is neither right nor proper that you should act thus. We are friends, but can no longer be lovers. Let that suffice you."

Gasping for breath, still I determined to persevere and urge my suit, and win her at last.

"Julia," I said, in tremulous tones, "you are unjust and cruel. Have I deserved such treatment at the hands of one who stands pledged to become my wife?"

I saw the rich blood mantle her face, and her eyes grew brighter.

"Remember, Charles," she said, "when I promised you my hand, it was with the understanding that you should give up your follies and silly pranks. Has such been the case? I pardoned your conduct at Kammaira, because you were under no vows to me. When you asked for my hand, I promised it to you under certain conditions. You recollect them — do you not?"

I did recollect, but man-like I pretended to have forgotten them, and assumed a look of surprise. She noticed the expression upon my face, and added, —

"Let me enlighten you, Charles. You promised me that, under all and every circumstance you would remain pure and good. Have you kept your word?"

"Of course I have," I answered, with a look of innocence. "O, how can you doubt me?"

The sweet eyes of my companion took one hasty glance at my face, and then gazed out upon the harbor, and the Helen, which was lying at anchor in the basin, and I recollected that Lilly was on board the vessel.

"O, Charles, Charles!" and then, to my horror, her fair face was bowed and covered by her hands.

I whispered a thousand words of consolation as I held her in my arms, and for the second time during the interview she suffered me to kiss the tears from her eyes. But she yielded only to a momentary weakness. As soon as reason returned, she withdrew from my embrace, and her tears ceased.

"Charles," she said, laying a hand upon my shoulder, and with her soft eyes looking me full in the face, "have you told me all?"

"Of course I have, you little darling," making an attempt to seize her hand and kiss it; but she repulsed the action with such firmness that I desisted, and looked quite humble.

There was a moment's silence, and then Julia spoke.

"Once more, Charles; have you confessed all?"

She did not look at me while speaking. Perhaps if she had I should have faltered. But her eyes were turned from me, and I gained courage to adhere to the monstrous lie which I had told.

"Of course I have informed you of all. Do not doubt me."

She sighed, and arose from the window, as though to leave the room. I noticed that she was deadly pale, and that her steps faltered. I sprang forward to assist her; but she repulsed me with such firmness and dignity that I was awed, and retreated.

"Here we part, Charles," she said; but the words came from her lips with an effort, and her form trembled as she uttered them.

"Part, Julia!" I exclaimed, in pretended astonishment. "O, no; do not pronounce so harsh a decree."

"It must be so, although my heart bleeds to utter the words. You are free to choose a wife where you please. I release you from the bonds which were imposed, and in doing so I also free myself. It is better for both of us. You are fickle, and I dare not trust my happiness in your keeping. You now think that you love me —"

"Think, Julia!" I exclaimed, interrupting her. "O, if you only knew the love which now stirs my heart, you would pity me, and not have listened to the tales of evil-minded persons while I was absent. They slandered me, and you have given me no chance for contradiction. Perhaps our engagement weighed heavily upon you, and you seek this means of annulling it. Well, let it be so. I am as proud as you, and shall cease my pleadings, now and forever."

Sharp as my words were, she did not become angry at them. Her cheeks flushed a little, and her eyes looked more humid, but that was all. In a moment she was as calm as ever.

"Your words pain me, but they do not anger me, Charles. I know your disposition much better than you think for. Come, let us be friends, but not lovers. We must inhabit the same house, and should treat each other courteously."

She extended her thin, fair hand, through which the blue veins could be traced like lines in marble; but I folded my arms, and stepped back.

"I thank you for the hint," I said, in a bitter tone. "This house, you think, is too small for both of us. I hope that I have money enough to find another shelter, and one, I trust, more agreeable than this."

"O, Charles, Charles," she moaned; but I was a beaten, baffled, furious wretch, and heeded not her scared looks or imploring gestures.

"Perhaps you think I have not wealth enough to support you in state," I cried, with a mocking sneer. "I have the pleasure to inform you that I am rich — rich beyond my wildest expectations. It was for your sake that I sought wealth, and now I am glad that you discarded me before you learned it is mine. Look!" and I tore open my vest, and brought to light a bag containing the diamonds which Mr. Wismer had bequeathed me. "These are worth forty thousand dollars. Do you know what I intended to have done with every one of them? They were to be strung upon your person, neck, bosom, and fingers, and I was to fall down and worship you."

O, the look of scorn which was impressed upon that fair face! I never saw such a glance before. It would have struck me dumb if I had not been filled with rage and conceit. She was silent. I saw that I had made no impression with my diamonds; so I thrust them into my pocket, and turned to leave the room.

"One moment, Charles," the lady said; and I stopped to listen to her.

"You have taunted me most unjustly, but I forgive you. I care nothing for your wealth and your jewels. I loved you for yourself, as I believed you loved me. This you are well aware of, for I promised you my hand when you were far from being rich. But let that pass. You think that I have treated you unjustly. On that point we differ. I asked you for a full confession. You equivocated, and gave me but half, and that the best. You did not speak of that miserable native girl who was on board your vessel when you first visited California, and who went with you to the Ladrones, where she was seen by one who knew her when she resided in the village of Kammaira. All this time she was dressed in boy's clothes, and occupied a portion of your cabin. Dare you deny that at this moment the girl is on board the Helen? Dare you deny the statements I have made? Charles, Charles, you have this day told me a monstrous lie. May God forgive you, as I do."

I felt as though the house was shaken by an earthquake. The air seemed dark, thick, and heavy. My frame trembled, and I gasped as though I should suffocate. I was weighed down by the crushing blow which had fallen upon me; and yet I was filled with fierce rage, and I knew that my eyes were bloodshot from passion.

"One word," I managed to gasp, although the effort nearly choked me. "Who informed you of all this?"

"I will answer on one condition."

"Name it, and be quick, or I shall suffocate in this close room."

"Is the report true? On your soul, Charles, is it true?"

"Every word of it. The girl did go with me, and she is on board at the present time."

Julia turned away her head, and I heard a sob as she answered, —

"Kamaka."

I waited to hear no more. I left the room, seized my hat, and dashed from the house with murderous thoughts in my brain, and my heart beating as though it would burst. As I reached the sidewalk in my headlong career, I fancied I heard some one call my name; but I did not stop. Down the street I rushed, intent only on finding the kanaka who had exposed me so many times, and crossed my path just as I supposed it was free from difficulties. I wanted revenge for the injuries which he had inflicted. His life, I thought, should be sacrificed to the shrine of vengeance, and I cared not what became of me if I could but crush the meddling rascal.

Just as I reached the corner of Queen and Kaahamaun Streets, who should I meet, face to face, but the tattooed rascal I was in search of. He did not notice me until I had my hand upon his throat, compressing his windpipe with no gentle grasp. Then he showed fear in every feature of his dark face.

"Dog," I said, in a hoarse whisper, "you have told tales regarding me, and now I mean to kill you."

He struggled to get away, but I held him firmly. His resistance was useless, and only enraged me the more. If I had had a weapon I should have taken his life, for I was hardly conscious of my acts. I only saw before me the man's face; and lifting my hand I struck it several times, and blood followed each blow. A crowd gathered around us; but I cared not, for it did not interfere with the fight, or attempt to rescue the kanaka from my angry grasp. I heard the man begging for mercy, but I was deaf to his entreaties. At last he fell, and with my foot I spurned him, and passed on.

"Look out," shouted some one in the crowd; "he has a knife."

But I did not heed the warning, and the next moment I felt a sharp sting near my right shoulder-blade; and the blow was so sudden and strong that I pitched forward and fell upon my hands and knees.

In an instant I was on my feet; but the man who stabbed me had disappeared in the crowd of natives, and I knew that I could not find him, for the kanakas would assist his escape.

"Kanaka did it," said a white man who was standing near me. "He struck hard, but I trust you are not hurt."

"No, not much, I think;" and I passed down the street towards the basin, for the purpose of reaching the Helen as soon as possible, and having my wound examined.

I felt blood trickling down my back, and began to experience a sudden feeling of weakness; but I persevered, and reached the deck of my vessel, and as I passed along towards the cabin, my blood stained the planks and alarmed my men. They rushed towards me, and assisted me into a state-room; and the last thing that I recollected, was feeling Lilly's lips pressed to mine, and her arms around my neck.

I awoke weak and feverish. I saw that I was lying in my state-room berth; and by my side was Lilly, cooling my head with a fan, which she waved without cessation. For a few moments I watched her face unobserved. It bore the traces of suffering and grief, but I knew that on my account she mourned; and the thought that I was loved by the kanaka girl caused a thrill of pleasure to pass through my feeble frame.; for I recollected that I was discarded by one whom I loved, and I would now show that I could be as indifferent and careless as herself. I did not know how long I had been insensible, but I thought it could not be a great while, although my shoulder was stiff and heavily bandaged. A slight movement on my part attracted Lilly's attention, and when she saw that my eyes were open, her face expressed the most intense joy.

"You will live," she cried, "you will live!" and she sunk upon her knees, and laid her fair face close to mine, and wiped the moisture from my brow.

Although I was grateful to the girl for her attentions, yet I could not help thinking how much more I should have preferred seeing Julia's head in the same place; so I could not prevent an expression of impatience, which I know caused pain to Lilly's heart — for I saw it reflected on her face.

"How long have I lain here?" I asked.

"Since yesterday. We feared that you would die, for you lost much blood. The doctor says you were not to talk much."

"Then give me a drink and leave me."

The girl raised my head and put a glass of lemonade to my lips. I drank, and then my kind attendant stole from the room and closed the door. I lay in my state-room in sullen silence, and thought of the past and the dreary future, until I fell asleep through weakness; and when I awoke I found Mr. Cherington by my side.

"Well, my boy, how do you feel?" he asked, in a tone of sympathy.

"Better, I think."

"You have had a narrow escape, Charles. The rascal aimed well, and only missed a weak spot by the breadth of a hair. We have had parties searching the island for him, but I fear that he has escaped."

"The next time I meet him he will not escape," I muttered.

My partner sighed, and was silent.

"There is one transaction connected with our settlement which I failed to mention," I said. "I intended to surprise you with the details at dinner, and see if you thought it just that the funds should go into the concern."

Mr. Cherington looked astonished and anxious; and then I told him how I had saved Mr. Wismer from a terrible death, and how he had bequeathed to me his fortune, amounting to some eighty thousand dollars or more. I then hinted how pleased I was with the thought that I should share all with Julia, and how terrible was my disappointment. My partner listened patiently, and after I had finished, he said, —

"I can't see how I can demand a share of the money. It was a private donation, and as such you are entitled to it. Keep the money and the diamonds, Charles, for I have no claim on them."

Of course I thanked him for his kindness, and then he left me, carrying on shore the gold and the diamonds which I had on board. He thought the treasure safer in the store than in the vessel, and I agreed with him.

Again in the afternoon Mr. Cherington came on board, and was glad to see that my wound was doing well, and that I was able to sit up, and even talk a little. He told me that the kanaka, Kamaka, had left the island in a canoe, and that no doubt he had gone to Lahaina, some eighty miles distant. If such was the case, the fellow would be arrested, for government had sent orders to that effect.

"Julia is quite anxious respecting you, Charles," my partner continued.

"Indeed! I am sorry that she should be disturbed for the fate of one whom she has ceased to regard."

"She has not ceased her regard for you, and she told you so. You have committed certain acts which she deems unpardonable. Ask your own heart if you do not think she is right. Every charge she made is substantiated; and with such an array of facts, what could she do?"

I was silent, for I knew that she had acted right and proper.

"She has heard with much regret that you refuse to be removed to my house on account of meeting her. She does not want you to experience any such feeling. It is foreign to your nature, and distresses my daughter as well as myself. You can be friends. You must be friends, and let us hope that time will bring matters right. Now, let me take you on shore, and you will find in Julia a sister."

"No, no, no!" I said, after a moment's reflection. "I could not see her near me without feeling the loss which I have sustained. Absence will, I hope, cure me of the passion which I entertain for her. I cannot now act towards her a brother's part. Will you tell her this? Let her know that at the present time, while suffering from this wound, my thoughts are of her and of the happy hours which we have passed together. I now know my own unworthiness, and esteem her many good qualities. If we do not meet for some months, we may, in a measure, forget each other. It will require an effort on my part. Heaven grant that she may be as happy as she deserves. If I could live my life over, I would act in a different manner."

"Then why not commence a new life from the present time, Charles? Show Julia that you are sincere in your repentance, and she may look with compassion upon your sufferings."

"How?" I asked.

"Send that kanaka girl on shore, and dissolve the connection at once. Julia knows that she is on board, and I suspected, but said nothing. If you are anxious for repentance, now is the time to show it."

The proposition startled me, and I required time to think of it. If I sent Lilly on shore, would Julia look upon me with more favor? I was inclined to doubt it, and with uncertainty why should I discard Lilly and break her heart? She was now my true friend, and I her only protector, and I should be base indeed if I suffered her to be thrust away. All these things I thought of while Mr. Cherington sat opposite me, watching my face.

"Well, Charles, what answer do you give me?" my partner asked.

"I cannot do it," I answered. "Julia has discarded me, and it would look weak to yield now. She would mistrust my motives, and think that I was inclined to play the hypocrite for the sake of winning her back."

"And did you not intend to send that kanaka girl home if you married Julia?" asked Mr. Cherington in a stern tone.

"Of course. How can you doubt it?"

"Then I cannot see your consistency, my boy," was the answer; and a moment's reflection taught me that he had taken just grounds.

I could not pursue the conversation further, for I felt fatigued and dissatisfied; and my partner saw it; so talked of other matters.

"I shall have a large number of passengers for you by the time you get able to sail. There is quite a fever in Honolulu for emigrating to the mines. I think that we can make more money by carrying passengers than we can by buying fruits at the present prices. What is your opinion?"

"The same. California will be flooded in a short time, and prices will droop. We have made all the money that we can make by trade, and now we must look out for other sources of revenue."

"Have you any suggestions to make in that respect?" my partner asked.

"Yes; but perhaps they will not strike you as favorable."

"Let me hear them, and then I will judge."

"You know, sir, that it would not be agreeable to me to remain long in Honolulu. It is better on Julia's account and on my own that I be absent. Now, I think that if I can sell the schooner at San Francisco, I had better do so, and take my party to the mines. They will follow me and stick to me. We shall incur but a trifling expense, and may make some money. In the mean time you can carry on the business here, and do as well as ever — perhaps better, for we have a large capital to operate with, and can take advantage of the market."

"I like the plan," said my partner, after a moment's thought, "and give it my hearty consent. You will write to me often, and I will keep you advised of matters at home. Besides, by every vessel that leaves port I can send you fruits and a few luxuries which you may like, and cannot obtain in the mines. Of course all the money that is made by either branch is to be shared equally."

"Of course," I said. "As far as the crew is concerned, I shall propose that they receive a percentage of all the dust which they gather, we finding provisions, tents, and tools."

The next day I was able to reach the deck, and my appearance caused much joy to my crew. They crowded aft to welcome me, and were ready to do anything to promote my comfort. I thought this a good time to mention the proposition which I had submitted to my partner; so I told the men the idea which I had formed, and inquired if they were willing to go with me. They all answered in the affirmative, and were eager that I should make my own terms with them. The crew went forward to talk the matter over, and left me with Lilly.

"Can I go with you to the mines?" asked the kanaka girl, in a timid manner, as though fearful of a refusal.

"Yes; if you desire to."

"And shall I meet many women there?"

"No; probably not one."

"I am glad of that," she said, with a happy smile.

"Why?"

"Because —" and then she hesitated, and stole a look at my face.

"Speak freely. What do you mean?"

"You won't see those whom you love more than you do me."

She appeared frightened at her temerity, and evidently expected a hasty word; but I made no reply, for I was thinking of Julia, and wondering if she would regret my absence. I wanted to see her and talk with her, but my pride would not permit me to ask the favor, neither would I visit the house before I sailed, much as I desired to. I would have given the world, if I had owned it, for the purpose of being pardoned; but I could not take the proper steps to secure such a desirable result. I was the most unhappy of mortals, and needed some stirring adventures to banish the past from my mind, so that I could look forward with some degree of calmness to the future; and while I was thus meditating, a boat came alongside, and one of Mr. Cherington's servants reached the deck, walked aft, and placed a note in my hand. I saw that it was directed in Julia's handwriting, and with trembling nerves I broke the seal, and read as follows: —

"DEAR CHARLES: Forgive me if I am too familiar, for you are still dear to me, although we are separated forever. I trust that you do not hate me for the course that I have pursued. It was dictated by high motives, and my conscience acquits me of all blame. O, Charles, why were you not good and honorable, and why did you not realize the expectations which I had formed of you? Could not the pure love of one suffice? You have wronged me, and I feel as though my heart would break; but I have sought consolation in prayer, and God has strengthened me

Why do you not turn to the same source of goodness, and ask support? O, Charles, if you had but avoided evil, — had but loved me as man should love his betrothed, — all this trouble would have been avoided, and we should now be happy, and beyond the danger of reverses. Can I not entreat you to avoid the course which you are now pursuing? My father tells me that you will soon sail for California, and be absent many months. I am sorry that such is the case, for, in that wild country, I fear you will not improve; but I pray you be as good as possible, and return as soon as you can. In me you will always find a friend, and one who hopes for your happiness. I wish that you were with us now, so that I could wait upon you while you are recovering from your wound; but my father tells me that you are obstinate, and refuse to leave the vessel. Under the circumstances, I cannot visit you, and you must not expect it; but let me see you before you sail, if only for a moment. Believe me, I shall not reproach you for your conduct. Reproaches are numbered with the past, and I will never bring them to light."

The reading of this letter affected me more than I was willing to acknowledge. It was evident that the dear girl still loved me, but her pride and self-respect prevented her from joining her fate with mine, and I knew her self-respect too well to think that argument would overcome the resolution which she had formed. I resolved to see the lady, and speak with her; but I did not dare to incur the fatigue until I had gained more strength. I answered the letter, but my reply was short.

"Miss Julia is not well," said the kanaka, who brought the note on board, speaking in his native dialect. "She looks very pale, and unhappy."

The rogue knew that we had quarrelled, and he was anxious for a reconciliation, for the house was not gay and festive while I was absent. I must confess that I longed for the time to arrive, when my health would permit me to visit Julia. I thought of the matter for a whole week, and at last the surgeon said that there was no danger of a relapse, even if I should become excited; and with this assurance, one afternoon, I dressed myself in a suit of light clothing, and went on shore. I found my partner's carriage waiting for me at the landing, and entering it, was driven to the house which contained the most precious treasure, in my eyes, that the whole island held. How my heart fluttered as I entered the house! I felt as timid as a young girl on the eve of her wedding, and I know that I blushed as I opened the parlor door, and saw Julia standing before me, with a hand extended, in the way of welcome.

CHAPTER XX.

AN INTERVIEW. — THE RESULT. — BEATEN AT ALL POINTS. — OFF AGAIN FOR CALIFORNIA. — ON THE PASSAGE.

I DID not augur much good from this reception. It was too kind, and yet too distant, to please me. I took a seat, and she placed a chair opposite to mine, and sat down. I saw that her face bore traces of suffering, and looked thinner than usual. Her color had fled, and her skin was as white as a Vermont snow bank. My illness had told upon me, also, and I saw the dark eyes of my friend scrutinizing my face, and noting the change which had occurred there. For a moment an expression of pity was seen in her glorious eye, — ah! so beautiful and gentle; and then it passed away, and nothing but sadness was left.

"When do you leave for California?" asked Julia, at length.

"In a few days."

"Shall you remain absent for a long time?"

"I really don't know. There is no occasion for me to return to Honolulu immediately. I think that I can do better for the firm in California than I can here. When I arrived I hoped that I should remain, but circumstances have occurred which will prevent me."

"Do you think that I have acted towards you in an unjust manner?" the lady asked.

"I think that you have been hasty. You should have listened to my explanations."

"I did so; but did the explanation redound to your credit? O, Charles, I did think you were different from other men. I looked upon you as a model; and what have I found?"

Perhaps my piteous look touched the heart of the gentle lady, for she added, —

"O, Charles, how could you act as you have done? You never loved me, or you would have conducted in a different manner."

"Never loved you, Julia?" I repeated; and in an instant I was by her side, and one arm was around her waist. I thought that she had melted, but I found to the contrary; for she released her form from my clasp, gently, but firmly, and pointed to the seat which I had vacated, for the purpose of taking up a position more congenial to my nature.

"Will you be seated, Charles?" she asked, still remaining on her feet, as though to show that she was determined to keep me at a distance.

"If such is your wish, I will;" and down I sat, but in rather a sulky manner; for I felt that the prize was not yet mine, and that it was still slipping through my fingers.

"Let us talk calmly as friends, not as lovers," she said, after I was quiet. "Remember we promised always to be friends."

"That was a safe promise on your part," I remarked, bitterly, "but not on mine. When I return I may be able to assume the part you designate. As it is, I cannot now. Let us part. This interview is not satisfactory to me, and must distress you. It will amount to nothing. The promises which I am prepared to make will not be received, and the vows which I am ready to utter will not be listened to. Let me kiss your hand and go, and when next we meet it shall be in the friendly manner which you prescribe. This I promise you. I will struggle with the love which now binds me to you, and tear it from my heart, even if life goes with it. Can I promise more?"

She was silent and thoughtful, yet I saw no sign of yielding in her calm face.

"If you think that such a course is best, I will not oppose it," she said, as I rose from the chair which I had occupied during the interview.

"Answer me one question," I cried. "If I should remain, would your feelings undergo a change?"

"In what respect?"

"Could you be induced to accept me as a husband?"

The lady shook her head.

"A long probation, Charles, would be necessary before I could consent to such an arrangement. Even then you would have to experience a change of heart and mind, to obtain my consent."

"O ——"

An oath was on my lips, but, thank fortune, I suppressed it. I turned impatiently from the lady, and strode towards the door.

"Farewell," I said. "You will see me no more."

A white hand was laid lightly upon my shoulder, and a gentle voice said, —

"Do not leave me in anger, Charles — not in anger."

I turned, threw my arms around her waist, and before she had time to think, pressed my lips to hers. She struggled to free herself from my embrace, but I held her fast.

"Is there no hope?" I whispered. "Do you doom me to banishment without a sigh?"

"Not without sighs and tears, Charles; but I dare not trust my happiness to your fickle nature."

I released her, and stifled my wrath in the best manner possible.

"Are you still angry?" she asked.

I made no reply. I took one last look at her sweet face, and left the house, much more miserable than when I had entered it. I walked slowly to the counting-room, and there found Mr. Cherington surrounded by an eager crowd, anxious to engage passage for California. My partner left the people, and came towards me.

"What success at the house, Charles?" he asked.

I could not tell him. He read it in my face without the aid of words.

"Poor boy! I am sorry, but let us hope for the best. There is time enough yet. When you return she may think differently."

"Yes; but I shall not return in a hurry," I answered. "Absence alone can heal my wounds."

"Let us hope so; but now to business. When can you sail?"

"To-morrow, if necessary."

"It is not necessary. Shall we say the day after?"

"Yes, the quicker the better."

"Then, gentlemen," addressing the passengers, "you must be on board at eight o'clock day after to-morrow. Now I'll receive the money for your passage;" and Mr. Cherington went to work counting gold and silver as coolly as though he thought of nothing but business, and cared only for that; but I could see that he was annoyed at my ill luck, and I knew that he wished matters had terminated in a different manner.

As soon as I had concluded my affairs, I went on board, and

commenced preparations for sailing. I was too weak and tired to attend to all the details; but the officers and men were not disposed to slight matters, and before night we had stowed our wood and water, and received on board such provisions as we needed, and when the day arrived for our departure, the passengers were on board, and eager for a start. The shore was crowded with natives and friends of those on board. A hundred boats plie l around us, filled with laughing, white-teethed kanakas, who, as they ventured near us, were pelted with oranges from the quarter-deck; and yells of laughter were heard, as the rich fruit struck and burst, as it came in contact with some poor fellow's head. During this time I was in the cabin conversing with my partner, who seemed unwilling to release my hand from his close clasp. I never saw him so much affected, not even on the night we rescued him from the burning ship.

"It is not too late, Charles, to give up this trip," he said. "In a few minutes I can find some one to take charge of the vessel. It is not necessary for you to go. You have enough wealth to satisfy your ambition, and what you lack I can make up. Consider well. I love you as a son, and hoped that you would be one some day; but I dare not interfere in your behalf. Neither do you wish me to. You must win Julia without my aid."

"Of course," I replied; "I want no one's aid. But by even remaining here, what do I gain? Is there any hope of winning Julia?"

"Not at present."

"Then why should I stay? Absence is better than home, especially with the conscious-ness of knowing that Julia despises the weakness which I have manifested. We must part. I see no hope of happiness here."

Mr. Cherington made no further effort to detain me.

"Go," he said; "and may you return, and then prosper in your suit."

We shook hands and parted, he to return to the shore, and I to sail towards that land where thousands met fortune, or disappointment, penury, and death. As we left the basin I looked towards the house, where I had passed so many happy hours. Not a window was open, not a face was to be seen. No one waved a handkerchief as a token of remembrance, and in bitterness of heart I contrasted my departure with the previous ones, when I possessed Julia's love and esteem. Onward we sailed, and the fair island which contained one so dear to me was lost to view; and then I truly felt that my voyage of life had really begun, and for the first time, for many months, it seemed as though I was alone, with no one to love or confide in me. Unconsciously I uttered the last words aloud, and as I did so I felt a hand laid upon my shoulder.

"I remain to love you, and confide in you," said a soft voice; and turning, I saw Lilly standing by my side, her eyes fixed upon the blue line on the edge of the water, many miles distant, which betokened the land we had left. "Let Lilly share your confidence and your love," she said. "Once she did; but something stepped between her and the light of your eyes, and then a shadow passed over her soul, for you no longer smiled upon her. Let me feel your hand."

I gave it to her, and she took it in her own.

"Once it was calm, and the pulse beat firm. Lately you have been feverish and fretful, and your flesh burns like fire. You are not as happy now as you were when you swam with me at Kammaira. Are you?"

"Not quite, Lilly; but I trust that I shall be, in time."

"And what has made you feverish and unhappy? Will you not confide in me?"

"I have had some trouble, Lilly; but I cannot tell you all."

She did not press me further. How could I tell her that it was owing to the love which I bore another? No, thank God, I did not have a heart so cruel as all that. If she knew nothing of Julia and my engagement, I did not feel disposed to enlighten her. Once more the girl laid her hand upon my arm, in such a timid manner that I knew she expected me to shake it off; but I did not.

"I did not visit my father while we were at Honolulu," she said. "I should have done so, but I had not the courage to leave you, even for a day."

I made an impatient movement, and she continued.

"I shall never see him again. I know that I shall not, for three different times have I dreamed of the *Malo*, and our people say that it is a sign of death. If I should die, let me expire in your arms; and then I know I shall pass to the other world, or to some pleasant islands where the sun ever shines, and the fruits are always ripe, and the clear streams cool and fresh. Perhaps

I shall go to your heaven, and if I do I will be your servant, and wait upon you, and gather flowers for your house, and I will select the ripest fruits for your table, and when you sleep I will fan you with feathers plucked from birds of bright plumage. When you walk I will be by your side, and hold back the branches of trees, if they impede your path. At night, while you smoke your pipe, I will sing to you, and place roses near your head, and cover you with soft cloths, and be near to hand you cool water, if you should desire drink. I will be your slave, and for all this I shall only ask a smile."

"Don't talk of death, Lilly," I said. "You have many years of happiness before you. Some day you will marry — and —"

"Will *you* marry me?" she asked, eagerly.

It was the first time she had ever put such a question, and I think that it startled me. For a few moments I paused to think what answer I should return. She knew not the difference in our position, and could I expect to make her comprehend it?

"You do not answer me. You would despise me as a wife;" and the kanaka girl withdrew her hand from my arm, and I saw more sadness upon her brow.

"Listen to me, Lilly," I said. "I have wealthy and proud parents. They would not think you were a proper wife for their son; and if I should marry you, they would be very angry, and refuse to receive me in their house. You would not have me disowned by my father and mother — would you?"

"No, I will do nothing that would give them pain; but when you landed at Kammaira, pursued by your enemies, hungry, and without a place to rest your head, I did not stop to ask if you had a father or mother. I made no inquiries regarding their wealth or position. I saw that you were in want, and my father, a chief among his people, the first in their estimation, did not stop to ask if you were any better than your companions. He listened to me, and received you in his house, and gave you food and shelter; he protected you, and there was no one to raise his hand against you. You remember this — do you not?"

"Yes," I answered; for I could not deny a single word that she had uttered.

"Well, if such is the case, why should your parents treat me in a different manner, provided I visited your country?"

I attempted to explain the difference of society in Boston and the Sandwich Islands; but the poor girl could not understand my meaning, and she shook her head as she puzzled over it.

"If I had asked you to marry me, when living at Kammaira, would you have consented?" Lilly inquired. "You told me then that you loved me better than life, and I loved you, and was happy, and thought not of the future. Would that we had always remained at my home, for now, alas! I shall see it no more."

The topic which she was anxious to discuss was disagreeable, and I was only too willing to avoid it. I was not sorry, therefore, when the girl turned from me and entered the cabin, with a sad face and tearful eyes.

The schooner struggled through the water, sometimes pounding the waves with her bluff bows, as though she was a driver, and had a certain amount of piles to drive before night. Again she rolled like a drunken sailor on shore, and sometimes moved along like a dainty lady, as though picking her course on a crowded sidewalk. One by one the passengers retired to their berths, some to dream of Fortune's favors, and others to think of home, and the friends they had left behind them. The watch paced the deck, smoking and laughing, and some of them spinning long yarns of the fun which they had experienced at Honolulu. Perhaps the stories which they told were a little colored, and hardly worth repeating; but sometimes I could not help smiling as I caught a word or two. Up and down the deck I paced until four bells, and then retired for the night; and just as the morning watch commenced preparations for washing down the deck, I heard some one shout the welcome cry of, —

"Sail, ho!"

It was not an unusual cry, but from the stir I heard on deck, I thought that the stranger must be something extraordinary; so I put on my clothes, and went up to take a look at him.

"There's the devil, sir," cried Jack, pointing to the leeward; and looking in the direction indicated, I saw the old whale-ship Sally, Captain Bunker, about three miles off, under easy sail, and heading in the same direction as the Helen.

"Put your helm up," I said to the man at the wheel. "We will edge off, and speak that fellow."

Mr. Topmall exhibited signs of tribulation immediately, but said nothing.

We ranged along off his weather quarter, and then Bunker, with his red hair and eyes, hailed us.

"Ain't that the Helen?" he asked.

"Yes; how are you?"

"Well, I'm so-so. Seen any whales lately?"

"Not a whale."

"Whar do you come from?"

"Just from Hilo. Come on board and see me. I've got some of the best whiskey on the Pacific coast."

"You ain't heard from Honolulu, then?" cried the whaler, a little suspiciously.

"No; have you?"

"Not much. I'll come and see you, and get some breakfast. Clear away my boat;" and while his men were obeying his orders, I called Jake to me.

"Our old friend," I said, "is coming to see us. I owe him a grudge, and want to pay him."

"Blast 'em, so do I," was the man's reply.

"Well, listen to me, and make no mistake. You have two coffee-pots — have you not?"

"Yes, sir."

"Well, in one you must have good coffee for the passengers and me to drink, and in the other coffee which has been *doctored*."

"Golly, cap'n; you ain't goin' to pizen 'em — is you?"

"No, but I intend to disturb him a little. Come with me, and keep your eyes open."

He followed me to the cabin. I took from the medicine chest a strong emetic, and told the darky to mix it with the coffee, and to give it to Bunker while breakfasting. The negro comprehended my intentions in a moment, and a broad grin spread over his face.

"Golly, cap'n, dat gib 'em fits for sure. Make dis nigger laugh."

He went forward with the emetic, and by the time he had reached the galley Bunker was alongside. The treacherous rascal jumped on deck, and came aft with a smile upon his face.

"Devilish glad to see you," he said, "I haven't forgot the turn you did me at the Ladrones."

Just at that moment the steward passed into the cabin with breakfast. Bunker needed no urging to join me. He thought I was not aware of his treacherous course and became confident and overbearing. He talked of whales, and the Sally; of my running away, &c., until at last Jake placed a cup of coffee before him.

"This is devilish good," Bunker said, sipping it, and looking satisfied. "I like good coffee. I remember I once commanded a ship called the Spouter, of New London. We were cruising for sperm whale near Japan, and one day the steward told me that we had run short of coffee. I didn't know what to do, but at last concluded to go on shore, and see if I could not buy some of the Japs."

"Do they raise coffee?" asked a passenger, who was eating his breakfast, and evidently much amused at the master's yarns.

"Oceans of it," was the reply, "and I determined to have some. I ran in close to the land, and went on shore with a boat's crew. The Japs came down to the beach, and motioned me to clear out, but I made up faces at 'em. They stood their ground, and swore that I should have nothing, and I swore that I would."

Bunker drank half a cup of coffee, and then continued: —

"When they said I shouldn't have what I wanted, I just took up a lance and pinted it at 'em, and by the Lord Harry if they didn't take to their heels then I'm a beggar."

"Fill the captain's cup," I said to the grinning Jake.

"Go on with the yarn," cried the passengers.

"Well, I will. I followed 'em to the village, driving 'em before me, and when I reached it, the old men came forward, and said I should have all that I wanted if I would spare 'em. I promised; so they loaded my boat with coffee and fresh truck, and off I went, and didn't have to pay a cent. That's what I call — "

He paused a moment, and placed his hand upon his stomach, while his face grew several shades lighter. The emetic was working slowly but surely.

"How many died with the cholera while we were at Hilo?" I asked a passenger, who knew that there was some mischief brewing, and answered, —

"About three hundred, I think."

"And how is that fellow this morning? Will he live?"

"O, he died half an hour ago, and the other one will go before noon."

Bunker began to stare. His color changed rapidly.

"What in the devil's name do you mean?" he gasped.

"O, nothing, excepting the cholera. We have it on board. It was bad at Hilo, but we are not much alarmed. We've kinder got accustomed to it. Only three or four of our kanakas have died, and some half a dozen are sick."

"Another is down since breakfast," remarked a passenger, whose name was Brick, — rather suggestive of his nature.

"Is he bad?" I asked, gravely.

"Rather — stomach all knotted, and feet cold. Vomits freely."

Bunker started up from the table with symptoms of alarm. His face was pale, and perspiration was standing on his brow.

"What in the devil's name do you mean by asking me to come on board?" he yelled.

"Why, to eat some breakfast, of course."

"Breakfast!" shrieked the victim; "cuss your breakfast! I've caught the cholera. I'm sick. Give me something."

"Take some more coffee," suggested Brick, who had been let into the secret.

"Is that good for me?" howled Bunker.

"Nothing better. I've known it to cure a man, after he was in the last stages."

"Let me have some, then. Quick, you nigger, or I shall bust."

Jake poured out a cup of coffee, and the whaler seized on it, and threw back his head. It disappeared in an instant, and as soon re-appeared; for the emetic commenced its work in the most powerful style.

"O God, I'm dying!" yelled Bunker. "My inards is all torn to pieces. Can't you give me something? A little brandy would be better than nothing. Do you think I shall die?"

"I think that brandy would save him," remarked Brick, in a low tone.

"Then let me have some. I need it. I shall die without it."

"Can't spare it. Must keep it for our own men," was my cool reply.

"O, do give me a little. If you knew how I felt!" and a fresh spell of vomiting stopped his utterance.

"On one condition you shall have the brandy," I said.

"Name it, and be quick; for I'm growing cold."

"You must sign a confession of your doings at the Ladrones, and entirely repudiate the falsehoods which you related to Miss Cherington. Will you do it?"

"I don't know. Do you think I shall die at the present time?"

"It appears as though you were sick, quite sick. If you think you will recover, don't sign any statement I shall draw up."

A fresh spell at vomiting decided the man. He wanted the brandy at all odds.

"I did tell some tough yarns about you," he moaned, "but it was some of my fun; I didn't mean anything. You know I didn't."

"I know that you injured me, you rascal; and I have a good mind to let you suffer or die without the least help. But I will assist you, and save your life, if you will sign a paper, in which shall be stated the lies you told concerning me."

"I'll do it; bring the brandy along."

I told Brick to administer it at the rate of a spoonful every five minutes, while I went to my state-room, and drew up a statement, which was strictly correct, respecting my conduct and that of Bunker's at the Ladrones. This I read to him; and to my surprise, he said that he would sign it immediately, and without modification.

"I did act a mean part towards you, and no mistake," he said, all his pride having left him; "and if I live I'll do the right thing. Botheration, how it gripes me! More brandy."

We gave him a dose, and then he signed the statement, and half a dozen of my passengers witnessed it. As soon as that was done, Brick poured out half a tumbler of liquor, and the master swallowed it without hesitation.

"That's all you'll get, old fellow," said Brick. "We want the rest for our punches. You won't die this time."

"You think there's hope for me?" timidly inquired Bunker.

"Hope; of course there is. Who ever heard of a man's dying after taking an emetic."

"After taking what?" cried Bunker, raising his head, and looking a little wild.

"An emetic," Brick repeated.

"Have I taken one?" yelled Bunker.

"I should think you had, from the evidence."

"Ain't I got the cholera?"

"Not that we know of, unless you brought it on board. We haven't seen anything of the disease."

Bunker sat up, and looked first at Brick, and then at me, in amazement and disgust. He felt better immediately.

"What's the meaning of all this?" he asked.

"It means that we have punished you for telling such rascally lies respecting me. Let it be a lesson which you will remember for the rest of your life. You have injured me in the estimation of a young lady, and I have retaliated. Now you can leave the vessel as soon as you please. I have done with you."

"Cuss your eyes!" the whaler muttered; "if I ever have a chance I'll make you pay for this; you see if I don't."

He left the cabin, but as he reached the deck, gave evidence that the emetic was still working, and with curses and groans entered his boat, and was pulled to the ship. We crowded sail, and continued our course for San Francisco. The whaler made no attempt to overtake us, and by night was out of sight. We had twenty days' passage to San Francisco, reaching there in the month of September. In a few hours after the anchor was dropped, my passengers left me, bag and baggage. They were fearful that they should lose even a day. They were fierce for gold, and gold only would satisfy their desires. I was not sorry to have the vessel free of a crowd, and saw them go without regret. As soon as they had left, I went on shore to pay my respects to my friends. The first place which I stopped at was the Connecticut House.

"Is Captain Myers in?" I asked of the bar-keeper.

"Don't keep here now," was the curt answer.

"What is he doing?"

"Has a store somewhere on Montgomery Street. Sold this place a month ago."

I left the hotel, and went in search of Hatch. He, too, had moved, and it was some time before I could discover his location. I found him at last, doing a large business. He was eager to hear from Honolulu, and had a thousand questions to ask me respecting people he was acquainted with.

"Why did Myers sell?" I asked.

"Because he had a good offer, and his wife urged him to leave hotel-keeping, gambling, and kindred vices. She is the leader of the fashions here, and is making him quite a good wife. I see them occasionally; but the captain is rather shy about inviting me to his house. He remembers that his wife had a partiality for me."

"Has Myers gone into any business?"

"Of course he has, and is doing well. He has quit selling lots of land, for the business grew dangerous. He stopped just in time. He has bought a new house out towards the Mission, and gives some good dinners; so I have been told."

I left Hatch and went in search of Myers, and was lucky enough to find him. The whaler was glad to see me, and insisted upon my going home with him, and chatting with Dorothea.

"Ah, my boy, what a treasure that woman is!" cried the captain, as we left the store for his house. "She is just the thing for this market. I can go away and leave her, and be certain of finding her when I return. No man dares make love to her in my absence. She is trumps, and no mistake. She leads the fashions in San Francisco. But you shall judge of her merits."

We reached the house after a quarter of an hour's walk. As soon as the front door was opened I heard a rustling of silk, and then saw a pair of very thin and dark arms thrown around the whaler's neck, and a large mouth pressed towards his lips; but the kiss only reached the jolly red nose of the captain. He received it as a matter of course, and after giving her one hug, said, —

"My little dovey, don't you see that I have brought home a friend?"

Dorothea withdrew her arms, and looked at me in silence. I thought that she intended to upbraid me for my presence, but I was disappointed, for she suddenly opened her arms, and came towards me, shouting, —

"O! to you I am indebted for this."

I dodged, but was not quick enough. She managed to get one arm around my neck, and held me fast. I struggled, but it was useless. She pressed me closer and closer, and at last showered down kisses upon my nose and mouth.

"Go in and win, old lady," cried the delighted whaler. "He's the author of our happiness; you can't do too much for him."

At length she became exhausted, and stopped her caresses.

"To think how much we owe him!" she murmured, looking at me and throwing her arms around the neck of the whaler.

"Yes, I know we do," he answered; "but he don't like your kisses as well as I."

I confessed as much, and then we entered the parlor and I found that it was well furnished, some of the articles being quite expensive. But the dress which the lady wore was not in good taste. She had on a heavy silk, flounced to her waist, low-necked, bare-armed, and short enough to show her ankles, which I am sorry to state were none too thin for symmetry. She was weighed down with jewelry, having an immense gold chain on her neck, made from native ore. Attached to the chain was a gold watch of large dimensions, and it protruded from her waist belt like an over-grown wart. On each arm she had two bracelets, one of them being studded with diamonds, and the other dotted with specimens of California gold. Each of them weighed about four ounces. On her fingers were rings of great value, diamonds and pearls, emeralds and amethysts. My attention gratified Myers immensely. He rubbed his hands and laughed.

"What do you think of her?" he asked. "Isn't that the way to dress a wife? Look at her. Note her jewelry. Has she got enough? I can buy her more."

"She might find room for a breastpin," I remarked.

"I never thought of that. I'll have one as large as my hand made for her, and it shall be of solid gold, too."

"What do you suppose Constance would say to see me now?" asked Dorothea, with a look of pride at her jewels. "Some day we intend to visit the Ladrones, and then I shall show her that I have forgiven past offences."

We had tea, and then they pressed me so hard to remain all night that I consented.

CHAPTER XXI.

UP THE SACRAMENTO. — OFF FOR THE MINES. — THE HEAT ON THE PRAIRIES. — AN ATTACK. — JOQUIN THE ROBBER.

We remained at anchor for a few days, until I had an offer to take a load of freight up the Sacramento, to the city of that name. As the terms were liberal, I accepted them, and commenced loading, which was completed in forty-eight hours. I secured the services of a good pilot, and one forenoon we left San Francisco, and arrived at Sacramento in good time. Here I received a very liberal offer for the schooner, — ten thousand dollars, — and disposed of her at that price.

The next day we discharged a portion of our freight, and the following day landed it all on the levee. As yet we had no idea where we should go, and thought that it was time that that important point should be settled; so one evening I wandered towards the gambling tents, where all the gossip was related and the news circulated, and mingled with the crowd, asking questions and listening to answers.

After some talk, I determined to attempt mining on the Yuba, calculating that if the location did not suit I could change to some other quarter with but little trouble, while the money which I had received for freight and by sale of the vessel, I invested in house lots, buying from the city authorities.

At four o'clock one morning, we left Sacramento City for Baker's Bar, on the Yuba. I hired a team drawn by eight mules, to take our freight, at the rate of ten cents per pound, and I also purchased horses and saddles for the use of Lilly and myself.

We left the city before many of its inhabitants were stirring. Our party consisted of seven persons, Lilly and myself, Jack, Will, Jake, Bushy, and two kanakas, the cook being one of them. The others had expressed a preference for remaining by the vessel, and I was willing that they should. They preferred a certainty to an uncertainty. We were all in good spirits as we wound our way among the tents and shanties, the driver and owner of the team cracking his whip, and yelling to his mules if they did not draw fair and square. At last we left the city behind us, and entered upon the prairie, the road leading past Sutter's Fort. Soon after passing the fort we forded the American River, where we stopped for a moment to drink of its cool waters, and bathe our faces and feet, which already began to show signs of travel.

By this time it was seven o'clock, and the sun commenced illustrating its power by drying up the dew and causing the prairies to steam like a boiling kettle of water. The teamster, a man named Hardcase, an Oregonian, dipped his head into the steam, and then, while the water was gently trickling down neck and back, spoke as follows: —

"Stranger, it's goin' to be all fired hot to-day, and no mistake. These prairies will bile by and by, and a man might as well set his foot on a hot brick as to touch 'em. I tell you it's so, 'cos I know 'em. I left old Illinois two years ago, and made a jaunt over land, and perhaps we didn't catch it at times. Wal, we did; now that's a fact. But that ain't here nor thar. The question is, shall I push on, or will you camp till near sunset and then start, travel in the cool of the night, and come out as lively as a lark in the morning?"

"Which do you think best?" I asked.

"Wal, 'tain't for me to say. I'm here to get you at the mines, and I'm going to do it; but I don't want to near kill you. Arter we leaves this river we don't strike water till we touches Bear Creek, about thirty miles from here, over a prairie that ain't got a bush as big as a bull-calf, nor a tree as large as a mule's hind leg. But you can take your choice; I'll risk the mules, but I won't risk the company."

I concluded to wait, and said so, for the heat was pouring down most unmercifully. In about half an hour we reached a grove of trees which completely sheltered us from the sun, while we were so near the river, — having followed its course, — that we were enabled to obtain all the water we desired.

We had breakfast, and then slept, and passed the day in the best manner possible. Towards night, after another hearty meal, — it is singular how much a man can eat in California, — we collected our animals, gave them as much water as they could drink, and just at sundown we started to cross a thirty-mile prairie, the soil of which was like heated bricks. But no sooner had the sun disappeared than a heavy dew commenced falling, which cooled the air and the ground, and enabled us to travel in a comfortable manner.

Lilly endured the fatigues of the journey much better than I anticipated. When she was tired of riding horseback she would walk until once more glad to seek the saddle. In this way we reached Bear River just at daylight, tired, thirsty, and hungry. But after a wash in the cool waters of that little stream we were much refreshed, and enabled to do full justice to the excellent breakfast which Jake prepared for us.

We slept through the day, and at night started as usual; but we had not proceeded two miles before we heard the sound of horses' feet advancing towards us, and almost before we had time to think, two men checked their animals and hailed: —

"Hullo, whom have we here?"

"Hullo yerself, and see how you like it," responded Hardcase.

"Who are you?" asked the horsemen.

"Honest men."

"It is easy enough to say that," was the sneering answer.

"And easy enough to maintain it; so stand out of the way, and let us pass."

"Patience, my friend," was the answer. "We mean no harm."

"Well, what do you mean?"

"To inform you that the Indians are in arms, and killing people on the route between here and the Yuba."

Hardcase gave a laugh of defiance and contempt.

"We isn't alarmed at that," he cried.

"But I have other news," said the stranger, advancing closer, as though afraid to communicate it at a distance.

"Spit it out," was the inelegant expression of Hardcase.

"Joquin and his gang are out."

"Are you sure?" demanded the teamster in a tone of some anxiety.

"Quite sure. He robbed and murdered four miners yesterday morning near the Ten Mile Reach, and where he is now the Lord only knows."

This was important intelligence, for Joquin was the most desperate robber that ever murdered travellers in California. He was a Mexican by birth, and entertained the most profound hatred for Americans, and if one fell into his hands he rarely suffered him to escape. He was noted for his boldness, cunning, his good looks, and splendid horsemanship, and brave men were cowed when his name was mentioned.

"How comes it that you travel alone at this hour of the night if Joquin is near?" asked Hardcase.

"Because we wish to leave the mines, where we are not safe, and seek shelter in the city. We have ridden hard, and think that now we are beyond danger."

"You can't tell about that," was the reply of the teamster. "Joquin has fresh horses, and rides like a whirlwind. But go on and inform every miner that you meet of the danger, and all will then prepare for it, and perhaps some bullet find a way to his heart."

"Good night, and Heaven protect you," was the answer of the horsemen, as they swept on and soon crossed the river.

"Shall we push on?" asked the teamster, as he gathered up the reins.

"Of course."

"That's my style," was the answer; and on we went.

"What do you think?" I asked.

"We must keep our eyes peeled, and look out for squalls. If Joquin attacks us we must beat him off, and if the Injuns come we'll sarve 'em out in a way that will astonish 'em."

"Then we had better look to our rifles and pistols, I think."

"Yes, and see that they are loaded carefully. If I can get a bead on Joquin he will never rob again."

I fell back a little, and ordered the men to take their weapons from the wagon and load them, and keep close to me, and on no account to stray away, all of which they promised; and then we pushed on through a thick wood, where it was so dark that we could hardly see the road, and where two resolute men could have destroyed us.

It was about twelve o'clock at night, and we had just reached the edge of the woods without meeting with any adventure worthy of note, save the rustling of leaves and the cracking of branches, denoting that some animal was moving or had been disturbed by the rumbling of the wagon, when we were somewhat surprised to hear a shrill whistle, which seemed to come from a dense thicket on our left, and it was answered on our right.

In an instant Hardcase struck his mules with his long and heavy whip, and they dashed along at a rapid rate; but just as the leading mules reached the open prairie, the report of a rifle or revolver was heard on our left, and a ball whizzed within a foot of the driver's head.

He made no reply to the shot, but yelled to his mules, and the next instant they were on the open ground, and the dark forest was behind us; but still we did not stop until my men were out of breath with running, and the mules were covered with sweat and foam, and unable to continue their headlong pace. Not until then did Hardcase draw up and await my coming, for I was some distance in the rear, for the purpose of seeing that my men made good their escape.

"Wal, cap'n, what do you think of that?" asked the driver, as I reached the wagon.

"I think that somebody was impertinent, and had designs upon your life."

"Wal, that's a fact, and no mistake. He aimed well, the tarnal skunk; but the wagon bounced over a log, and took me out of the range. Blast their picturs, let 'em come on now if they want to."

"Who do you suppose is concealed in that wood?" I asked.

"Wal, it's hard to tell; but I shouldn't wonder if it was Joquin, and some of his beauties. It's jist like him; and we ain't seen the last of him yet, I know. But now to business, cap'n. We shan't escape in this way. The gang that attacked us want provisions, and they will fight for them. They don't dare visit the towns for grub, so make forays on trains. Shall we fight or run, and let 'em take what they want from the wagon?"

"Fight," shouted Will, Jack, and Bushy.

"What do you say, cap'n?" asked the driver.

"Fight until we are whipped or whip the rascals," I answered.

"That's the talk. Then I'm with you. Come on, and we'll soon see what kind of stuff the robbers is made of."

He had hardly finished speaking when from the woods galloped half a dozen horsemen; but instead of advancing towards us, they kept close to the trees on our left, as though they desired to gain the road which we would have to pursue if we continued our journey, and which wound around the base of some high hills covered with a growth of large pines, affording some lovely spots for an ambush, where an attacking party could pick us off with impunity.

"Stay by the wagon, some of you," shouted Hardcase. "Cap'n, you come with me."

The speaker, rifle in hand, ran towards one of the hills, so as to cut off the robbers and drive them back into the woods, and leave us in possession of the road. I followed him, but he ran so swiftly that I had to put forth all my speed to keep within speaking distance. But we reached the position we desired, and before the robbers gained the road, owing to the latter stopping for some time to make out the movements and force of those around the team.

"Now, then," cried Hardcase, as he threw himself upon the ground, "do you feel cool and steady?"

"Not cool after such a run as that. I am covered with perspiration."

"But your narves — how is they?"

"Steady enough to hold a rifle."

"And use it?"

"I think so."

"Wal, we'll tell better by and by. We must knock over two of them peeps, or they'll go for us. Can you shoot?"

"A little," I answered, modestly.

"Humph. We'll see how much that little amounts to. Take a careful aim and cover your man. We can't afford to waste a shot. Imitate me."

"I will, all except the running."

"Wal, we may have some of that to do afore we is through with these fellers. Ah, what is they up to now, I wonder?"

The horsemen had stopped, and were grouped together for consultation. They had not seen Hardcase and myself when we crossed the level spot between the woods and the wagon; for when we ran we were somewhat sheltered by the latter, and while we were under the shadow of the trees, of course we were out of sight of those on the plain.

"I hope they is not a goin' to make a dash at the wagon," muttered the driver. "If they does will your men fight?"

"Two or three of them will, I am certain, and the others will strike a blow if cornered."

It seemed as though the horsemen were determined to make an attempt at capturing the team, for one of them rode rapidly towards it, and did not draw rein until he was within fifteen or twenty fathoms of it. Then he halted and examined the wagon, and the men who where clustered around it.

This movement we watched with some anxiety, for we feared a sudden dash.

"That is Joquin," whispered Hardcase, in a tone that savored somewhat of admiration. "I know it's him, the cunning rogue."

"How are you so certain?"

"Don't you see that feller ain't still for one second. See him move fust one way and then another. Allers in motion."

"What is it for?" I asked, in my simplicity.

"What for?" re-echoed the driver, in a tone that savored somewhat of contempt; "why, he don't want a bullet through his skin — he don't. Your men must be mighty smart on the trigger to hit him, now I tell you. O, he's an old head, I'll warrant you."

The night was not so dark but we could see the movements of the man quite plainly, and I must confess that they were worth noting, for I never saw a more graceful piece of acting. Now the horse would bound forward, now retreat, the body of the rider swaying to and fro, so that it was almost impossible for any one, except an experienced marksman and an old hunter accustomed to the business, to hit him. The horse and rider appeared to understand each other most perfectly, and a motion seemed sufficient to guide the beast.

"Blast the feller! I hope some one will have a crack at him, if only to let him know that we ain't asleep."

Hardly had the words escaped the mouth of the driver than there were two loud reports, and we could hear the whistling of balls as they flew across the plain.

"Them ain't rifle shots," cried Hardcase, with an expression of disgust.

"I know that. Jake has a pair of horse-pistols, and some one has fired them."

"And much good they has done. But I don't know, though. See, Joquin is off like a deer."

In fact, the robber had suddenly wheeled his horse and dashed towards his comrades, as though he thought time was precious just then.

"We can tell in a minute what the cusses will do," said Hardcase; and his prophecy was correct, for, after a moment's consultation, the gang trotted towards us, evidently determined to capture the wagon in the easiest manner possible.

"Now for it," cried the driver, raising his rifle. "Wait till I tell you, and then fire."

We waited for a minute. On came the horsemen, galloping rapidly, and some of the men chatting and laughing in a pleasant tone, as though the business on hand was of a light and easy nature. I think they were talking of the recent shots, and making merry over them, for I heard several words in Spanish that gave me such an impression.

"Take the feller on the right," whispered Hardcase. "Don't miss him. Now, then, are you ready?"

"All ready!"

"Let her rip, then."

We fired, and I had the satisfaction of seeing the man whom I had aimed at fall from his horse, while the animal galloped towards us, and stopped just as it reached the woods where I afterwards secured it.

Hardcase was not so fortunate with his shot, much to my surprise and his disgust. Just as he fired, or a second before the bullet left the rifle, the robber had turned in his saddle, and consequently saved his life; but his horse paid the penalty, for the rider had drawn the curb rather tight, and the animal reared, so that the ball struck his neck, and down he went, throwing the robber over his head, where he lay for a moment, stunned and confused by the suddenness of the shock.

"A miss, by the Lord," cried the driver, with an imprecation; but still he did not neglect to load his rifle while grumbling at his ill luck — an example I was not slow to follow.

But we did not have a chance for another shot immediately. The robbers were not fond of such sport, and before we had time to charge our rifles, the horsemen had turned and fled towards the place from whence they came, sheltered from observation and pursuit by the thick pine woods through which we had passed an hour before.

"Now is our time," said Hardcase, starting up. "Catch the hoss and come with me."

"But the wounded man? What shall we do with him?"

"Let him remain where he is."

"But he may die."

"Let him die and be hanged; it's no business of ours. Come along with me. We must get through these woods afore the shunks cut us off. Have you got the hoss?"

"Yes."

"Then mount and gallop like the devil to the wagon. We must stir our stumps or we'll have our throats cut afore mornin', blast 'em, for that Joquin isn't the man to give it up so."

The wagon creaked and groaned as it started, thus informing our enemies that we were under way. I kept in the rear of the team, with my eyes constantly turned towards the woods, thinking that I should see the robbers leave them and pursue us; but all was still and quiet, and no sign of the ladrones was visible. I had Lilly for a companion, and she chatted until we again entered more woods, and then we followed the wagon in silence, expecting every moment that we should be attacked, but from what quarter we could not tell.

The road was terrible, filled with gullies, stones, and fallen timber. Half a dozen times did we stop to remove obstructions from the trail, and once to chain the wheels so that the wagon should not be dashed to pieces in sliding down a ravine, which the winter rains had gullied out. How we escaped I do not know, for the trees made the road dark and it was almost impossible to see the leading mules. Hardcase must have felt some joy to have extricated us from our perilous position in safety, for had the wagon capsized, we should have been compelled to leave most of our goods and chattels on the road, for we would not have dared remain and protect them, with a gang of robbers hovering in our rear.

After an hour's hard work we had the satisfaction of emerging from the woods and striking a prairie; and as we reached it we found that there were indications of daylight in the east, and the signs were hailed with the most intense satisfaction by all of our party.

"A few miles more, cap'n, and we'll fetch water," said Hardcase, as I rode towards him, after leaving the woods, for the purpose of congratulating him on his skilful driving.

"We shall have to camp," I said, "for the mules look too tired to tramp much further. They need rest."

"Of course they does, and they shall have it, although we must keep our eyes peeled all the same. I don't think we've seen the last of Joquin. He ain't the man to give up in that manner. He is like a bull-dog, and if he ain't got better business afore him, he'll try his hand ag'in as sure as you're a live man."

"How far are we from water?" I asked.

"Not more'n three miles; but we will fetch and give the mules somethin' to line their bellies. It's no use to talk. I'd rather run the risk of a fight than kill my mules, 'cos they is worth, each on 'em, three hundred dollars, and I can't afford to lose that sum, you know."

I did not urge the man, for I thought he knew his own business best. Besides, to tell the truth, I did not really think we should have another attack. I supposed that the Mexicans, finding we were well armed and ready, would haul off for some other party, and let us go on our journey in peace; and as my men were tired, and Lilly began to droop, I had no great objections to halting and refreshing.

We were some time in moving three miles, when we struck a branch of the Yuba, the water of which was pure and cold. Here we halted beneath the shadow of a grove of trees, where we could protect ourselves in case of an attack, and be well covered from the fire of an enemy.

By the time our mules were turned loose, the sun had made its appearance, and we were enabled to take a full survey of the prairie; but no one was in sight, even from the top of the tallest tree, which Jake climbed for the purpose of being assured that neither Indians nor robbers were lurking near, before he could commence a fire for breakfast. After the negro was satisfied, he turned to with a will, and in half an hour we had an excellent meal; and then we lighted our pipes and lay down under the trees, intending to talk over the events of the night, before we posted a picket and went to sleep. While we were thus engaged, it suddenly entered Jake's thick head that it would be a good thing if he took a bath in the river, which was only a few rods distant, and sheltered by bushes and trees. He did not ask my consent, — and indeed it was not needed, — but off he started, and was not missed. We supposed that he was busy with his pots and pans; but while smoking our second pipe we heard a shrill yell, and then a succession of yells, which startled us to our feet in short order, and made us grasp our rifles and pistols in expectation of an immediate attack.

Hardly had we gained our feet and collected our arms, when we were astonished with the sight of a dark, naked form, bounding from the bushes near the river, and rushing towards us."

"Good God!" I thought; "the Indians are upon us."

"The Injuns! the Injuns!" yelled Bushy, and with the words up went one of the venerable horse pistols, while the man shut his eyes and fired. Then, as though satisfied with the result, he dropped the weapon on the ground, and made for the nearest tree, up which he went with wonderful rapidity.

I don't know where the ball from the pistol went. I know this much, that it did not go near the strange-looking being who was approaching us, for he continued to run and to yell with most astonishing vigor; and he kept it up until he was within a rod or so of us, and then he stopped, and suddenly fell upon his knees, and stretched out his hands as though asking for protection. The cause of this was on account of the number of rifles he saw pointed at him, and it is a wonder that the man was not shot, for we were all ready to fire, when the person who was making such an indecent exhibition of himself, shouted, —

"De Injuns! de Injuns! Dey is on us wid knives and tomahawks."

It was Jake. We could not fail to recognize his voice; but we did not know his form, especially when it was not covered with clothing.

I turned to caution Lilly about remaining near the front; but she had already taken the alarm, and was under the wagon with her head covered with a blanket.

"You rascal!" I shouted, "what do you mean by frightening us in this manner? Where are your clothes?"

"Over dar, sir."

"Why didn't you put them on before you came here?"

"Couldn't, sar. De Injins see me and fire de arrers at me. Come precious near dis child, too, dat I tell you;" and Jake arose from his knees and wrapped a blanket, which Will had thrown him, around his form, and then hurried to the shelter of a tree, and commenced relating his troubles to Bushy, who had taken occasion to descend to *terra firma*, while we were occupied in questioning Jake. I looked around for Hardcase, but he had vanished as soon as he had heard Jake announce the presence of Indians; and while I was wondering what I should do, he reappeared, leaving the bushes which grew on the banks of the river with hasty strides, as though there was work before him, and it was time to commence it.

When Hardcase joined me, after reconnoitring the body of Indians on the opposite bank of the river, who Jake declared "were one hundred strong and terrible savage, with no clothing except a mat around their loins," he motioned me to step aside so so that we could converse without the men listening to what we said. As soon as we reached a convenient position, the driver said, —

"I've taken a look at them black divils, and I don't like the way they carries themselves. No, I must confess I don't."

"How many of them did you make out?"

"About two dozen bucks, but nary a woman or child."

"Of course if we are attacked we must fight," I remarked.

"I know that; but all our folks won't fight. If they would we might whip 'em. If we can keep the Injuns off, well and good; but can we lick 'em, and Joquin and his gang?"

"We can try," I responded.

"And we *will* try," cried Hardcase, enthusiastically. "I tell you I feel a little fightish, and afore I gives up my mules and wagon, I'll empty my rifle a dozen times or more. The cusses is waiting on the other bank of the river, and they won't attack us till dark. That we can rely on, 'cos they fear our rifles."

"Now for our plans of defence," I remarked.

"Wal, what do you propose?"

"That we fortify ourselves in the best manner possible."

"Them's my sentiments. We has got to do it, and wait and see what the Injuns is goin' to do. Will you leave it all to me?"

"Certainly. You have the command, and I'll act as assistant."

"Then we must go to work. Out with the axes, and down with some of these trees. With 'em we'll form breastworks and shelter; and if we don't keep the Injuns and Joquin at bay, I'm much mistaken."

"But they'll run our mules off."

"No, they won't, 'cos we will have 'em with us. You'll see how I'll fix 'em."

We got out our axes, and all hands set to work using them. If Jake and Bushy did not know how to manage fire-arms, the same could not be said regarding the manner in which they handled the pioneer's weapon of civilization, the axe; for the stately trees fell with such heavy crashes that the ground trembled for rods from our camp, and the Indians on the other side of the river must have wondered what we were doing, making such a noise. They did not cross over to see, however, and the work went on until we had laid low some thirty trees, and then the axes were put aside, and we commenced the formation of our fortification. We piled the trees, one upon the other, at right angles, until we had formed a square, the wagon helping to form one side. Our walls were about five feet high, and so covered with green leaves that we could look over them and run no risk of being seen by the enemy. One side we left open for the entrance of the mules; and when we were ready for them Hardcase took his rifle, mounted my horse, and went in search of them. They were feeding on the prairie, some distance from the river, and were very reluctant to leave the wild oats which grew so plentifully there. But at last Hardcase started them, and galloped towards the river for the purpose of giving them a drink before they were subjected to a siege which we did not know how soon might terminate, or how long it would last.

During the afternoon Hardcase and I were occupied in various things appertaining to our safety. The driver visited the prairie and cut several large armfuls of oats to feed the animals with, while Mr. Topmall volunteered to bring water from the river and fill all our canteens and all the empty vessels, so that we had enough to last us for twenty-four hours, although the animals would suffer unless we could find some means of supplying them in the course of a day or two.

At last we were ready, and just at sundown, while we were drinking a pot of cold tea, and eating pieces of bread and meat, we saw two or three dark forms steal along the bank of the river and shelter themselves in a clump of bushes. They were noting our position, and getting ready for an attack if they thought one likely to succeed. We were ready for action, but waited for the black rascals to commence the fight if they saw fit. As darkness stole over us we stationed our men, with strict orders to keep awake and watch for the foe. We held our weapons ready for use, but hour after hour passed and there were no signs of an attack, and we began to hope that we should escape a fight; but we were doomed to disappointment, for Hardcase came to my side and whispered, —

"I can hear the tramp of horses on the Yuba road, and they are coming in this direction."

The sound of the horses' hoofs grew more distinct, and at last, just as the riders were opposite our camp, they suddenly stopped, as though they had lost the trail of our wagon, and were somewhat puzzled to find it.

"Ah," muttered Hardcase, "you may bet high that Joquin leads that party;" and I thought that the driver spoke in rather an enthusiastic tone, as though he felt proud to be near such a man.

"What reason have you for thinking so?" I asked.

"Wal, I'll tell you. You see our wagon trail didn't go no further than this," pointing with his hand in the direction of the prairie.

"Yes, I'm aware of that."

"Wal, Joquin can foller a trail in the dark as well as most men can in daylight. He's a great scout, and knows his business. Yes; I'll give him the credit of knowing what he's about as well as any Mexican that lives in this part of the country. He has follered us right along, but the instant the trail ceased he stopped. O, he's got an eye like a hawk, that feller has. Can't fool him, not easy."

"Then you suppose that he'll pay us a visit before long."

"He'll come this way, I'll bet. He will want to see if we has crossed the river, or is camped and sound asleep. If he should —"

The driver ceased speaking, for at that moment there was a rustling in the bushes just outside of our fortifications, and at the same instant arose the shrill yelp of a prairie dog, or cayote; and very mournful it sounded, as it floated along through the calm air, and was taken up by cayotes, near the river, and the howl repeated with all sorts of cadences and variations.

Hardcase raised his rifle, and let it rest for a moment in the direction of the bushes. But the next instant he removed it from his shoulder, and muttered, —

"Let the poor devil go — he ain't worth powder and ball. It's a poor trick, and a risky one, as the scamp will find out some day if he ain't keerful."

"What do you mean? You wouldn't fire at a dog or wolf at such a time as this — would you?"

"And you really thought that noise was caused by a dog — did you?" asked Hardcase, with a low laugh.

"Of course it was. Didn't I hear him howl?"

"O, Lord, how easy you sailor chaps is fooled! 'Twan't no dog that made that noise, I tell you. 'Twas an Injun, and a bold one at that. He come to see what we was doin', and if we wan't asleep. He made more noise than he meant to, and he must have thought that we was awful green, or he'd been more keerful. But when he found that we was awake, and that he'd been imprudent, he thinks to turn it off by a howl; but I'd make him howl to a different tune if Joquin wan't near us. Blast him, let him go; but I hope the Injuns won't think I was cheated by so shallow a trick."

In the mean time, it was evident that the party on horseback were slowly and cautiously approaching our camp, for the purpose of discovering if we had crossed the river, or had halted for the night. It was evident that the robbers did not suspect the close proximity of the Indians; if they had they would have been much more circumspect in their movements, and avoided an ambush, for while the gang was coming towards us the sounds of the prairie dogs ceased, and all was quiet on the bank of the river.

"Had we not better give the horsemen a salute?" I asked, while Hardcase and I were peering over the barricade, watching their movements.

One of them was dismounted and searching for the wagon trail, and the others were sitting on their horses, quietly smoking, waiting for a report.

"Not for a hundred dollars would I fire a gun at the present time," was the answer. "Keep still, and perhaps we shall see some fun afore we is much older. The Injuns is quiet now — they is much astonished at the appearance of them men, and don't know whether they is our friends or enemies. Even now the black rascals is examining them from every bush, and you will see fun in a few minutes, unless the robbers take the scent and make off."

Presently the ladrone who was dismounted announced that he had found the trail, and then the whole party came towards us. We counted them — there were nine, and all well armed, we had no doubt.

"A few seconds more, and our camp will be discovered," whispered Hardcase. "As soon as they see it they'll turn tail in a hurry. Had we better give 'em a shot?"

Before I had time to reply there were yells to the right and left of us, and then we heard the twang of bowstrings, and the whiz of arrows. Some of the shots told, for we saw two of the horses plunge wildly and then fall; while one of the robbers uttered a pious exclamation, a call upon the saints for mercy, and fell to the ground; and then his companions drew their pistols, charged with a rush towards the bushes, fired several shots from their revolvers, and wheeled their horses and fled, leaving the dead or wounded man upon the field.

We could not tell if the gang of Mexicans had inflicted any injury upon their opponents, for they kept very quiet after the retreat of the horsemen, and seemed to be waiting for further developments. They evidently thought that the Mexicans were re-enforcements for our party.

At last, when we found that there was no probability of an immediate attack, we proposed that half of our number should lie down and get some rest, which was much needed, and that the balance should keep watch. The instant this was proposed, Lilly suggested that I should sleep while she stood guard in my place.

"But your eyes will grow heavy," I remarked.

"Look at them, and see if they are not bright enough to distinguish an enemy many yards distant."

In fact they did look bright, and she was eager to take my place. I was tired, and needed a little sleep; so, after a moment's consultation with Hardcase, who seemed to be more watchful than ever, and disdained the thought of closing his eyes, I lay down under the wagon, and soon fell asleep; and while I was dreaming of Julia, and that our quarrel had been settled in the happiest manner, and that I had again ordered a wedding suit, a hand was laid on my shoulder, and starting up, I found that Lilly had awakened me.

"Hush," she said. "Don't make a noise. The driver told me to arouse you. The robbers are close to us."

In a very short time I was by the side of Hardcase, who was listening and peering through the branches of the trees, quiet but watchful as usual. "What is up?" I asked.

"That is more than I can tell. Some movement is going on

near the bank of the river, but what it is I cannot imagine. The scamps may intend to carry our place by storm; and if such an attempt is made, we must give the rascals a warm reception Call up the men and get them ready."

It was rather hard to start some of our people, for they were tired and sleepy; but at length we had them in proper position, with guns in their hands, and orders not to fire until they saw something to fire at. By the time this was accomplished, we could hear stealthy movements in the bushes, as though the Indians were attempting to take up good positions near our defences, under cover of darkness. All at once, while we were listening, there was a sudden lighting up of the bushes, and then followed a pistol volley, and we could hear the balls ring as they tore their way through the bushes. Joquin and his gang were again at work determined to revenge the injury which they had received at the hands of the Indians. As yet the former did not suspect the presence of our force and fortifications, for not a bullet came in our direction.

The discharge of fire-arms was answered by a yell, one of the fiercest and loudest that I ever heard, and then from a dozen different directions could we hear the whizzing of arrows, showing in the most conclusive manner that the dark-skinned natives were neither surprised nor intimidated by the attack on the part of the Mexicans. They must have approached each other by crawling from bush to bush, and poured in their fire when they found they were at close quarters.

For a few minutes all was silent, with the exception of a few groans which came from some person wounded. The Indians remained in ambush, waiting an attack, and the Mexicans did the same, satisfied their revolvers would make short work of the natives when they chose to show themselves. But this the red men were not disposed to do. They preferred remaining where they were until such time as their weapons could be used in an effectual manner. They had the advantage of numbers, and knew that at short distances their arrows would be as effectual as pistols; and while they waited the Mexicans crept from the bushes, passed around a grove of trees towards the banks of the river, intending, in military parlance, to flank the Indians; but the latter, by the aid of their scouts, learned the design, and therefore fell back to the river, taking a stronger position than before. As soon as the Mexicans saw that they had failed, they fired a few shots for the purpose of feeling the natives, and then retreated, the Indians close upon them, and discharging their arrows rapidly. The conflict was thus carried some distance from us, and raged quite warm; and while it was going on, Hardcase adopted a new resolution.

"We must leave this place," he said. "Now is our time to start, and without a moment's delay. Them fellers will fight all night, and neither party will whip. While they is at work we can reach the Yuba, and be out of their reach. They won't know we has gone."

We hurried the mules over the prairie, and struck the road which wound along the bank of the river, and as we reached the top of a hill, paused a moment to look back. We could see the flashes of the pistols, and hear the reports of the weapons; but which side was getting the best of the battle we could not tell, and cared but little.

"Let 'em fight," said Hardcase. "May the Lord keep 'em at it for four hours, is the only prayer I can utter at the present time. Now, then, look out for the wagon, and keep it on its legs;" and the mules started, and away we went down hill, the wagon swaying to and fro, and creaking as though it would give out every moment; and faith, appearances were correct, for just as we reached the foot of the hill, one of the wheels came in contact with a stone which was lying on the trail, and with a crash down fell the wagon, some spokes having yielded to the pressure, and tumbled to pieces.

24

CHAPTER XXII.

A BAD POSITION. — OFF FOR HELP. — OLD NAT BAKER.

Our situation was not so pleasant as the one we had left, and we could not help regretting that we had started.

"What shall we do?" asked Hardcase, as we walked aside to consult.

"We can leave the wagon and cargo, and effect our escape on the mules," I answered.

"Yes, we can do that; but I don't believe in such desertion. We'll stick by the wagon as long as we can, and when we can't defend it we'll leave it. Blast the luck! who'd have thought that confounded wheel would give out jist as it did. A few miles farther and we'd been all right — for the varmints don't dare to get within the sound of old Nat Baker's rifle. Blast it! I wish that he was here, or we had his team."

"Why can't we have it?" I asked.

"I don't know. I s'pose we could, if I should see him. Old Nat would do most anything for me. We come from Oregon together, you know."

"Did you?"

"O, yes; we're like brothers."

While the driver was speaking I was thinking of an interview I once had with Baker at the San Francisco post-office, when the old man expressed much indignation at the conduct of one of the clerks on duty. I remembered how warmly the Oregonian had invited me to visit him at his ranche on the Yuba, and had promised me all the assistance in his power, in case I needed it.

"I will go for the wagon," I said. "I am acquainted with the man, and can borrow or hire it."

Hardcase thought of the proposition for a moment, before he said, —

"It's the only way to save the groceries. Mount your hoss and be off, and don't let the grass grow under your feet."

"And the road?" I asked.

"Is straight ahead until you reach the Forks, then turn to the left, and foller the trail for a mile, and you'll see Baker's house. It's on the bank of the Yuba, and the only house to be seen for miles."

"I will take the boy for company," I said, knowing that Lilly would fret during my absence, and would be of no use in case of an attack.

"Wal, we can spare him. Now be off, for we may need help afore you can get back. Tell old Nat how we is placed, and ask him to come to us. If he refuses, tell him that we have a keg of the best whiskey to be found in Sacramento City, and that it is liable to fall into the hands of the Indians. That will start him, I guess."

I was enabled to reach the Forks just at daybreak, about four o'clock. Then I turned as directed by Hardcase, and after following a trail for two miles, I gained the top of a hill, and was enabled to obtain a fine view of the valley which lay at my feet, and also the course of the Yuba, which wound its way among the hills, through prairies, and over rocks, foaming and roaring as though in a terrible hurry to reach the Sacramento River. Nestled in a grove of trees was a rudely built house, plastered over with mud which the hot sun had baked hard, until it looked capable of resisting the storms and rains of winter. On the opposite bank of the river were some ten or twenty tents and huts, occupied by those who were engaged in mining, and before each habitation was to be seen a thin spire of smoke, showing that the miners were preparing their morning meal before commencing work. I descended the hill at a rapid rate, and did not draw rein until I was opposite the door of the adobe house; and no sooner did I stop than two large dogs saluted me with ferocious growls, as though my visit was unwelcome, and entirely too early. As the animals looked threatening, I did not dismount, but sat on my horse until the noise which the dogs made brought to the door a tow-haired young fellow, six feet or over, thin, but muscular, with a face so freckled that it was difficult to tell the color of his skin.

"Hullo, old hoss," asked this specimen of young America, "what is up?"

"Does Mr. Baker live here?" I inquired.

"Wal, he don't live anywhere else."

"I would like to see him, if he is at home."

"Wal, he's at hum, and I s'pose you can see him. Here, dad, somebody is arter you."

"What does he want?" I heard a voice inquire.

"Wal, can't you come and see?" asked the young man. "I ain't goin' to ax him his business."

I heard a growl which sounded like that of a dog, and then the tall, lank form of old Nat Baker — the man whom I had met in San Francisco — hove in sight, and scanned me with a pair of eyes which age had not dimmed.

"Wal, stranger, what is it?" asked Baker, after a keen glance at my person. He did not recognize me, although I knew his weather-beaten face in a moment.

"Do you recollect meeting me at the San Francisco post-office many months since?" I asked.

The old fellow shaded his eyes with his huge black palm, and took a long look, and as he gazed I saw the expression of his face change from that of indifference to one of pleasure.

"By thunder!" he exclaimed, leaving the doorway and advancing towards me, "if it ain't you than I hope to holler. Give us your paw, old feller, and git right off that hoss, and come into the house. Here, Sam, Bill, where is you?"

I dismounted, and Lilly did the same, while the young men took charge of the animals.

"Don't take the saddles off," I said; "I must leave you in a few minutes."

"Nonsense!" cried the old man. "You don't do no such thing. We holds on to you for a few days. Come in and have a cup of coffee. You and your friend is welcome."

"But —"

"No buts here. In you come."

I entered the house, thinking it was the easiest way to stop discussion. The three men crowded around me to learn the news from a world which they only heard rumors of.

"Tell us somethin'," cried Nat. "How's things in the city?"

"Let me first tell you something that will interest you all."

"Yes, yes," they exclaimed; "that suits us. Let us have it."

"Within a few miles of here is a band of Indians. They are on the war-path, and mean mischief."

"Let 'em come," muttered old Nat, glancing at his long rifle, which was in a corner of the room.

"But I have more news."

"Good! let us have it."

"Joquin and his gang are not far from here."

"Ah, the varmints! I heard they was at their work agin. This is serious. The Injuns ain't of much 'count, but the Mexicans is sharp, and must be looked to. Did you see 'em?"

"Yes, and had a brush with them."

"The devil! Not you two?"

"No. A few miles from here is my party, under the charge of one Hardcase, a teamster."

"Not Bill Hardcase?"

"The same."

"And what does Bill want?"

"Your team and your help, and to obtain them without delay he sent me forward. His wagon has broken down, and not more than two miles in his rear are Joquin and the Indians, fighting. As soon as they cease fighting, one gang or the other will attack Hardcase for the sake of plundering his freight."

The three men listened to me in silence, and did not lose a word. As soon as I had concluded, old Nat said, —

"Bill, go and toot that horn. Sam, drive in the mules, and put the harnesses on 'em. We start in fifteen minutes for Oak Holler, where I s'pose Bill is waiting for us. Now eat."

By the time Lilly and I had satisfied our hunger the two boys came in.

"Wal, what does the miners say?" asked Nat.

"All right, dad. Six of 'em will be here in five minutes," answered Bill, seating himself at the table.

"And the mules, Sam?"

"They is hitched in, dad, and jumping to be off."

"That's well. Now I'll examine the shooting-irons while you is eating. Go on, lads, and line your ribs. I'll see that the lead and powder is right."

While he was speaking, half a dozen stalwart fellows entered the cabin, each man armed with a revolver and a rifle. They were all welcomed in a warm manner by old Nat, but declined the breakfast which he offered them, on the ground that they had eaten enough.

"Then take a nip of whiskey," said the host; and all agreed to that, without a single dissenting voice. "Come, let's move," cried Nat, as the tin pot returned to him emptied of its contents. "P'aps Bill Hardcase may be wanting us."

I found, on emerging from the house, that all the miners had joined us with horses, which stood ready saddled, and hitched to a fence. The animals which Lilly and I rode had been taken care of during the time we were breaking our fast. The boys had taken off the saddles, fed the brutes, and rubbed them down with wisps of straw. Consequently the brutes were in good condition for the journey.

"Better let that boy remain here," said old Nat, pointing to Lilly, who was waiting for me to arrange her saddle. "He won't be of any use to us."

"O, no; please take me with you," cried Lilly, speaking in her native tongue. "I should die if left here with no one to talk to. I won't give you any trouble, you know; you know I won't."

"But you are too much fatigued for the journey."

"O, no. See how smart I am!" and she leaped into the saddle so quickly, that even the grim men who stood near her did not suspect her sex, and were compelled to shake their heads, and acknowledge that he was smart, even if he was but a mere chick.

"Sam," cried old Nat, "you jist look arter that ere team and the mules, and come on arter us as fast as possible."

"But, dad," whined Sam, "if there's any fighting, I shan't have a hand in it; I don't think that's fair. You know I want a crack at Joquin for stealin' my hoss, some two months ago; dod rot his pictur."

"Never you mind that, my boy. You just cotton to them mules, and mind your daddy. Who knows but the Injuns may give you a chance for a shot on the road?"

Sam's face brightened at the idea. He made no further remonstrance, but took his seat upon the wagon, and placed his heavy rifle by his side, where he could lay his hands upon it at a moment's notice. Then he gathered up the reins, and started his mules up the long hill which I had descended an hour before.

"You Bill," shouted old Nat, as the wagon started.

"Wal, dad," answered the young man, leaving a miner, with

whom he was conversing regarding a bear hunt a few days before.

"You mount your nag, and start out ahead. We want some scouting done, and you is jist the boy to do it."

"All right, dad. Shall I draw a bead on the varmints if they show themselves?"

"Not if you see more'n one. Remember that, Bill. No risk, you know."

"All right, dad. I'm off;" and the young giant threw himself into the saddle, and went off at a gallop, waving his rifle as he reached the top of the hill; and then with a yell put spurs to his horse, and disappeared from sight.

By this time all were mounted, and ready to start. Old Nat locked the door of his house, and leaving the dogs in charge, announced that he was off. We started at a brisk trot, and soon passed the wagon, which caused Sam to groan and complain that it "wasn't fair, and he'd be gol darned ef he stood it much longer."

The miners yelled at him as we dashed on, and in a few minutes had left him far behind, and reached the Forks. Then, for some miles, our course was over a trail that was good. We could see Bill far in advance, glancing to the right and left, as though his keen eyes were searching for ambushed Indians; but he did not appear to encounter any, and on we went until the hot sun warned us that our horses needed rest, or a breathing-spell at least. Then, while we were walking our animals, I conversed a few moments with Nat. We rode on for some time, and just as we gained the top of a hill, we saw Bill in the valley coming towards us at a gallop; and then the sound of rifle shots met our ear, causing us to touch our horses and quicken our pace. In a few minutes we joined Bill, whose freckled face expressed the news which he brought us.

"Wal, Bill, what is it?" asked old Nat, as he checked his animal.

"Wal, dad, the Injuns is over the hill. There's a right smart squad of 'em, and they is pressing Hardcase pretty hard, I reckon."

"On we go," shouted old Nat; and we dashed along, each man looking at the cap on his rifle as we climbed the hill which overlooked the valley.

We swept on to the top of the hill, and reached there just in time to see the Indians dodging from tree to tree, as though they were preparing to surround Hardcase and his men, and then crush them with a rush.

Our leader glanced over the battle-field with his keen gray eyes, saw Hardcase's position, and in what manner the Indians were assailing him. After he had seen all this, he turned to his companions, and said, —

"Boys, you won't make much of a mistake if you hit any of 'em; so come on and pitch in."

We charged down the hill at a run, and with a yell which must have encouraged Hardcase and my men, as they answered our shout, and then fired a volley at the Indians, which caused several of them to drop or limp towards the nearest clump of bushes. But we saw that the natives returned the fire with their bows and arrows, and showed no signs of retreating as we expected they would; and this fact became so strongly impressed upon the mind of old Nat that to my surprise he raised his voice and shouted, "Halt," when we were not more than fifty or sixty yards from the natives.

"Boys," he said, as we checked our animals and demanded the meaning of such an order, "there's some blasted ambush here, and I don't bite at it, I don't."

"Nonsense," was the cry from the miners. "The Injuns is in sight and waiting for us. Let's give 'em thunder and lightning."

"Don't be blind as bats," roared old Nat. "Do you think I'm a fool? Whar did I come from? Wasn't it from Oregon? Didn't I cross overland? Answer me that and be hanged to you."

"Yes, yes," was the exclamation; for no one could dispute the assertions.

"Then jist trust to me, 'cos I know what I'm about, I does."

The miners appeared willing to listen to any suggestions which might be offered.

"Do I see seven or eight hosses in the brush jist off there to the right?"

We all looked in the direction indicated, but I could not make out the animals.

"I seed 'em," said one fellow, whose vision was sharper than mine.

"Wal, them hosses wern't rid by Injuns — was they? Answer me that."

"No, no."

"Wal, I should reckon not. Them hosses was rid by Mexicans, and them Mexicans is not far from us. They is ambushin', boys, as sure as you is alive. Lord, any one with common sense can see through such a trick. Do you s'pose them Injuns would stand there and wait for us unless they know'd they had some one between 'em and the fire we could pour in?"

His argument did look reasonable, and if true, would place old Nat at the head of his profession — as a scout of rare abilities.

"Now, boys, you jist see how we'll draw the varmints. Follow me."

He turned the head of his horse and dashed away to the right, towards the animals which were nearly hid by the bushes. We followed him, but had not rode more than one hundred yards before we saw eight men, dressed in the Mexican costume, leave the bushes which had sheltered them, and run towards their horses, fearing that we should secure the latter, and thus, in a measure, impede their movements.

"Whoop!" yelled old Nat, rising in his stirrups and waving his hand; "didn't tell yer so?"

We had the start of the Mexicans, and the rascals saw it; so they strained every nerve to defeat our intentions; but seeing that it was impossible, they stopped, raised their revolvers, and gave us a volley of bullets. Some of the missiles passed in close proximity to our heads, and one struck a horse, breaking the animal's leg; and as he fell his rider went over his head in a series of evolutions which provoked roars of laughter from his companions, although the men did not know whether the fellow was injured or safe in his rapid flight to the ground.

As we charged towards the horses I was fortunate enough to pick out a splendid-looking stallion, of a dark bay color, full of fire, and fit to carry an emperor. As we swept down upon the animals, I seized his rein, and the prize was mine; but the others were nearly as fortunate, for each man obtained a horse.

"Follow me," shouted old Nat, as he threw the bridle of the animal which he had secured over his arm, and dashed off at a smart canter towards the hill on our right.

We followed our leader until we reached the summit, and then halted and dismounted. We found that Sam, with his wagon, had arrived, and was impatient for a chance in the conflict; but old Nat was deaf to his entreaties.

We left the animals in Sam's charge, and after a look at our rifles and revolvers, plunged down the mountain, or hill, sheltered by trees and bushes, so that those on the plain should not see us or understand what we were doing. We separated and scouted down the hill until we reached the plain, keeping under cover as much as possible, while our foes did the same. As we advanced, the firing ceased, for the Mexicans did not wish to betray their positions unless they were certain that every shot would tell, and we were equally as cautious.

We crept on our hands and knees for some two hundred yards, and were nearing the position held by Hardcase, when on our left arose a wild yell, and there was a rush of Indians towards us. I saw one fellow, daubed with clay and yellow paint, taking very fair aim at me behind a bush, and to save him some trouble I raised my rifle and fired. The naked savage threw up his arms and fell back, and then on either side of me I could hear the sharp crack of fire-arms; and each discharge told of the death of an Indian.

After an attempt to flank us, and the death of several Indians in the rush, the latter fell back discouraged and disgusted, desirous of allowing the Mexicans an opportunity to show their hand; but this the wily Joquin was not disposed to do; so, when he found that the Indians were retreating, he signalized his men to do the same. Of course we followed them, but at such a slow pace, for fear of an ambush, that I thought the Mexicans would escape us entirely. I wanted to rush on them, and decide the battle by quick blows; but my companions were not to be hurried in their operations. They fought to win, and manifested no signs of impâtience while crawling on their bellies, hands, and knees, behind bushes and trees, taking advantage of all inequalities of ground, now skulking behind a rock, and anon climbing a tree, to overlook the field, and obtain a shot.

In this manner we worked our way towards the wagon, and when within one hundred yards of it I heard a yell on our right, and then several shots were fired in rapid succession. We went in the direction indicated, and found that the Mexicans, fearful of being cut off, had attempted to break through our line, and were rewarded by a loss of two killed.

We pressed forward as before, examining each bush and tree, but seeing nothing to excite our suspicion until we were within one hundred yards of the wagon, and then we caught sight of two or three dark skins dodging amidst the wild oats; but before we could obtain a shot, they disappeared.

On we went, and at last saw the wagon. We gave a cheer, which was answered by Hardcase and his party, and then started to our feet to walk towards our friends, thinking that danger was passed; but just at that moment old Nat yelled, —

"Down with you, you tarnal fools! Do you want to be shot like dogs?"

We dropped on the instant, and it was well for us that we did so, for a shower of arrows flew over our heads, sent to us by the Indians, who were concealed on our right in a thick clump of trees and bushes, which had not been examined by those whose duty it was to attend to it.

Hardly had the arrows flown over our heads, when the crack of some seven or eight rifles was heard, each man firing at random, or in the direction of the bushes where the Indians were supposed to be concealed. The shots were productive of some result, for we heard several yells, and then all was quiet, as though the wounded had subdued all expression of pain for the sake of those who were uninjured.

"Load and for'ard!" shouted old Nat; and with a cheer we charged on the bushes, but found no enemy to encounter. They had vanished, carrying their wounded with them; and so quietly had they left, that we did not suspect their retreat.

"Blast 'em," muttered old Nat, scratching his head, "they is cute, and no mistake. They knows somethin', they do."

"Let us push on for 'em," cried Bill, blazing with excitement, and eager for a fight.

"Stop your noise, you fool," replied the old hunter. "You don't know what you is talkin' about."

"But, dad, I want to fight 'em real bad," whined the son.

"And don't I want to fight 'em too? Answer me that."

"I s'pose so, dad."

"You 'spose so. Do you think that I want to get killed, or have an arrer shot through me?"

"I hope not, dad."

"Wal, then, you jist mind me, my son, and don't go off half-cocked. I knows what I'm about. I don't push on arter them Injuns and get ambushed, I don't. We can't chase 'em through all the brush of Californy."

Old Nat gave the word for an advance towards the wagon, but, in doing this it was necessary to act very cautiously, for Hardcase was on the watch, and might mistake our party for that of the enemy; and if such was the case, we should receive a broadside that would do us much injury.

"Here, you Bill," said Nat; "put a white rag on your rammer, and go for'ard and shake it; and if Hardcase sees you, tell him we is comin'. Mind your eyes, now."

"Whar can I find the rag?" asked Bill, with a grin, as though he had puzzled his parent.

"Eh, well, I don't know; that's a fact. We must have one. Our friend here has got on a white shirt, and perhaps he can spare a piece for a short time. That will do," said old Nat, with a grin. "'Tain't white, but it looks some like it. Let a piece come off."

I was about to comply with the request; but just at that moment I heard a yell, loud and piercing, and then the discharge of a rifle, and a second yell.

"By thunder, boys, something is the matter with Sam. Come on;" and old Nat rushed through the bushes towards the hill on which we had left Sam and the mules, team and horses.

As we dashed along there was another yell, and a shot; but these only quickened our steps, and at last, breathless and nervous, we reached the foot of the hill, and saw that Sam was coming towards us, wagon, mules, and horses, yelling at every step; while forty rods in his rear were four Mexicans, running as hard as possible, in hopes of getting a shot at our friend, and making a brilliant capture of their property and our own.

"A smart trick," roared old Nat, as though in admiration of the audacity of the Mexicans; and then he laughed, and the next instant Sam was in our midst, yelling like a Camanche while charging on a herd of buffaloes.

We all expected that we should be ordered in pursuit of the Mexicans, and were not disappointed.

"Mount!" shouted the old man. "Give 'em thunder. No quarter for the sneaks. Kill 'em if you can."

We dashed up the hill; but the Mexicans, suspecting our pursuit, had disappeared before we started. We thought that we could find them, so continued on, but when we reached the summit we could see no one.

"Separate," shouted Ned; and we did, to the right and left, and plunged into the woods; but after galloping for a few minutes were compelled to give up the pursuit, for the robbers were nowhere to be seen. They had disappeared in some manner that excited our surprise, and although we searched in all directions, we could not even find their trail.

We slowly wended our way towards the wagon which Sam still had charge of, and as we passed down the hill Hardcase and my men came out of their shelter, and cheered us until they were hoarse. After mutual congratulations old Nat took me aside for a confidential talk.

"You've got a nice lot of traps on that wagon — hain't you?" he asked.

"O, yes; provisions and other things."

"And a keg of whiskey, of course."

"Yes — a ten-gallon keg, for medicinal purposes."

"That's it. Now, you see these poor fellers what has fit for us?"

"Yes."

"You know the day is warm, and they is putty well tuckered out — don't you?"

"They look tired."

"That's a fact. Now, don't you think that a leetle whiskey would do 'em good — kinder bring 'em up and make 'em feel nice?"

"I have no doubt of it. They shall have a drink as soon as we come to the keg. It is at the bottom of the wagon."

Many hands made the work light. In ten minutes' time we had got hold of the whiskey keg, and it was welcomed with a yell of triumph. I tapped it, and gave the boys a big drink all round.

"Moderation," shouted old Nat, taking the quart pot from his mouth, and drawing a long breath. "Drink decent, men. Don't make hogs of yerselves. A pint of whiskey is as good as a quart, if you only think so."

Some of them did not think so, for they cast longing glances at the keg, and continued to eye it until it was repacked upon the wagon.

"They've had enough," said old Nat, in a whisper. "If they drink more they'll be uproarious. Me and you can take some quiet nips arter you has got settled. That's what we'll do, hey?"

Up the hill we went, the miners singing songs of triumph, and anxious for more fighting, when Will came to my side and whispered, —

"Where is Lilly, sir? I have not seen her since your return."

The information was enough to stagger me, for I had not missed her, being so busy with other matters. I had sent her to the rear while the fight was raging, and I certainly thought that she was with Sam, and therefore safe.

Will saw by my face that I was unconscious of her absence.

"Good God!" the lad exclaimed, "it is not possible that she has fallen into the hands of the Indians."

I could not imagine anything so dreadful. I dashed to the side of Sam, who was still driving his wagon, and endeavored to learn some particulars of Lilly's fate.

"What — that little feller?" asked the man. "Why, yes; I seed him and talked with him but a few minutes afore them Mexican thieves come sneaking round. Arter that I don't know what become of him. I had to look out for the hosses and myself, you know."

"Then the Mexicans must have made him a prisoner. Poor boy, I'll find him if I have to go alone."

I turned my horse's head, but as I did so Sam called to his father and whispered to him, and then the old hunter bolted towards me.

"You lost that little boy, hey?" he asked; "and you is goin' to search for him all alone. Now don't you do that, 'cos it's dangerous. If they've got the boy they'll keep him, and he must take his chance to escape the best way he can. You can't do no good in huntin' for him; so you just come along with us, and let things settle for a while."

I learned, by questioning Sam, that Lilly had left her horse after fastening him to the wagon, and sat down upon the brow of the hill overlooking the valley. Sam had spoken to her but a few moments before the Mexicans appeared, and that was the last he had seen of her. I would have turned back and searched for her, but old Nat would not permit it; so I was compelled to ride on, with a heart so heavy that it seemed like lead. Will made an attempt to cheer me up by relating the incidents which occurred after my leaving the wagon. He told me how the Indians had attacked them, confident of success; and how Jake had used the horse pistols with great bravery, having got so accustomed to gunpowder that he refused to shut both eyes when he fired.

We were compelled to move slowly, owing to the crippled condition of one of the wagons; therefore we were not more than three miles from the valley where the fight occurred, when I heard a loud shout, and on riding forward to ascertain the cause, saw, to my great joy and surprise, that Lilly had made her appearance, suddenly emerging from the woods, and crossing our path.

The rude miners frightened her by their boisterous acclamations; for her quiet, shy manner had won the regard of the men, and they were shaking hands with her and patting her on her shoulders with heavy palms when I reached the circle which surrounded her. I feared that she would demonstrate the joy which she felt at our reunion, and thus betray her secret; but she did not. She only smiled, held out both of her hands, and said, in her native language, —

"Did you miss me much?"

"More than words can tell."

"I thought you would;" and she made an attempt to conceal the tears which would flow from her eyes. "I want to talk with you alone," she remarked, seeing that two or three men hovered near us.

I sent them away, and then fell back so that no one could hear what was said.

"I have had a strange adventure," Lilly remarked, when we were alone. "You will hardly believe it. While you were fighting in the valley I was on the hill praying for your success and welfare; and so much was I occupied that I did not know the Mexicans were stealing on us, until the man who had charge of the wagon fired his rifle and started his mules. Then I saw that I should be captured if I remained where I was, and the robbers would shoot me if I ran down hill. I thought for a moment, and then crawled on my hands and knees in the bushes, and then into the woods, where I secreted myself by piling branches upon me, leaving a little place so that I could look out. I remained quiet, listening to the shouts of men and the firing of rifles, until I was surprised to see four Mexicans pass close to me, running as though they were in a hurry, but stopped close to where I was concealed. While I watched I saw one of the men pull aside some bushes, and look behind them; and then they stood there listening until they heard the shouts of your men as they reached the top of the hill. Then they laughed, and went into the bushes and disappeared. I was so afraid that I did not dare to speak, for I thought that the robbers would fire at me if I moved. You did not come near me, and none of the men offered to, so I had to remain concealed; and at last, to my dismay, you left the woods. I should have followed you, but just as I was about to clear away the branches, one of the robbers thrust his head from the bushes and watched your retreat. Of course I lay perfectly still, but I was terribly afraid that I should be discovered and killed. At last the man who was observing your movements spoke to his companions, and then they left the bushes and laughed. They talked for a few minutes, and walked off, going in an opposite direction from your friends. I waited to see if they would return, but as they did not I crept from my place of concealment. At first I thought that I would run to you, but my curiosity prompted me to examine where the robbers had hid. I pushed aside the bushes, but saw nothing; so I walked on, thrusting aside the brush at every step, and at last I came to a small mound. I did not think that it was worth while to go farther, and I turned back; but while turning, I put out my hand to steady myself, and seized a young pine. It yielded to my touch and fell; and then I saw, right before me, directly under the mound, a large hole, big enough for a man, on his hands and knees, to crawl into. I was frightened, but you know I am curious; so I crawled into the cave."

"You are a brave little girl," I said, in admiration of her conduct.

Her eyes sparkled at my praise. No wonder — she had not recently received much of it.

"I noticed that the cave grew large as I advanced, and I smelt the fumes of a burning wick, as though the Mexicans had used a candle while in the place, and had blown it out when they got ready to leave. I should like to have learned more, but I did not dare remain and run the risk of the Mexicans' returning."

It was evident, from what I had heard, that the Mexicans made the cave a rendezvous for their leisure hours; and if such was the case, was it not probable that they concealed a large portion of their stolen property there?

"Lilly," I said, as we reached the Cross Forks.

"Yes," she answered, looking up.

"Don't mention a word about the cave to any one."

"No, I won't."

"Not even to our own companions."

"I understand," she answered; and then we were joined by old Nat, who was in fine spirits after the adventures of the day.

"Allspice," said he, "do you want me to pick you out a place to camp, on the bank of the river? If you'll jist say the word, I'll find a spot that can't be equalled on the Yuba. I wouldn't do this for every one; but my boys has taken a shine to you, and I kinder like you; so we'll have you near us for company."

"It is a favor that I would ask, if not too much trouble."

"No trouble, my lad, no trouble. We must help each other sometimes. Near my ranche is a good bar that ain't been worked much. You go there and camp."

"Is there any gold there?"

"Gold!" repeated the old man, in tones of astonishment; "you can't stir the sand without finding gold. You mustn't expect to take it out in handfuls, 'cos that's agin natur; but the more you dig, the more you'll take out."

It was near three o'clock when we arrived at old Nat's house. While the men were dismounting from their horses, I whispered to old Nat, and said, —

"Shall I offer to pay these men for their trouble in saving my traps?"

"Don't mention such a thing," was the answer. "They lend one another a helping hand, and don't make any charge of it. But if" — and here old Nat's voice fell — "you have a drop of whiskey which you can spare, bring it out, 'cos it's awful hot, and the fellers has worked hard — now ain't they?"

I was glad to oblige them. Once more the ten-gallon keg was made to bleed, and once more the miners drank success to them selves and all their friends, and then to Oregon; and while they were doing so, Hardcase started the wagon, and we continued on our journey towards the bar which Nat had pointed out. It was not more than half a mile from the house, on the same side of the river; and just back of the bar was a fine grove of trees, and amid them we commenced unloading our team and pitching our tents, and before sundown our kettles were on the fire, singing merrily.

CHAPTER XXIII.

OUR CAMP ON THE YUBA. — THE SEARCH FOR GOLD. — A HUNT AND WHAT CAME OF IT.

Even before we pitched our tents old Nat had visited us, and gave us friendly advice, lending a helping hand when he could do so, and expatiating upon the beauties of our location. The next afternoon, after the intense heat of the day had passed, we put our two rockers together, and took them to the bar in front of our camp for trial. Every man was anxious to dig the first gold, yet we did not know how to go to work to insure success. We supposed that any of the sand and dirt would pay, but after washing out some five or six buckets full, we found only a few specks of dust, which induced us to think we had not struck rich dirt. Fortunately for us old Nat and his two sons visited us just at this time, and laughed at our efforts.

"What is you fellers at?" the old man asked. "You is washing out dirt what has been through a cradle afore. Didn't you know any better than that?"

We confessed that we did not.

"Wal, then, we must show you. See here; you must skim off the top dirt. Gold don't stop thar. It settles, and goes down and down till it reaches a ledge of rocks, or hard, blue clay. Thar it stops, and thar you must look for it."

"But suppose we don't find the clay or the rocks until we dig ten feet down?" I asked.

"Then you must dig to that depth. It's hard, I know, but without labor you'll not find gold. Come, let me show you how to do it."

He took a shovel, and after a careful examination of the bar, commenced work near an elbow of the river, at the foot of a gulch which lay between two high mountains. My men saw that the old man was in earnest, and lent their assistance in rolling out of the way some large stones, and then scraping off the surface gravel. In a short time a space a rod square was cleared, and after going down two feet we reached blue clay.

"Thar," cried old Nat, "now you can find the dust, if thar's any thar. But it's hard work, and me and my boys is dry, awful dry."

I understood the hint. I led the way to my tent, and brought out the whiskey keg. All hands took a strong pull at it, and left me. While I was putting away the whiskey Jake burst in upon me like a crazy man.

"Glory to God!" he shouted; "we found 'em — lots of it, too, cap'n."

"Found what?" I asked.

"De gold. I see it, and all see it. Whole handful."

The man found his breath, after a while, to tell me that, after washing out a few buckets of dirt, they had seen considerable gold in the cradle — much more than they expected. I hastened to the spot, and found that after panning out the dust, we had secured just one ounce of coarse gold, which was doing remarkably well, and showed that the dirt was rich, and well worth working.

A week passed away, at the end of which time we found we had made good California wages at gold-digging, averaging some two hundred dollars per man. Besides this, we had learned much in the short time we had been on the river, and we felt more confidence in our resources. We prospected in different places, and found that gold was to be obtained wherever we struck a shovel. We had taken up several claims, and held them in reserve against the time we should require them; and although people were flocking to the mines, yet our claims were not disturbed until we were surrounded by miners, and that happened some months after our commencing gold seeking.

One morning, about five o'clock, while we were taking our coffee, Sam and Will Baker called to see me, each of them armed with a rifle and revolver.

"What's in the wind?" I asked, as they sat down, and helped themselves to a dish of coffee.

"We are on a hunt," they said, "and we want you to go with us."

"What kind of a hunt?" I asked.

"Wal, principally deer, although there's no tellin' what we shall meet with afore we returns."

It did not take me long to get ready, and off we went, the two huge dogs, which belonged to old Nat, keeping us company. We had not travelled far before I chanced to look back, and saw Jake dogging my steps. We were then a mile from camp. I stopped, and the guilty-looking negro came towards me.

"Who told you to come?" I asked.

"No one, cap'n; but den I s'posed as you wanted some one to carry de game."

"But who is to cook the dinner?"

"O, dat all prepared, and dey can eat 'em widout me."

"Let him come," said Bill. "He won't do any harm."

So I agreed to let Jake go with us, and very glad the negro was to hear that such was the result of my deliberation. He pointed in a significant manner to his horse pistols, which he had placed in his belt, and intimated that he would "make 'em tell afore de day was out." We scaled the side of Mount Misery, — a steep hill, which separated us from the next valley, — and after much sliding, and some bumps and bruises, were enabled once more to follow the course of the river, which we did for a mile or more; and then we skirted a mountain, whose sides were almost perpendicular, and up which it would have been nearly impossible for a fly to crawl. At the foot were huge pines, and some small oaks, the latter gnarled and stunted, as though crushed by the former. At the foot of one of the latter we sat down to rest. The solitude of the place struck me as extremely oppressive. Probably no human foot had ever trod that dark, gloomy valley before our party had entered it, and certainly none would desire to, walled in as it was between the mountains, whose towering heights prevented the sun's rays from penetrating until near noon. I could conceive of no place more suitable for the home of grisly bears, and I said so.

"Wal, I s'pect they is near here," remarked Sam, in a cool, lazy manner, as he lighted his pipe, and puffed out huge volumes of smoke.

During the time we rested, I noticed that the dogs had

crouched at our feet, in obedience to commands; but at the same time they had manifested strong symptoms of rebellion, fretting for a dash into the woods, and uttering low, savage growls, because they were restrained of their liberty. When, therefore, we arose to our feet, the dogs bounded forward with delight; but Sam speedily recalled them.

"You poor fools," he said, addressing the brutes, "do you want to be chawed up in less than no time? If you do, just run right plump into the mouth of a bear. That's all you've got to do."

I thought that the animals looked as though they were willing to take their chance of the encounter, for they were of the bull-dog breed, tough and wiry, with courage which no man could doubt. We penetrated the forest of pines. The trees did not stand close together. They were in clusters, with some vacant spaces between them, as though the monarchs of the forest did not brook familiarity, but preferred to stand alone. In these vacant spaces were oaks, bearing acorns, such as the Indians gather for their winter supply of food. On these acorns bears feed, but I was not aware of it at the time. We had passed one or two of these places, when Sam pointed to a pine, and called my attention to it. The bark was torn off in large strips, as though done with a hatchet, and the fragments lay scattered around the trunk of the tree. It looked as though it had been chopped into little pieces.

"What do you think of that?" asked Sam. "Ain't that an exhibition of power?"

I asked for an explanation.

"That's the mark of a grisly," he said. "Some old feller has been sharpening his claws on that tree. While he was doing it he got kinder mad, and bit things, and I s'pose afore he was through, he was ready to fight any one, even if it had been his own daddy. Go smell 'em, Bose."

One of the dogs approached the tree, smelt of it, turned up his nose, and then uttered a low growl, as though he would like to catch sight of an animal that sharpened its claws in that manner.

"Come along," cried Sam; "we'll find that bear afore long."

"But don't you tink," said Jake, "dat it would be better if de bar come in search of us, instead our goin' in search of de bar?"

"What! are you afeard?" demanded the boys, who were anxious for a little sport.

"No, I's not afeard; but den I don't tink dat it's best to be too for'ard in dis matter. Let de bars alone, and den dey let you alone."

We laughed and passed on; but I thought Jake had spoken words of wisdom, and wished that my companions had heeded them. As far as I was concerned I did not care to take any active part in the hunt; but if I had said so, it would have been known to every miner on the river.

"Don't be too anxious," said Sam, speaking to me. "We might stumble on a feller afore we knows it, and then you'd be snapped up in no time."

I was glad of this advice, because it showed that they had not detected my reluctance to engage in the hunt.

"Why don't you turn the dogs loose?" I asked. "If there's a bear in these woods, they will be sure to find him."

"And the cuss would kill the dogs afore we could get to 'em. But I's a good mind to try it. What do you say, Bill?"

"Remember what the old man told us, Sam. If we lose the dogs, we'll get particular thunder."

"We'll run the risk, by jingo;" and as he spoke the young men loosened the straps of hide which were fastened to the collars of the animals, and away they bounded towards a clump of bushes; and just as we were preparing to follow them, I heard a roar like thunder, and then caught sight of the two dogs, retreating towards us, closely pursued by a monster, all black and white, shaggy, and strong, large as a cow, and twice as heavy. It was a grisly.

"De debil," yelled Jake, jerking out his horse pistols, and firing them; and then he struck for an oak tree, and that was the last I saw of him for some time.

When the animal was first discovered, he was not more than three rods from me; consequently I had to do my thinking mighty quick, and make up my mind whether I should run or stand up to the rack like a hero, and be clawed in less than two minutes. I concluded to run, but not until I had fired, and this I did in a great hurry; and I had the satisfaction of seeing the fur fly from the bear's head, but it made no difference in checking the speed of the monster. On he came, and back I went, turning like a flash of lightning, and running like a race-horse; and as I sped on I had the satisfaction of seeing Bill and Sam take aim, and heard them discharge their rifles; but I did not stop to see with what effect. I think, however, that the bear did not stop; for I have a distinct recollection that the Oregonians suddenly ranged alongside of me and attempted to take the lead, but my legs were too quick for that; so I put on steam, and as I did so I glanced over my shoulder, and saw that the bear had stopped at the foot of the tree on which Jake was posted; and the reason for such a halt, which was acceptable to us, was because Jake had shouted in loud tones, —

"Golly! don't run away and leave dis child all alone. Don't act as cowardly as all dat. Stick by me."

The dark-complexioned gentleman seemed to have forgotten that he had run first for the purpose of saving his skin, and that we had followed his example with the best of motives. But his strong appeal stayed the course of the bear, and enabled us to pick out trees near each other, and to climb them; but we were compelled to leave our rifles on the ground, and trust them to the mercy of the bear, and our existence to the efficacy of our revolvers.

It did not take me long to reach the first limb of a pine tree, and after I had obtained a seat glanced around to notice the position of my companions, and found that they were safe, perched on the boughs of trees near me, and apparently quite contented with their situations, although I noticed with extreme regret that they were several feet higher than myself.

In the mean time the bear stopped and cast long and wishful glances at Jake, and such delicate attention nearly drove the negro frantic.

After one or two growls, as though undecided what to do, the bear came towards our trees, and when within a rod of us, halted, squatted on his haunches, and looked up at his prisoners, as much as to intimate that he knew he had us, and was determined to enjoy our position; but while he was thus licking his chops, and uttering some gentle growls, which sounded as though he had a cold, caught by staying out late nights, the two dogs, which must have had some good training, silently crept up and attacked the grisly's rear, and I think they nipped him with their teeth, for the bear uttered a roar that made the trees tremble, and turning, aimed a blow at one dog which would have felled an ox, but the animal was too quick. He dodged and retreated, and then the second cur was chased a short distance; but as he could run two feet to to grisly's one, of course he escaped; and the bear, seeing that pursuit was useless, turned and came towards us, growling and grumbling as though disgusted with such trifling.

"Look here," I said, hailing Sam and Bill, who were chewing tobacco, and composedly squirting the juice at the eyes of the bear, but not hitting within ten feet, "do you call this hunting grislies?"

"We don't call it anything else," was the reply.

"I think that it looks as though the grisly was hunting us," I remarked.

"Wal, 'tis open to that objection," Bill answered; and just at that moment the bear walked near the tree as though to hear more distinctly, and while he was cocking up one eye, Bill let fly about a gill of juice, strong as cavendish tobacco could make it. The saliva struck old bruin on the eye that was upturned, and such impoliteness was followed by a roar that partook of rage, pain, and fright, all combined.

The bear rolled over on his back. He kicked and wiped his face — he clawed it, and bit the ground; and while he was suffering so much, the dogs once more attacked him, and the rascals bit his rump most unmercifully, to Jake's great delight. For a short time there was a confused mass of leaves, dirt, fur, and broken branches; and then from a circle up in the air flew a dog, and when he struck the earth lost no time in seeking safety in flight. His companion followed suit, and then the bear removed as much of the tobacco from its eye as possible, sat on its haunches, and growled at us.

"Are we to stay here all day?" I asked.

"We shall unless we can kill the cuss," was the answer.

I did not wait for further light. I drew my revolver, took careful aim, and fired. I saw the ball strike the monster's breast; and in return he gave us a very fair specimen of boxing, rearing up on his hind legs and waving his fore ones, as though he expected a blow, and was prepared to ward it off, even if it came as quick as lightning.

"What in thunder are we to do?" I asked of my companions.

"O, take it easy," was the reply.

"But the blasted bear will starve us to death."

"I shouldn't wonder," was the answer.

Perhaps I had better have remained silent, for the monster turned and came towards my tree, grumbling and shaking his head in an angry manner. He looked up at me, then stood on his hind legs, laid his fore paws against the trunk of the tree, and faith, commenced moving towards me, but at such a slow rate, owing to his size, that I thought he would tire of it before he reached the bough on which I was seated.

Heavens, how old bruin snorted as he worked his way up the tree! His breathing sounded like the puffing of a high-pressure steamer, and his breath was hot and far from perfumed, for I could smell it even where I sat, looking down at the monster. I was fascinated by the grisly's movements — his blazing eyes and foaming jaws; and as the bark which he had ground between his teeth had colored the froth issuing from his mouth, it resembled blood, and added a terrible interest to the rascal's open countenance.

I think that the bear had climbed about two feet from the ground, when the dogs made another rush, biting his rear in such a vigorous manner that the old fellow could not stand the pressure; and once more he dropped to the earth, and made an angry rush for his tormentors. Of course they vanished in an instant, and after feeling satisfied that such was the case, bruin once more turned towards his human enemies; but this time, by some mistake, he struck the tree upon which Jake was perched, and commenced nearing the negro, to the great terror of the latter.

"Now, Jake, look out," said Bill; and he fired at the bear. The animal was about three feet from the ground, and seemed to be at a perfect stand-still, unable to advance, and unwilling to recede.

The ball struck the animal near the fore shoulder, and must have broken some of his bones, for he released his hold of the tree and tumbled to the ground, falling upon his back; but he only lay in this position for a few moments. The dogs again advanced to attack him, and this insult added new fury to his rage. He was up and striking at them to the right, but I noticed that he did not use his left paw, and that he growled when he rested on it, as though the pain was more than he could bear without manifesting some feeling.

As usual, the dogs vanished the instant there was a chance for a free fight, and then the bear licked his wounds, smelt of them, and gathered new rage by the act. He looked up and saw Jake, and that look was sufficient to make the darky shake in his shoes.

"Gemmen," he said, with chattering teeth, "please kill dat ole cuss afore he gets at dis nigger. He's arter me, I know. He tinks I's more tender dan de rest ob you."

We could not withstand that appeal. Three revolvers cracked at the same time, and three balls struck the bear. His rage was terrible. He tore up the ground in all directions, and howled until the valley re-echoed his cries.

I could not help pitying the brute, for his great courage made me respect him. But our lives were more precious than his; so death was sure to overtake him. We knew that he would not leave us, yet all felt that the work was nearly finished, and that death would relieve the brute of his suffering. Once more we fired. The bear received the balls with a shudder. Fresh wounds were opened, and fresh streams of blood flowed to the ground. Flesh and muscle could not stand it. The monster sunk upon his haunches, and looked around with an expression as though asking what we meant by such treatment. But he had not lost all his fierceness. He still shook his head and growled, and when the dogs ventured near him mustered strength enough to aim a blow at them, and to pursue them a few steps. But it could not last. Down he went with a crash, made a desperate effort to rise, failed, and then tumbled upon his side, and as he went over the dogs fastened upon him; but the old veteran was not entirely powerless. By a sudden blow he struck one of the curs, and sent him howling through the air, to the great indignation of Sam and Bill. So mad were they that they once more fired, and the shots seemed to have finished the career of the brute. His head drooped, his legs straightened out, he gave a gasp, and was motionless.

"Hurrah for us!" yelled Jake. "We finished 'em at last;" and down the tree slid the negro.

After gaining *terra firma* he danced "Juba" for a few minutes, keeping time with his hands, and still dancing approached the bear.

"Yer didn't get a chance at dis nigger — did yer?" asked

the fellow, with an insulting gesture and a kick. Then turning, he called to us, "Come down. Don't you be afeard. He's a goner."

He stood with his back to the bear as he spoke, and the insults which he had heaped upon the animal seemed to have recalled its life, for it suddenly raised its head, lifted its paw, and with one mighty blow tore away the seat of Jake's trousers. With a yell, loud and piercing, the negro bounded into the air, clapped both hands behind him, and run for the nearest tree, shrieking for help. But there was no occasion for assistance. It was the last, expiring effort of the bear. We left the shelter of the trees, and gathered around our prize, wondering at the strength of its limbs, the length and massiveness of its teeth, and the enormous bulk which it presented. We skinned the monster, and having slung the pelt upon two sticks, placed the latter upon our shoulders, and commenced our march for home. It was terrible hard work, creeping over the mountains, with a skin which weighed more than a hundred pounds; but we accomplished it, and reached camp just at sundown.

The morning after the bear hunt, I noticed that the faces of my men wore a jubilant expression, as though they had heard some good news; but as they did not immediately communicate it to me, I supposed that it was nothing that affected my interest. Besides, I was too tired to ask many questions. The hunt had used me up, and I felt as though I wanted rest. But after breakfast Will and Jack lighted their pipes, and sat down by my side under a tree, near our tents. They looked so mysterious that I was inclined to think something strange had happened, and I was not long left to conjecture what it was.

"While you was gone, yesterday," said Jack, "somethin' happened to us."

"Something of importance," chimed in Lilly, who was close at hand.

"Something that will make you stare," remarked Will.

"Only us knows it," continued Jack.

"No one else," echoed Will.

"Now tell me what you mean," I cried, looking from one to the other in astonishment.

"You tell him, Will," said Jack. "You can do it ship-shape."

"I will," answered the lad. "You see, sir, after you was

gone, yesterday, we went to work as usual, until about eleven o'clock, when the kanakas knocked off labor, and laid down under a tree. It was hot, and no mistake, and we were all thinking of following the kanakas' example, when Miss Lilly paid us a visit."

"Yes, yes; go on," cried the girl, impatiently.

"She sat down, looked at us for a few minutes, and then said she wanted to try her hand at digging for gold. We laughed at her, but she insisted, and at last we consented. She took the smallest pickaxe, struck a few blows into the earth, and then —"

"I found this," cried Lilly, taking from a bag a large lump of pure gold, and placing it in my hands.

I was so astonished that I could only look at the girl and at the gold, bewildered at the magnitude of the treasure which she had found.

"I knew you would be surprised," laughed Lilly. "I wanted to tell you last night, but you were so tired that we all agreed to postpone it until this morning. Now, ain't you glad?"

Of course I was pleased, for the lump of gold, which was entirely free of foreign substances, was the handsomest specimen that I had seen, and weighed within a few ounces of six pounds troy.

"We thought it best to say nothing about it, sir," Will continued. "Even the kanakas don't know it. We don't want the miners crowding round us, and staking out claims near our bar. Now, I think that we can keep the secret. At least we can try it."

CHAPTER XXIV.

JOQUIN'S CAVE. — A BARGAIN. — AN EXPLORATION. — DEAD MEN. — A RATTLESNAKE. — FASCINATED. — TREASURES OF THE CAVE.

For several days we had heard nothing of the doings of Joquin, and his gang of robbers. So I thought it high time to visit the cave which Lilly had discovered, and see if large stores of treasure were not concealed there. But first I consulted as to the expediency of informing old Nat of my project, and obtaining his powerful aid. The more I thought of the matter, the more inclined I was to trust him; and when I had settled on the right course to pursue, sent Jake over to the old man's ranche, with a request for the Oregonian's company for a short time. He readily obeyed the summons, for he smelt whiskey as soon as the message was received. Therefore, in a few minutes old Nat was grasping my hand in his hard palm, and licking his lips in anticipation of the drink which he knew I would invite him to.

"What is it, my hearty?" he asked, as he threw back his head, and drank something from a quart pot which Jake handed him.

"Uncle Nat," I said, "I have a secret which I wish to confide to you, and I want your assistance."

"Well, fire away;" and the old man once more looked at the tin pot, snuffed it, and put it down with a sigh. I motioned to Jake, and the negro once more tapped the keg, and gave some of its contents to the trapper. A pleased smile stole over his rough face as he wet his lips, and then prepared to listen to what I had to say.

"You recollect the time we gave the Mexicans a touch of our quality?"

"Don't I?"

"Well, on that day my boy was lost."

"I know. You was terribly puckered about it, and wanted to go off arter him."

"Yes, but I did not, because we picked him up an hour after he was lost."

"Yes, I recollect."

"Well, while he was absent he saw some Mexicans go into a cave, and that was the reason we could not find them."

"I see. Go on."

"Now I have been thinking that we had better visit that cave, and see what it contains. If we find anything of value, how shall we share it?"

"Halves," answered the veteran.

"No, that would not be fair. You furnish your two sons, and then you shall have one third of all that we capture."

The old man mused on the offer. He thought of the risk, and the advantages, and then closed with the proposition.

"I'll do it," he said. "When shall we start?"

"To-morrow morning, at an early hour."

"Good. I'll be ready. But not a word of this to the other fellers on the river. We must keep mum."

"I understand. We can say that we have gone out on the prairies for cattle."

"Yes, so we can. Now I'll go home and get ready, 'ces if we meet the Mexicans we shall have to fight for it."

I selected Mr. Topmall and Will to accompany me, besides Lilly to guide us to the cave. All of us were mounted, and all excepting Lilly carried rifles and revolvers. Those I left in camp had not the slightest idea where we were going. I feared that they might talk of it, and thus expose the whole project. We joined old Nat and his sons at the ranche, and left the house about five o'clock, before the dew was off the grass, and before the sun had shown its hot face in the valley. On we dashed, and at last the woods, which Lilly had fled through, were gained. We saw nothing suspicious near them. No signs of Mexicans or Indians, although we scouted in all directions in search of fresh trails, and then met beneath a huge pine, and reported to old Nat that the coast was clear, and the veteran gave the word to push on. Not for a moment did Lilly hesitate about the course to the cave. She pointed out the way as confidently as though she had lived in the vicinity all her life, and knew each tree and bush by name. At last she stopped, and pointed to a heap of dried branches.

"Under those," she said, "I concealed myself when the Mexicans entered the woods."

"And the cave?" I asked.

She dismounted from her horse, and we followed her example. She led the way through a thicket, the twigs of which looked as though a deer had broken them in passing or browsing. We pushed on, and a few paces brought us to the quartz mount which Lilly had spoken of. As yet I saw no evidence of the cave. I only saw a few dead bushes, and those were piled up in a heap, in a careless manner, as though some one had contemplated setting them on fire, and had abandoned the purpose for some cause.

"Whar's the cave, youngster?" asked old Nat, with a sarcastic grin upon his face. He began to doubt her power to find it.

"Wait a moment," she answered; and then she commenced throwing aside the branches. Will and Sam assisted her, and in a few seconds what we sought was before us. The entrance was not larger than the end of a barrel, dark and gloomy; but still there was evidence that it had been inhabited, for on the ground we picked up a silver bell button, such as Mexicans wear upon the legs of their trousers.

"Wal, by hokey!" ejaculated old Nat, with an expression of wonder upon his face.

"There is the cave," I said. "Shall we enter it?"

"Of course," all cried, in one breath. But who would lead the way was the question.

We looked at each other, and then at the dark entrance to the cave. No one spoke. How did we know but that the place was filled with Mexicans, who would pick us off, one by one, as we entered?

"Here, Bose," cried old Nat to one of the dogs which we had brought with us.

The animal went to him. It was only necessary to point a finger. The dog understood him. He entered the cave, was gone one or two minutes, and then returned, his tail between his legs, and every appearance of abject terror in his looks. The animal was naturally bold. He did not exhibit signs of courage now.

"What does this mean?" roared old Nat, looking around upon the group which surrounded him.

We could not answer the question. It puzzled us as much as it did our leader.

"Go in, Bose," said Nat; but the dog shrank away in spite of threats and blows.

"Blame me, if this don't beat all creation!" muttered Bill, with a look of wonder upon his freckled face.

"It's the fust time that dog ever refused to go anywhere," said its owner, in tones of astonishment.

"Wal, dad, it shan't be said that one of the family was afeard," cried Bill. "I'll lead the way and see what's in thar."

The father thought of the matter for a moment, and then gave his consent. He lighted a candle, and with a revolver in his breast, and the candle in his hand, Bill started on his explorations. We waited one, two, three minutes, and then heard a yell which satisfied us that Bill had encountered something of an extraordinary nature. Was it a yell of triumph, or a cry of fear?

The question was soon solved. While we waited, listening eagerly for more demonstrations, we saw Bill's head, and then his body, emerge from the cave. His face was pale, and his limbs trembled as he gained his feet and looked at us.

"Bill, my son," asked the father, in a soothing tone, "what is the matter with you?"

"I seed, dad, O, I seed —"

"What, you fool?" roared the affectionate parent.

"Two fellers what is dead, and ain't got no clothes on. I seed their ribs and bones, and then I dropped the candle, and left in a hurry."

The old man looked at his son in a scornful manner, and then lighted a candle.

"Come on," he said. "I'll show you that I ain't afeard. Allspice, you foller me."

We left Bill and Lilly outside to keep guard, and the rest of us entered the cave, crawling on our hands and knees for some distance; the light of our candles disturbing several bats, which flew over our heads and dashed at our lights, extinguishing one or two, and provoking oaths of the most emphatic character from old Nat and Mr. Topmall.

"On we goes," cried old Nat; and after relighting our candles, crept along until we were suddenly stopped by a suppressed oath from our leader, and a peculiar whirring sound, like that produced by a child's rattle.

"What is the matter?" I asked.

"Matter!" repeated old Nat; "why, there's a cussed big rattlesnake, standing on its tail, all ready for a jump, within ten feet of me. That's what's the matter. Don't move, or the reptile will make a spring. We must deal gently with him. Jist keep quiet, and I'll see what can be done."

I obeyed his instructions, but those behind me did not. They commenced retreating as rapidly as possible; and I would have done the same if it had not been through shame from deserting the brave man in front of me.

"Are you still near me?" asked Nat.

"Yes."

"Wal, don't make a noise. Keep quite cool, and we'll yet fix the varmint. He ain't goin' to make a spring jist yet, 'cos he don't like the looks of this lighted candle. He's a little fearful of it. I've got my eyes on him, and I's watchin' all his motions. O, I tell you he does look putty; that's a fact. If I could only get my revolver out, I might shoot him; b-u-t I c-a-n-'t. He looks — all covered with — sparkles — diamonds — I don't fear him —"

He paused as though lost in astonishment and admiration at the spectacle before him. The last few words which he had uttered were so disconnected, and spoken in such a monotonous tone that I was astonished, and feared he was falling asleep. He no longer seemed to have care or fear — he was indifferent to his own fate and that of others.

"Nat," I said, in a low tone; but he paid no attention to my voice.

As I spoke I heard the ominous rattle of the snake's tail, as though the reptile was angry at the sound of my voice.

The old man did not move. He did not even answer me.

"Nat," I said; and I spoke louder this time.

There was no response, although once more I heard the rattles and an angry hiss. The snake did not like my interference. What did the silence on the part of old Nat mean? It alarmed me. I touched him, but he took no notice of me. I raised my body as high as possible, and looked over his shoulders. He still held the lighted candle in his hand, but I noticed that the arm was rigid, as though stiffened by a stroke of paralysis.

As I raised my head the snake uttered an angry hiss, and its eyes were like flaming carbuncles. Its head swayed back and forth, and its tongue quivered like an aspen leaf, and while looking I suddenly heard Lilly's voice at the entrance to the cave, calling on me to come out and save myself.

Her voice aroused me to thoughtfulness. I no longer looked at the snake, and as soon as I averted my eyes, the old feeling of dread and disgust took possession of me. I should have instantly made my escape, but would not leave old Nat behind.

"Come," I said, speaking so loud that he could not help hearing me.

As I spoke I laid a hand upon his shoulder; but he did not move. Suddenly it came to my mind that the man was under the influence of the snake. What could I do? Old Nat was incapable of helping himself, and I would not desert him. There was but one way, and that I could attempt. If I failed, my friend and myself were liable to be destroyed. If I succeeded we were safe.

I nerved myself for a task. I took from my belt the revolver which I carried, cocked it, and rested my elbow on old Nat's back; then aiming at the fiery head of the snake, I fired. The report was deafening. The candle dropped from the old man's hand, and we were left in darkness and smoke; but before I could move I felt my friend's body tremble, and then a sigh, as though of relief, escaped him.

"Thank God," he ejaculated, as though from the bottom of his heart. "You didn't do that none too soon."

"Is the snake dead?" I asked, anxious and excited.

"His head is all smashed up. But I can't talk now. I want some air, and a drop of whiskey. I'm all of a tremble."

The man was shaking as though suffering from an attack of ague.

We commenced retreating out of the cave. Old Nat moved rather slow, but at last succeeded in reaching the air, and it seemed to revive him, or, if that did not, about half a pint of whiskey did.

"Boys," said the old fellow, "I don't know what come over me arter I had looked at that snake a bit. It seemed as though I couldn't turn my eyes. It was a putty sight. I never seed a handsomer one in my life. The cuss was all speckled over with sparkles like gold dust, and the more I looked the more I wanted to. I've heerd tell of sich things, but I never 'spected to meet with 'em."

"Did you know that I was near you?" I asked.

"Yes, I could feel you all the time; but, to tell the truth, I wanted you out of the way, 'cos I feared you would stop the fun I was having in lookin' at the varmint."

Once more we lighted the candles, and again commenced our preparations for the exploration of the cave. Before we entered, however, we took a drink of whiskey, and the liquor inspired Sam with so much courage, that he volunteered to enter the cave and bring out the body of the rattlesnake, and see that no more of the same kind were in our path. This proposition was accepted, and the bold young fellow crawled in, and in five minutes returned with the snake which I had slain. It was five feet long, and had ten rattles. The shot which I fired had passed through its head, just below the eye, and killed the reptile almost instantly.

Again we entered the cave, in the same manner as before, with lighted candles, and on our hands and knees. We crept cautiously, looking to the right and left, for fear that we should encounter another snake, but did not; and after crawling for some twenty feet, suddenly emerged into a spacious cave, large enough to hold thirty men, with ease. We raised our lights and looked around us, and although we were somewhat prepared for the scene which met our eyes, yet we could not repress a shudder, for our glances fell on two skeletons, both lying upon the earth, with hands folded upon their breasts, as though they had died praying. There was no clothing on the upper part of the bodies. The flesh had fallen from the bones, and the grinning skulls appeared to welcome us to their strange sepulchre with a unanimity far from pleasing. After satisfying our curiosity, as far as the dead were concerned, we commenced an examination of the premises. We found boxes of claret wines, stolen from the stores of miners and traders, two bundles of jerked beef, some garlic, olive oil, and other things which were not of much use to the thieves. But we found no gold, although we examined every article that was in the cave. We began to think that the Mexicans were too shrewd to leave their valuables behind them, and gave up the search; but Will continued it, and at last commenced stirring some dirt which he found in one corner of the cave. We watched him without interest, but all at once he uttered a shout which brought every one to his feet.

"I've found something!" he said; and in a few minutes he moved from the dirt a tin box — such a one as Boston crackers are packed in.

"Rip it open!" shouted Bill and Sam; and they crowded up to see the contents, but we forced them back until all hands were close to the two skeletons, the horrible grins of which were unnoticed by the excited men, all strongly impressed with the belief that a rich prize had been discovered.

"Open! open!" was the cry; but for a moment the fastening to the box could not be forced, and while Will was searching for it, we were startled by hearing a groan of so unearthly a character, that we imagined that the fiends of the other world had visited the cave for the purpose of making us relinquish our prize.

"What's that?" asked old Nat, with a slight tremor in the tones of his voice, while Will stopped his work to listen.

There was no answer to old Nat's pertinent question. Who could reply to it? The sound did not seem of this world.

"Open the box if the devil stands at the door!" roared old Nat. "It's full of gold dust. I know it is by the weight. Rip it open!"

But as Will was about to obey the order, to our intense consternation, a second groan, more loud than the first, greeted our ears, and one or two rushed for the passage-way, as though to leave in a hurry; but old Nat recalled them.

"Fools!" he shouted; "what is you afeard of? The devil will get you in the open air just as quick as he can here. Don't be afeard — I ain't."

But in spite of the man's brave words, he showed some signs of agitation, and, I must confess, if it had not been for the love of gold, all of us would have left the cave in short order. Curiosity and hope of gain alone kept us there. We looked at each other, as though attempting to fathom the mysterious sounds which we heard; but I could see nothing but astonishment depicted upon the faces around me. Had the Mexicans left the dead to guard the treasure? and were the dead performing their duty in as gentle a manner as possible? The groans were faint reminders that we were trespassing. If we persisted, what was to come next?

"Blast the grunts!" cried old Nat, as soon as we recovered from our astonishment: "Open the box. I'll do it if the dead vagabonds rise up and oppose me."

He rushed forward to seize the box, but had to pass the skeletons in so doing. It seemed to me as though something dreadful was about to happen, and therefore my eyes were turned towards the dead bodies. What was my horror to see the bony arm of one of them raised in a slow, cautious manner until it had reached an altitude of forty-five degrees, then it paused a moment, waved two or three times in a threatening manner, and fell with a crash! This was too much for old Nat. He uttered an oath, dashed his candle to the earth, and rushed for the passage that led to the open air, and would have gained it if some others had not been before him; so there was a jam, a struggle, and an immense amount of fearful oaths, and yet no one could escape. The only candle left burning was the one held by Mr. Topmall. I had dropped mine, and stood staring at the skeletons with astonishment and terror combined. Perhaps I was too much alarmed to speak or run, although I know that I most sincerely wished that I was on the bank of the Yuba digging gold, instead of stealing it in a cave. In the mean time old Nat nearly forgot his terror, and blasphemed in his usual lively style.

"You infernal brutes!" he yelled, "if you don't get off of me I'll cut some of your throats — I will, by the jumping jingo!"

There was no response to this stirring appeal. Bill and Sam seemed to disregard the feelings of their respected parent, and while they were struggling I thought I saw a chance for escape. I rushed forward to improve it, but just at that moment a heavy hand was laid upon my shoulder, and I was held back. I turned, expecting to see a grinning skeleton by my side, but to my surprise I only saw the smiling face of Mr. Topmall.

"Don't be afeard," he said; "it was me. 'Twan't one of the dead fellers. It was one of my tricks to try 'em."

I looked at Jack, and then at the two skeletons lying on the ground. Could it be possible that the former had managed in such an adroit way as to frighten us almost into fits by his unearthly groans and demonstrations?

"Yes, sir; I did it," said the man, in a whisper. "I jist wanted to try 'em. No harm done, you know."

I was not so certain of that, for near me was a surging, raving mass, struggling to escape, and there was a fair prospect that all would ultimately succeed.

"Jist hear me give 'em one," said Jack, when he saw that we were likely to be left alone, with the exception of Will, who, in spite of his terror, would not leave me, for fear I should be spirited away, and lost to him forever.

"Yes, I must give 'em one for the fun of the thing," continued Jack; and he did produce the most awful groan that I ever heard, it was so unearthly.

"They is arter us," yelled Sam; and he renewed his efforts to escape, even crowding his father in doing so; but the old man launched out with one foot and kept the boy at a respectful distance; so in a few minutes they passed from sight.

"That's good groaning—ain't it?" chuckled Jack, who was highly amused at the success of his experiment.

"Yes; but the next time you practise, let me ask as a favor that I know something of it beforehand. I don't want you to enjoy all the fun."

"All right, sir; I won't forget. I'm some in the groaning line. I larned it on board the ship-of-the-line St. George, when we groaned the admiral out of the vessel."

"But how did you manage that the dead should raise one of its arms?" I asked.

"Nothin' easier, sir. While you was all engaged in getting at the box, I jist slipped a piece of marline over the bones of the feller, and then stood back and pulled. In course the hand would go up, and by a jerk I could make it shake its fist. That's how I did it. Frightened 'em—didn't it?"

I was forced to confess that it had rather startled me, also those who possessed more courage than I could boast of. The trick had driven old Nat and his sons from the cave, leaving Will, Jack, and myself to get along the best way we could. Luckily after Topmall's explanation I did not have that fear of the dead I had experienced when I saw the skeleton's hand raised; so there was nothing for us to do but to examine the contents of the box, and see if we had found a prize.

"Remember," I said to Jack, as we laid hands upon the box, "you must keep this trick to yourself. It would only cause trouble if it was exposed. Old Nat would be furious if it was known. Let it pass as something extraordinary. You understand?"

"'Sartin, sir. No more tricks. I is on honor now."

We turned the tin box over, and at last found an opening. We ripped off the cover and saw that we had indeed captured a prize, and one of much value. There were about two quarts of gold dust, and mingled with it were gold coins, and some few pieces of silver. I judged that there were about five hundred dollars in gold coin, and some twenty thousand dollars' worth of dust. After admiring our prize for a few minutes, we shut the lid, lighted our candles, and examined every part of the cave, but we could not find another concealed deposit; and we came to the conclusion that the Mexicans had placed all the gold which they had stolen in one box, thinking that it was quite safe, and could be reclaimed any time.

While we were thus occupied we heard some one at the entrance of the cave, shouting in a lusty manner; and, recognizing old Nat's voice, we answered.

"Hullo!" he said. "Is you dead or alive? Jist answer me that."

"We are all right, and shall be out in a short time."

"Wal, come as quick as you can. We has had a big scare, and had enough of it."

We took the box, and left the dead and the cave. We were some minutes in gaining the open air; but when we found ourselves surrounded by our friends, and exposed to them the box which contained the gold, they were delighted at the success of our expedition, and congratulated us in the most enthusiastic manner.

"You desarve success," cried old Nat, as he weighed the tin can in his hands, and mentally calculated the amount which it was worth. "We fellers cut and run jist 'cos a dead man jerked up one of his bones. I don't understand it yet, and I don't see why you wasn't scared jist like us."

"We were; but we could not run, because you blocked up the passage-way. After you were gone, the groans and manifestations ceased. Of course we were no longer frightened. We remained and secured the treasure."

"And a great prize it is, and no mistake. But we won't stand here talking all day about it. Let's back to camp afore them sneakin' thieves, the Mexicans, comes on top of us, and makes us pay for what we has done. Pour the stuff into bags, and then we'll be off. And remember," said Nat, as we halted for a moment on the hill which overlooked his valley, "no one must even hint at what we has done. If you does, our throats will be cut some fine night, and we shan't know nothin' about it."

We all promised to keep the secret, and then we plunged down the hill, and separated at old Nat's house; the Oregonian promising to look over in the evening and settle the dividend, feeling perfectly confident that the dust was safe in my hands. We rode on and reached my tents just about three o'clock in the afternoon.

CHAPTER XXV.

I AGAIN MEET JOQUIN. — A SIGN SAVES ME. — A RANSOM DEMANDED, AND WHAT CAME OF IT. — A RESCUE.

And now I come to one of the most painful portions of my erratic life. That very night I was called from my bed to visit a sick miner, a mile below my quarters. In passing through a thick wood, I suddenly found myself in the midst of a party of Mexicans, and a commanding voice shouted, "Halt!" On the instant I discharged two barrels of my revolver, — a preconcerted signal of danger, — for I saw that I was surrounded by Joquin and his gang.

"So," said I, quietly, to the chief, "we meet again."

Joquin started back a pace or two, but quickly recovered his presence of mind, and seemed ashamed of having shown surprise.

"You are a cool one," he said. "Who are you? — not a Mexican, I swear."

"No; I'm an American."

"I thought so. Are you wounded?"

"Thank the saints, no;" and as I spoke made the sign of a cross. The robber chief noticed the act, as I intended that he should; but his men did not, and when they heard me say that I was an American, two of them drew their knives and rushed towards me.

Luckily for me, Joquin's eagle eye fell upon them as they advanced, and he shouted, —

"Halt! What do you mean?"

The robbers stopped, and pointed with their long knives to me.

"He is a Yankee and lives. Remember our vow — death to all Yankees."

"Peace, you fools!" returned Joquin, fiercely. "Don't you see that he is a Catholic."

The scoundrels sheathed their knives in an instant, and I uttered a sigh of relief at the sight, and vowed that I would make some recompense to the first Catholic church that I saw, for thus borrowing a little of its religion.

The party took me to a fire, which was replenished by throwing on some dry branches, and, as the flames shot up, the light fell upon my face. My eyes met those of Joquin. We looked long and earnestly at each other. I knew what his thoughts were, but I did not interrupt them. I wanted to see if he would recognize me; but he had seen too many faces to identify me.

"Where have I seen you?" he asked, at length.

"Can you not call to mind the time and place?"

"No."

His men crowded around us to hear the conversation.

"A few months since a train was on its way to the mines, when it was attacked. The miners fought long and well, and after receiving re-enforcements, beat off the attacking party."

"We should have beaten you had not the Indians ambushed us," the Mexican said, extending his hand.

"You are right," I answered; and then I accepted his hand, red though it was with the blood of my countrymen.

"We came north," said Joquin, "for the purpose of removing the treasures which we had collected in a cave, but some of your countrymen have saved us the trouble. My men feel disappointed, for they are anxious to spend some portion of their time in the cities and enjoy themselves. They have worked hard, and need a little relaxation. Our visit south has not been a pleasant one. The Yankees have hunted us a little too close for comfort. In fact we have made but little money, I am sorry to state; and on this account my men feel in no good humor. Now we have a proposition to make, and I think that it is a reasonable one. You shall furnish us with some five thousand dollars, and then we will release you."

Willingly would I pay the money if I could but escape. Circumstances might occur, however, which would release me from all obligations, and I silently prayed that such might be the case. If Nat and his men heard my signal, I should be free, and the gang would be destroyed by daylight. Already there were indications of day breaking, and it seemed to my impatient spirit that my friends must be on their way, and near at hand. Every moment of time was precious to me; and as I knew it, and the Mexicans did not, I concluded to waste as much of it as possible.

"You must write to your friends," said Joquin. "They will send the money if they value your life."

"But who will take the letter?" I asked.

"Carlos, here. You can trust him — can't you?"

"Yes; but where will he find you when he returns?"

"We will take care of that point. Do you write the letter, and mind that you word it strong; and state that if any attempt at a rescue is made, it will result in disaster to you. Now write, for here is paper."

I commenced a note to Will and Jack, stating in fair terms that I was a prisoner, and that the money must be handed to the Mexican without delay, as my captors were impatient to leave the country. I also stated that no attempts must be made to find me, as I had pledged my word to that effect. I put in the latter clause more for the purpose of killing time than anything else, and it was a most fortunate circumstance that I did so; for, having finished the letter, Joquin asked, —

"Have you written all that I requested?"

"Yes."

He smiled as though he had caught me, but said nothing, merely turning to one of his men, whom he called "Pedrez," and handing the note to him, ordered him to translate it, word for word.

The cunning fox! He had not informed me that he had a man in his gang who could read and speak the English language quite fluently.

"Read! read!" cried the Mexicans; and thus urged, the man translated the note, word for word.

"*Diablo!*" they exclaimed; "it is as we said; he is an honest Yankee — he is not disposed to trick us;" and even Joquin suffered his features to relax, as he nodded in approval of my honesty.

"*Bien*," cried Joquin; "let Carlos start at once. He has no time to lose. Pedro can accompany him most of the way."

Hardly had he ceased speaking, when the woods opposite to us seemed alive with jets of flame; and then came loud reports, and through the air whistled half a score of bullets, which struck all around me, and yet I escaped. I saw the Mexicans leap in the air, and fall flat on their faces; and then my eyes sought Joquin, who was standing beside me. For a few seconds he seemed irresolute and undecided what to do. His hand was upon his pistol, and he half drew it from his belt; but just at that moment the men in the woods uttered a yell of triumph, and dashed towards the fire, discharging their revolvers as they advanced. I saw a light form bound towards me with outstretched arms — I noted the look of joy upon her face — I heard her utter an exclamation of gladness; and then, before I could speak or interfere, the Mexican chief drew his revolver and fired at the advancing girl. The next instant he had plunged into a piece of woods on his left, and disappeared from sight.

I sprang to my feet, and rushed towards the kanaka girl, but I was too late to catch her form in my arms. She had sunk to the ground, and by the aid of the fire I saw drops of blood trickling from her breast.

"I dreamed of the '*Malo*' last night," she whispered. "It was for the third time. I do not fear to die, but I am sorry that I must leave you, for I do love you so dearly."

"You must not die, Lilly," I cried, in an agony of sorrow and grief. "You must live and be happy."

"No more happiness for me on earth," she murmured. "The bullet has struck home, and my hours are numbered. The *Malo* never deceives his children."

I bent my face to hers, and she touched my cheek with her lips, sighed heavily, and then remained silent for a few moments. I raised her head and placed it in my lap; and then, for the first time, I was aware that Jack, and Will, and Bushy were near me, gazing with sorrowful eyes at the scene before them.

"She would come with us, sir," whispered Will. "We tried to have her remain at the tent, but it was useless. And to think that she is the only one of our party injured, and yet two thirds of the Mexicans are killed or fatally wounded."

Low as he spoke, Lilly heard him, and opened her large black eyes.

"You were in danger," she murmured, "and I could not remain behind. I hastened to find you, and as soon as I saw you I did not think of bullets or the robbers. I wanted to throw my arms around your neck, and say how glad I was at seeing you."

"But if you had waited a minute you would have been safe."

"It was not the will of the *Malo*," she murmured, in a faint tone, as though her life was failing fast. "If you ever see my father, tell him to pardon me for leaving him alone in his old age."

"And do you forgive me, Lilly?" I asked, as I kissed her cold lips.

A smile passed over her face, and as it fled, she murmured, —

"I loved you;" and with the words her gentle spirit fled to its Maker, and I held in my arms cold clay.

It was broad daylight when I arose to my feet, and looked around the late scene of strife. All the dead were buried in one common grave, while the wounded were nowhere to be seen, although I was confident that I had seen some before Lilly fell.

"They are all dead," whispered Will, who read my thoughts. "The men were so mad that they didn't spare one of the wounded robbers. Only two out of the ten escaped. One of them was the captain, I suppose. He shot Lilly, and we chased him for half a mile, but he was too quick for us. I would like to have killed him for your sake, and the sake of the girl, but we shall yet meet him."

Poor Lilly! how life-like she looked, as she lay under the shadow of a stately oak. It seemed as though she had fallen into a pleasant slumber, and was dreaming of some merry scene, for a half smile was on her lips, and had rippled all over her face. We formed a couch of blankets, and laid her form in the wagon, and then I took a horse, and rode to the front of the cortége for the purpose of being alone, but I was not so fortunate. Old Nat and Sam joined me, and opened a conversation by handing me a hunting flask filled with whiskey.

"Don't be afeard to drink it," said the Oregonian. "It is good. It came out of your keg."

I looked at him for an explanation.

"Drink," he said, "and then I'll tell you what I did."

I really felt the need of some stimulant, for I had passed through so many scenes during the last twenty-four hours, that my nerves were shaken, and my mind wandered. It is not to be wondered at, therefore, if I did put the bottle to my lips and drink quite freely, and I felt better for it.

"Yes," cried old Nat, as he followed my example, "this is some of your whiskey. When the signal startled us, I sent over to your camp, and found that you were gone, and borrowed a quart of this stuff to last me till I met you, 'cos I knew you would be faint and need it. 'Twas on your account, you know."

I nodded approval of his course, and the old man went on: —

"It didn't take us long to muster a force; the men came on horseback, and were anxious to lick all the Mexicans in creation. I gave 'em a drink of my whiskey, — mighty mean stuff, — and off we went at a gallop, and we didn't allow grass to grow under our feet till we halted in the woods, where we tied our horses and stole forward. To our surprise we heard, when we came in sight of the fire, Mexican lingo, and we didn't know what it meant; but arter a while we understood it, and then we come the Injun over 'em, and over they went, and you was free; but it was rather hard to lose the boy."

Upon reaching the camp, Will and the others had removed the body of poor Lilly from the wagon, and deposited it in my tent, where it was prepared for the grave. Bushy, who was useful as a carpenter, made a coffin of such pieces of board as could be found on the river, and the kanakas visited the valleys, and collected flowers, and strewed them on the body and the box containing the remains. We found a suitable spot for the grave. It was near a waterfall, and at the foot of a giant pine, which reared its tall head aloft, and spread out mammoth branches, as though asking for weaker things to seek its protection. It was a fitting place for the burial of the gentle girl, for, when in her native land, she loved the water and its music, as it rippled over falls and ledges, and sang, on its way to the sea, sweet hymns of praise to the Creator. It was a favorite resort for the girl when living, and such a place as she would have selected for her grave.

Days passed, and we again settled into the usual routine of life; but the place had become distasteful to me. I saw that our supplies of provisions were getting low, and that it was necessary they should be replenished, if we intended to remain at the mines during the wet season; so one morning I called the men together, and asked them what course they chose to adopt. We had been in the mines three months, and during that time we had made some fifteen thousand dollars, including the nugget which Lilly had found. This did not include the sum which we had taken from the Mexicans, and I feared we were collecting too much dust to render it altogether safe, in case of an attack. Somewhat to my surprise, they all declared that they preferred to remain at the mines through the winter, provided they could be assured of a supply of provisions; and when I informed them that I intended to procure all that was wanted, they agreed unanimously to build a house, and pass the wet season as comfortably as possible. I then unfolded my plans. I would visit Sacramento City, and invest some money in provisions, and the balance of the cash I would place in some securities, where interest could accrue.

This was agreed to, and after I had completed my business I went to San Francisco, where I met the ex-whaleman, who declared I must take up my quarters at his house, and I did not decline. One day I was walking towards home, about dinner time, when a hand was gently laid on my arm, and a sweet voice, speaking in the Spanish language, said,—

"My dear friend, how glad I am to see you!"

I looked around, and my gaze fell upon as lovely a face as I had ever seen. I stared at her in astonishment, for I could scarcely believe that I saw before me the mischievous, roguish, coquettish Constance of the Ladrone Islands, who had once played me as pretty a trick as ever woman was guilty of.

"May the saints preserve me!" I managed to articulate; "but am I asleep or awake?"

"Let me pinch you and see," was the laughing response. "Well," she continued, "if you are awake, let me introduce you to my husband. Don Pedro, Don Carlos."

For the first time I glanced at the gentleman at her side. He was a tall, dark, finely-formed fellow, with a handsome face, and Spanish cast of features. He had listened to our conversation with all the dignity of a hidalgo; but when his wife mentioned my name, his face relaxed its sternness, and a smile ruffled it, as he extended his hand and grasped mine.

"I can most heartily congratulate Don Pedro on the possession of so much goodness and beauty," I cried.

"It gives me much pleasure to meet Don Carlos," the Spaniard said. "I have often heard of him, and desired to see him. He is not forgotten at Guam."

"No, I should think not," cried Constance. "His bull ride is still remembered by all the tailors, and mothers of the town. O, didn't I laugh that day! But it is wrong to laugh at a relative;

may the saints pardon me for my mirth. Tell me, dear uncle, how is your wife."

It was my turn, now, to laugh, and I did so, to her astonishment.

"Speak!" she exclaimed; "didn't you marry Dorothea?"

"Not much."

She looked at me with astonishment and some anxiety.

"We heard at the islands that aunty married a sea captain, and we supposed that it was you. The governor was delighted with the match."

"And yet I assure you that I am unmarried."

"And Dorothea?" cried the young lady. "You did not deal harshly by her?"

"The saints forbid. You know me better than to suppose that."

She smiled faintly, just enough to show her white teeth, but looked anxious, nevertheless.

"Come," I said, "explain how you came here, and I will relate some matters of interest to you."

"Willingly," she answered; and then she glanced at her husband with a look of pride and affection, that caused me to remember the time when she coquetted with me on board the Helen, while lying in the harbor of Guam. I stifled the sigh that sought to find utterance, and listened to her words with marked attention.

"Don Pedro," she said, with a blush, "commands a Spanish ship. He sailed from Manilla for San Francisco, by the way of Guam. At the latter place he landed passengers and supplies, and of course stopped at my father's house."

"And there I learned to love her," said the captain, interrupting his wife. "I courted her for six days, and on the seventh married her."

"And now tell me of Dorothea," pleaded the young wife.

"Come with me," I said, "and you shall see her."

"She is married and happy?" asked Constance.

"Yes; united to a rich man, and one who thinks she is perfection. He is no stranger to you. But come with me, and you shall see your aunt."

"Is she as pleasant as she used to be?" asked Constance. "I know that I bothered her, but it was natural enough. She used to fuss so much, and was so anxious for a husband!"

I remembered the days she spcke of well enough, and I knew

that she thought of them, for her red lips curled as though she wanted to laugh, but did not think that it was proper.

"Don Carlos," said the lady's husband, "you must have passed some pleasant days in Guam, if all that I hear is correct."

"The happiest in my life," I answered, with a low bow.

"Tell me," she cried, "what did you do and say, when you found that aunty was on board your vessel instead of myself?"

"Don't you suppose that I knew the trick which you played me? Of course I pretended ignorance, but —"

"That won't do," she cried, with an expression of fun. "If ever a man was deceived, I know that you were. Don't deny it, for I shan't believe you."

"As you please," I answered. "Your aunt will give you all the particulars."

By this time we had arrived at the house. I let the party in with a latch-key, seated them in the parlor, — which they surveyed with astonishment, for it was elegantly furnished with rich curtains and carpets, paintings and statuary, — and then went in search of Dorothea, who was in her chamber dressing for dinner.

"Come in!" cried Mrs. Myers, as I knocked at the door; and in I went.

I found Dorothea was dressed, and just putting on a collar.

"Can you guess who is down stairs?" I asked.

She shook her head.

"Don't ask me such Yankee questions. You know I can't guess."

"What if I should tell you that some one from the Ladrones had arrived, and was in the parlor?"

Dorothea turned from the glass, and looked at me in astonishment.

"Who is 'em?" she managed to ask.

"A lady."

"Constance?"

"Yes."

She flew towards the door, but suddenly stopped on the threshold, and meditated for a moment.

"She must see my diamonds," she cried, and turned back to open the box which contained them.

I could not help laughing, and Dorothea noticed it; but she liked me too well to feel offended.

"I don't care for your laugh," she said. "I want her to see that me rich, and have plenty of money. Then she think that I have good husband."

"She won't deny that after she has seen him," I replied.

But Dorothea paid no attention to me. She slipped on her bracelets, ear-rings, and breast-pin, and then went down stairs. I did not accompany her, but I heard the relatives rush into each other's arms, kiss, cry, make explanations, and all in the same breath. You or I might not have worn diamonds in profusion at the dinner table, but I have no doubt we should have shown them as soon as an opportunity occurred, and that we should have listened to their praises in the most complacent manner, and assumed an indifference which we did not really feel. But the reader will hardly believe that Constance, in her childish simplicity, did not know a diamond from a piece of cut glass, such as whaling captains used to present her when desirous of expressing warm sentiments. Poor child! she had never seen a diamond; consequently, when the light struck Dorothea's jewels, and a hundred jets of flame flashed from their centres, Constance looked at them in wonder and delight. At last the could no longer control her admiration, and exclaimed, —

"O, what pretty pieces of glass you have on your fingers and in your ears! Where did they come from?"

"Glass!" repeated the horror-stricken Dorothea.

"Yes; such as we used to have given us at Guam," continued Constance.

"Glass!" Dorothea again exclaimed; "why, they are diamonds, my dear child."

Constance had heard of diamonds, but she did not know their value.

"Are they worth much?" she asked.

Dorothea smiled in pity at her ignorance — such a smile as women assume when men tell them they can see no difference between a camel's hair shawl and a common cotton and wool affair, worth about five dollars.

"These ear-rings cost fifteen hundred dollars, and the pin two thousand, while my rings are valued at various sums."

Dorothea spoke in as indifferent a tone as possible, but the pride would show itself by the flash of her eyes.

Constance clasped her hands in astonishment.

"Here, my dear child," said the aunt; "wear this for my sake;" and she slipped upon her niece's finger a magnificent brilliant.

The "dear child" commenced crying, and her tears were only dried upon the entrance of Myers. He welcomed his niece and her husband in the most hearty manner, called for some of his best champagne, and made Constance drink until her eyes sparkled like the diamonds which Dorothea wore.

On going to the post-office next morning, several letters were handed to me, and on one I recognized the handwriting of Julia. I hurried into a saloon, and tore the letter open, and read an epistle that caused me the most intense anxiety and anguish. Julia informed me that the past was forgiven and forgotten — that she was sick, and desired to see me with as little delay as possible. She did not know if I yet loved her; but she would candidly confess that she loved me, and had never ceased to feel that I was all the world to her. She now believed my conduct was not so bad as it had been reported to her.

Mr. Cherington's letter did not add much to my comfort or happiness. He said that Julia was ill, and that it was best that I should return to Honolulu as soon as possible, closing up business entirely, and be prepared to settle on the island. He thought that we had wealth enough to last us through life; but he cared not for it, unless he could see his child well and happy.

I thrust the letters into my pocket, and returned to the house. The first person I encountered was Myers.

"How soon does a vessel leave for Honolulu?" I asked.

"A Spanish ship, commanded by Don Pedro, my nephew, will sail in the course of a week."

"Is it the first one that leaves?"

"Yes. Don Pedro is now in the house."

I turned away, but Myers laid a hand on my arm.

"You look agitated," he said. "Have you received bad news?"

"Yes."

"Can I assist you?"

"You can. Engage me a passage in the Sacramento boat. I leave this evening for the mines."

"I will do so. Is there anything else?"

"Nothing at present;" and I left the room to get ready for my journey to the mines, for I could not leave the country without making some arrangement with the men I had on the Yuba.

In the evening the Senate worked her way through the shipping and across the bay. I looked over the passengers, and could find no one whom I knew; so I retired to my state-room and rested until morning, and then found that we were at Sacramento City, and that many of the deck passengers, men who had just arrived in the vicinity, were preparing for a start to the mines, as though fearful all the gold would be dug before they could reach them. I advised them to try the Yuba, but they feared that I was a speculator, so refused to listen to me. I did not waste words with them, but went direct to the person who had agreed to take charge of my horse, the same one I had captured from the Mexicans, found the animal safe and in good condition; and, after breakfast at the hotel, started for the Yuba.

My people were eating their supper when I arrived. I entered the room where they were seated, and suddenly said, —

"How are you all?"

"O, de Lord!" yelled the negro Jake; and over he went with two huge feet in the air.

"Blast my eyes, but it's him!" roared Jack and Bushy, while Will sprang up and shook hands with me in the most enthusiastic manner.

"O, golly! whar did you come from?" asked Jake, who managed to get upon his feet after a desperate struggle.

I answered all their questions in due time, and then intimated to Jake that I should like a specimen of his skill in the cooking line, as a ride of a hundred miles in twenty hours' time, including all stoppages, was well calculated to give a man a sharp appetite.

"By golly, you shall hab chickens!" cried Jake; and he left the room to seize on them, while the kanakas took charge of my horse, rubbed it down, and housed it in the storehouse, with an ample supply of barley and wild-oat straw.

"Now, boys, tell me what has happened to you during my absence," I remarked, as I took a seat before the fire, and waited for supper. The fumes of a broiling chicken were very pleasant to a hungry man, and I was congratulating myself on the prospect before me, and prepared to listen to the yarn which the boys would reel off, when suddenly there was a loud knock at the door; but before one of the men could answer the summons, the door was forced open, and in walked a grisly bear about as large as a yearling heifer, and ten times more disagreeable in look and form.

"O, de debil!" roared Jake, and jumped for a rafter, and we all followed suit.

When the animal first entered the hut, it walked towards the fire quite boldly, never having met such a sight before; but as soon as it got within heating distance it stopped short, and uttered a grunt of surprise, and then looked around, as much as to ask us what it meant. Receiving no answer, and the fumes of the burning chicken proving too strong, the bear stretched out a paw and made a pass at the gridiron; but meeting the hot coals, it uttered a howl that bespoke rage, wonder, and disappointment.

"Good!" yelled Jake, when he saw the brute smell of the singed paw. "You jist luff dat chicken be — will you?"

The bear turned its head towards him, and exhibited a remarkably fine set of white teeth, and then poked its nose towards the fire; but meeting with a warm reception, the shaggy brute looked reflective for a few minutes, and then thought, most probably, that a fight was wanted, and without the slightest reluctance Bruin pitched in. The first blow he struck sent the gridiron, chicken and all, flying across the room, and a lot of coals after them, which prodnced a yell from the gastronomic Jake. As that blow did not mend matters, or prevent the grisly from feeling the effect of the fire, another blow was aimed at the flames, and then another, until at last the animal pitched in with full power, and sent the brands flying in all directions. But teeth and claws were no match for the flames; for although the grisly rolled over the coals, and stamped them with his huge feet, and bit them, the fire conquered at last, for the brute drew off and uttered a roar of agony, and that roar was answered by a sharp report, and looking down, I saw that Bushy, who had dove for the window at the first appearauce of the grisly, had reappeared and shot the brute with an old musket which carried a two ounce ball.

"Hit 'im agin!" cried Jake. "He ain't got no friends nor nothin'."

But there was no occasion for a second discharge. The aim had been true, and the ball had sped home, and after a few kicks the brute tumbled over on his side and breathed his last. Order was soon restored. The kanakas removed the grisly, and commenced skinning it; and when supper was over, and we were seated at the fire, with lighted pipes and a steaming glass of hot coffee, the question was once more asked as to the work which the men had performed during my absence.

"We have done somethin'," returned Bushy. "We has been purty lucky, takin' all things in account. We has raked out some dust and some chunks, but no such pieces as that poor gal found."

He alluded to Lilly, who was buried but a short distance from the hut; and I felt my eyes grow moist as I thought of the poor girl, and the love which we had entertained for each other.

"Yes," continued Bushy, "we has made things pay while you was gone. You see we struck under the bank, and found some pockets what held out purty well. Get the buckskin bag, Will, and let us see how much we has got to show for our work."

Will arose, raised a plank near the end of the hut, and took out a bag, and emptied its contents on the table. I looked it over, and was somewhat surprised at the amount of dust which they had collected. I estimated that there was nearly twenty thousand dollars worth, and said so.

"Yes," replied Bushy, quite gravely, "we think there's as much as that. But we has some more. Show him the nuggets, Will."

The lad emptied on the table about three pounds of nuggets, some of them weighing an ounce, and the whole combined, formed about as handsome a lot of specimens as I had seen in California.

"You have done nobly," I said. "I did not anticipate such luck. But it is hard work, this mining, and I am tired of it."

No one answered me. They all sucked away at their pipes in silence.

"When I think of the comfort and luxuries to be obtained at Honolulu, it makes me feel homesick," I continued.

All hands uttered a deep sigh. They had thought of them as well as myself.

"I have received urgent calls to return to the Sandwich Islands," I continued, "and I have already made arrangements to leave California. If you desire to remain, we can make a settlement, and part company on the best of terms."

"How much might be comin' to us?" asked Jake.

I looked over the account-book, and found how much each man was entitled to, after deducting all expenses.

"Four of you are entitled to six thousand dollars each, while the kanakas will receive about three thousand each."

"I don't work here any more," cried Jake, executing a break down in the Virginia style. "I'm goin' back to Honolulu, where I can see some fun. I've got money enough to last me through life, I has."

"The same for me," cried the Englishman. "I ain't goin' to stop here and be eat up by bears, when I has as much money as all that."

"Where Captain Allspice goes I go," said Will, in a quiet tone.

"We all say that!" was the exclamation.

"You had better think of the matter," I replied. "At the present time you are making money, much more than you can hope to obtain in any other business. I will leave you here with provisions and tools, and you can pass the winter as pleasantly as you please."

The men shook their heads, and said that they were firm in their determination; and after a little more talk I retired to my bed, and slept so sound that I did not wake until long after sunrise. When I arose I found a good breakfast awaiting me, and to keep me company was old Nat Baker, the Oregonian.

"You've got back safe from that den of thieves," said the old man, as the first salutation, alluding to the city of San Francisco. "I'm powerful glad to see you. How's whiskey sellin' down there?"

I answered the inquiry as well as I was able, and then the old man joined me at the table, when I announced to him my intention of leaving the country.

"Then you'll want to sell what truck you has here," he remarked.

"Yes, I suppose so."

"Wal, I'm your man to buy it. I'll take your claim, and all the truck you has, at your own valuation. I can sell at a profit, if you don't ax too much."

So it was settled that Baker should take the hut, provisions, and tools, and pay a fair profit on them; and that forenoon we commenced taking an account of stock, and before dark the property was transferred, and the money paid in dust, at the current rate of sixteen dollars per ounce.

Nothing of note occurred on our journey to the city. If Joquin and his gang were on the road, they took good care not to show themselves; so we passed Bear River unmolested, and there I left the party and galloped towards the city, and made arrangements for a passage to San Francisco. The next morning the men arrived, and at night we were on board the Senator, and steaming down the Sacramento River, with every standing and sitting place occupied with passengers, who were fleeing from the mines, as though they feared plague and famine combined. The winter rains were considered unendurable by a large class of miners, so they were rushing towards San Francisco, for the purpose of securing some kind of employment, even if they had to work for their food, and hundreds were unable to obtain even that poor privilege, consequently there was much distress in all the large cities during the winter months, and beggars were met at every turn. We had a hard passage down the river, for the decks were so crowded that men could not move or turn, and thus wedged in they vented their wrath in curses loud and deep. We had several fights on board, but no lives were lost, although one or two men were somewhat cut with bowie knives. I think that I was thankful when we landed at San Francisco.

I saw that the gold dust which I had brought with me was placed in a safe and locked up, that my men were quartered at some place where they could be comfortable, and that my horse, my gallant bay, which I would not part with at any price, was safely stabled, and then I turned my steps towards Myers' house. I found Constance and Dorothea, both of whom welcomed me in warm terms, while the beautiful Constance, bewildering with her great black eyes, very politely offered me her cheek for a salute; but I got the start of her, and obtained a taste of her red lips, — an act which caused me to receive a box on the ear, thus showing the lady possessed all the spirit of her early days. I gave them an account of my adventures, and had the satisfaction of describing my encounter with Joquin in such a vivid manner, that the ladies looked the apprehension which they felt.

That evening I met Constance's husband, and he informed me that he should leave for Honolulu in the course of two days, and that he would take my men and their effects at a reasonable rate, and would gladly give me a passage for the sake of company; which offer I would not accept on any consideration; so, after some mutual expressions of good will, a price was agreed upon.

CHAPTER XXVI.

AT HONOLULU. — JULIA AND HER FATHER.

One morning — a bright and pleasant one — I went on deck, and found that we were close to Honolulu, and that a dozen boats were pulling towards us, each one containing a pilot, thinking that the Cortez would enter the inner harbor, which Don Pedro had no intention of doing.

It seemed to me, as I looked at the town, that I was returning home after an absence of several years. All the familiar objects were noted, and the few changes that had occurred were observed at a glance. By the aid of a glass I could discover Mr. Cherington's house; and I saw, with a feeling of dismay, that all the blinds were closed, as though it was desirable that the apartments should be protected from light.

"Perhaps Julia is very sick," I sighed, as I closed the glass and turned to the pilots, who were climbing over the side.

One of them, a fellow with wonderful white teeth, which were always to be seen on account of his smiling face, came aft. I knew him, and he recollected me, and the whole of his ivory was displayed as he bowed, and touched his apology for a cap.

"Want a pilot, sir? I takey you in, and no touchey rocks. Me berry good pilot, sir."

"I can vouch for that, John," I said; "but the captain does not want a pilot."

I determined to go on shore with the kanakas, and thus gain an hour or two; for the wind was light, and it would be some time before the ship could come to an anchor. I announced my intention to Don Pedro, and invited him and his wife to take up their residence with me while they remained in port, and to be sure and land in time for dinner, which they promised to do. Then I gave the men who looked to me for orders a few directions about the baggage and other property, and over the side I went.

At last I reached the store, and looked in. I saw two or three of the clerks at work arranging goods; but I could not tell whether Mr. Cherington was in his counting-room, on account of the door being closed. For a few minutes I hesitated, and walked up and down the street; but at last I pulled my hat over my eyes and entered the store. One of the young men looked up and came towards me, thinking that I was a customer. I saw that he did not recognize me, so much had I altered in the course of a year; so I pushed on towards the counting-room.

"Do you wish to see Mr. Cherington, sir?" the young man asked.

"Yes."

"He is in the counting-room, and very busy. Unless your business is of some importance —"

I did not answer. I pushed on and opened the counting-room door, much to the astonishment of the clerk, who stared after me with open mouth, surprised that I did not take the hint and confide my business to him.

As I opened the door I saw Mr. Cherington sitting at his desk, with his back towards me. He did not appear to be occupied, but seemed reflecting; for although a ledger was open before him he was not looking at it, neither did he have a pen in his hand.

For a moment I stood at the door and looked at him. He thought that a clerk had entered, and, without looking around, asked, —

"Is it known what vessel is in the offing?"

"A Spanish ship," I answered, in a voice resembling the clerk's.

"O!" and the old gentleman manifested a sign of impatience. "I don't suppose Charles would come from California in a Spanish ship. If he were as impatient to come home as I am to see him. he would have been here a month ago."

"But he is as impatient as yourself," I said, in a natural tone, which caused Mr. Cherington to start up in surprise, to turn around, to utter an exclamation of joy when he saw my face, and then to seize both of my hands and shake them, as though he had entered into a contract for exercise, and was determined to do his duty.

"Charles, where *did* you come from?" asked Mr. Cherington, as soon as he could speak; and he patted me on the back, and rubbed his palms, and then shook hands once more, and would not wait for me to answer him, but continued to ask questions in the most insane manner, the whole interspersed with the waving and frequent use of a red silk handkerchief.

"In the first place, I arrived in the Spanish ship which you noticed in the offing this morning," I replied. "I took the first vessel that left San Francisco; and here I am, delighted to see you, yet fearful of asking one question."

"Ask it, my boy, ask it," cried Mr. Cherington.

"Julia," I said, in a faltering tone, — "tell me of her."

"She is better, and your return will render her recovery complete. Come and see her. Let us lose no time, for I know that you are impatient."

I looked at my dress, and wondered if I appeared well enough. The old gentleman read my thoughts, and laughed at them.

"Come along, you foolish boy," he said; "your dress is good enough."

"Perhaps Julia is not ready to see me, and she may not care to."

"Nonsense! She is not strong, but she is up and dressed, and has been since six o'clock. Come along. All the past will be forgotten. Let the future be bright, and I am content."

He seized my arm, and left the counting-room; and as we walked through the streets, asked me innumerable questions regarding the course which I had pursued in California; for, in spite of his eagerness to have me reach home, he was not deaf to all ideas of pecuniary considerations, and was, therefore, quite delighted when I told him that my success had been of the most satisfactory nature.

But suddenly the old gentleman stopped in the street and laid his hand on my shoulder, while he looked me in the face very attentively and very seriously.

"Charles," he said, "before you see Julia, answer me one question. Is that kanaka girl on board the Spanish ship?"

"No, sir; she is not."

"Ah! I am glad to hear it. Have you parted company?"

"Yes," I answered; while a feeling of sadness stole over me, as I recollected that the remains of the poor girl were lying on the bank of the Yuba.

"There is no prospect of your meeting once more?" asked the old gentleman.

"Not unless we meet in heaven, sir," I answered.

"Ah! I am willing to run that risk;" and I thought that the old gentleman looked quite satisfied. "She is dead — is she?" Mr. Cherington continued.

"Yes, sir."

"Ah, well! we must all die some time, and must feel resigned to it. If that girl had come with you I don't think Julia would have cared much for a reconciliation, for you know that you have acted wrong."

"Lilly was as pure as —" I commenced replying, but Mr. Cherington stopped me.

"I know all that you would say. It is customary for the people of Honolulu to make mistakes and excuses. It's the climate, I suppose; but sometimes young ladies doubt assertions which young gentlemen make. If Julia does not speak of the girl, I don't think I should allude to her. You understand;" and we resumed our walk.

"Tell me how it happened that Julia changed her mind in regard to my doings," I said.

"We received letters from a Mr. Myers and his wife, stating that they had known you for a long time, and that you had been most shamefully misrepresented. The lady said that your constancy was of the most enduring kind; and so earnestly did she write, that Julia was satisfied you had been wronged, and I really began to take a different view of the matter. But who are the parties? do I know them?"

"Very respectable people, and very rich," I said.

"O, I am glad to hear it. I should be most happy to see them in Honolulu."

I thought that the reputed wealth of Myers would touch the old man's fancy; but before he could ask another question we were at the door of his house.

"You wait here for a few minutes," the old gentleman said, pushing me into the parlor. "I will find Julia, and prepare her for the interview. She is not strong, you must recollect."

He left me, and was gone ten minutes. When he returned, he said, —

"She will come to you in a minute. Now I will take myself off;" and he was about to leave me, when I requested him to send his carriage for Don Pedro and wife, and to receive them in case I was not at the landing; all of which he promised to do, and then left the house.

I waited with a beating heart for a few moments, and then heard a rustle on the stairs, a light step, and the next instant Julia had entered the parlor, was encircled in my arms and folded to my heart.

For some time we did not speak. How long we remained silent I have not the slightest idea, for under such circumstances as my meeting with Julia hours seemed like moments, so quickly did time fly. I know that I kissed her lips, and as I did so her eyes were shedding tears, for I felt the drops on my cheeks. I led the precious girl to a sofa, and took a seat by her side; as I did so, she softly whispered, —

"You have returned to me in good health — have you not, Charles?"

"Yes; I left San Francisco as soon as I could obtain a passage after receiving your letter."

"And you do not think me bold in writing such a letter as I did?" she asked.

"No, indeed. I was delighted with it. How could I help being so?"

"I don't know. We did not part the best of friends."

"But we meet as friends."

"Yes! O, yes!"

"As lovers?" I whispered.

She pressed my hand, but did not reply. I considered that a sufficient answer for all practical purposes, and so did Julia; for she smiled at my demonstrations of delight, and rebuked me for daring to kiss her.

"You have been ill, darling?" I asked, as I marked how thin was her face, and how pale it looked.

"Yes; I was quite ill."

"And what caused your sickness?"

"I do not know, unless it was thinking of our parting," was the candid answer.

"Then you did allow that to prey upon your mind?"

"Yes; I could not help thinking that I had been hasty in my treatment of you — that you did not deserve it."

"I am so glad that you arrived at such a conclusion," I answered, quite eagerly, delighted to find that she took such a view of the case, and beginning to entertain an idea that I was really an injured individual, although I could not tell in what light my injuries were to be placed.

"O, yes!" answered the innocent girl; "I thought of all that you told me, and I found that you were not so much to blame as I supposed. Then I received a letter from some of your friends in San Francisco, and they spoke in such high terms of you that I felt sure you were not really bad; but if you were," — and the dear girl looked at me in the most thoughtful manner, — "you must promise me not to be bad after we are married."

"I will make a thousand promises," I cried, with rapture; perfectly delighted with the manner in which I was to escape.

"And keep them?" she asked, with a roguish smile.

"And keep them," I answered, most solemnly; wondering at my good fortune, and hardly daring to believe that I was awake.

"Then I will trust you;" and she put her hand in mine, and I took the gift as the greatest treasure that I could own. But even with all my happiness I did not forget that I had friends on board the Cortez, and that I had invited them on shore, and that it was near time they arrived. I told Julia that such was the case; and she was delighted, and volunteered to ride to the beach with me, and welcome Don Pedro and Constance.

In ten minutes the carriage was at the door, and Julia and I were rolling towards the landing. While we were on the way I had an opportunity to examine Julia's face by the strong sunlight. It looked delicate, and most wonderful in its clearness and transparency; and I could but confess that even if she had lost a little flesh, her beauty was as great as ever. On our way to the beach we overtook Mr. Cherington, and stopped to speak with him.

"I was just going to meet your friends," he said. "I ordered the carriage to the landing, but I see that you have taken possession, so you may go together. I'll return to the house, and look after the dinner."

The old gentleman waved his hand, and beamed on us a pleasant smile, and then turned in the direction of the house. We reached the landing just in time to welcome Don Pedro and his wife. I introduced Julia to them, and she was delighted with Constance; and the frantic efforts which the ladies made to understand each other, while one spoke in Spanish and the other in English, were so amusing that I was compelled to laugh, despite my efforts to maintain my gravity.

"O, you may laugh," said Constance; "but if I could speak English I would tell the lady some of your actions, and then we should see how much you would smile. I know that she is too good for you."

"What does she say?" demanded Julia, as we took our seats in the carriage.

"She says that she thinks we are just suited for each other," I replied, with a slight perversion of truth.

Julia seized the Spanish lady's hand and pressed it very warmly, to the astonishment of the latter.

"I know you have told her something that reflects credit on yourself," cried Constance. "It is just like you;" and then she turned to Julia, and said, —

"You no knowey dat man muche. He berry good."

All of which Julia construed into a compliment for me, and bowed and smiled in the most genial manner. But it was astonishing with what rapidity the ladies learned to like each other; and although they could not comprehend a dozen words uttered, they managed to get along very well, and by the time we reached the house they were fast friends, and would have exchanged confidences, if they could have done so. We had a most pleasant dinner party, and it was none the less agreeable because it was confined to our family and Don Pedro and wife. The two latter were particularly pleased with their reception and entertainment. After dinner we rode out, and showed our guests the best part of Honolulu. When we returned I found all my men at the house, waiting for me. They had landed all of the property belonging to the firm, and had deposited the gold and gold dust in the safes at the store, and now they wanted to know if there were any further orders for them, because if there were not they would like to take a cruise for a few days. I had no orders for them, but I told Jack to select a number of articles from the store, and take them to Lilly's father, and to tell the old chief that his child was dead, but that she died happy, with the hope of meeting him in the kanakas' heaven. This mission I desired him to keep secret; and it was so kept, for Jack understood my ideas of what was just and proper. He nearly loaded a boat with presents for the old man, and so delighted was he with them, that his grief was of short duration. He lived for many years at his native village, and while alive I saw that he never wanted for any of the necessaries or luxuries of life.

But I must return to my story, for I recollect that my yarn is nearly run out, and that time is pressing. Jack and Jake left for the village which they called their home, while Will and Bushy found quarters at a respectable boarding-house, and waited patiently for something to turn up. They had money enough to live on, and they determined to enjoy it; and I think they did, for I saw them every day the first week of our arrival, mounted on horseback, riding about town in a quiet manner, and wondering how they should pass away the hours. Don Pedro and Constance remained with us for three days, and then sailed for Manilla, at which city, I am informed, Constance is a belle, and has often danced with the governor. Her husband is rich, and loves his wife as devotedly as ever. I hear from them twice a year, in the shape of letters and *piney* dress patterns.

On the fourth day of my arrival home I met Julia in the parlor, and determined to press her to appoint the day of our marriage, — a subject that neither of us had alluded to during the visit of Don Pedro.

"Julia," I said, as I ranged near her, "I suppose you know that I love you very much."

"I know that you say so," was the answer.

"Are you not certain that I do?"

"Well, yes, I think you like me pretty well;" and the young lady's cheeks were dimpled with a smile.

"And loving you, of course I feel as though I should like to marry you," I continued.

"I don't see the necessity for it," the little coquette replied, with a toss of her head.

I was determined to humor her, so I pleaded for the appointment of a day on which we could be united; but to my surprise she did not seem to agree with me on that point.

"Why can't we remain as we are for the present?" she asked. "We are happy now, and see each other as often as desirable. Don't let us think of marriage for a year or two."

Now I knew that this was all uttered for the sake of effect, so I resolved to change my tactics.

"To tell you the truth, Julia," I said with a grave face, "I think that you are right. We are both too young for married life. We will wait for each other a year or two, and in the mean time I will strive to increase my fortune."

I saw that she stole a look at my face, as though wondering if I could be in earnest. I maintained my gravity, and seemed to be engaged in some mental calculation.

"Yes," I continued, "I can return to California, and engage in trade, and in two years' time, with prudence and attention, I can add to my wealth."

"Then you had better go," she said, in a petulant manner, for she did not like the position which I had suddenly taken.

"I mean to, dear. When I started for Honolulu I thought I should soon own a wife. As I have made a slight mistake, I will go back."

I arose from the sofa and walked to the window. I can't say that I felt very pleasant, for I feared that we should carry the joke too far, and that what was intended for a little coquetry would end in a serious quarrel.

"How long before you will leave us?" asked Julia.

"As soon as a vessel sails for California."

"Are you serious?" and I saw her black eyes open to their widest extent.

"Yes."

She left the sofa and came near me, standing by my side.

"Charles," she asked, "do you want me to marry you very much?" and she laid her hand on my shoulder, and looked up in my face with such a loving glance that I was tempted to yield, but did not.

"I am not particular about it, if you prefer to wait a year or two."

This was so unkind and unexpected that the dear girl could not restrain her tears. They flooded her eyes in an instant, and burst all the barriers of reserve.

"O, Charles!" she moaned, "I begin to think that you do not love me."

"I should suppose that charge might be proved unfounded, if you would but take time to think of my conversation this morning."

"I don't recollect it," sobbed the dear girl.

"Then I won't remind you of it."

"Did you say you wanted me to marry you?"

"Something of that nature."

She made an effort and shut down the flood-gates of tears, and then looked up, and asked, —

"Do you suppose that papa would be willing?"

"I am certain that he would."

"Then I don't think that I shall make any objections;" and she smiled in her usual roguish manner, and held out her hand.

In an instant I was at her side, her little hand clasped in mine, while an arm was around her waist.

"Did you think that I was in earnest?" the lady asked, with a smile.

"At one time I thought you were."

"I was only testing your temper;" and the little coquette laughed. "O, haven't you a temper!"

"Yes; but please don't test it in that way again."

"Then you won't go back to California?"

"Not at present."

"Did you intend going?"

"No, indeed. I came here to marry you, and I mean to."

"Why, you bold, impudent boy!" she said. "What shall I do with you?"

"Name the day, and then we will discuss that question at some future time."

"Well, say three months from the present time."

"No; I'll listen to no such suggestions."

"Then two months will have to answer."

"No."

"Aren't you cruel? Then one month, and not another day will I take off."

"Yes, you will. You will say two weeks from to-day — and I will commit my life, my happiness, my honor, to your keeping; and may God have mercy on me if I do not esteem the precious charge."

She gave me her hand, put her red lips to mine, and then I knew the bargain was consummated, and that unless some accident intervened, I should own the handsomest wife in Honolulu. What a happy forenoon we passed! We sat and planned for the future until Mr. Cherington returned home for dinner, and then we walked directly up to him, and told him what we had agreed to do, and asked his consent.

"You have it, my dear children," he said. "Most readily do I agree to your marriage. It is the principal wish of my heart to see you united and happy. God bless you, my children, and may you be patient in affliction, considerate in your joy, and loving in your old age. And now let's have dinner."

The day before the wedding a large ship appeared off the harbor. Will, Bushy, and I were fishing at the time, and we noticed that those on board made signals for a boat, so we up anchor and ran towards the vessel, and as we passed under her stern the captain asked, —

"Will you take two passengers on shore? I can't stop, for I'm bound to China, and don't want to lose this wind."

"Yes," I answered, thinking that I could accommodate some one, and seeing that the vessel was from California, which place I very much desired to hear from.

The ship backed her maintopsail, and I ran alongside.

"Come up, sir," cried the mate, as he swung me the man-ropes. "We will have the luggage in the boat in a few minutes. But it takes all day for a woman to get ready."

I went up the side and landed on deck, and to my surprise the first person I met was my old friend Myers.

"Charlie, my boy, how are you?" cried the ex-whaler, with a rush, and a strangle in his throat. "How glad I am to see you here!"

We had a most hearty hand shaking, for I was really delighted to see the man.

"And Dorothea, where is she?" I asked.

"In the cabin, packing up. We won't interrupt her, if we do she will have one of her fits, laughing and crying, you know, and then nothing will be done."

"I am really glad to see you, but had no idea that you would visit me."

"O, Dorothea wanted a change. You know her condition, so I left business and started. Passage don't cost me anything. I own the ship. Bought her for the China trade, and mean to make a heap of money with her. But are you married yet?"

"No; you are just in time, for to-morrow the joyful event occurs."

"Good! Then I have arrived none too soon."

Just at this moment Dorothea made her appearance, and with a yell she rushed into my arms and kissed me.

"Gently," whispered Myers; "remember she is delicate;" which I was not so ready to believe, for the lady seemed as lively as ever.

I saw that the captain of the ship was a little impatient, for fear of losing the breeze; so I hurried Myers and his wife into the boat, with their numerous trunks, and then started for the shore, leaving the captain to steer for India, and to crowd sail alow and aloft for the purpose of making a quick passage in his clipper.

"Charlie, where shall I stop in Honolulu?" asked the ex-whaler.

"O, with me, of course."

"Shan't I be in the way?"

"Not in the least. We have a spare room, and plenty of seats at the table."

"All right, my boy. If I'm in the way I'll go to a hotel."

But I had no idea of that. I was under too many obligations to my friend to permit him and his wife to seek a hotel when I could command a room; so to the house they went. I managed to find Julia, and introduce her, and then all hands were quite happy; while Dorothea was enthusiastic because she had arrived in time to see me married, and because Julia carried her off to see the wedding dress, — the greatest treat that one woman can give another.

If my future happiness depended upon omens, the bright sun which greeted my eyes the next morning, as I raised the curtains of my windows, was emblematic of bliss, for a more lovely day I never saw in Honolulu; and this was the more remarkable because it was during the winter months, when severe storms sometimes swept over the islands. And this is my wedding-day, I thought, as I stood at the window and looked towards the outer harbor; and as my gaze roamed from point to point, I thought of the time when I shipped on board the Sally at New Bedford, a lad, without friends, and without hope, a victim to a boyish passion, having been jilted by a heartless little flirt, whose black eyes and red cheeks had been too much for my susceptible heart. Many years had passed since then. I was over twenty-two years of age, rich, and to be married to the loveliest young lady in Honolulu — one whom I prized most dearly, and who loved me; and as I thought of the enviable position which I occupied, I could not help uttering a sigh as my mind reverted to poor Lilly, and I wished that she was alive and happy, with some man of her choice.

I must pass over the many incidents that took place, until we were dressed and ready for the ceremony. At three o'clock visitors began to flock to the house, and they continued to arrive until all the parlors were filled; and when every one was crowded to suffocation, the king and his cabinet entered, so of course they had to have the best places.

I have a confused recollection of taking Julia by the hand — of looking at her with admiration, and of kissing her, which caused all the bridesmaids to utter a little scream, and declare that I had "rumpled" the young lady's clothes; of the manner in which Julia laughed, trembled, and blushed; of my declaring that she resembled an angel, and one of the bridesmaids asking if I had ever seen one; of floating into the parlor, with Julia by my side, and of hearing a hum of admiration at the beauty of the bride. I have a distinct recollection that a tall, venerable missionary, who had made a fortune by his piety and shrewd bargains with the kanakas, on the ground that he was saving their souls from endless punishment, rose up before me and said something. What it was I have not the slightest idea; but I bowed my head, and wished that it was over so that I could get a breath of air, for the rooms grew warm, and the company looked in a perspiring mood. I felt the little hand that I clasped tremble, and then tried to follow the minister in his prayer; but could not, for my thoughts would revert to the last speculation in which he indulged, and I wondered if he had made much by it. From this state I was aroused by hearing the missionary pronounce me a married man; and then there was a rush towards us, the whole company anxious for congratulations.

CHAPTER XXVII.

LIFE IN A STEAMER. — IN BOSTON ONCE MORE. — CONCLUSION.

LIFE on board a Pacific steamer was not pleasant years ago. In the first place, every part of the vessel was crowded, so that there was not room enough to move. The heat was intense, and unless you had a state-room, you had better be in purgatory, for there was no comfort, ease, or convenience. Luckily for Julia and myself, we had a splendid state-room, the best one on board; but then I had to pay for it, and a good price, too, although I did not regret it after I saw the motley collection on board.

We steamed on, day after day, and at last arrived at Panama; were transported across the country, and found a steamer ready to take us to New York, which place we reached without accident. As Julia had never before visited New York, we remained there a week, to enable her to recruit, and obtain a supply of fashionable clothing, without which women seem to think it is impossible to exist.

I had not sent word to my parents that I intended to return home. I thought I would surprise them, so I was in no hurry to leave the city, where my wife enjoyed herself so much; and I was happy in seeing her pleased. But at last her robes and flounces were completed, and then, one Monday evening, in the month of June, just ten years from the time I had shipped on board a whaler at New Bedford, we left New York on a Sound steamer for Boston.

We were late in reaching the city, on account of some delay of the train, so that it was near nine o'clock before we arrived at the Providence depot.

"Where do you want to go?" asked the hackman.

I had forgotten the number of father's house.

"Take us to the residence of Alderman Allspice," I said, hoping that the man would know where he resided.

"Yes; he lives on Beacon Street;" and the man slammed the carriage door and started.

We were not long on the way; but short as was the time, I

was enabled to think of the many adventures I had passed through since I had been absent. At last the carriage stopped, and the driver opened the door. I rang the bell, and a smart-looking colored servant appeared.

"Is Mr. Allspice at home?" I asked.

"No, sir; you will find him at his place of business."

"Mrs. Allspice is at home?" I asked.

"Yes, sir."

"We will see her;" and in we walked, and entered the drawing-room, the furniture of which was most magnificent.

"Your cards, if you please," the servant said.

"We have none."

"Your names, then," and the servant almost looked contemptuous at a party who did not carry cards.

"Never mind the names," I answered. "Tell her we want to see her; that's enough;" and then, to the surprise of the servant, I walked to the windows, jerked up the curtains, threw open the blinds, and let a stream of daylight into the room.

"Beg your pardon, sir, but missis don't allow that, sir; and perhaps, sir, you have made a mistake. There's other Allspices in the city, sir."

"O, Charles," pleaded Julia, "do explain."

I laughed at her fears, and opened another blind. The servant thought that we were the most free and easy people that he had ever seen.

"I beg your pardon, sir," he said; "but couldn't you tell me your name?"

I answered him in the dialect of the Sandwich Islands, and, after one stare of astonishment, he left us to inform my mother that there were pert foreigners down stairs, and that they didn't know much, and he rather thought they wanted offices under the city government.

My dear mother sighed and descended the stairs, intending to be curt and to the point. I heard her steps, and knew them, and I thought I should betray myself as soon as she entered the room, for I felt like springing to her arms and kissing her. But I managed to quell the beating of my heart, and awaited her entrance.

Then she stood before me. Her face had not grown old, but it seemed more thoughtful than when I saw it last, and the threads of silver in her hair seemed a little brighter than when I left home. But the eyes had not altered. They looked as kind as ever, and if it had not been for them I should have remained firm. But I remembered how often those eyes had stood between my father and myself, when the old gentleman had come home hungry and angry; and how she had excused my faults, and endeavored to persuade him to do the same, which he was not always inclined to do, I am sorry to say, as my back can testify. Therefore, when my mother looked at me with her dark-brown eyes, so mild, yet so unconscious, I could no longer restrain myself.

"Mother," I said, and rushed towards her and clasped her in my arms.

I saw the look of surprise which she gave — the quick, anxious glance at my face, which had changed much during the ten years that I had been absent, and then she sighed, put her hand to her forehead, as though she felt, for the moment, overwhelmed, and I feared that she would faint.

"Bring a glass of water," I said to the tall servant who had resented our entering the parlor, as far as looks were concerned, and who now stood in the entry, apparently bewildered at the scene before him.

He ran towards the dining-room as fast as his long legs could carry him; but mother did not faint. She rallied immediately, and found relief in a flood of tears; but they were happy ones, for, as soon as she could speak, she said, —

"O, Charles, why didn't you give me some warning of your coming?"

"Because I wanted to surprise you, and I think I have."

"You almost made me faint, you naughty boy;" and half a dozen motherly kisses proved that I was forgiven.

But I did not let her ask questions. I took her hand and led her to Julia.

"*I* have not only come home, but I have brought a daughter for you. Of course you will love her as well as myself."

"Full as well," was the hearty answer; and then my dear little wife found herself clasped in my mother's arms.

"You are full as handsome as I have been led to expect, my dear child," mother said, as she looked at the sweet, blushing face, and kissed it half a dozen times.

"You know, my dear mother, that I was always noted for my

taste in that line. You did not suppose that I would choose a homely bride — did you?"

"I had no idea that you would choose any, until we received your letters. But I am glad that you are married, and that you married the daughter of such a dear old friend as Mr. Cherington. I could not have wished for a better wife for my son."

"Nor I," was my reply.

"And you are both happy?" asked my mother, as she scanned us with her calm eyes, as though to see if such was the case.

I put an arm around Julia's waist and kissed her.

"This is my answer."

"And a good one it is. May you always be faithful to it, my dear child."

She rang the bell for the housekeeper, and in a few minutes we were in elegant apartments, and everything convenient for comfort; and after we had changed our dresses we descended to the dining-room, and found an excellent breakfast awaiting us.

"I hope that father is as well as usual," I said, as we took seats at the table.

"Yes; his health is excellent, although a few months since he had a touch of the gout, and was rather cross in consequence. He will be delighted to see you, for he has boasted enough of your exploits and success in making money, although I don't see how you could do it, and so young and inexperienced when you left home. Was it all true about that German, Mr. Wisner?"

"It was all true, mother, and Julia will show you some of the precious stones, besides a costly ring which she intends as a present for you. The brilliant is really beautiful."

Mother looked pleased, but finally said, —

"I'm afraid that you can't afford such an extravagant present for me. Besides, I'm growing old, and don't need diamonds. They will do for young people, but not for me."

Julia arose and walked softly to the old lady's side, and laid her young and blooming face against mother's cheek, and whispered, —

"We love you, and because you are older than we are we take pride in seeing you happy. Only love us as well as we love you, and our days will pass very happily."

The young wife was clasped to a mother's breast, and from that moment they loved each other most dearly.

As soon as our breakfast was completed, I left Julia to chat with mother while I went out in search of my father. I passed through the store, and saw old Penchard, the bookkeeper, laboring at his desk just as I left him ten years before. He looked up, stared at me for a moment, wondering, I suppose, if I dealt in groceries; and apparently satisfied that I did not, dropped his eyes to his ledger.

I passed on towards my father's private office, entered, and found myself in his presence; and then through my mind rushed all the incidents of our last interview — how I, a trembling boy, had stood before him, and dared to resist his demands, even when threatened with a severe flogging. I recollected how I had stolen raisins and figs to feed that little coquette, Jenny Fairchild, and how, rather than reveal her name, I had run away from home. All these things I thought of as I saw before me a stout, bald-headed old gentleman, with dark-brown hair; or what there was around his temples and ears was brown, and curling in quite a careless manner; but the face had not changed. There was the same dogged resolution and firmness, with a little more thoughtfulness around the corners of his mouth.

"Well, sir," he said, as though anxious for me to state my business in as brief a form as possible.

"You do not know me?" I asked.

"No, sir, I have not the honor."

"Did you ever see me before?"

"No, sir; not to my knowledge;" and the answer was a little curter than before.

"I have called to bring you information of your son," I said.

"Of Charles! my boy Charles?" he cried, in an eager tone.

"Yes, of him."

The old gentleman jumped from his chair, and came towards me; but looked so eager that I could no longer remain grave. I was compelled to smile, and when I did, my father stopped, looked surprised, and then roared, —

"Charles! Charles! you rogue! is this you?" and before I could answer, his stout arms were around me, and he was hugging me to his breast, and uttering all manner of exclamations of delight.

"You shall never leave me again, you young dog! Not a bit of it. But where is your wife?"

"At the house."

"Good! But come here. Old Penchard will be delighted to see you."

He seized me by the arm, and dragged me into the store.

"Look a-here, Penchard," cried my father, his voice a little husky, although he attempted to be stern; "do you know this young man?"

"No, sir; I do not. I never saw him before."

"Ha! ha!" roared my father. "Why, you old fool, this is my son, Charles."

"God bless me! you don't mean it!" cried the old clerk, starting up and throwing down his pen.

"And to think that you didn't recognize the boy. That is a joke. Why, I knew him at once;" which assertion I think was an aldermanic one, to be received with some allowance for excitement.

The old clerk took off his glasses, wiped them, and then put them on and looked at me.

"Yes," he said, at length; "it is him, sure enough. I know him now. But he has changed so much."

"Of course the boy has changed. Blast it, do you suppose that ten years can pass away without changes? Penchard, you grow stupid."

The old clerk took no notice of the remark, but continued to look at me in silent wonderment.

"To think that he should return to us after all," the old fellow sighed. "And he is married, too. Well, well, I'm growing old, I suppose; but it don't seem but last week that I stuffed his little pockets with raisins, and charged them to profit and loss. He was always fond of raisins, you know."

"Yes, I know he was," replied my father; "and it is but a few months since I discovered the reason why Master Charley ran away. Miss Fairchild told me. It seems that you purchased her love by the aid of my stock of fruit, and then felt too proud to inform me of it. What do you think of that, Penchard?"

"Just like him," answered the old clerk.

"Of course it is; but you come and dine with us to-day. You want to hear the boy talk, and see his wife. I know you do, so don't say another word. Come, Charles," and the old gentleman seized my arm, and dragged me on 'change, and introduced me to all his friends, and made me talk until I was tired, and glad to get home.

"Charles," said my mother, as I entered the house, "Miss Fairchild is in the parlor. Do go and see her. She wants to laugh with you over childish days."

"Perhaps that would be a dangerous experiment," I muttered, as I thought of her handsome face and bright eyes, and recollected how much I loved her at one time; but I entered the parlor, and then a young lady of wondrous beauty arose and extended her hand. I should have known her if I had met her in the wilds of California. She still possessed the same clear pink and white skin, the same sweet eyes, and red lips.

I took the hand and held it for a moment, while we looked at each other long and earnestly.

"You have changed so much, Mr. Allspice," and then she laughed and withdrew her hand.

"And you have changed, for I left you a beautiful girl, and you have grown up a lovely woman."

"O, what a naughty man," and she pretended to look sober; but the effort was not successful.

"Do you remember the night I parted from you?" I asked.

"I shall never forget it," she sighed, and then looking up, exclaimed, "What a goose you were to run away!" and to my surprise all sentiment left her, and she was a wild, laughing girl, full of fun and nonsense.

"I want to see your wife," she said; "and so I intend to dine here. Do go and ask her to come down."

I went in search of Julia. She was dressing for dinner; and as she held up her beautiful face for the usual kiss on my return home, I could not help thinking that she was full as handsome as Jenny Fairchild, and that I loved her more dearly.

"Look your prettiest," I whispered, "for you will meet several strangers at dinner."

This information did not dismay her. She was too much accustomed to society to feel timid at meeting strangers, therefore when she did appear in the drawing-room there was a general murmur of admiration.

My father kissed her, blessed her, and was delighted with her and Jenny whispered to me as I waited upon her to the table, —

"I love your wife most dearly."

"And the husband?" I asked.

"O, dear, I did love him; but time has changed my feelings. We are friends; but love is something of the past."

"Amen!" was my answer, as I glanced at my wife, and thought of her good qualities and rare beauty.

One word, and I have ended my yarn. Will, whom I left at Honolulu, returned to California, and amassed a fortune in buying ships and fitting them out for Panama with passengers. Bushy was concerned with him in the enterprise. Jack and Jake took to farming at Honolulu, and now own a large sugar and coffee plantation. Myers and his wife are still residing in San Francisco, while my respected father-in-law is with us, and occupies his time in playing with his grandchildren.

www.ingramcontent.com/pod-product-compliance
Lightning Source LLC
Chambersburg PA
CBHW031348290326
41932CB00044B/555

* 9 7 8 3 7 4 4 7 1 2 4 9 1 *